Economics of
OUTDOOR RECREATION

Economics of

OUTDOOR
RECREATION

By Marion Clawson and Jack L. Knetsch

Published for
Resources for the Future, Inc.
by
The Johns Hopkins University Press, Baltimore and London

The Johns Hopkins University Press, Baltimore, Maryland 21218
The Johns Hopkins University Press Ltd., London

Library of Congress Catalog Card Number 66-16040
ISBN 0-8018-0121-4 (cloth)
ISBN 0-8018-1302-6 (paper)

Originally published, 1966
Second printing (cloth), 1969
Johns Hopkins Paperback, 1971
Second printing (paper), 1974
Third printing (paper), 1975

RESOURCES FOR THE FUTURE, INC.
1755 Massachusetts Avenue, N.W., Washington, D.C. 20036

Resources for the Future is a nonprofit corporation for research and education in the development, conservation, and use of natural resources and the
improvement of the quality of the environment. It was established in 1952
with the cooperation of the Ford Foundation. Part of the work of Resources
for the Future is carried out by its resident staff; part is supported by grants
to universities and other nonprofit organizations. Unless otherwise stated,
interpretations and conclusions in RFF publications are those of the authors;
the organization takes responsibility for the selection of significant subjects
for study, the competence of the researchers, and their freedom of inquiry.

This book is one of RFF's studies in land use and management, which are
directed by Marion Clawson. At the time the book was written, Jack L.
Knetsch was an RFF research associate. The illustrations were drawn by
Clare O'Gorman Ford.

RFF editors: Henry Jarrett, Vera W. Dodds, Nora E. Roots, Tadd Fisher.

Foreword

The demand for outdoor recreation is booming today, as is obvious to anyone even modestly familiar with the situation. Less publicized but no less impressive has been the enormously heightened interest in outdoor recreation as a field for professional study in the last decade or so. Park lovers and administrators, dedicated conservationists, and others deeply interested have long written and spoken about parks and recreation, and they have often been influential in securing public action to reserve or manage parks and other areas in ways which they thought desirable or essential. But this type of concern has not really been a professional one, and it has rarely included research, especially research in the social sciences, about outdoor recreation. These park and recreation people have been advocates of a point of view or of specific actions; they have not generally been concerned with analysis of social and economic processes.

All of this has changed greatly; there has been a major upsurge of professional interest in outdoor recreation. In a recent bibliographical survey, Wolfe has listed some 160 books and articles, in addition to the studies of the Outdoor Recreation Resources Review Commission, nearly all of which have been published within the past decade.[1] This upsurge of professional interest has not been confined to any single professional group; economists, sociologists, geographers, lawyers, foresters, landscape architects, park and recreation executives, and other groups have shared in it. For many of these men, outdoor recreation has not yet become, and perhaps never will become, a professional field in and of itself;

[1] R. I. Wolfe, "Perspective on Outdoor Recreation—A Bibliographical Survey," *Geographical Review*, Vol. 44, No. 2, 1964.

rather, it is subject matter for workers from various professional fields. National interest in outdoor recreation was given a major boost by the work of the Outdoor Recreation Resources Review Commission.[2] One outcome of its work was the passage in 1964 of the Land and Water Conservation Fund Act, under which substantial sums will be granted by the federal government to the states for aid in acquiring and improving park and recreation areas. The requirement that the states have a recreation plan will give much increased weight to the usefulness of research in the general field, and we may well expect to see further proliferation of research in response to this stimulus.

Our concern with outdoor recreation is, we think, a natural one. Outdoor recreation requires natural resources, sometimes rather large amounts, and the mounting demand for outdoor recreation will bring major pressure for shifts in resource use. In the coming years, money is going to be invested in outdoor recreation—large amounts, by all indications. Decisions affecting recreation are going to have to be made. We think that they would be better made if more were known about the subject and about the outcomes of alternative ways of dealing with it.

Numerous issues of public policy on outdoor recreation are now before the American people. Shall government (at any level) try to meet the apparent demand for outdoor recreation on an essentially free entrance basis? Are we prepared to pay the price required to maintain the quality of the recreation experience? Can some means be devised to obtain effectively co-ordinated planning among the numerous private groups and public agencies? Shall natural resources be allocated to recreation and to competing uses on the basis of their comparative value for each purpose? If on some other basis, which one? How can the public use of privately owned land and water areas for recreation best be stimulated and assisted? How is the nation going to pay for the outdoor recreation it demands? More specifically, who is going to pay for it?

These are some of the policy issues which we raise in this book; we do not try to solve them, much less to advocate a line of policy on outdoor recreation. In the solution of issues of social policy, the value standards and philosophy of the persons concerned may be as critical as the technical and economic aspects of the issues. But the latter do set limits or raise problems of cost which often condition, if not determine, the answers. We think the general analytical framework erected in this book, and the methods of analysis outlined, can be very helpful in

---

[2] *Outdoor Recreation for America: The Report of the Outdoor Recreation Resources Review Commission to the President and to the Congress* (Washington: U.S. Government Printing Office, 1962). See also the twenty-seven Study Reports of the Commission.

enabling any individual or group to arrive at a sounder decision on recreation policy issues.

This book has been written by economists, but it is not directed primarily toward economists. Instead, it is aimed primarily at park and recreation workers, and at students in these fields. There are many employees of federal, state, and local park, forest, and recreation agencies who will be, we think, interested in the ideas and the approach we have developed herein. Most of these men and women are not economists, and we have tried to write in a nontechnical style that does not introduce economists' jargon unnecessarily and which tries to explain the concepts used in analysis. At the same time, there is a growing interest among such workers in the economic and social aspects of recreation, and we hope this book will thus be of value to them. Many nonprofessionals—citizens deeply concerned with recreation—may find the book useful in the same way. At the same time, we have tried to present ideas, concepts, and data that will be considered valuable by other economists and social scientists generally. In particular, we hope to stimulate university and other professional workers to initiate research on some of the problems we outline, and thus to test our ideas.

Our main concern has been with the United States. The analysis we make, and the problems we raise, are generally directly applicable to Canada also, although we have explicitly introduced but little of the Canadian experience into our discussion. The situation is different in the older countries of Europe and Asia where comparatively little land has been set aside specifically for outdoor recreation and where settlement on the land is often heavy. The situation is still different in many low-income countries, where incomes, transportation facilities, and leisure do not permit the kind of mass outdoor recreation we have in the United States. Yet, we believe that similarities are growing and that many parts of our analysis could fruitfully be adapted to the special problems of all these countries where the resource and population situations are so different from our own.

This book presents our views on the economic and social aspects of outdoor recreation, *as of now*. It brings together many ideas, analyses, and viewpoints which are scattered through other writings; but it also includes much new material, presented here for the first time. Its greatest virtue, in our eyes, is that it puts numerous specific materials into a reasonably consistent and comprehensive framework.

Outdoor recreation is a growing and changing field, and a definitive book simply cannot be written today. What is written here will be partially out of date in five years, or at least we hope it will. The basic principles and approaches should stand the test of time; but there should be amplification, enrichment, and change as these basic ideas are applied in specific situations of widely varying kinds. We badly need more research, in many areas and kinds of situations, both to test and modify ideas and to provide a body of quantitative research results.

We encourage other researchers to develop, challenge, modify, and amplify the ideas and concepts we advance in this book. We hope that it, and our earlier studies, will serve to stimulate many workers in various professional fields, as well as to provide useful and workable ideas to those in the administration of outdoor recreation.

We owe thanks to a very large number of persons who have contributed, often indirectly, to this study. Over the past several years, it has been our privilege to meet with many workers on outdoor recreation problems, either individually or in groups, and these have broadened our viewpoint and increased our interest, possibly to a greater degree than even we realize. Several of our colleagues at Resources for the Future have been especially helpful: Joseph L. Fisher, Irving K. Fox, Allen V. Kneese, Robert K. Davis, Harvey S. Perloff, John V. Krutilla, Henry Jarrett, and Hans H. Landsberg, in particular.

Much of the material for this book was assembled by Mary A. Holman, without whose intelligent and diligent assistance the authors would have had a much more difficult task. During the 1959–60 academic year, David N. Milstein carried on research along somewhat similar lines, under RFF auspices, and his ideas have been very helpful.

A draft of several chapters of the present book was circulated for review in the summer of 1961; comments on them were received from the following persons (the agency with which they were associated at the time of review is shown for identification only): Elmer Aldrich, Division of Recreation, State of California; W. M. Baker, Department of Northern Affairs and National Resources, Ottawa; Charles K. Brightbill, University of Illinois; George D. Butler, National Recreation Association; Charles B. Cranford, Department of Recreation, Philadelphia; Charles E. Doell, Superintendent of Parks, Minneapolis; George R. Hall, Technical Review Staff, U.S. Department of the Interior; William J. Hart, State Park Commission, Nevada; Irvin Hoch, University of California (Berkeley); H. Clifton Hutchins, University of Wisconsin; M. M. Kelso, University of Arizona; Karl S. Landstrom, Bureau of Land Management, U.S. Department of the Interior; J. Karl Lee, Bureau of Reclamation, U.S. Department of the Interior; Morris Miller, Department of Northern Affairs and National Resources, Ottawa; James Munger, Economic Research Service, U.S.D.A.; Edward B. Olds, Health and Welfare Council of National Capital Area; Richard H. Raymond, of Harris, Kerr, Forster and Co. (San Francisco); James C. Rettie, U.S. Department of the Interior; Harry A. Steele, Agricultural Research Service, U.S.D.A.; L. F. Twardzik, Michigan State University; Raymond D.

Vlasin, Economic Research Service, U.S.D.A.; Robert E. Waugh, University of Arizona; William W. Wells, State Parks and Recreation Commission of Louisiana; Ellis T. Williams, Forest Service, U.S.D.A.; Nathaniel Wollman, University of New Mexico; Gene Wunderlich, Economic Service, U.S.D.A.

A draft containing all the chapters in this book was circulated for review in the spring of 1965, and comments were received from the following persons (the agency connection is again shown for identification only): Rendel B. Alldredge, National Park Service, U.S. Department of the Interior; Ronald Bird, Economic Research Service, U.S.D.A., Columbia, Missouri; Charles K. Brightbill, University of Illinois; Edward P. Cliff, Forest Service, U.S.D.A.; Robert M. Coates, National Park Service, U.S. Department of the Interior; Johannes Delphendahl, University of Maine; Philip A. DuMont, Bureau of Sport Fisheries and Wildlife, U.S. Department of the Interior; Ed V. Dwyer, Division of Beaches and Parks, State of California; Winston A. Elkins, Bureau of Sport Fisheries and Wildlife, U.S. Department of the Interior; Herbert Gans, Columbia University; Don Goldman, National Park Service, U.S. Department of the Interior; John S. Gottschalk, Bureau of Sport Fisheries and Wildlife, U.S. Department of the Interior; Paul F. Graves, State University College of Forestry at Syracuse University; R. J. Hildreth, Farm Foundation, Chicago; William J. Hart, Resources Planning Associate, Washington; Edward D. Hollander, Robert R. Nathan Associates; Alfred B. LaGasse, American Institute of Park Executives, Inc.; T. R. Lakshmanan, Alan M. Voorhees and Associates, Washington; John J. Long, Bureau of Sport Fisheries and Wildlife, U.S. Department of the Interior; Robert C. Lucas, Lake States Forest Experiment Station, University of Minnesota; Neil W. Newton, National Park Service, U.S. Department of the Interior; Roland N. McKean, University of California (Los Angeles); A. Allan Schmid, Michigan State University; G. D. Taylor, Department of Northern Affairs and National Resources, Ottawa; Betty van der Smissen, National Recreation Association; S. V. Ciriacy-Wantrup, University of California, Berkeley.

We are glad to acknowledge our debt to these people, and to any others whom we may have inadvertently omitted. Full responsibility for errors, omissions, viewpoints, and conclusions rests with the authors, of course.

MARION CLAWSON
JACK L. KNETSCH

May 1966

Contents

CONTENTS

CONTENTS

List of Tables

Table

Appendix Tables

List of Figures

LIST OF FIGURES

I

The Setting

1

Introduction

The purpose of this book is to present a review of outdoor recreation in the United States with particular concern for the significant policy issues of the next decade or two. From the extremely large number of subjects or topics that could be involved in questions of outdoor recreation, we have chosen those which seemed to us, conditioned by our own particular interests, to be most useful for dealing with the important policy and operational decisions.

If the problems and opportunities of outdoor recreation are to be properly understood, they must be seen in terms of the whole society and whole economy. Accordingly, considerable attention is given to the role of leisure in the total life and economy of the United States today and in the future, and to the role of outdoor recreation as one of many uses of leisure.

The discussion at many points will emphasize the limited nature of our present knowledge about outdoor recreation. With a few notable exceptions, the various physical, economic, social, political, and other problems relating to outdoor recreation have not been the subject of serious research and study. In no small part, this has been due to the fact that recreation has been equated to a degree with play, and both have been considered beneath the dignity of serious research effort. Fact-gathering and fact-analysis have been infrequent enough, but sound theorizing has been especially lacking. The shortcomings of many years of neglect obviously cannot be made good in any single book. We hope that some new ideas, new methodology, new facts will be found here. But, perhaps most of all, we hope that this book will serve to clarify and to organize what is known, or believed to be known, and that it will stimulate others to greatly extend present knowledge.

Major emphasis is placed in this book upon the economic and social aspects of outdoor recreation. This emphasis arises out of two considerations: (1) these seem the most important and at the same time the most neglected aspects of outdoor recreation at present, and (2) these are the aspects on which we feel best qualified to speak.

We approach outdoor recreation as social scientists. The starting point of the whole analysis is people and their wants and demands for outdoor recreation; from this, the resource and institutional problems are considered, and lastly the major policy issues—as we see them—are posed. Other authors, with different professional backgrounds, might well include somewhat different ranges of subject matter under the same title.

Our objective is not to present, much less to advocate, an "action" program; rather, the purpose is to suggest things to be considered in developing any program and to raise what seem to be significant issues for public discussion and hence for ultimate resolution. Increasingly in the future, conflicts of value and dynamic changes in our society are going to require a better awareness of what is happening and a better analysis of recreation alternatives.

Major attention is focused throughout upon outdoor recreation on publicly owned land and water areas—the areas that have been of major importance in the past and about which more is known. Much of the discussion, though illustrated by examples from public areas, is equally applicable to private areas, which may well increase in importance.

THE SHAPE OF THE FUTURE

Since outdoor recreation is but a part of the total life of the nation, and since the demand for outdoor recreation will be determined in large measure by factors external to recreation itself, a brief consideration of our social and economic structure may be helpful at the outset.

Most would agree that the society and economy of the United States during the next several decades will evolve gradually, and in directions now rather evident, from the present society and economy. Radical departures and drastic changes are ruled out; but continued modification, which over a period of decades will bring changes so great in magnitude as almost to be changes in kind, is definitely assumed. To anticipate a little the discussion which follows, a "more so" society and economy is forecast. There will be more people, more income, more leisure, more travel, more opportunity for individual choice and growth, and more varied activities generally. But the change each year will be comparatively modest; the forecast is evolution, not revolution. We also assume that developments in science and technology will be evolutionary in nature. A constantly increasing volume and variety of consumer goods is probable. Some of these goods will add to the enjoyment of outdoor recreation; others will compete with recreation for the time, interest, and money of the average citizen.

Of prime importance among the factors affecting outdoor recreation are population trends. Steady growth in population is probably the most persistent social change in this country. But growth is not the only kind of population change that has an impact on the recreation situation. People are also becoming better educated and healthier. Shifts are taking place in the age distribution of people and in their locations or places of residence. This last includes the steady movement of people westward and the all-important movement of people from rural areas to urban areas. These trends have been subject to minor fluctuations, but the directions are clearly indicated by long periods of observation and they will surely continue.

Another important change is the increase in leisure time (a subject explored in more detail in Chapter 2). The average workweek has decreased from around 70 hours in 1850 to about 40 hours today, and there are signs that it may well become shorter in the future. Changes are also occurring in the timing and sizes of pieces of leisure. Annual vacations are becoming the rule for workers in nearly all occupations, and the average length is growing. Retirement years are also increasing owing to increased longevity and changes in retirement programs. Again, the future will see more changes in the amount and arrangement of leisure time.

The population is also becoming more mobile. Total travel per capita has increased from around 480 miles annually in 1900 to over 5,000 miles in 1956. Better roads, more automobiles, and the airplane are among the contributing factors. This upward trend is also expected to continue.

Incomes are also increasing. The trends here, though more irregular than others, are clearly upward, and are expected to continue. Per capita disposable incomes have increased, in 1958 dollars, from about $1,236 in 1929 to $2,200 in 1965.[1] Along with changes in average incomes, there are shifts in the distribution of income, which make it economically possible for more and more people to engage in different kinds of outdoor activity.

The indications are imposingly those of a more-so society. And so it is with recreation. Attendance and use figures for outdoor areas are

[1] Economic Report of the President, January, 1966.

already reflecting the trends of related factors and are rising at continued high rates. National park attendance rose from about a million in 1920 to 102 million in 1964. Total state park attendance increased from about 69 million to 285 million over the years 1942 to 1962. Some areas, particularly those which are water-oriented, are experiencing even higher rates of increase in use. In view of the trends in recreation participation and in the factors having a direct relationship to outdoor recreation, greater pressures on recreation resources seem inevitable.

A FEW DEFINITIONS

Discussion about recreation matters has been plagued by much misunderstanding and vagueness, in no small part because the same word means quite different things to different people. For this reason, a few definitions seem desirable; those that follow are a prelude to discussion in following chapters.

Recreation, as the word is used in this book, means activity (or planned inactivity) undertaken because one wants to do it. In a deeper psychological sense, recreation refers to the human emotional and inspirational experience arising out of the recreation act; we use the latter to stand for the whole. Recreation contrasts with work, which is done primarily to earn money or otherwise to provide the "necessities" of life, or what have come to be so considered, for one's self and one's family. It also contrasts with the mechanics of life, such as eating, sleeping, housekeeping, and personal care.[2] There is no sharp line between recreation and all other activities. The same activity may be work at some times and recreation at others. Cooking, dressmaking, embroidery, furniture making, and other specific activities may fall into either classification. Even some jobs which are the chief source of income may be essentially recreation. One college professor friend of the authors has admitted that, had he other income, he would gladly pay for the opportunity to do a modest amount of college teaching.

The distinguishing characteristic of recreation is not the activity itself but the attitude with which it is undertaken. When there is little or no feeling of compulsion or "ought to," an activity (or inactivity) is almost surely recreation. In the modern, complex world, where so many aspects

[2] Others have included as leisure, and hence perhaps inferentially as recreation, time spent eating and sometimes in other activities that would be excluded by the above definition. For instance, see George A. Lundberg, Mirra Komarovsky, and Mary Alice McInerny, "The Amount and Uses of Leisure," in *Leisure: A Suburban Study* (New York: Columbia University Press, 1934). Reprinted in Eric Larrabee and Rolf Meyersohn, ed., *Mass Leisure* (Glencoe, Ill.: The Free Press, 1958).

of life are socially ordered, recreation is often a major opportunity for self-expression. However, elements of social compulsion are present even for recreation, as we shall see in later chapters.

Recreation is closely related to leisure. Briefly, if leisure is taken to mean time in which activities (or inactivity) consciously decided upon are undertaken, then the relation of recreation and leisure is very close. On this basis, mere idleness is neither leisure nor recreation.

Outdoor recreation is simply recreation that is typically carried on outdoors. As such, it contrasts with the various forms of recreation typically carried on indoors. There are some borderline activities, that can take place either outdoors or indoors. Basketball courts are typically indoors, yet on occasion are outdoors. Track activities are typically outdoors, yet often are held indoors. Outdoor recreation obviously requires space and resources, sometimes large quantities, for its enjoyment. Some kinds are best carried on where the natural landscape has had the minimum modification, others require extensive investment.

Natural resources for outdoor recreation include areas of land, bodies of water, forests, swamps, and other natural features, and even air spaces, which are in demand for outdoor recreation or likely to become so. The physical characteristics of these natural elements of the landscape affect their use for outdoor recreation, but they become resources for outdoor recreation only as they are useful for this purpose. Land, water, forests, and other natural features which for any reason are not or cannot be used for recreation are not part of the present outdoor recreation resource, although they may have future value for this purpose. In this respect, outdoor recreation is no different from any other use of natural resources such as farming, forestry, grazing, and mining. There is nothing in the physical landscape or features of any particular piece of land or body of water that makes it a recreation resource; it is the combination of the natural qualities and the ability and desire of man to use it, that makes a resource out of what otherwise may be a more or less meaningless combination of rocks, soil, and trees.

Recreation activities include those specific actions undertaken as part of recreation, whether indoors or outdoors. Some activities are relatively formal, as is the case with many organized games and other group activities. But most activities—picnics, hikes, fishing expeditions, and many others—are characterized by their informality. Very often it is the informality, the formlessness, the absence of order and pressure, and the spontaneity that give outdoor recreation its appeal and its value. In our modern urban and industrial society the job and the workday have relatively a lot of order and form, and as a relief from them many people seek outdoor recreation. This is one reason why outdoor recreation "activity" must always include a large measure of inactivity; many people stress the opportunity merely to lie around, loaf, talk informally, or merely rest.

PLAN OF THIS BOOK

As a means of organizing ideas and facts on this general subject, we have divided this book into five major parts and into sixteen chapters. There is to us, and we hope to our readers as well, a logical progression from chapter to chapter.

Part I: The Setting includes three relatively short chapters. There is this introductory one, with a little general setting and some definitions. Chapter 2 considers leisure in modest detail; recreation is so peculiarly a time-oriented activity, that it seems essential to consider first the limitations of time available for recreation. There has been much interest, and much misunderstanding, about leisure. On the one hand, we judge there will be more leisure in the future, as a result of numerous aspects of modern life which are described in the chapter; but, on the other hand, we judge that productive work to earn income will still dominate most of the life span for most people, either for themselves or for their married partner. Outdoor recreation will be a growing use of leisure, but only one use of it. In Chapter 3, we describe some general aspects of outdoor recreation, including the "whole experience" and the nature of outdoor recreation areas, which are basic to the analysis of later chapters.

Part II: Demands for Outdoor Recreation is the longest single part in the book, and in some respects the most important part. In our judgment, demand for recreation is always important and sometimes it is crucial, but it has often been neglected. Although demand and supply are closely interrelated, as is pointed out at several places in this part, here we focus on demand, leaving a more detailed consideration of supply for later.

Chapter 4, Some Elements of Recreation Demand, is designed to show the noneconomist how the powerful tool of demand analysis, developed by economists over several decades, can help solve some of the difficult problems existing in outdoor recreation. The best solution to such practical problems as to how much land to buy for parks, its best location, the allocation of costs among project purposes, the best level of development of a park, and others can often be facilitated by a good demand analysis. The chapter is also designed to show economists some of the practical problems within recreation to which demand curve analysis is applicable. Chapter 5, The Nature of the Demand for Outdoor Recreation, applies this general demand approach to specific recreation situations of the general kinds described in Chapter 3, with illustrative examples. The value and limitations of this demand approach are also discussed here.

In Chapter 6, Behavior of Some Causal Factors in Demand, we temporarily put aside the analytical demand approach, to look again and in more detail at some of the factors which have underlain demand for outdoor recreation in the past—population, leisure, transportation, and income, which we had more briefly mentioned in Chapters 2 and 3. Chapter 7, Alternative Methods of Estimating Future Use, takes up a number of alternative ways of making the necessary but difficult projections of future use which must underlie the planning of any outdoor recreation area. All the methods we consider are based to some degree on the demand analysis of preceding chapters. No method is infallible; each method considered may have value under some circumstances. The difficulties of projection lie not in the lack of suitable methodology, but rather in the dynamics and uncertainty of the future.

Part III: Recreation Resources is largely concerned with resource supply aspects of outdoor recreation. Chapter 8, Use of Resources for Recreation, applies economic concepts about resources, which have proven fruitful for other uses, to the problems of recreation. Chapter 9 deals with preservation of recreation quality, a matter that must receive much more attention if increasing use is not to be offset by declining quality. Chapter 10, Existing Areas and Their Use, is primarily factual and descriptive, summarizing data from a number of sources. But the synthesis of these data produces some new conclusions about the regional distribution of recreational resources in relation to need.

Part IV: Some Economic Considerations brings the whole demand and supply approach to outdoor recreation a little closer to the solution of a number of current policy issues. Chapter 11, The Value of Land and Water Resources When Used for Recreation, considers the best methods of measuring these values in ways that will be comparable with value measurements for competing uses of the same resources. Chapter 12, Economic Impacts of Outdoor Recreation on Local Areas, gets into a subject of intense interest to localities, regions, states, and even the national government. How far can outdoor recreation provide economic salvation to depressed areas? (The answer: often, not very far.) Chapter 13, Cost and Investment Considerations in Providing Public Outdoor Recreation Facilities, provides some guidelines for investment decisions. In Chapter 14, Pricing and Paying for Public Outdoor Recreation Facilities, the inescapable problems of who pays and how, are considered in modest detail; issues and methods of analysis are presented, not pat answers.

Part V: Outdoor Recreation for the Future is the brief concluding part. Chapter 15, Research for Outdoor Recreation, analyzes the need for research in this general field, makes a number of suggestions for lines of research, and some suggestions about how best to secure the desired research. Chapter 16, Major Issues of Public Policy, seeks to pose, as sharply and clearly as possible, the really significant issues of public policy; but it does not try to answer these issues, much less to advocate a line of action.

2

Leisure in Modern America

Merely to maintain life, man must sleep, eat, and have time for some minimum personal hygiene. In order to subsist, he must work. In our modern society, this means work at a job or jobs. With the income obtained from this work, he buys goods and services produced by other men. For better lifetime subsistence, he must be trained for higher productivity, which today means he must go to school. Beyond these general categories, his time is discretionary. Leisure is largely discretionary time, to be used as one chooses.[1] It excludes existence and subsistence time, and time spent in socially or group determined activities in which the individual would prefer not to participate.

These categories are not completely watertight. Time for existence, if the latter is strictly interpreted, is fairly clear; yet time spent in eating may be for pleasure as well as existence. In subsistence, one may choose

[1] Leisure is a subject which has evoked a large body of writing by those concerned with its psychological and social aspects; our concern in this book is primarily with the availability of time for outdoor recreation, and the factors affecting it. Some general references which underlie this chapter, and which in turn contain additional references, providing more consideration of the psychological and social aspects of leisure, include: Nels Anderson, *Work and Leisure* (New York: The Free Press, 1961); George Barton Cutten, *The Threat of Leisure* (New Haven: Yale University Press, 1926); Sebastian De Grazia, *Of Time, Work and Leisure* (New York: Twentieth Century Fund, 1962); Johan Huizinga, *Homo Ludens: A Study of the Play Elements in Culture* (London: Routledge and Kegan Paul, Ltd., 1949); Eric Larrabee and Rolf Meyersohn, ed., *Mass Leisure* (New York: The Free Press, 1958); Martin H. and Esther Neumeyer, *A Study of Leisure and Recreation in Their Sociological Aspects* (New York: A. S. Barnes and Co., 1949); Arthur Newton Pack, *The Challenge of Leisure* (New York: Macmillan Co., 1934); G. Ott Romney, *Off the Job Living—A Modern Concept of Recreation and Its Place in the Postwar World* (New York: A. S. Barnes and Co., 1945).

11

a minimum of income in order to have a maximum of leisure, or one may seek maximum income at the cost of leisure, or one may choose some intermediate position. The individual is not completely free in the modern world because the time requirements of jobs are largely group determined; and some nonjob activities are so closely determined by social custom or pressure that little discretion is left to the normal individual. Yet many major choices are possible within discretionary time.

Discretionary time is similar to income. It is what is left after necessary obligations are met; its use connotes a large degree of purposefulness or choice. Mere idleness is not leisure, any more than lack of expenditure is use of discretionary income. This does not exclude a purposeful decision to do nothing; but it does exclude idleness which arises out of lack of something desirable to do.

Leisure time may be completely filled, or like discretionary income it may even be overcommitted. A person may wish to do so many things, or may have agreed with others to do so many things, that he either has no free time left, or is unable to meet his commitments.

A classification of time as work or leisure raises some difficulties. Broadly speaking, leisure is the time left over after sleep, necessary personal chores, and work. It is time available for doing as one likes, within the range of one's interests and abilities. But it is not synonymous with idleness. The use made of leisure—and, in fact, the distinction between leisure and idleness—depends upon the general economic situation in the society and for the individual. In many low-income societies, the bulk of the population has idle time which could be turned into leisure, given modest outlays for leisure activities, including training for them. Leisure and recreation are highly correlated, but they are not the same. Leisure is *time* of a special kind; recreation is *activity* (or inactivity) of special kinds. Recreation takes place during leisure; but not all leisure is given over to recreation. We return to recreation in more detail in the following chapter.

The way people use their leisure can shape a society as much as the way they work. Until recent decades, leisure as we define it was the privilege of the few. It is still that way in much of the world today, but meaningful leisure has become available to the bulk of the population in the United States and in the western world generally. Many students of the subject have been frightened at the prospect of mass leisure because it provides time for socially undesirable activities as well as for constructive ones. Clearly, some people have used leisure badly, often because they did not know how to put it to better use.[2]

[2] James C. Charlesworth, ed., *Leisure in America: Blessing or Curse?* Monograph 4, American Academy of Political and Social Science, Philadelphia, April 1964.

Man's activities in the western world today extend over a long continuum, from the most unattractive drudgery to the most delightful leisure, and also from the greatest activity to the sheerest inactivity. Attractiveness or satisfaction and degree of activity are not necessarily correlated at all. The distinction between job and fun has narrowed for some parts of the population, but widened for others. Some people must today seek such physical activity as they wish at times and places other than on the job. Others find their jobs physically tiring, and look to leisure for rest. Even when they engage in a specific outdoor recreation activity, such as picnicking, people are motivated by different forces and seek different kinds of satisfactions. All of this adds to the complexity of the job for the planner or administrator of outdoor recreation.

LEISURE VERSUS WORK

By and large, leisure and work are competitors for time. If one increases, the other decreases. This is so for the individual and for society as a whole.

The number of hours of work performed by an individual worker, and thus the opportunity to balance work against leisure, is to a large extent socially determined. The nature of production and also commercial processes often preclude individual variations in working hours. The limits to which individuals must conform to the group pattern are extended in cases of those self-employed and those taking part-time work or two jobs. Individuals may join together in an attempt to modify their working hours.

It is within these limits of choice that the individual attempts to balance hours of work and hours of leisure. The choice will in part be dependent upon the wage rate he anticipates. While the desire for leisure may be great, the incentive to work longer hours lies in increased money income, and the taking of more leisure time consequently becomes a "cost." As the wage rate is raised there is no assurance of how individuals will react in their desire for more or less work. Higher wage rates and unchanged working hours mean higher income, and the individual is able to buy better food, more clothes, and more of other consumer goods; but a higher wage per hour would also permit the recipient to choose more leisure while maintaining total income unchanged. It depends upon the individual and his income which of these desires will dominate.

Historically, workers have been able to increase incomes and take more leisure as well, owing largely to increases in economic productivity. Over the past century, workers have taken about half of this increased productivity in more income and about half in more leisure; from 1920 to 1950, it was 60 per cent for more income and 40 per cent for more leisure.[3] Taking more leisure is certainly one of the ways we have chosen to enjoy the fruits of technological progress, and no doubt future workers will choose to work still shorter hours. More time will be taken for leisure, not so much because it improves productivity while on the job, but mostly because people get a great deal of enjoyment from it.

TIMING AND SIZE OF PIECES OF LEISURE

Time is one resource which every human has in equal measure—24 hours a day, 365 days a year, as long as he lives. But the use made of it varies greatly. The amount of leisure, in the sense we use the term, depends upon life expectancy and labor force participation, upon length of the typical workweek, upon reliance on part-time and second jobs, upon vacations and other paid time-off, and perhaps upon other factors. As far as outdoor recreation is concerned, the timing and size of pieces of leisure are as important as the total amount of leisure. Just as the possible use of land may be greatly affected by the size of the parcels into which it has been subdivided, so may the use of leisure time be equally affected by the size of the pieces. In each case, excessive subdivision may reduce a total value.

Because of improved medicine and better economic conditions generally, the life expectancy of babies born in this country has increased substantially. The average life expectancy for boy babies rose from 48 years in 1900[4] to 65.5 years in 1950; and is expected to reach 73 by the year 2000. The greatest change has been made in reduction of death rates among babies and small children, so that a larger proportion of those born live to grow up; but progress has been made in extending life at the older ages. Many students think that greater progress will be made along the latter line in the decades ahead.

In 1900, the average boy would spend about 13 years in getting educated and growing up before entering the labor force, 32 years in the labor force itself, and about 3 years in retirement. By 1950, each of these figures had risen: to 18 years becoming educated and growing up, 42 years in the labor force, and nearly 6 years in retirement. By 2000, the figures are expected to be: nearly 20 years growing up and getting educated, 45 years in the labor force, and nearly 9 years in retirement. Thus, the effect of increased longevity will continue to be felt in each of

[3] Clark Kerr, discussion of paper entitled "The Shortening Work Week as a Component of Economic Growth: The Alternatives," by Charles D. Stewart, *American Economic Review*, Vol. 46, No. 2 (May 1956), pp. 218–23.

[4] Seymour L. Wolfbein, "The Changing Length of Working Life," in *Mass Leisure, op. cit.*

these three broad phases of the life cycle. Longer and presumably better preparation for life is possible; more working years; and at the end of life a longer period of retirement provides a major opportunity for enjoyment.

For women, the picture is somewhat similar, but more complicated.[5] The life expectancy for women is greater than for men, by about 6 years; it, too, has increased over the years, from the same general causes. But the employment pattern for women varies considerably from that for men. Girls enter the labor force in considerable numbers in the years up to 20, and women enter much more slowly after that age. For women between 20 and 25 years of age, the number who leave the labor force greatly exceeds the number who enter it; marriage and child-bearing take a large proportion of the total. It is at this age that marked differences begin to show up between the women who marry and those who do not, and between those whose marriages are broken by death or divorce and those remaining married. The women who do not marry before the age of 30 are likely never to marry. Most of them stay in the labor force unless ill health forces them out. Widowed and divorced women are often forced back to a job, and are likely to remain there for economic reasons. The average age of women when the last child is born is 26 years, and between 35 and 44 years of age the number of women who enter the labor force is larger than the number who leave. Those entering at this time are, for the most part, women who formerly worked and whose children are now enough older so that their family situation permits their return to work. The need for additional income or the desire for the stimulus of a job are the major reasons for their working. At older ages, women begin to leave the work force. But many married women with children will work 20 or more years during their lifetime.

Interestingly enough, the average woman who has worked spends about twice as many years in retirement, after work, as does the average man. Although historical data on work force participation are less complete for women than for men—in part because of more complicated life work histories—there is good reason to think that present trends will continue. There will almost certainly be a longer period of growing up and getting educated for the average young woman; some will work for a relatively short period, marry, raise children, and then re-enter the labor force when they still have many active years ahead; a modest

[5] Stuart Garfinkle, "Tables of Working Life for Women, 1950," *Monthly Labor Review,* Part II, Vol. 79, No. 8 (August 1956); and Part III, Vol. 79, No. 10 (October 1956). See also U.S. President's Commission on the Status of Women, *American Women* (Washington: U.S. Government Printing Office, 1963), for a generally similar analysis.

number of career women will work continuously; and the number of retired women will be larger. All of this has its implications for outdoor recreation.

The typical workweek and the average workweek are not exactly the same. For instance, most workers may be working a 40 hour week, and thus this is typical. But in some occupations, workers may have either a longer or shorter week; overtime lengthens the week for some, lay-offs and operations at less than capacity shorten it for others; and paid time off the job, in vacations and for other reasons, also affects the time actually at work. Some of these differences vary according as boom or prosperity affect the demand for labor.

The average workweek has declined greatly in the past 100 years or more.[6] In 1850, the average workweek was 70 hours—about 72 hours for agriculture and about 65 hours for all nonagricultural employment. By 1900, the average was down to 60 hours, and by 1920 to 50 hours, and today to about 40 hours. Part of the declining trend was due to the rise of nonagricultural employment, which typically has shorter working hours, but agriculture also shows a declining trend. The average has declined because typical hours per day have shortened, from 10 or 12 to 8 or less; because typical days per week have declined from 6 or 7 to 5 or less; and because of the rise of the paid time off. Declines in the average workweek have varied from industry to industry, and from occupation to occupation.

Some men and women work only part time. Students, housewives, and others may have other demands on their time which permit them to work only a portion of the week. Pay and working conditions in part-time jobs are often not attractive to workers. Moreover, there are major obstacles to a wider use of part-time workers, especially in industry. In wartime or when labor is short, employers may be driven to a greater use of part-time workers, but revert to employing full-time workers when labor conditions are normal again. In the service occupations, part-time work is more practical.

A special situation is the worker who has two or even three jobs.[7] In 1963, 3.9 million persons in the United States, out of a total labor force of about 75 million, more or less regularly had two or more jobs.[8]

[6] J. Frederic Dewhurst and Associates, *America's Needs and Resources—A New Survey* (New York: The Twentieth Century Fund, 1955); and Joseph S. Zeisel, "The Workweek in American Industry 1850–1956," in *Mass Leisure, op. cit.*

[7] Gertrude Bancroft, "Multiple Jobholders in December 1959," *Monthly Labor Review,* Vol. 83, No. 10 (October 1960).

[8] U.S. Bureau of Labor Statistics, *Special Labor Force Report No. 29,* "Multiple Jobholders in May 1962" (1963); *Special Labor Force Report No. 39,* "Multiple Jobholders in May 1963," by R. A. Bogan (1964).

Nearly half of these workers were self-employed at their second job—a farm for many of them, or a small business or profession. Some types of public service, as the postal service, are characterized by second job-holding. In New York City, it has been asserted that 60 to 70 per cent of the policemen and 50 to 60 per cent of the firemen hold a second job. Most of the double jobholders are men; the highest rate is for men in the 25 to 54 year age bracket, who often have heavy financial obligations. This seems a clear case where added income is valued more highly by the worker than is added leisure.

Another major development has been the increase in the paid vacation, or, more generally, in paid time off the job. The total number of weeks of paid vacation in the nation rose from 17.5 million in 1929 to 78 million weeks in 1959; or, based upon all members of the labor force, from 0.37 week in 1929 to slightly more than 1 week in 1959 per member of the labor force[9] and has continued to rise in more recent years. However, substantial numbers of self-employed, casual, and non-unionized workers have no paid vacations; this means that those with a paid vacation actually have far more time than these figures indicate. The paid vacation has long been a privilege of the managerial or upper professional employees in industry, education, and other major activities. For the hourly employees in industry, less than half had paid vacations before the war, but now almost all have them.[10] There has been a strong trend toward longer paid vacations. Length of paid vacation is often correlated with length of service with the company. In addition, hourly workers get paid vacations on holidays during the year. Nearly all workers get six such paid holidays and a substantial proportion get eight or more.[11] Also, in some companies, workers are allowed time off with pay for various personal matters such as a trip to the doctor or for voting, or for civic activities such as jury duty. There is considerable evidence that the full-time regular employee in a unionized plant, or in one with similar employment conditions, enjoys as much paid vacation time as do the managerial employees. The situation is different for the casual worker, for the typical nonunionized worker in service activities, and for the self-employed; they typically get no paid vacations.

A number of studies have been made in the past as to the daily living,

[9] Economic Report of the President, January 1960, and for earlier years.

[10] Harold Stieglitz, *Time Off with Pay* (Studies in Personnel Policy, No. 156), National Industrial Conference Board, New York, 1957.

[11] Bureau of Labor Statistics, *Wages and Related Benefits: All Metropolitan Areas, United States and Regional Summaries, 1962–63,* Bulletin No. 1345–83, Part II.

work, and leisure schedules of various classes.[12] The typical employed male in the United States today arises between six and eight in the morning, showers and shaves, eats breakfast, and departs for work, usually with no leisure except possibly scanning the morning paper or listening to the radio. The journey to work—varying from a very few minutes to more than an hour in the largest cities for some workers—possibly averages half an hour. For those who drive in a car pool with fellow workers, visiting en route, the trip to work is at least partly leisure; for those who take public transportation and read while traveling, the ride to work has a strong leisure content. At work there are some opportunities for visiting with co-workers, perhaps during coffee breaks. Lunch, especially for business and professional men, may be a combination of business and pleasure. A journey home after work completes the working part of the day. From three to six hours is likely to remain before bedtime, for eating, necessary personal chores, and leisure. The latter may be used in one of many ways—at home or away, outdoors or in, actively or passively, at a wide variety of activities. On the weekend, maintenance of home, car, and yard, and other chores will occupy some time. So may church and civic activities. But as much as four to twelve hours can be found for leisure pursuits on each of the two weekend days.

There are many variations in this pattern. Some men work shifts other than the normal daytime one, and therefore have entirely different daily schedules. However, for them, too, daily leisure is typically after work. The daily pattern for the child or youth going to school is roughly similar, with generally less time spent in travel, shorter hours at school than on the job, but more likelihood of homework from school than from job. The married woman has a somewhat similar schedule also, in part because the demands on her time are partly established by the activities of her family. She may arise earlier or later than the male, but usually must get her children their breakfast and get them off to school. During the day, her work schedule is more easily varied. Coffee with a neighbor may intermix leisure with work. Shopping may combine necessary household duties with pleasure. Many housewives do a considerable part of their daily work in the late afternoon, in getting dinner and in clearing up afterward, thus working later than other members of the family. For them the weekend days are similar to weekdays, and they have less additional leisure than the other members of the family.

The whole family, together or in various groupings, is likely to take an annual vacation, usually in summer, although winter vacations are

[12] For an early study of this type, with a comprehensive bibliography of published studies up to that time see Pitirim A. Sorokin and Clarence Q. Berger, *Time Budgets of Human Behavior* (Cambridge: Harvard University Press, 1939).

becoming more common. Spring and fall vacations may become increasingly popular in the future. The vacation may be spent at home, at a mountain or shore resort, traveling, or in other ways. Children of certain age groups often go to summer camp. A major problem is to find a vacation which is reasonably enjoyable to each member of the family. For example, the man and boys may enjoy camping and fishing, while the women and girls find the outdoors a particularly inconvenient place to do necessary housework.

For most persons from ages 6 to perhaps 65 years, leisure time comes in one of three major forms: (1) daily, for the approximately 180 school days or for the approximately 240 work days, in amounts of perhaps 3 to 6 hours each day, not necessarily all continuous, after the demands for sleep, work or school, and personal chores have been met; (2) on weekends, for about 100 days a year, when work is typically absent, and the time may run as high as 12 hours per day; and (3) annually, for vacations extending over a period as long as 75 to 90 days for school children and as long as 20 to 30 days for workers, when the whole pattern of family life may be different, and oriented largely to the leisure activities. The pre-school and retired ages have different patterns, less regular and less geared to the weekly and annual cycle; to a lesser extent, so do housewives. But all members of a household are affected by the schedules of the school and working members.

As we shall see in later chapters, differences in the amount and timing of leisure are directly reflected in the kinds of outdoor recreation that people engage in.

NATIONAL TIME BUDGET

As far as we can ascertain, very little work has been done on a compilation of a national time budget for the United States. Certainly there is no authoritative continuous series of annual time budgets showing how total time is used for the whole nation. National money income accounts, showing how national income originates and how it is used, annually, have been in existence for several decades. Perhaps "time is money," but the statisticians have never attempted to account for time. In a sense, this is curious, for in an advanced industrial society such as the United States the real wealth is very much in the time of its members, and not merely in the dollar accounts. It is altogether possible that in the future the competition for consumers' time will be more severe than for their money. This is possibly true on TV today; it may well be true for outdoor recreation tomorrow. Money can be used to buy time-saving measures and hence money is translatable into time, within limits. The fact that goods and services are sold in some kind of a market place, with money price tags attached, makes money national income vastly easier to estimate than a national time budget, since the use of time is so much a personal affair. However, a national time budget has been estimated for 1900, 1950, and 2000 and is shown in Table 1 and Figure 1.[13] Total time (population multiplied by hours per year) is broken down by use, including leisure, and then leisure time is further subdivided. How time is used depends in part upon the number of people in various age and activity classes, and upon what the typical person in each class does with his time. Although our information is relatively good on the first point, it is poor on the second, and our estimates are only approximately accurate.

By far the largest use of time at each period is for sleep—approximately 40 per cent of the total time is used in this way at each date. The time spent in work has declined from 13 per cent of total time in 1900 to 10 per cent in 1950, and is expected to decline further to only about 7 per cent in 2000. Only a part of this decline is due to average working hours per week; part is due to differences in participation in the labor force. Other readjustments in use of time have occurred or seem probable. For instance, the time spent in housekeeping has risen less than proportionately to the increase in total time, less than proportionately to the increase in paid work, and very much less than the rise in leisure.

Our particular concern is with leisure. It has risen greatly in absolute terms; with total time roughly doubling in each 50-year period, total hours of leisure for the whole population increased nearly threefold between 1900 and 1950 and are expected to increase 2.5 times between 1950 and 2000. Leisure time has also increased relatively, from 27 per cent of total time in 1900 to 34 per cent in 1950, with an expected further increase to 38 per cent by 2000. There have also been some changes in the distribution of leisure among its major types. Daily leisure remained a relatively constant proportion of total leisure from 1900 to 1950, but is expected to drop in relative terms by 2000 as other types of leisure increase relatively more. In contrast, weekend leisure has risen greatly in relative terms, and promises to continue to do so. Curiously enough, vacation leisure had hardly kept pace with the rise in total leisure up to 1950; a comparison to 1960, however, might show a different result as this type of leisure is expected to rise greatly in relative terms by 2000. The change in total hours of the whole population plus the changes in time distribution of leisure will mean a tenfold increase in total vacations and total retired time between 1900 and 2000.

[13] Mary A. Holman, "A National Time-Budget for the Year 2000," *Sociology and Social Research,* Vol. 46, No. 1 (October 1961).

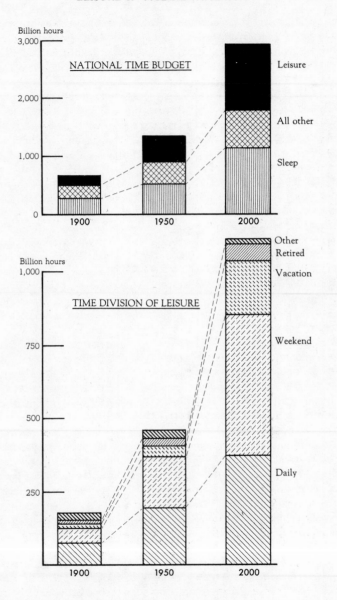

Figure 1. National time budget and time divisions of leisure, 1900, 1950, and 2000.

21

TABLE 1.
NATIONAL TIME BUDGET AND TIME DIVISION OF LEISURE, 1900, 1950, AND 2000

Use of time	1900 Billion hours	1900 Per cent of total time	1900 Per cent of leisure time	1950 Billion hours	1950 Per cent of total time	1950 Per cent of leisure time	2000 Billion hours	2000 Per cent of total time	2000 Per cent of leisure time
1. Total time for entire population	667	100		1,329	100		2,907	100	
2. Sleep	265	40		514	39		1,131	39	
3. Work	86	13		132	10		206	7	
4. School	11	2		32	2		90	3	
5. Housekeeping	61	9		68	5		93	3	
6. Preschool population, nonsleeping hours	30	4		56	4		110	4	
7. Personal care	37	6		74	6		164	6	
8. Total (items 2–7)	490	73		876	66		1,794	62	
9. Remaining hours, largely leisure	177	27	100	453	34	100	1,113	38	100
10. Daily leisure hours	72		41	189		42	375		34
11. Weekend leisure hours	50		28	179		39	483		44
12. Vacation	17		10	35		8	182		16
13. Retired	6		3	24		5	56		5
14. Other, including unaccounted	32		18	26		6	16		1

SOURCE: Adapted from Mary A. Holman, "A National Time-Budget for the Year 2000," *Sociology and Social Research*, Vol. 46, No. 1 (October 1961).

These comparisons of 1900 and 1950 are based upon the best available estimates of what has actually happened over this period. The comparisons of what may happen between 1950 and 2000 are based upon certain assumptions as to the form of leisure in the latter year.[14] The total leisure then available is likely to be about as estimated, but of course some of it might be shifted from one category to another.

The combined influence of many more people, of more of them in leisure age groups, and of more leisure for the working ages all combine to suggest a very great increase in total leisure in the decades ahead. The effect of such changes upon outdoor recreation will continue to be very great.[15]

Table 1 and Figure 1 present data on leisure for the whole population; this will be shared unequally among individuals. Not every individual, or at least not every individual in every year, will necessarily experience an increase in leisure over the next few decades. Professional and white-collar adult workers, during the weeks they work, may well work as long hours as now; but they may enter the labor force at a later age than now is common; they may have longer paid vacations, including perhaps "sabbaticals" of several weeks duration at intervals of a few years; and they may have more years in retirement. In recent years, blue-collar workers have perhaps gained relatively more leisure than white-collar workers, as union contracts have frequently included more paid time off, as well as shorter workweeks in some instances. While the variations among individuals will be important to the persons concerned, the total demand for outdoor recreation will be affected

[14] These are discussed in Holman, op. cit.

[15] It is only fair to warn readers that not everyone accepts our findings, either as to past trends in leisure or as to outlook for the future. Those who criticize our interpretation of the past do so mostly on the grounds that other demands of our modern urban society take so much time that the increase in genuine leisure is much less than we estimate. Sebastian De Grazia, in Of Time, Work and Leisure (New York: Twentieth Century Fund, 1962) almost goes so far as to deny that there has been any increase in leisure. Various reviewers of an earlier draft of this manuscript think that the extent of leisure today is exaggerated. We can only reply that we think our statements are correct in terms of our definition of leisure. Those who criticize our views of the future do so on directly contrasting grounds. On the one hand, Donald Michael in Cybernation (Santa Barbara: Center for the Study of Democratic Institutions, 1960) and Work and Free Time (Philadelphia: American Recreation Foundation, 1962) and Robert Theobald in Free Men and Free Markets (New York: Clarkson Potter, 1963) think that science and technology will so reduce labor requirements for most types of economic enterprise that the amount of unemployed time will rise enormously more than we estimate. Taking the contrary view are various persons who think that consumers' demands for goods, plus the necessities of the international situation, will require that leisure be kept to a lower level than we have estimated, in order that more productive work be done.

primarily by the total volume of leisure, and very little by its distribution among individuals.

The past and prospective increases in leisure per capita are sharply at variance with the past and probable increases in real income per capita. For the 1900–1950 period, leisure per capita rose about 27 per cent, while real incomes per capita increased about 150 per cent; for the 1950–2000 period, the contrast may be still sharper—a rise of about 12 per cent in per capita leisure to be contrasted with an anticipated rise of at least 150 per cent in real income per capita. The total supply of time per person is absolutely fixed; while leisure has increased, and is expected to increase further, there are rather definite limits to the increase per person. On the other hand, real incomes per person can rise more or less indefinitely, and in fact have risen sharply in the past. The leisure-income balance is shifting toward much more income and to only slightly more leisure, each on a per capita basis. People will be under increasing incentive, and will increasingly have the means, to spend part of their larger income on making the most of their limited leisure. The vacationist will fly to his destination and rent a car, rather than spend time in driving there, for instance. It is this divergence in prospective trends of per capita real income and of per capita leisure which has led us to state that the competition for time will become more severe than the competition for leisure.

How have people used their available leisure time? Our information on this point is even less complete; we find it impossible to present an estimated division of total leisure time into various activities. However, some rough estimates can be made for total time spent on certain outdoor recreation activities for which information on numbers of participants and estimated time per unit of participation is available. At best, the margin of error for each figure is considerable, but perhaps the general magnitudes are correct. Our estimate of leisure time spent in certain primarily outdoor recreation activities in 1960 is as follows:

	Million man-hours
Travel for pleasure	5,330
Visits to public outdoor recreation areas (excluding travel time):	
National park system	660
National forests	2,285
Federal wildlife refuges	150
Reservoirs of Corps of Engineers	900
TVA reservoirs	432
All state parks	1,620
All municipal and county parks	5,000
Fishing in all areas	1,500

	Million man-hours
Hunting in all areas	1,125
Boating of all kinds	600
Bowling	660
Organized sports, such as baseball, football, basketball, etc., but excluding golf and tennis—spectator as well as participant time included	600
Horse racing	150
Total of enumerated activities, 1960	21,012

There are some duplications in the above listing. For example, fishing and hunting, which are listed separately, are the purpose of some visits to national forests; and some boating is for the purpose of fishing. But there are many omissions also, because even approximate data were lacking. Many kinds of sports and outdoor activities are excluded; no allowance is made for gardening and work around the home, which possibly are larger uses than any single item included. Since our concern is with outdoor recreation, most indoor recreation activities (movies, watching TV, reading, and the like) are not included. Likewise, no allowance is made for visiting with friends, or for resting and relaxing.

The items enumerated amount to roughly 3 or 4 per cent of the total leisure probably available in 1960. Even if our estimates of time spent on each activity are much too low—and we tried to avoid exaggeration —it still seems probable that the major outdoor recreation activities use but a relatively small part of total leisure. In view of the age of various parts of the population, the time-size of various pieces of leisure, and other factors, one could not expect a major share of all leisure to be used for these purposes. However, it would seem possible for a large increase in outdoor recreation to take place within the available amounts of leisure, as well as by increases in it.

For purposes of comparison with 1960, estimates were made of the total time spent in the previously enumerated activities in earlier years. The results are shown below. Data on attendance and on average time

	Million man-hours
1900	300
1910	650
1920	2,100
1930	5.300
1940	7,850
1950	12,200
1960	21,012

per unit of participation being even less complete for earlier years than for 1960, the individual activities are not listed separately. Even the totals are far from precise, but they do suggest the enormous rise in time spent on outdoor recreation over the past two generations.

These estimates indicate that about 70 times as much time was spent in outdoor recreation in 1960 as in 1900. Automobile travel for pleasure, which makes up more than a fourth of the total today, was inconsequential as late as 1920; fewer publicly-owned outdoor recreation areas existed, and use of those that did exist was much less prior to about 1930; and many activities such as water skiing that are popular today were unknown a few decades ago.

From 1900 to 1950, while total leisure increased less than three-fold, our estimates indicate that time spent on the enumerated activities increased more than 40 times. It is possible, though by no means certain, that time spent on some other outdoor activities decreased over these decades; but one is hard put to suggest an example. Although there may be fewer farm boys hunting and fishing today, there are probably more people in other occupations who now engage in these activities. More work was done outdoors, and most people lived closer to nature in the earlier period, but outdoor recreation in the sense we use the term was much less common than today.

We have not hazarded an estimate as to the precise amount of time that will be spent by the total population on outdoor recreation in 2000; but it seems almost certain that the increase over the next 40 years will be far more than proportional to the increase in total leisure. Whereas less than 0.25 per cent of all leisure was used for these enumerated activities in 1900, perhaps between 3 and 4 per cent was so used in 1960; this may well increase to higher proportions in the future. If it were to increase to 8–10 per cent by 2000—a proportion by no means unlikely—this would amount to 900–1,100 billion hours in outdoor recreation then, or 40 to 50 times the total time spent in this way in 1960.

As noted earlier in this chapter, the increase in leisure or discretionary time is not inconsistent with increasingly tighter time budgets for individuals. Although the amount of discretionary time has increased, the desire to engage in outdoor recreation and in other leisure-time pursuits has risen even more. Many individuals are today forced to make more difficult choices among alternative uses of their time; many undoubtedly feel harried by the necessity for such choices, and will say they have no leisure. Yet many of them have more time left after the basic necessities of life are taken care of than did their parents.

3

The Role and Character of Outdoor Recreation

Recreation, as we use the term, is the activity or activities (including inactivity if freely chosen) engaged in during leisure time.[1] Leisure is time, recreation is activity. The two are closely related but not synonymous.

Some writers have stressed the emotional and intellectual experiences involved in recreation, and their highly personal nature; these writers define recreation in terms of those experiences. We prefer to focus attention upon the activity—upon what people do, in observable ways—and to use the term "experience" to describe the activity.

Just as the individual has choice in use of leisure so he has a choice in

[1] General references for this chapter, in addition to those listed at the beginning of Chapter 2, most of which are not specifically cited in the text, are as follows: Harry Elmer Barnes, *Social Institutions* (New York: Prentice-Hall, Inc., 1942); C. K. Brightbill, *Man and Leisure: A Philosophy of Recreation* (New York: Prentice-Hall, Inc., 1961); George D. Butler, *Introduction to Community Recreation* (3rd ed.; New York: McGraw-Hill Book Co., 1959); Foster Rhea Dulles, *America Learns to Play* (New York: D. Appleton-Century Co., 1940); Henry Durant, *The Problem of Leisure* (London: George Routledge and Sons, Ltd., 1938); Herbert J. Gans, "Recreation Planning for Leisure Behavior: A Goal-Oriented Approach" (A dissertation in city planning, University of Pennsylvania, 1957); Luther Halsey Gulick, *A Philosophy of Play* (New York: Charles Scribner's Sons, 1920); George A. Lundberg, Mirra Komarovsky, and Mary Alice McInerny, *Leisure, A Suburban Study* (New York: Columbia University Press, 1934); Harold D. Meyer and Charles K. Brightbill, *Community Recreation—A Guide to Its Organization* (2nd ed.; Boston: D. C. Heath and Co., 1956); and *State Recreation: Organization and Administration* (New York: A. S. Barnes and Co., 1950); Martin H. Neumeyer and Esther Neumeyer, *Leisure and Recreation* (rev. ed.; New York: A. S. Barnes and Co., 1958); Allen V. Sapora and Elmer D. Mitchell, *The Theory of Play and Recreation* (rev. and enlarged ed.; New York: Ronald Press, 1961); Jesse Frederick Steiner, *Americans at Play* (New York: McGraw-Hill Book Co., 1933).

recreation activity. Individuals choose their recreation activities within the range of opportunities physically and economically available to them. Their choices are conditioned by their social environment and by their knowledge of the opportunities. Recreation activities which require substantial outlays of cash are practically unavailable to those whose incomes are low. Recreation choices are heavily influenced by age and sex; what one chooses as a child or youth may no longer appeal when one is older, and the strenuous activities engaged in by the young adult may be more than the older person either can undertake or wishes to undertake.

A complete listing of all kinds of recreation activities is not necessary for our present purpose, but the simple division of recreation into indoor and outdoor types must be recognized. Indoor types compete for the time and money of consumers, and to this extent are of direct concern to outdoor recreation. However, it is also true that most other forms of consumer expenditure compete for money and sometimes for time.

A common characteristic of the many forms of recreation considered, be they informal play, organized games, water sports, or any of the many diverse and interesting other types, is their need for areas of land or water—often for relatively large areas. In its use of land and water, outdoor recreation competes with other uses of the same resources—forestry, agriculture, grazing, homesites, factories and other uses of land; flood control, hydroelectric power production, irrigation, water supply, and other uses of water.

THE NEED FOR OUTDOOR RECREATION

The nature and severity of the emotional stresses and strains of modern life have been emphasized by many writers. Although this viewpoint may sometimes be overstated, it does seem clear that modern life is more ordered in terms of time than was life in earlier periods. Mumford has put it very well:

> The clock, not the steam-engine, is the key-machine of the modern industrial age. For every phase of its development the clock is both the outstanding fact and the typical symbol of the machine: even today no other machine is so ubiquitous. . . .
> . . . the effect of the mechanical clock is more pervasive and strict: it presides over the day from the hour of rising to the hour of rest. When one thinks of the day as an abstract span of time, one does not go to bed with the chickens on a winter's night: one invents wicks, chimneys, lamps, gaslights, electric lamps, so as to use all the hours belonging to the day. When one thinks of time, not as a sequence of experiences, but as a collection of hours, minutes, and seconds, the habits of adding time and saving time come into existence. Time took on the character of an enclosed space: it could be divided, it could be filled up, it could even be expanded by the invention of labor-saving instruments.

28

Abstract time became the new medium of existence. Organic functions themselves were regulated by it: one ate, not upon feeling hungry, but when prompted by the clock: one slept, not when one was tired, but when the clock sanctioned it. . . .[2]

We have noted that most of the working man's leisure in the United States today falls into one of three major categories: on workdays after work; on weekends; and on vacations, usually annually. A fourth category of leisure is added when he retires. The demands of the job and the necessity of earning a living greatly restrict the individual in his ability to take leisure whenever he wishes. He must be guided by the accepted social and economic pattern of work, sleep, personal chores, and leisure. In the case of younger persons, even the freedom to refrain from going to school has been taken away by society, in the form of compulsory school attendance laws. The modern society is more highly productive of material goods than older and simpler ones; the average worker is able to consume more and to live better, but his life is a more ordered one.

In this generally ordered life, recreation in general and outdoor recreation in particular stand as opportunities for free choice. True, there are some restrictions. Television programs are tightly scheduled, as are most spectator activities. Group activities, such as organized sports, require some agreement among the participants as to timing. Many outdoor recreation activities require daylight although electric lighting of outdoor areas is increasingly removing this obstacle. But the individual still has great freedom in choosing both the activity and the time. This is one of the appeals of recreation.

Many sociologists, psychologists, social workers, outdoor recreation specialists, and others have emphasized the psychological and emotional need for outdoor recreation—need for relief from the tensions and emotional strains which modern urban living place upon the individual. To recreation in general and to outdoor recreation in particular they ascribe great value, of almost a therapeutic kind. Some stress that in outdoor recreation the individual can test his physical fitness and his ability to cope with Nature. Still others emphasize the opportunity which outdoor recreation gives for self-fulfillment and individual choices. Recreation is also considered by some to have significant value in combatting or preventing juvenile delinquency.

A moderate expression of a common viewpoint in this connection is given by Butler.

[2] Lewis Mumford, *Technics and Civilization* (New York: Harcourt, Brace and World, Inc., 1934), pp. 14 and 17. Margaret Mead has made a similar point: "The Pattern of Leisure in Contemporary American Culture," *The Annals of the American Academy of Political and Social Science*, Vol. 313 (September 1957.)

Recreation has always afforded an outlet for self-expression, for release, and for the attainment of satisfaction in life. During the last few decades, however, the marked and rapid changes that have taken place in our social, industrial, economic, and political life have magnified the importance of recreation and have greatly affected the recreation life of the people.[3]

Most, perhaps all, of the authors referred to at the beginning of this chapter would endorse this statement, or a stronger one. Butler goes on to outline the effect of growth of cities, changing home conditions, increase in leisure, specialization and automation in industry, population changes, the rising economy, technological developments, and other factors which he had in mind when referring to rapid changes.

A stronger statement of the same general viewpoint is that by Romney:

This highly mechanized industrial age with its materialistic accent has transfigured the working lives of most human beings. Millions of men (and, in wartime, women) work at assembly lines looking all day long at a monotonous parade of identical objects going by, perhaps screwing on nut 272, or attaching part 48b, using one tiny set of muscles while starving all the rest of the physical body of activity, finding no challenge for the mind or imagination, no exercise for the emotions. These whole human beings are not only entitled to an opportunity for full living, but are in need of a variety of experience to lend balance and refreshment and to stimulate growth. . . . The wholeness of all these human beings cries out for release from the suffocation of dwarfed experience. It is in his time-off-the-job, his free choosing time, his earned leisure, that man must find compensation for the deprivations of his work. It is then that he may discover his potentialities and may venture into chosen pastures at the dictates of his appetites and talents.[4]

A still more emphatic statement is that by Pack:

Deprive man of intimate relationship with the soil or some equivalent, and his bodily powers, as well as his spiritual and mental fiber, weaken and decay. Surrounded by steel, concrete, asphalt, and glass, doing the same meaningless, repetitive job day after day, with no feeling of creating something in its entirety, the worker becomes ill-adjusted, unhappy and unstable. . . . Because agriculture embodies hard work, it builds character, tenacity, ruggedness, and individualism. Because it envisions the changing seasons and nature's moods of friendliness, of beauty and creation, it feeds the very soul of man and raises up his eyes to the infinite possibilities of wider horizons, until he is no longer a cog of man-created machines, but a living power at one with creation itself.[5]

[3] George D. Butler, *Introduction to Community Recreation* (3rd. ed.; New York: McGraw-Hill Book Co., 1959), p. 14. (Used by permission.)

[4] G. Ott Romney, *Off the Job Living—A Modern Concept of Recreation and Its Place in the Postwar World* (New York: A. S. Barnes and Co., 1945), pp. 2–3.

[5] Arthur N. Pack, *The Challenge of Leisure* (New York: Macmillan Co., 1934), pp. 80 and 82.

With the exception of Pack's glorification of agriculture, the spirit of these quotations is repeated in scores of books and articles addressed to professional and popular audiences. It is generally agreed by writers of this type that serious tensions exist, that they are increasing because of various economic and social developments, and that recreation, especially outdoor recreation, is a major solution for the grave problems arising out of such tensions.

Since these views are widely held by able and sincere men and women with extensive experience in outdoor recreation, they obviously must be taken seriously. The present authors, with different backgrounds of training and experience, do not so readily come to the same conclusions as a result of their personal knowledge. One need not be a cynic to be sceptical about some of these statements, or at least about the more extreme of them. That serious emotional and nervous tensions exist today, no one can deny; and that some people find release in outdoor recreation is equally obvious. But it is by no means clear that everyone, or even a majority of persons, suffers from severe strains and stresses; moreover, a substantial proportion of the population apparently rarely or never engages in outdoor recreation. It is at least arguable that it is the well-adjusted, not the ill-adjusted, who both experience outdoor recreation and gain most from so doing. Although much is made of the increase in tension and strain, yet it is a fact that no comprehensive continuous efforts have ever been made to measure these factors—indeed, it might be extremely difficult to do so. One can express serious doubt that there has in fact been a rise in such stresses and strains; early life, including that of the bucolic and frontier societies, was not without its special problems. Pack seems unaware of the bestial conditions in which the typical Negro sharecropper of the South was living at the time he wrote (1934), and even today many thousands of farm families live in intellectual and emotional, as well as financial, poverty. Moreover, while the therapeutic or tension-relieving aspect of outdoor recreation is often stressed and is widely accepted by most workers in outdoor recreation, a verified scientific or research base for this view is weak if not wholly lacking.

A variant of the foregoing views may be described, in economists' terms, as the externality argument. This asserts that recreation lessens juvenile delinquency, mental illness, and other undesirable consequences of modern life so that those not directly involved nevertheless gain a better total community life. Even though you and I are neither juvenile delinquents nor mentally ill, according to this argument, we nevertheless benefit if these ills are diminished in the community at large; and for this reason we should be willing to expend public funds, derived in part from taxes we pay, to reduce or alleviate these social ills. To the extent that recreation in fact does help overcome serious social problems, it is worthy of public expenditures and one can justify use of taxes paid by those indirectly rather than directly benefited.

The case for the psychological and emotional *need* for outdoor recreation may, therefore, have been somewhat overstated or wrongly stated. We do not pass judgment on these views; on the one hand, we recognize that they are widely and firmly held by many able people with experience; on the other hand, the evidence in their support is not wholly convincing. We do, however, feel that the *demand* for outdoor recreation —in the economists' sense of the term—is very strong and is clearly demonstrable. When people are free to choose how they will spend their time and money, many will choose outdoor recreation. By their actions, they make it clear that they value recreation highly—more highly than other activities which would have used the same time and money. The demand and the need approaches are not necessarily in conflict. If there exists a psychological need not measurable in conventional economic terms, then there also exists some form of value in addition to any direct monetary value that may be estimated.

There is perhaps another attribute of outdoor recreation which should be mentioned; this is the effect of recreation as a democratizing force. By world standards, the United States has a relatively open society. That is, its members are to a very great extent free to choose their occupations, their mode of living, and their associates on the basis of individual abilities and tastes. The forces of caste, class, and custom are less restrictive in our society than in most contemporary societies in the world. Yet it is also true that our society has many groups—racial, ethnic, religious, economic. The boundary lines of these classes are not always hard and sharp, but still they exist. There are many divisive forces in our society, as well as cohesive ones.

Because outdoor recreation takes place in a less formal atmosphere, where the customary restrictions of job and home are less evident, it may be that it can serve to bring divergent groups together, to provide a broader basis for common understanding. There is some evidence that sports have served to do this. The star halfback will receive a measure of social acceptance regardless of the occupation and wealth of his parents, or of his race, for instance.

If outdoor recreation is to serve in this capacity, all or most public outdoor recreation areas must be freely available to all classes within the population. Some segments of the population would resist this bitterly, as they have fought school integration. Obviously, the problem is not simple, and no easy answer exists. If outdoor recreation serves to a significant degree to lessen social tensions and to promote true democracy within the nation, this is a most important function and advantage.

MAJOR PHASES OF OUTDOOR RECREATION EXPERIENCE

Most writing about outdoor recreation seems implicitly to assume that the actual outdoor recreation activity on the site is the total recreation experience.[6] Actually, the total recreation experience is almost always much broader than this; at least five rather distinctly different phases can be identified.

First. An outdoor recreation experience begins by *anticipation,* including planning. The thinking may be very brief, as when a small boy responds to the invitation of his group to play ball on a playground; or it may extend over weeks or months, as in the planning of the family summer vacation. Anticipation may far outrun the later reality. A fisherman may get more enjoyment from tieing his own dry flies through the winter than he will later get from the actual fishing itself. Pleasurable anticipation is almost a necessity—certainly travel agents cannot be charged with underestimating the attractiveness of the areas they advertise! But excessive optimism in the anticipatory stage may lead to later disappointment and frustration. By and large, advance planning should be based upon realistic factors. If the anticipation and planning lead to a positive decision, the outdoor recreation experience goes farther.

Second. The second major phase of an outdoor recreation experience is *travel to* the actual site. In almost every instance, some travel is required, even if it is only a short walk or bicycle ride to a local playground. The time required for travel, both absolutely and relative to the time spent at the site, may vary greatly; so may the cost of the travel. These variations have a major effect upon the amount of recreation experience, as we shall try to show in a later chapter. Less obvious, but perhaps of greater significance, the satisfactions and dissatisfactions of travel to the site vary greatly between individuals, between routes, and between end objectives or areas visited. At the best, some persons or groups may enjoy the travel itself. This attitude seems to have been more prevalent in an earlier day, when travel was less common and many persons traveled for the sheer enjoyment of the trip. Even today, a majority of the visitors at many recreation areas give "sightseeing" as their major purpose; certainly, many of these must value the travel positively. On the other hand, many travelers seem to regard the trip itself as a necessary nuisance. We have almost no objective data on how

---

[6] Many of the general writings cited earlier take this position, explicitly or implicitly.

outdoor recreationists evaluate travel incident to their outdoor recreation, and on variations among individuals in this regard; indeed, we know little about how to go about measuring their satisfactions and dissatisfactions from travel.

Third. On-site experiences and activities are the third major phase of the total recreation experience. These are the activities we usually think of when we consider outdoor recreation—swimming, hiking, camping, picnicking, hunting, fishing, playing games, and all the other myraid activities engaged in at outdoor recreation areas—and the satisfactions from them. This is what many seem to think is the total outdoor recreation experience; this is the part which is usually discussed, and sometimes studied, in most detail. But this third phase may be less than half of the total, whether measured by time involved, expense incurred, or total satisfactions gained. It may be the basic reason for the whole outdoor recreation experience, and the remaining parts of the total experience may be built around it. But it is only a part. As a matter of convenience, we often describe the total experience in terms of what happens during this third phase. "I went camping on Willow Creek." This method of description tends further to confuse the nature of the whole experience, but it is often a simple way to describe it.

In some outings, especially those taken during vacations, several sites may be involved, with intermediate travel between them. A family may visit a few national parks, perhaps a state park or two, and some relatives or friends during a single vacation trip. Each of the sites is important and the experience at each contributes to total enjoyment. For the typical one-day outing, usually only a single site is involved.

Fourth. Travel back is the fourth phase of the total outdoor recreation experience. It is unlikely to be a duplicate of the travel to the site. Even when the route is the same, the recreationists are different. If it has been an all-day outing, they are now tired, while they were fresh traveling to the area. If travel is back from a vacation, memories of the vacation and anticipation of the job are certainly different from the thoughts on the outbound trip. Even the small boy, called home for dinner from the playground, is likely to proceed at a different pace and in a different frame of mind, as well as in a different state of cleanliness, compared to his travel toward the recreation area. As pointed out, we know little of the role travel satisfactions or their lack play in outdoor recreation, and we know still less about the difference between the going and the returning trips.

Fifth. The fifth major phase of the total recreation experience is *recollection*. After the experience is over, the person or persons concerned recalls to memory one or more aspects of the total experience. He may share these recollections with friends, relatives, and associates—

sometimes beyond the point of their maximum interest. When the total recreation experience makes a major impression, as a first camping trip or a first visit to a distant national park often does, the recollection will be strong and lasting. If the experience is a brief and common one quickly followed by a similar one—as with children playing on a playground—then each experience will make only a dim impression. Recollection may produce feelings quite different from the actual experience; rain and a leaky tent, or poison ivy, or any one of many other events that seemed catastrophic at the time may provide much fun and conversation later.

Recollection of one outdoor experience often provides the starting point for anticipation of another, by the same person or by others. And recollection of many experiences in time builds into knowledge, or assumed knowledge, which provides a basis for choosing among different areas and different activities.

In many ways, the whole outdoor recreation experience is a package deal; all parts are necessary, and the sum of satisfactions and dissatisfactions from the whole must be balanced against total costs. Pleasurable parts of the experience must more than balance the unpleasant parts, if any, if the same kind of experience is to be repeated. Later, where we consider demand for outdoor recreation, the whole experience is the unit of study; the same is true, to some extent, when we consider the value of natural resources for recreation.

Although the whole recreation experience is the unit of study and analysis, different parts of it respond differently to various causal factors. The two travel phases provide an opportunity to substitute money for time, for the man whose time is limited but whose income is high. A combination of flying and car rental is an obvious means of reducing travel time to distant places. Personal effort can reduce money expenditures, and many families camp rather than spend money for motels or hotels. One might even have a travel agency plan his trip for him, although for many recreationists this would mean losing half the fun. Presumably no one would go so far as to hire someone to take over the on-site part of the experience for him! But use of guides and conducted tours is a means of seeing more in a limited time than can be achieved by poking around by one's self. Although all phases of the total experience are necessary, the means for carrying out some of them vary.

Research, planning, and operation of outdoor recreation programs and areas should be concerned with all five of these major phases, not merely with the on-site phase. Research might well reveal ways in which each major phase could be made more enjoyable and less costly in both monetary and human terms. Adequate information and advice might help recreationists to plan their outings better. This seems particularly important for vacations in which a family makes a major investment in money and time. Travel to and from the site might be made more pleasurable.[7] People might be aided in developing more accurate recollections of their experiences. All in all, each phase of the total experience seems to merit serious, if not equal, attention in research, in planning, and in operations. The effort might be less directed to advising people than to providing them with the kind of information that helps them discover for themselves what they most want to do. In this way, the content of the total outdoor recreation experience could be materially enlarged.

CLASSIFYING OUTDOOR RECREATION AREAS

Publicly owned outdoor recreation areas have a bewildering variety of names—parks, forests, nature preserves, monuments, historical areas, playgrounds, wildlife refuges, waysides, and many others. The nomenclature is based in part upon the physical characteristics of the area, its chief uses, its history, and in part upon the administering agency, and, perhaps, in large part upon historical accident. In addition, there are many kinds of privately-owned areas that are used for outdoor recreation either by their owners or by a larger public. Public and private areas each have their own special problems. But they also share problems, for although areas may differ in ownership and in name they may be similar in nature and use.

Because there are so many physically different kinds of outdoor recreation areas some classification into fewer groups is helpful for understanding and analysis. Our classification is a threefold one, and the three classes—user-oriented, resource-based, and intermediate— are described in detail later in this section, and summarized in Table 2. Others have devised different breakdowns for their particular purposes. The classification in the *California Public Outdoor Recreation Plan, Part I* (State Printer, Sacramento, California, 1960) is somewhat similar to ours, but includes four classes of area, as does the one used by E. G. Pleva in his studies in Ontario, Canada, while the Outdoor Recreation Resources Review Commission established a sixfold classification. The various systems are not without similarities, even when the primary basis of distinction is different.

The following listing describes the ORRRC classes, which are based in part upon management criteria and in part upon physical charac-

[7] Marion Clawson, "Implications of Recreational Needs for Highway Improvements," Paper at Department of Economics, Finance and Administration, Division of Economic Studies, Highway Research Board, January 1961.

TABLE 2.
GENERAL CLASSIFICATION OF OUTDOOR RECREATIONAL USES AND RESOURCES

Item	Type of recreation area		
	User oriented	Resource based	Intermediate
1. General location	Close to users; on whatever resources are available	Where outstanding resources can be found; may be distant from most users	Must not be too remote from users; on best resources available within distance limitation
2. Major types of activity	Games, such as golf and tennis; swimming; picknicking; walks and horse riding; zoos, etc.; playing by children	Major sightseeing; scientific and historical interest; hiking and mountain climbing; camping, fishing and hunting	Camping, picnicking, hiking, swimming, hunting, fishing
3. When major use occurs	After hours (school or work)	Vacations	Day outings and weekends
4. Typical sizes of areas	One to a hundred, or at most to a few hundred acres	Usually some thousands of acres, perhaps many thousands	A hundred to several thousand acres
5. Common types of agency responsibility	City, county, or other local government; private	National parks and national forests primarily; state parks in some cases; private, especially for seashore and major lakes	Federal reservoirs; state parks; private

SOURCE: Marion Clawson, R. Burnell Held, and C. H. Stoddard, *Land for the Future* (Baltimore: The Johns Hopkins Press, for Resources for the Future, Inc., 1960), Table 20, p. 136.

teristics of the areas, and indicates how these relate in a general way to our classes, which are distinguished primarily on the basis of economic similarities.

"Class I—High-density Recreation Areas; areas intensively developed and managed for mass use." (These would, in general, resemble our user-oriented areas.)

"Class II—General Outdoor Recreation Areas; areas subject to substantial development for a wide variety of specific recreation uses."

"Class III—Natural Environment Areas; various types of areas that are suitable for recreation in a natural environment and usually in combination with other uses." (These two would, in general, resemble our intermediate type areas.)

"Class IV—Unique Natural Areas; areas of outstanding scenic splendor, natural wonder, or scientific importance."

"Class V—Primitive Areas; undisturbed roadless areas, characterized by natural, wild conditions, including 'wilderness area'."

"Class VI—Historic and Cultural Sites; sites of major historic or cultural significance, either local, regional, or national."

(These latter three categories would, in general, resemble our resource-based areas.)

User-oriented areas. At one extreme in our classification are the user-oriented areas, such as city parks or playgrounds. Their most important characteristic is their ready accessibility to users. Their chief time of use is after school for children, after work for adults, and during the day by mothers and small children. For these purposes, it is essential that such areas be close to users, both in order to keep the travel time down and to permit some users to go from home to the area unaccompanied by adults. The use of these areas is closely correlated with the free time available each day. Such areas are often individually small, frequently ranging from a few to a few hundred acres; their physical characteristics are not too demanding.

Resource-based areas are at the other extreme. Their dominant characteristic is their outstanding physical resources. Resource quality for recreation is largely a subjective matter, yet most people would agree that some areas are inherently more attractive and outstanding than others. This applies to historical as well as to natural sites. The major areas of this type are mountains, desert, sea and lake shores, and swamps—areas that usually lie at considerable distance from concentrations of population. For most people, a visit to a resource-based outdoor recreation area involves considerable travel, and thus both time and money in moderately large amounts; as a result, such visits are typically vacations. Except for the historical sites, which are often small, most resource-based outdoor recreation areas are fairly large units, generally of several thousand acres or more. Typical of this group are the national parks and monuments, the national forests, federal wildlife refuges, privately owned sea and lake shore areas, and the like.

Intermediate areas lie between these extremes, both geographically and in terms of use. They must be well located with respect to users—typically within an hour's driving time, almost certainly within two hours' time—and they should be on the best sites available within this range. Such areas are typically used for all-day outings, and on weekends. Visits to them involve less travel time and expense than visits to the usual resource-based areas. Many such areas are state parks; federal reservoir areas also fall into this general category. Tracts of this type often include a few hundred acres; they are much larger than the typical user-oriented area, but much smaller than the typical resource-based area.

Although by far the greater number of areas and by far the greatest use falls into the general patterns described above, there is, in fact, a continuum from one extreme to the other, by any measure or characteristic that may be used. In size, for instance, some city parks will be larger than many state parks, but some of the latter will be larger than some federal resource-based areas. In the matter of timing of use, a few people will be located so near a national forest that they can use it for an after-work picnic, much like most people use a city park for this purpose. On the other hand, a few persons may be willing to spend their whole vacation going quietly each day to the local neighborhood park. In many other ways, some usage or characteristic outside the main pattern is possible. Nevertheless, outdoor recreation areas of various sizes, locations, and characteristics form an interrelated system.

The pattern of use of these various areas is closely affected by the amount and timing of available leisure. A shortened workday enables the worker to spend more time in the park, on the golf course, or in some other user-oriented outdoor recreation. A longer number of years in school before getting the first job also contributes to the number of youths seeking outdoor recreation during the school year and in vacations. The increase in household appliances and the transfer of many domestic activities such as baking and sewing from the home to an industrial establishment give the housewife more time to take her small children to such areas. The shortening of the workweek to five days freed the worker and his family for all-day outings in an intermediate outdoor recreation area. Most such outings now take place on Sunday; yet it seems clear that it is the availability of Saturday for doing the necessary family chores and for resting which makes possible many of the Sunday outings. The great rise in the annual paid vacation has been largely responsible for the great increase in use of resource-based outdoor recreation areas. Larger incomes, which enable families in the middle income brackets to afford a vacation trip, have also been a major factor.

The use of the three types of outdoor recreation areas will be affected by a reduction in total hours worked and by the way the reduction is brought about. If the typical workday is shortened, the demand for user-oriented outdoor recreation areas will increase greatly. If the typical workweek is shortened to four days, much of the demand will fall upon the intermediate areas. Many workers will seek a day of hunting or fishing, often without the family, since the children will be in school. If the reduction largely takes the form of longer paid vacations, then the greatest demand will fall upon the resource-based areas, since these are the vacation areas of the nation. Increased annual vacations might mean more vacations in fall, winter, and spring, as well as in summer, with consequent increased demand on natural resources suitable for such seasonal vacations. Increases in average income and improvements in travel facilities will also be particularly important for resource-based areas.

Later chapters will show that somewhat different factors, or the same factors in somewhat different proportions, affect the demand for each of these three major kinds of areas. When we seek to establish demand curves for outdoor recreation, we must distinguish among the various kinds of areas. Likewise, many of the policy issues differ greatly according to the kind of area. For instance, the most appropriate level of user charges for outdoor recreation areas depends primarily upon the kind of areas.

II

Demands for Outdoor Recreation

"Demand," as applied to outdoor recreation, is a word with several meanings; in the popular sense, as applied to a specific area or facility, it means the total number of visitors; to the economist, it means a schedule of volume (visits, user-days, etc.) in relation to a price (cost of the recreation experience). Our primary concern is with the latter meaning, yet we show how a demand approach can be used to estimate the recreation use of an area.

Though demand and supply are closely interrelated, as the discussion in this part makes clear at several points, here we focus on demand topics in a series of four chapters. Chapter 4 provides an analytical and descriptive background to demand analysis *as applied to outdoor recreation*. There exists a rich economics literature on the complex problems of demand and its analysis, in general; we have not tried to introduce this. We have tried to keep the discussion of demand to the minimum needed for the noneconomist to understand the later specific applications of this approach. We hope that this chapter will suggest to the economist some of the lines of inquiry where he might use his general tools, when he considers outdoor recreation. In particular, we have tried to show the great importance, for outdoor recreation, of the geography of demand.

In Chapter 5, we illustrate this general approach by use of specific examples, for which data existed, for intermediate, resource-based, and user-oriented areas, as these were described in Chapter 3. We apply demand analysis first to the whole outdoor recreation experience, also discussed in Chapter 3, and from the demand curves so obtained we derive demand curves for the natural resource itself, which is used for recreation. While we feel that this is a highly valuable approach, it does have its limitations and its problems, which are also discussed.

In Chapter 6, we look again and in more detail at the historical record of the basic factors of population, leisure, transportation, and income, which we briefly mentioned in Chapter 1. We conclude that the factors have had a marked joint effect, the upward trend in each tending to reinforce the importance of the other. In Chapter 7, Alternative Methods of Estimating Future Use, we emphasize methodology, but give some results of using each approach. We provide our projections, on a national basis, of future use of the three major kinds of outdoor recreation areas. The difficulties of making projections are stressed. But it is also pointed out that projections are often unavoidable; when a public agency or private individual makes an investment, buys a new area, erects buildings, trains people for future professional activity, or does any one of various other things, some estimate of future use and demand is implicit in their actions.

4

Some Elements of Recreation Demand

If the physical opportunity for outdoor recreation exists, and if people are given a free choice, a large majority of them will spend some of their money and some of their time on outdoor recreation. The available statistical information shows that millions of persons in the United States are doing this, and the numbers are rising sharply each year. The magnitudes involved can be seen in Figure 2, which shows attendance at major types of recreation areas from 1910 for the national park system, and from various later dates for other major kinds of areas. Visits to the national parks increased all through World War I; the Great Depression of the 1930's did hardly more than slow down growth in visits to the national park system and to the national forests. Minor variations in rates of growth occur in other years for some kinds of areas, but the whole record is one of surprising uniformity in the persistence of the growth rate. The only major interruption was during World War II, when travel and other restrictions existed.

Figure 2 has lines at 8 per cent and 10 per cent growth per year, for contrast. By and large, the growth in use of the major kinds of outdoor areas is 10 per cent per year,[1] or possibly a little more for some areas, and definitely more in some years for the TVA system and the reservoirs created by dams built by the Corps of Engineers. Since population growth over these decades was generally below 2 per cent annually, it is evident that the per capita visitation rate rose markedly. The data in Figure 2 indicate the increased public use of outdoor recreation areas, and reflect changes in their supply as well as the increased demand. For

[1] Figure 2 is plotted on semilogarithm or ratio paper; lines of equal slope indicate equal rates of growth.

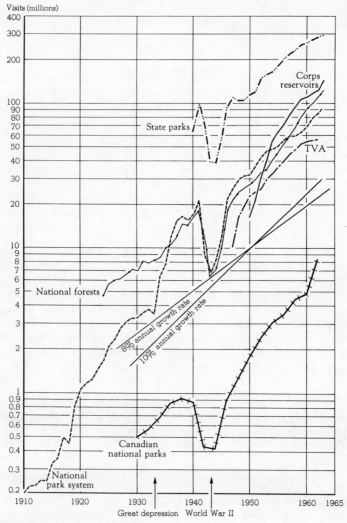

Figure 2. Attendance at major types of outdoor recreation areas, years of record.

each of the kinds of areas shown on the chart, there were increases in area—substantial ones in the case of the Corps reservoirs, relatively small ones in the case of the national forests, and intermediate ones for most other areas. Although there was relatively little increase in the total acreage of the national forests, there was a great increase in the amount available for recreation as new roads opened up additional areas.

The tangible expressions of personal values reflected in the attendance figures are more significant for our purposes than judgments by specialists as to the role of outdoor recreation, as would be the case with any other good or service. The people who chose to visit public outdoor recreation areas presumably weighed the costs of doing so against the costs of other goods or services they might have bought with the same money. Theirs was a personal choice, dependent in large measure upon their personal value scales and preferences, but conditioned also by many social factors in the society of which they are a part. Without attempting to appraise the role which this activity plays in the emotional and intellectual lives of the persons concerned, we may simply say that people demand outdoor recreation.

We know all too little about why different persons seek outdoor recreation, or what they hope to gain from it. And too often we have thought of recreation administration and management in terms of the physical area, and not enough in terms of demand, and of the user public. Just as modern marketing is turning to a study of what the consumer wants, expects, and is willing to pay for, so must modern recreation administration turn to a study of its consumers.

APPLICABILITY OF ANALYSIS

While professional workers and others directly interested in recreation have developed a large body of information on many aspects of the subject, most would agree that there has been far too little analysis of outdoor recreation in terms related to planning; to making decisions, particularly decisions on how to use scarce resources to obtain desired goals and objectives; and to facility management. This is both unfortunate and unnecessary.

The initial need is a modest one: a description of actual facts in ways that are useful. There are limitations to what can be done, to be sure, but there is immense merit in proceeding.

Economic analysis is of particular applicability here, as it is largely a study of human reactions, actions, and choices. It deals with the implications of subjective evaluations and intrinsic characteristics of recreation sites and experiences, not as such, but in terms of how such things affect what man does or is willing to do. Economic comparisons deal with physical and other characteristics of goods and services only to the extent that these affect human decisions.

Statements that the reactions to recreation experiences are personal and highly variable between individuals are true enough. But it is misleading to contend that economic analysis is therefore inadequate and inapplicable and that it is impossible to measure the economic worth or value of either the recreation experience as such or the recreation site. The personal values of recreation are reflected by what people are willing to give up to obtain them. Indeed, nearly any good or service has satisfying qualities which are highly particularized and almost completely personal and varied. However, the economic system takes account of these varied satisfactions, arrives at prices for individual goods and services, and gives order to the whole structure. It may seem contradictory that bread, which is one of man's most important and valuable foods, sells for but a relatively few cents a loaf, while diamonds, which most certainly are not a necessity of life, sell at a high price. Such seeming contradictions are resolved when the pricing mechanism—the way things are valued—is looked at more closely. The price does not value the worth of the total quantity but only the worth of the last unit put on the market. Thus because bread is plentiful relative to our wants and needs it commands but a small price.

In choosing to use parks and other recreation facilities and to spend time, money, and trouble in so doing, people behave in a way that is not fundamentally different from the way they purchase other items. In a good many ways we can think of society, or the economy, producing good parks, playgrounds, and other recreational facilities and enjoying the benefits in much the same way it produces and enjoys automobiles, dishwashers, roads, and nearly everything else. Economic analysis is as applicable to outdoor recreation as it is to any other of man's wealth-getting or income-spending activities. It is a particularly useful vehicle for focusing on two important aspects of outdoor recreation: the question of worth or values, and the determination of patterns or regularities.

BASIC ELEMENTS OF DEMAND CURVES

No doubt the most important and productive tool of economic analysis is the notion of demand. While the term has been used with considerable ambiguity, we use demand statements primarily as a means of expressing the reactions of consumers to given commodities or services. If the basic underlying relationships can be established with some degree of confidence, various other productive analyses are possible to provide at least partial answers to many difficult problems.

Reduced to its simplest terms, a demand schedule or curve is simply a statement of the amount of a particular good or service that will be purchased in a given period of time at specified prices per unit. Other things being equal, the lower the market price the more units people will buy. This is true for bread, apples, tents, ice cream, bus fares, park entrance fees, and for almost all commodities and services. As a result of a given price increase, sales will fall off more quickly for some goods and services than for others, but the quantities sold will be reduced for nearly all.

This information can be presented in a simple table where two columns would relate the quantity that would be taken or bought at alternative prices. We can also present the identical information graphically on an arithmetic scale in a demand curve obtained by plotting the observed points and drawing a smooth curve through them. After doing this we would observe that, importantly, for most goods and services the curve slopes downward to the right, reflecting the fact that the lower the price the greater the quantity demanded and conversely the higher the price the smaller the quantity demanded. These same data can also be plotted on paper with double logarithm scales (sometimes referred to as ratio scales); while superficially the curves would look different, in reality they would be the same. In later chapters, we shall plot some demand curves on double log paper, but this will be a matter of expository convenience, not one of basic difference in relationships. Frequently, the data can also be expressed in a mathematical formula. These are different ways of expressing the same basic information.

Although a table showing quantities of any good or service purchased at given prices, or a chart presenting the same data, may seem rather cold and impersonal, each in fact summarizes many intensely human reactions. The small boy agonizingly trying to decide whether to spend his dime for an ice cream bar or for a coke is but the reflection in miniature of the man or the couple trying to decide whether to buy a new car or have a vacation in Europe. Virtually unlimited combinations of competing goods or of choices exist when the whole population is considered. Although the competition between alternative choices is more clearly revealed for money, yet it also exists for time, as we noted in earlier chapters. In this book, following the custom of economists generally, we shall use data on demand in a rather impersonal way; yet the human choices and tastes which underlie actions of consumers should not be lost sight of.

We may also note that demand for a good or service has only limited meaning when not associated with some price or cost notion, for demand might be reduced to nothing at sufficiently high prices, or alternatively, it might be stimulated to great proportions at sufficiently low prices.

In its simplest form, a demand curve is instantaneous; that is, it expresses the relationship between prices and quantities at any moment, with other factors constant or unchanged. Even if one can imagine all other factors remaining unchanged over considerable periods of time, the full response to major changes in price might take an appreciable time to become fully manifest because past habits of buying and consumption might persist for some time. In point of fact, factors other than price and quantity do change over longer time periods, thus introducing changes, or shifts, in the basic demand curve. For instance, the price or the quality of competing goods or services might change, thus inducing consumers to pay higher or lower prices for the commodity or service under study; or the tastes or attitudes of the public might shift. Some of the ways in which such changes can be isolated, at least approximately, and thus the basic or underlying demand curve estimated in the case of outdoor recreation will be suggested in Chapter 5.

One other particular factor, however, deserves mention at this point—the effect of changes in income upon demand. If prices were to remain unchanged over a considerable period of time and per capita income were to rise, then it is highly probable that quantities demanded would also rise. For some commodities or services the quantities demanded are highly responsive to changes in income. For others, change in income will bring only minor changes in quantities bought. There are some commodities whose consumption actually falls as incomes rise; these are the economically inferior goods, which are replaced by more desired goods as income permits. As we shall see in later chapters, outdoor recreation is generally very responsive to changes in real income per capita, but not uniformly so.

In this introductory discussion of demand, we have focused on the consumer's willingness to pay for given quantities of a good or service. However, the importance of supply must not be overlooked, even in this consideration of demand. Every market transaction involves a meeting of supply and demand at a price. A lowering of price may bring forth demand for a larger volume, but this demand cannot be translated into actual purchases unless supplies also increase. The use of park and recreation areas could not have increased as much as it did, if the supply of park areas had not also increased.

APPLICATION OF DEMAND CURVES TO OUTDOOR RECREATION

Without attempting to develop these elementary ideas of demand theory further, we may see how they may be applied, first on a purely hypothetical basis, to outdoor recreation.[2] Let us assume that the illus-

---

[2] A number of articles in professional journals and various reports have presented methodology for measuring recreation demand. Among them are: Lloyd Brooks, "The Forces Shaping Demand for Recreation Space in Canada,"

trations which follow in this section are for recreation on the intermediate type of outdoor recreation area described in Chapter 3, that is,
for areas used primarily for day outings. The same ideas can be applied
to either user-oriented or resource-based types of areas, and in fact we
do so in Chapter 5. However, various difficulties exist in so doing and
these ideas find their clearest application for intermediate areas. On the
one hand, a visit to such areas requires a definite decision, often a carefully considered one, to spend both time and money in this particular
activity, whereas a visit to a user-oriented area is usually more casual.
Also, a visit to an intermediate area is likely to be the single purpose of
the trip, whereas a visit to a resource-based area is often part of a
vacation trip which may also include visits to other areas.

In the discussion which follows in this section, the *whole recreation
experience* as described earlier, is the unit of study. That is, anticipation,
travel to, experience on the site, travel back, and recollection are all
included. Our discussion pointed out that all of these phases are present
in every major outdoor recreation experience. One part cannot meaningfully be separated from the others, in terms of cost or volume. We
measure what people do, in terms of amounts of recreation consumed
and of prices paid; we do not attempt to measure their psychological or
emotional reactions.

Background Paper, Resources for Tomorrow Conference, *Proceedings,* Vol. 3,
Ottawa, 1962; Marion Clawson, *Methods of Measuring the Demand for and Value
of Outdoor Recreation,* Reprint No. 10, Resources for the Future, Inc., Washington, 1959, and *Dynamics of Park Demand,* RPA Bulletin No. 94, Metropolitan
Regional Council and Regional Plan Association, New York, 1960 (out of print);
Allen V. Kneese, "Measuring the Benefits of Developing and Maintaining Recreation Resources: Issues and Approaches," in *Recreation Research in the Great
Plains,* Proceedings of a seminar sponsored by the Resource Economics Committee
of the Great Plains Agricultural Council, South Dakota State College of Agricul-
ture and Mechanic Arts, Brookings, 1962. Jack L. Knetsch, "Outdoor Recreation
Demands and Benefits," *Land Economics,* Vol. 39 (November 1963), pp. 387–96,
and "Economics of Including Recreation as a Purpose of Water Resources
Projects," *Journal of Farm Economics* (December 1964). Lionel Lerner,
"Quantitative Indices of Recreational Values," *Economics in Outdoor Recreation
Policy,* Report No. 11, Committee on Water Resources and Economic Develop-
ment of the West, Western Agricultural Economics Research Council, 1962.
Robert K. Davis, "Value of Outdoor Recreation: An Economic Study of the
Maine Woods" (Unpublished Ph.D. thesis, Harvard University, 1963). Andrew H.
Trice and Samuel E. Wood, "Measurement of Recreation Benefits," *Land Eco-
nomics,* Vol. 34 (August 1958), pp. 195–207. Edward L. Ullman and Donald J.
Volk, "An Operational Model for Predicting Reservoir Attendance and Benefits:
Implications of a Location Approach to Water Recreation," *Papers: Michigan
Academy of Science, Arts and Letters,* Vol. 47 (1961), Ann Arbor, 1962. E. Boyd
Wennergren, "Valuing Non-market Price Recreational Resources," *Land Eco-
nomics,* Vol. 40, No. 3 (August 1964), pp. 303–14. William G. Brown, Ajmer
Singh, and Emery N. Castle, *An Economic Evaluation of the Oregon Salmon and
Steelhead Sport Fishery,* Technical Bulletin 78 (Corvallis: Agricultural Experiment
Station, Oregon State University, 1964).

As the simplest practical case, let us assume that all consumers or potential users of the recreation area or facility are located in a town or city, that they are close enough to one another to be considered as centered at a single point, and that they are interested in outdoor recreation at a specific point some distance away. For purposes of the numerical examples which follow, we assume a city of about 25,000 people, of customary mixed ages, sexes, incomes, occupations, and other characteristics. Let us assume further that we are considering a single brief space of time, probably not exceeding a year in length, in which all factors other than cost per visit and number of visits are fixed or given. That is, changes in population, income, tastes, transportation, and the like are ruled out of this first case.

Before we can construct a demand schedule for this example we need an expression of price or money outlay per unit of recreation "consumed." For this purpose we use the cost of the whole recreation experience. The people who use any particular area for outdoor recreation will incur various money costs in doing so, perhaps small ones, perhaps large ones. These costs will be made up of many items, including the cost of transportation, the cost of food in excess of what it would have been at home, and any entrance fees. These are the added expenditures which the individual, or family, must make in order to take part in the whole recreation experience. They are the "price" per unit of recreation experience; the fact that this price is paid to many suppliers—the service station operator, the grocer, and others, as well as to the gatekeeper (if any) at the park—often confuses some people as to the nature of the money price paid. This is not to say that time costs of the recreation activity are unimportant—they certainly are important and may impose more of a restraint than money costs. In this chapter, however, we use primarily money costs; time and other costs are discussed in the next chapter. We can assume that visitors find the experience is worth to them at least as much as it cost, especially when they continue to come in ever larger numbers.

In this particular case, we might find that if the cost per visit (the "price" of the whole recreation experience) were as high as $25, owing to high entrance fees or high travel costs, no visits would be made to this area. We might also find that no more than 50,000 visits would be made even if the costs were to fall to zero. Between these two extremes, the number of visits declines as cost per visit or price per unit increases. For the simple case, the demand schedule is given in the first two columns of Table 3. The data are also plotted on an arithmetic scale in Figure 3.

They might also have been plotted on a graph using a double logarithmic scale. They may alternatively be expressed in a mathematical

TABLE 3.
SCHEDULE OF VISITS, COSTS PER VISIT, AND TOTAL EXPENDITURE,
HYPOTHETICAL RECREATION AREA

Cost per visit	Number of visits	Total expenditures (1,000)
$25.00	0	$ 0
20.25	5,000	101
16.00	10,000	160
9.00	20,000	180
6.25	25,000	156
4.00	30,000	120
1.00	40,000	40
0.00	50,000	0

expression. The relationship is exactly the same in each case. These are merely different ways of saying the same thing, with different modes of expression useful for different purposes. The choice will be made for convenience, not because the relationship is different.

It should be noted that the unit of volume is *visits,* not visitors. This means that when the data show an increase in the number of visits we do not know whether it represents more visitors, more visits by the same people, or some of each. In this respect, data for recreation are not unlike those usually available for other services and commodities. When beef consumption rises, for instance, we do not know how much of the increase is caused by more people eating beef and how much by greater consumption per person by former customers. It would help greatly, as far as understanding possible future developments is con-

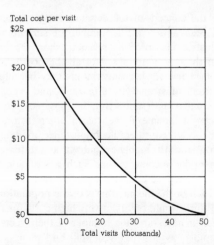

Figure 3. Number of visits and cost per visit at a hypothetical recreation area.

cerned if we knew the extent to which the increased recreation patronage was due to each factor.

It is of interest to note the total amount of money expended with different costs per visit. The total expenditure at this hypothetical site is given in the last column of Table 3. As costs per visit fall from the maximum that anyone will pay, the number of visits increases, and total expenditures increase until the cost per visit falls below about $11. After this, the total expenditures are reduced because the increase in number of visits is insufficient to offset the lower costs per visit.

The degree to which quantity decreases with increases in price is referred to as the price elasticity of demand. This is usually expressed as the percentage change in quantity associated with a given percentage change in price. Thus, if an increase in price produces a change in quantity that is large enough to result in a higher total expenditure, we speak of an elastic demand curve; if the change in quantity is slight in spite of considerable changes in price, we speak of an inelastic demand curve. In each case, elasticity and inelasticity are relative, not absolute. The dividing line between relatively elastic and relatively inelastic is where changes in price are exactly offset by proportionate changes in quantity, so that total expenditure or gross income or revenue remain constant. A demand curve may be—and in fact often is—relatively elastic in some volume and price ranges and relatively inelastic in others.

EFFECT OF DIFFERENT DEMAND FACTORS

To illustrate the concept of the demand curve of recreation we used a hypothetical area and made a number of simplifying assumptions. Many other illustrations could be given to show the effect of relaxing one or more of these assumptions. Not all the possibilities can be considered here, but a few further illustrations may be helpful.

In the situation illustrated by Figure 3 and Table 3, the entire populace was treated as a unit. But, in most communities, there are major differences in income as well as in other factors. It is generally felt that income is of considerable importance in determining recreation participation, and it is highly probable that a different demand curve exists for each major income group. Such a situation is illustrated in Figure 4. For the purpose of this illustration, it has been assumed that we know how each of the income thirds of the population will react. The highest income third would pay relatively high costs for recreation at our hypothetical site, if necessary; the number of their visits would rise, but perhaps not rapidly, as cost per visit fell; and their demand would be fully satiated even at zero costs with about 16,000 visits annually. The middle third of the population may begin to use this recreation area

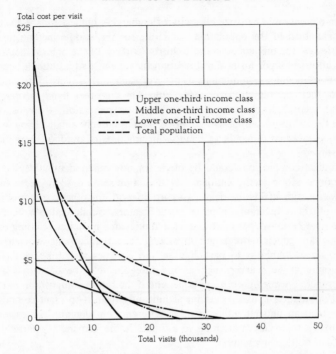

Figure 4. Demand for total recreation experience in a hypothetical area, by broad income classes.

when total costs declined to about $12; their use would also expand, but probably more rapidly, as cost per visit fell; their point of satiety, at zero cost per visit, might be at about 25,000 visits. The lowest income third of the population would not visit this recreation area at all until cost per visit fell to about $4.50; with each successive decline in cost, their use of the area would increase greatly, and their point of satiety at zero cost would not be reached short of 33,000 visits annually.

The demands by these three groups can be summed (laterally, in the figure) to yield a total demand curve for the entire population. Thus, at a cost of $3 per visit, the demand from the highest income group is for a little more than 10,000 visits, from the middle income group for about 12,000 visits, and from the lowest income group about 8,000 visits; or, for all three groups combined, about 30,000 visits in all. Although this illustration is based upon a division of the total population into thirds, it should be apparent that it might have been divided into any groupings, not necessarily equal in size.

Figure 4 also illustrates the effect of income on the demand for outdoor recreation. The price elasticity of demand is highest for the lowest income third of the population, moderate for the middle income third, and lowest for the highest income third. People with the highest incomes can afford most or all of the recreation they want, and additional increments of income, or reductions in price of each unit of recreation, would affect their consumption relatively little. On the other hand, people at lower income levels are able to afford less recreation; their use of facilities is more responsive to price, and relatively small changes in income produce rather large changes in amounts of outdoor recreation consumed.

Similar comparisons could be made for any other identifiable socio-economic group in the entire population. For some outdoor recreation activities, age affects the degree of participation; for others, sex; and for still others, education or other social factors. Small children cannot engage in certain types of strenuous activities, for instance. Hunting and fishing are much more common among men than among women. If data are available as to participation and cost per visit for any socio-economic group, curves such as the foregoing can be drawn. If the differences between groups are large, and if the future composition of the total population is likely to differ significantly from its present composition, then an understanding of these differences in demand curves may be highly important in attempts to estimate future demand for particular kinds of outdoor recreation.

The simplest illustration necessarily included some assumption as to available leisure time of the residents of the town or city involved. The effect of different assumptions as to leisure time are shown in Figure 5. In this illustration, other factors such as number of persons, transportation facilities, and income are assumed unchanged. If the average work-week is 60 hours, relatively few persons will have the free time to visit our hypothetical recreation area. Even when costs are no higher than $10 per visit, no one will be willing to spare some of his limited time to visit this area; as costs per visit decline, more and more visits will take place, but even at zero cost the total number of visits might be less than 10,000. If average hours of work per week are reduced to 40 hours, people will become accustomed to more leisure, and their desire to visit this area will increase. Use will now begin even at a cost of over $16 per visit; it will increase as cost falls, but the point of satiety at zero cost is now about 23,000 visits annually. If there are further declines in the average workweek, some people will be willing to pay even more per visit. The curve will then shift upward and to the right even farther.

Our simplest illustration also made certain assumptions as to travel facilities. The probable kind of effect of differences in kind of road is shown in Figure 6. If there is only a dirt road leading from the city to

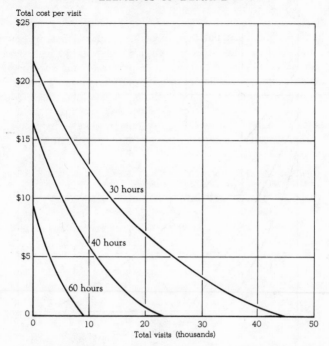

Figure 5. Demand for total recreation experience in a hypothetical recreation area, according to length of average workweek.

the recreation area, relatively few people will be willing to make the trip. This is in many respects a self-regulating mechanism; as use increases, so does dust and discomfort, and as the use declines the dirt road becomes less annoying. At any rate, in this hypothetical example, use is responsive to cost per visit, but at a comparatively low level of use. If the road is gravelled, and perhaps widened and straightened, more people will be interested in visiting the area, or the same people more frequently, or some of both. The new curve is now higher and to the right. If the road is later paved, and perhaps also improved in other ways, use would no doubt rise much higher at any level of cost.

The number of visits to a recreation area is generally influenced by the intensity of management, including such matters as water supply, sewage facilities, development of water areas for boat landings and for swimming. The amount and kind of advertising is likely also to affect the number of visits to the area. In our simplest example, we implicitly assumed certain levels of management and improvement for our hypothetical area. The effect of modifying these assumptions is illustrated in

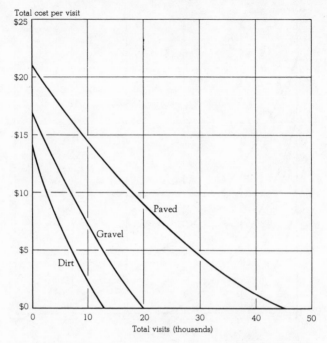

Figure 6. Demand for total recreation experience in a hypothetical recreation area, according to type of road leading to it.

Figure 7, which shows demand for two different areas under two sets of management conditions. For a relatively remote but only moderately attractive area, there is a definite relation between number of visits and cost per visit. A higher or more intensive development of such an area leads to some increase in use at each level of costs, but the differences are not great. For a closer area, where travel time would be less, and where the attractiveness of the area is perhaps greater, use is higher at each level of costs for the relatively extensive management; intensive management greatly increases the use of this area at a given cost. Many recreationists desire relatively improved areas, and flock to them in great numbers. The more attractive and desirable an area, the more likely is use to increase in response to increased intensity of management.

A change in access or management creates a somewhat different recreation "product." Camping at the end of a dirt road is in some degree a different activity than camping near a paved road. To use our earlier terminology, the content of the whole recreation experience has been changed. Similarly, boating or fishing at a lake where there is a

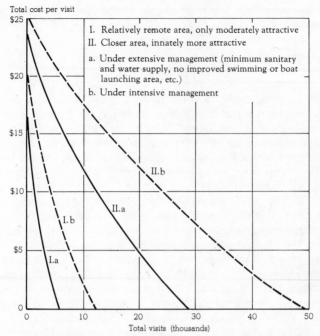

Total cost per visit

I. Relatively remote area, only moderately attractive
II. Closer area, innately more attractive

a. Under extensive management (minimum sanitary and water supply, no improved swimming or boat launching area, etc.)
b. Under intensive management

II.b

II.a

I.b

I.a

Total visits (thousands)

Figure 7. Demand for total recreation experience in two hypothetical recreation areas, according to innate attractiveness of area and intensity of management.

good launching ramp is in some degree different than boating or fishing at a lake where such facilities are missing. In this respect, outdoor recreation is not unlike many other commodities and services. The manufacturer who puts his product in a fancy box, advertises it actively, and prices it to appeal to snobs, has a somewhat different commodity than he had when he sold the same article more plainly wrapped, without promotion, and priced to provide a "bargain" appeal. Outdoor recreation not only includes a great many specific activities, but within each activity there is a wide range in "quality."

The foregoing illustrations by no means exhaust all the possible modifications of or additions to our simplest demand model for outdoor recreation. They do illustrate some common situations. The reader should not forget that these are all hypothetical or illustrative examples —believed to be reasonable, but not yet drawn from actual data for a specific area. It would be possible, we believe, to measure all of these and other relationships in some actual field situations, in ways useful for forecasting the effect of certain management and development combinations.

THE GEOGRAPHY OF DEMAND FOR OUTDOOR RECREATION

The location of customers is important in the demand for any good or service, but it is particularly so in considering the demand for outdoor recreation because travel from home to the recreation site and back takes time and money, sometimes relatively a lot of each. As a result, the demand for outdoor recreation is peculiarly affected by the location of the customers for each area and by the location of rival recreation areas.

In our simplest illustration of a demand curve for outdoor recreation, we assumed that all the people were in one spot or in a single city, and the recreation opportunity all at one spot such as a park. Actually, of course, the situation would almost always be far more complicated, both as to location of the users (or the demand) and as to the location of the recreation areas (or the supply). People are likely to live in clusters, commonly cities or suburbs, with a few living in patterns of very low density in the interstitial areas. Parks or other recreation areas occur in specific locations, but often there will be several accessible to a single city, and often each park may draw visitors from several cities.

If a park has many potential customers living nearby, then it will have a relatively large number of visitors, other factors being equal, because costs of visiting it will be relatively low in terms of both money and time. Contrarily, a closely similar park located at some distance from most of its potential customers will have relatively very few visitors because money and time costs of getting to it will be high. At first glance, the Grand Canyon National Park might appear to be a special case because more than half of its total visitors come from over 1,000 miles away and incur relatively large time and money costs. However, it must be remembered that the total population nearby is relatively small.

To remove the influence of the population distribution within the potential zone of use, visits to a park or recreation area are generally put on the basis of per capita or per 1,000 base population in each tributary zone. This is comparable, statistically, to putting the consumption of food or any other commodity on a per capita basis. By putting visits on a per 1,000 of base population basis, the underlying relationships between numbers of visits and cost per visit can be ascertained rather clearly in most cases; when this is done, the underlying relationship between visits and costs is evident also in the case of Grand Canyon National Park.

In our simple illustrative cases earlier in this chapter, we considered only one park to which recreationists went. Often, or usually, the residents of any city or other area will have the opportunity to visit other parks or recreation areas, perhaps several others. The different areas may lie at different distances from their users and may also vary in attractiveness. Two or more areas may be competitive for the time and money of a given group of recreationists; in this situation, an increase in visits to one area will be offset by a reduction in visits to the others. Different areas may also be complementary to each other; a man may buy a boat and other equipment if there are several lakes or reservoirs to which he can go, but not if there is only one. More complex models, more nearly resembling the situation likely to prevail in a system of parks and recreation areas, can be built, and the effect of other variables studied.

The geography of both demand and supply must be carefully evaluated in any outdoor recreation situation. In the planning of a new park, the location of its potential users and the location of alternative parks may be critical in estimating the demand for it, or the number of visitors to it. These are part of the "givens," or of the existing situation. Some people may move to take advantage of a particularly attractive new park or recreation area, but factors other than recreation will determine where most people live.

FACTORS IN DEMAND FOR A PARTICULAR RECREATION AREA

Our simplest demand illustration showed the relationship between number of visits to an area and the price of the whole recreation experience (as measured by the costs involved in that experience). We suggested further some of the factors that might affect the simple relationship between cost or price per visit and number of visits—income, roads, management, and leisure, particularly. If one knew all the relationships involved, and had reasonably accurate data for the magnitudes of each factor in a given situation, he could estimate the volume of recreation that would be demanded, or how many visits a particular area would receive in a given time period. Some of the relationships or factors would be relatively constant, at least over a year and sometimes for much longer; some would change more frequently—even daily, as far as weather is concerned. While it is probably impossible to enumerate, much less to measure, *all* the factors that might be involved, it would appear that each of the following factors might well influence attendance in some degree at a particular outdoor recreation area in a specified time period such as a year, a summer season, a week, or even a day:

1. Factors relating to the potential recreation users, as individuals:
   (a) their total number in the surrounding tributary area;
   (b) their geographic distribution within this tributary area—how many are relatively near, how many relatively far, etc.;
   (c) their socioeconomic characteristics, such as age, sex, occupation, family size and composition, educational status, and race;
   (d) their average incomes, and the distribution of income among individuals;
   (e) their average leisure, and the time distribution of that leisure;
   (f) their specific education, their past experiences, and present knowledge relating to outdoor recreation;
   (g) their tastes for outdoor recreation.
2. Factors relating to the recreation area itself:
   (a) its innate attractiveness, as judged by the average user;
   (b) the intensity and character of its management as a recreation area;
   (c) the availability of alternative recreation sites, and the degree to which they are substitutes for the area under study;
   (d) the capacity of the area to accommodate recreationists;
   (e) climatic and weather characteristics of the area, the latter during the period under study.
3. Relationships between potential users and the recreation area:
   (a) the time required to travel from home to the area, and return;
   (b) the comfort or discomfort of the travel;
   (c) the monetary costs involved in a recreation visit to the area;
   (d) the extent to which demand has been stimulated by advertising.

In practice, the problem of estimating park use is somewhat less formidable than this list may suggest. The effect of some of the factors listed above may parallel or be subordinated to other factors. As we shall see, several factors have changed more or less proportionately in the past, so that it is nearly impossible to estimate the separate effects of each. For other factors, changes from year to year or from any other time period to the next are likely to be small and in predictable direction and amount. In particular, during any given year, most of these factors are relatively fixed. On the other hand, over a considerable span of years various factors may change to new ranges not experienced in the past, so that attempts to project into the future require extrapolation beyond any past experience.

5

The Nature of Demand for
Outdoor Recreation

The concept of a demand curve is applicable to each of the three major types of outdoor recreation which we discussed in Chapter 3—user-oriented, intermediate, and resource-based; but the quantitative estimation of the relevant demand curve for a specific area or situation is not easy. The approach first must estimate the demand for the whole recreation experience (as we have defined it), and then proceed to estimate the demand for the recreation resource itself. Efforts to derive a quantitative demand curve are at best only estimates of the true curve. There are several major difficulties, in addition to the common one of a lack of accurate, relevant data.

First of all, the various factors affecting the position and shape of the demand curve are likely all to change at the same time, in either a correlated or in a haphazard way, so that it is extremely difficult to isolate the effect of any one factor, such as cost per visit (or price of the recreation service) acting alone. The various methods devised for dealing with this problem work well in some cases and not so well in others. Moreover, there is always the chance of a sleeper—a factor which appeared to be unimportant, or whose effect was covered up by changes in other factors in the past, but which in the future may be important.

In empirical demand studies, we are necessarily limited to the past range of experience and combinations of factors. If per capita income should rise by 50 per cent or some other relatively large amount, or if leisure or some other factor should be greatly different than in any past period, then past relationships between other factors, such as between cost per visit and number of visits, may no longer hold.

Even if we could measure past relations with complete accuracy, future relationships may differ. In particular, personal tastes for all or a particular kind of outdoor recreation might change. As a result, some people would be willing to spend more for certain kinds of outdoor recreation than has been true in the past, even after allowance for the effect of higher incomes, more leisure, and other observable variations. This is a problem to which we shall return in Chapter 7.

Outdoor recreation presents some peculiar problems for demand analysis, in addition to the foregoing which have their counterpart, more or less, in the demand for other goods and services. For most commodities and services, "price" is directly and easily measurable in dollars; we buy a steak, a hat, an auto, or a house, for a specified sum in dollars. Time and trouble are involved in such purchases, but they are generally ignored or subsumed under the price in dollars.

In contrast, outdoor recreation always involves cost in three kinds of coin: dollars, time, and travel. The dollar cost must be for the whole recreation experience, not simply for the admission to the recreation area, as we have noted. There are often problems of estimating such costs for visitors and of getting reliable data on costs; but the analysis itself is straightforward. Recreation is a peculiarly time-consuming activity, as we noted in Chapters 2 and 3; indeed, the very measure of volume or amount of recreation is often measured in units of time—visitor-days, etc. Wealthier people can often afford the money but not the time, while poorer people may have the time but lack the money. Trade-offs between time and money are possible, as we have noted. Outdoor recreation also always involves travel, of varying distances; it may be pleasurable or burdensome. If it is the latter, then travel clearly represents a further cost, additional to the cost in dollars and in time.

For a great deal of outdoor recreation, dollars, hours, and miles as measures of cost are closely correlated; in such cases, dollars may well serve as the index for all three. But there are circumstances when these three measures diverge, or might be made to do so; then each could well exert a significant separate effect. We carry the analysis through, first, in terms of dollar cost alone (or of miles as an index of dollar cost); in the last two sections of the chapter we come back to the relationship of dollar, time, and distance costs.

If it is so difficult to estimate demand curves, and if the results at best are only estimates which may turn out to be rather inaccurate, why bother to try to estimate such curves at all? The answer is clear: because such curves are enormously useful in answering all manner of practical questions. On the basis of such curves, one might well be able to say: a moderately attractive outdoor recreation area with a small body of water lying within 30 to 50 miles of a city of roughly 50,000 population will have an annual use running between X and Y thousands of visits; or an entrance fee will have a certain effect on attendance at an area and will yield a revenue of about some figure; or development of various kinds of areas or facilities will alter use in some way, or alternatively, perhaps, development of more land or other areas will have some other given effect; or the value of resources used in different ways will vary in some way that can be generally estimated such that if used for one purpose they may have a general value of X as opposed to Y in the alternative. Demand curves can provide some highly useful rules of thumb. They are like the rules of thumb an engineer uses when he says that the crushing strength of a certain kind of rock is between X and Y thousand pounds; or when a forester says that forests of a certain density on certain site classes will produce between A and B feet of sawtimber per acre per year; or when a rural land appraiser makes general statements as to land values in a certain area. In each case, more precise determinations are necessary for many purposes, but estimates of the ranges within which the data will usually fall are also valuable. This type of generalization about demand and value will not be possible for recreation areas until a great deal of research under varying conditions has been carried out.

It should be noted that statistical demand curves have long been estimated for many commodities and services, and that they have long since proved their worth. Difficulties generally similar to those described for outdoor recreation, have been encountered elsewhere and surmounted with sufficient success to yield practically usable results. Early attempts to estimate the demand for agricultural commodities were crude by modern standards, but with the passage of years methods have become increasingly more sophisticated and perceptive. Early studies were plagued by insufficiency or inaccuracy of data, as well as often by incomplete theoretical concepts or by mathematical tools of limited power.

In some ways, the study of demand for outdoor recreation today is about where the study of demand for agricultural commodities was 40 years or more ago; but it should be possible to draw on the experience in other fields and to make much more rapid progress in applying concepts of demand to outdoor recreation. The data problem for outdoor recreation is now especially serious, but use of the best presently available data may aid in pointing the way to collection of much more suitable data in the future.

ESTIMATED DEMAND CURVES FOR THE WHOLE OUTDOOR RECREATION EXPERIENCE

Intermediate Type Recreation Areas

To estimate a demand schedule or curve for a given recreation area, we cannot look at just the total attendance for a single year and at the average cost for all visits to the area, as this gives but a single line in the tabular data and a single point of the curve. We need a range in the observations in order to trace out a significant portion of the curve. For this purpose, we rely primarily upon geographic analysis, using differences in numbers of visits and in cost per visit from different areas or distance zones to estimate the basic relationship.[1] In so doing, we obviously must accept the pattern of population distribution, of distribution of recreation areas, of income of the population, of transportation facilities, and other factors as we find them. We must also accept use of recreation areas as we find it, but measure it and costs as carefully as possible. By careful selection of areas, a wider range in these various factors may be found.

In our first example we use data for Lewis and Clark Lake in South Dakota, which is illustrative of intermediate type recreation areas in general.[2] The lake is actually a large reservoir created on the Missouri River by the Gavins Point Dam. It is located in a region which has relatively few natural bodies of water. Although there are some artificial lakes and some state parks with water bodies in the general region, on the whole, Lewis and Clark Lake has relatively few competitors nearby. The population around the lake is distributed irregularly, with only a few people nearby, more in the next distance zone, relatively fewer per unit of area in the third zone, and a large city population in the fourth zone (Table 4). The lake has become highly popular, and thousands

---

[1] The use of travel costs as a means of estimating demand curves for recreation areas was probably first suggested by H. Hotelling, and reported by Roy A. Prewitt in "The Economics of Public Recreation—An Economic Survey of the Monetary Evaluation of Recreation in the National Parks," National Park Service, Washington, D.C., 1949 (mimeo). This formulation assumed an implausible relationship—that all people have identical preferences with respect to visiting a given recreation area. All visitors and potential visitors were held to value the area identically, and this was taken to be equal to the travel costs of the most distant visitor. The present formulation allows a more realistic view that individuals value parks differently.

[2] Carlton S. Van Doren, *Recreational Usage and Visitors Expenditure, Gavins Point Dam and Reservoir, Summer, 1959*, Bulletin No. 65, February 1960, and John S. Evans and Carlton S. Van Doren, "A Measurement of the Demand for Recreational Facilities at Lewis and Clark Lake," Business Review Supplement, February 1960 (Vermillion, S.D.: Business Research Bureau, School of Business, State University of South Dakota).

NATURE OF DEMAND

[handwritten: # of visits made to park for every 1,000 pop. — used frequently]

TABLE 4.

VISITS TO LEWIS AND CLARK LAKE IN RELATION TO TOTAL
POPULATION, AND EXPENDITURES PER VISIT (PARTY OF
FOUR), BY DISTANCE ZONES, SUMMER 1959

Distance zone[1]	Population 1950 (1,000)	Estimated visits June, July, August 1959 (1,000)	Visits per 1,000 base population	Average one-way distance (miles)	Estimated cost per visit (party of four)
1. Less than 50 miles	88	333	3,784	18	$3.70
2. 50 to 100 miles	407	363	892	70	13.80
3. 100 to 150 miles	474	50	106	123	27.10
4. 150 to 200 miles	1,055	161	153	175	37.90
5. Over 200 miles in Survey area	5,558	20	4	228	41.25

[1] Determined from state highway maps; distance from county seat to power house at Gavins Point Dam.

SOURCE: Adapted from Table 1 in "A Measurement of the Demand for Recreational Facilities at Lewis and Clark Lake," by John S. Evans and Carlton S. Van Doren, Business Review Supplement (Vermillion, S.D.: Business Research Bureau, School of Business, State University of South Dakota, February 1960).

of boats have been sold in the surrounding area. In 1955, the first year the lake was open for recreational use, there were about 100,000 visits; by 1959, there were nearly a million.

The number of visits (party of four) from each of five distance zones is recorded in Table 4. The table also records the number of visits per 1,000 base population in the zone, which is a more meaningful measure of attendance as it takes account of differences in the population and, as noted previously, is analogous to data on such things as per capita consumption of various food items.

The relation between numbers and cost is shown in Figure 8. Here, as in our earlier hypothetical models, the number of visits in a given population increases as the cost per visit decreases. For this particular area, it seems that no one is willing to pay much in excess of $40 per party of four.

The "kink" which appears in the curve toward the left side of Figure 8 indicates that although the distance—and thus cost—is greater in the fourth than in the third zone, the number of visitors per 1,000 base population is also higher. Aside from possible data discrepancies, if all other things were equal, this would be contrary to expectation. A closer inspection of the data suggests an explanation. Relatively larger cities are particularly important in the second and fourth zones. It is altogether possible that per capita incomes average higher in these larger

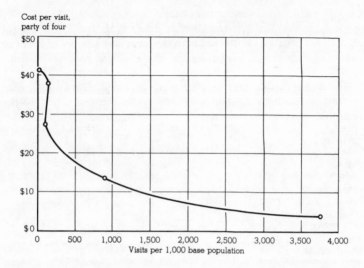

Figure 8. Visits per 1,000 base population, according to cost per visit, Lewis and Clark Lake, summer 1959.

cities than they do in the smaller cities and open country more characteristic of the third zone; moreover, there are likely to be more people who can afford a motor boat. This suggests that it is necessary to take account of differences such as income in attempting to ascertain an accurate picture of the demand situation.

The data for Lewis and Clark Lake are highly suggestive of the probable true demand relationship for the whole outdoor recreation experience for the intermediate type of outdoor recreation area. But they are deficient in at least two respects: (1) too few distance zones were established; if the total area of origin had been divided into ten or more zones, rather than five, the shape of the curve would not have been so nearly indeterminate in large portions, and we could have judged its reliability more readily; and (2) the study included no data on the income of users of the area, their other characteristics, etc. Had such data been available, it might have been possible to relate the use of the area by different income groups to the relative numbers of such persons in the base population.

This attempt to estimate the true demand curve for this type of outdoor recreation in this general area illustrates some of the practical problems that may arise from such an undertaking. Should one "smooth" the whole curve on the hypothesis that the kink resulted primarily from errors in data? Or should one draw two roughly parallel curves, the one based primarily on distance zones 1 and 3, to represent open country and small towns, the other on distance zones 2, 4, and 5 to represent larger towns or cities? But if one does the latter, the number of zones or observations, already too small for the whole sample, becomes absurdly small.

This South Dakota area may be more or less typical of the broad class of intermediate outdoor recreation areas. Approximately 80 per cent of the visitors spent one day or less at this area; fishing, picnicking, sightseeing, and swimming comprised more than three-fourths of all activities carried on at the area. Although the study does not provide direct evidence on the point, it seems highly probable that the experiences at this site were the sole or at least the chief motivation for the whole recreation experience. This means that there are no problems of cost allocation, as all the costs incurred for the whole recreation experience are chargeable to this site.

Evidence of the demand for an intermediate area is also available from a study of three artificial lakes in southwestern Nebraska.[3] Visitors come from Nebraska, northeastern Colorado, and northwestern Kansas. The study reports the origin of visitors by county, but does not reveal how many visitors were from towns and how many from farms or rural residences, or what their income levels were. Data were obtained on approximate distances traveled, but not on costs. It is highly probable that costs per visit are closely correlated with distance, and in analyzing demand for this area we use miles as a measure of cost.

This general region is one of small towns and relatively sparse rural population. Total population in most counties is about 5,000. One or a few small towns contain half or more of the total population of a county, with the rest in little settlements and on farms. The residents of some counties have two or more opportunities for water recreation within moderate distances; others have only one such opportunity, or even none nearby. There is nothing in the published study to indicate the *quality* of the recreation opportunity at each spot. Presumably each of the three lakes studied is somewhat similar, since fishing, boating, swimming, and other water sports were engaged in at each. The same may be true for the other water bodies not studied.

The study included some 6,000 interviews at the lakes themselves. While this is a moderately large sample, it does not provide many respondents for several counties. However, some interesting and perhaps significant conclusions can be drawn from the available information.

---

[3] Reported in *Recreational Aspects of Three Nebraska Lakes,* by Edgar Z. Palmer, Community Study Number Three, Studies in Community Economics, Bureau of Business Research, University of Nebraska, for the National Park Service and the Bureau of Reclamation, 1960.

The population of the nineteen counties and the visits reported per 1,000 are given in Table 5 for one of these lakes, Swanson Lake, Nebraska. This information is plotted in Figure 9.[4]

A number of things may be noted from this figure. Few visits were reported from counties more than 60 miles away, suggesting that this distance is about as far as people in this area were willing to travel for this type of recreation. The points do not fall in a smooth curve that would indicate a simple clear-cut relationship between distance and numbers of visits. Some of the deviation is no doubt due to such things as differences in per capita income levels and other socioeconomic factors, as suggested in the examination of the Lewis and Clark reservoir. However, for Swanson Lake, much of the deviation is accounted for by the existence of other lakes. This is true of County 3 (Dundy), which lies far below the line in Figure 9. Because many of its residents are closer to another lake and prefer to go there, the number of visits from the county is much less than expected.

It is impossible from this analysis of the data to come to a firm conclusion as to the degree to which one lake substitutes for another. However, the experience suggests that the lakes are in fact competitive with each other, and because they are generally similar physically, one would expect this to be true. Where lake recreation opportunities are nearby, as many as 100 visits per 1,000 of total population are experienced— this is true for County 5 (Hitchcock), at least. In this example, such a level of visitation occurs at a single lake within the county. Visits from counties 4 (Hayes) and 7 (Frontier) are distinctly lower, but it may well be that residents of these counties are going to other lakes to the north, not studied in this survey. Residents of counties 8 and 9 (Gosper and Furnas) may be visiting lakes to the north and east, although their distance from Swanson Lake would keep visits to it low in any case. This study raises many interesting questions on which further information is needed before final answers are possible.

We have suggested that cost per visit may be related to distance.

---

[4] The visit rate, though the dependent variable, is on the horizontal axis to conform with the plotting of visitor and cost information in previous figures and with the usual convention of plotting price on the vertical axis. In this case, distance is treated as cost.

A regression analysis of the visit rates resulted in an equation and the line drawn through the points. This type of statistical analysis takes into account the values of distance, in this case associated with each visit rate observed. It yields an equation which on the basis of all these values, establishes a relationship between miles and visit rate. The equation in this case was $V + 91.66 - 2.70 M + 0.02 M^2$, where V is the visit rate in hundreds per thousand population, and M the distance from the county to the lake. While only mileage is considered here, other factors could be simultaneously taken into account as determinants of visit rates in a similar way.

TABLE 5.
POPULATION 1950, AND VISITS AND DISTANCE TO SWANSON LAKE,
NEBRASKA IN 1958, BY COUNTIES IN SOUTHWESTERN NEBRASKA,
NORTHWESTERN KANSAS, AND NORTHEASTERN COLORADO

| | | Visits | | Estimated |
County	Population 1950	Reported in survey	Per 1,000 base population	distance (miles)
Nebraska				
1. Perkins	4,809	0	0	55
2. Chase	5,176	81	15.6	34
3. Dundy	4,354	125	28.7	10
4. Hayes	2,404	28	9.6	25
5. Hitchcock	5,867	595	101.4	4
6. Redwillow	12,977	716	55.2	21
7. Frontier	5,282	35	6.6	40
8. Gosper	2,734	0	0	68
9. Furnas	9,385	18	1.9	68
Kansas				
10. Sherman	7,373	71	9.6	59
11. Cheyenne	5,668	166	29.3	38
12. Rawlins	5,728	171	29.9	23
13. Thomas	7,572	247	32.6	46
14. Sheridan	4,607	4	.9	59
15. Decatur	6,185	123	19.9	35
16. Norton	8,808	31	3.5	59
Colorado				
17. Sedgwick	5,095	0	0	76
18. Phillips	4,924	13	2.6	59
19. Yuma	10,827	125	11.5	50

Certainly some costs are so related; others may be more or less fixed regardless of distance. Total costs per visit possibly vary proportionately less than do costs associated with distance alone. However, on the basis of the latter only, the curve shown in Figure 9 is quite elastic for distances in excess of 20 miles, relatively small differences in distance cost being associated with relatively large differences in use per 1,000 population. For shorter distances, where costs are lower, the number of visits is less responsive; people are apparently more nearly surfeited with this type of recreation, and factors other than cost may be determinative. Patronage of this type of outdoor recreation area is thus sensitive to distance, especially beyond some minimum distance, and thus to the population within different distance radii. It seems probable that usage of such areas would also be sensitive to charges for their use. Comparatively modest entrance fees might well lead to relatively large decreases in numbers of visits, particularly if alternative lakes were available, and if entrance fees for them were not also raised.

An examination of the data for the other two Nebraska lakes reveals generally similar results and also similar data deficiencies.

This method of estimating demand for outdoor recreation may be

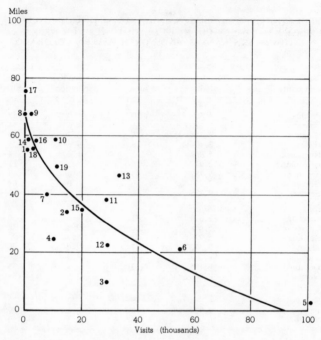

Figure 9. Swanson Lake, Nebraska: recreation visits per 1,000 base population in relation to distance (county basis), 1958.

further illustrated by the case of the John H. Kerr Reservoir,[5] a Corps of Engineers hydropower and flood control project on the Virginia-North Carolina border. A number of campgrounds, parks, and marinas have been established on the shoreline, and the reservoir attracts a good deal of recreation use. It, too, is more or less typical of the intermediate type of outdoor recreation area. Data on the origin of recreation visitors to the project for the year July 1, 1963—June 30, 1964 were available from sample surveys (Table 6).

Calculations were made of the effect of distance—the only factor examined in this instance—on the number of visitor parties originating in each of twelve distance zones. A consistent relationship was observed in which the visit rate varied from a high of 1,814 visits per 1,000 base population in the nearest zone (1–20 miles), to 0.087 visits per 1,000 in the farthest zone (401–500 miles). This is shown in Figure 10, which for expository convenience is on a double-log scale (an arithmetic scale

---

[5] Jack L. Knetsch, "Economics of Including Recreation as a Purpose of Water Resources Projects," *Journal of Farm Economics,* December 1964, pp. 1148–57.

TABLE 6.
POPULATION, PARTY VISITS, AND YEARLY VISIT RATES TO KERR
RESERVOIR, NORTH CAROLINA AND VIRGINIA, 1963–64,
BY ZONE OF ORIGIN OF VISITORS

Mileage limits of zone of origin	1960 population (1,000)	Total party visits[1]	Visits per 1,000 population	Two-way travel cost @ 5.16¢ per mile
1–20	91	165,104	1,814.33	$ 1.34
21–40	97	60,338	622.04	3.10
41–60	225	56,284	250.16	5.16
61–80	642	37,606	58.58	7.22
81–100	875	19,600	22.40	9.29
101–140	2,503	46,869	18.73	12.38
141–180	1,245	17,213	13.83	16.51
181–220	2,693	11,914	4.42	20.64
221–260	3,795	3,541	0.93	24.77
261–300	2,861	2,327	0.81	28.90
301–400	15,141	1,925	0.13	36.12
401–500	29,037	2,529	0.09	46.44

[1] Number of vehicles.
SOURCE: Calculated from unpublished surveys of the U.S. Corps of Engineers.

which would accommodate the highest visitation rate would bunch 9 of the 12 observations at one end of the volume scale).

The mileage figures were converted to cost figures, using the American Association of State Highway Officials' operating cost estimate of 5.16 cents per mile. A statistical regression analysis of the relationship between visit rates of the several distance zones and cost per visit resulted in the following equation:

$$\log (V+0.80) = 3.82462 - 2.39287 \log C$$

where V is the visit rate per thousand population in the zone of origin,

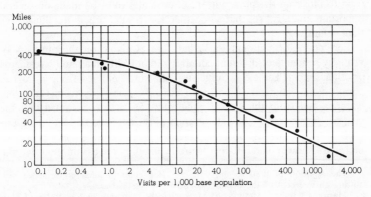

Figure 10. Yearly visit rates for various distance zones to Kerr reservoir, 1963–1964.

and C is the dollar cost of travel per visit.[6] This expression accounted for 97 per cent of the statistical variation in visit rates between zones.

Resource-Based Recreation Areas

For recreation experiences at resource-based areas, using our classification shown in Table 2, it is harder to assign a single cost and a single set of satisfactions. Some people on vacations go to a single spot and stay there for their entire vacation; this is the sole or chief purpose of their recreation experience. For them, the analysis can be similar to that presented above. For others, several places may be visited during the course of a vacation trip. This is especially true when the purpose of the recreation experience is largely sightseeing. The tourist may wish to see several places but would be unwilling to make a relatively expensive trip to see only one. The direct costs of seeing a particular place, such as travel off the main route, meals, lodging, etc., in the particular area, should of course be chargeable to this experience. But family satisfactions at each place must yield some surplus above direct costs of visiting that place, if the "overhead" or main trip costs are also to be offset, or more, by total trip satisfactions. One might attempt to allocate the general costs against each of the attractions visited, but numerous questions would arise in such a division. The results would necessarily be somewhat arbitrary, but might still provide the best possible approximation of relevant costs.

Data on the use of resource-based outdoor recreation areas are usually seriously deficient in costs incurred by visitors; and even when such data have been obtained, other deficiencies severely limit the kinds of economic analysis possible. Out of a number of studies made, four can be used to illustrate the procedures; but estimates must be made on several important matters, so that altogether the results are more illustrative than definitive.[7]

For Yosemite National Park, data are available on the numbers of visits by residents of different counties within California and by residents of other states (Table 7). Sufficient data were obtained from visitors to permit some estimates of costs per visit. For the visits from California counties and from the closest circle of states, it was assumed that the visit to Yosemite was the sole or chief purpose of the recreation experience. For visits from the more distant groups of states, two cost estimates are shown. The full-cost figure is based on the assumption that the

[6] The addition of 0.80 to the visit rate is a computational convenience permitting an intercept of the demand curve on the vertical axis.

[7] Marion Clawson, "Methods of Measuring the Demand for and Value of Outdoor Recreation," Reprint No. 10, Resources for the Future, Inc., Washington, 1959.

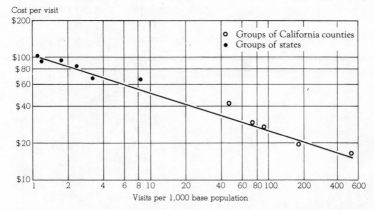

Figure 11. *Estimated costs ("shared") per visit to Yosemite National Park in relation to number of visits per 1,000 base population, 1953.*

trip was made for the sole purpose of visiting Yosemite. The shared-cost figure is based on the assumption that the trip was made for more than this purpose; it therefore includes all the direct costs of the side trip to Yosemite but only part of the costs of the main trip.[8]

It should be emphasized that the sharing of costs as shown in Table 7 and Figure 11 is wholly an intuitive matter. It seems reasonable to expect that persons making longer trips would include, on the average, more other purposes than persons making shorter trips. But we have no direct evidence that this is so, nor the extent of the difference.

The number of visits per 1,000 base population is highly correlated with the shared cost per visit (Figure 11). (This chart is on double logarithm paper for convenience. Had arithmetic scale paper been used, a scale adequate to include the highest visitation rate would have thrown more than half of the symbols into a meaningless cluster at the left side of the chart.)

The five observations on the right side of the chart represent groups of California counties. The group of counties with the lowest visitation rate (highest cost per visit) deviate somewhat from the line of average relationship. This may well be due to the fact that the counties included here are all southern California seacoast counties. Residents in these counties cannot go westward for outdoor recreation, except for sea types of recreation; they are less likely to go south, because that involves a trip across the border into Mexico; to the east the desert areas provide more

[8] In this latter respect, the analysis which follows differs from that in the original report.

TABLE 7.
NUMBER OF VISITORS TO YOSEMITE IN RELATION TO TOTAL POPULATION AND
EXPENDITURES PER VISIT, BY DISTANCE ZONES, 1953

Distance zones[1]	Average one-way distance[2] (miles)	Population of group of counties or states, 1950 (1,000)	Visits to Yosemite in 1953[3]		Estimated time required to complete a visit[4] (days)	Estimated cost per visit	
			Total number	Per 1,000 of base population		Full cost basis[5]	Shared cost basis[6]
1. Groups of California counties[7]							
less than 100 miles	81	70	35,250	505	1.4	$ 16.65	$ 16.65
100–150 miles	120	641	114,500	178	1.6	20.40	20.40
150–200 miles	190	1,588	143,400	90	1.95	27.05	27.05
200–250 miles	211	1,624	119,400	73	2.06	29.05	29.05
300 and more miles	350	5,206	245,000	47	2.75	42.25	42.25
2. Groups of states[8]							
300–500 miles	500	3,120	25,520	8.2	3.5	66.50	66.50
500–1,000 miles	800	5,856	19,030	3.2	5.0	85.00	69.80
1,000–1,500 miles	1,300	14,448	34,610	2.4	7.5	132.50	83.10
1,500–2,000 miles	1,800	38,649	66,450	1.7	10.0	180.00	94.50
2,000–2,500 miles	2,300	32,330	39,750	1.2	12.5	227.50	96.40
2,500 and more miles	2,900	44,910	51,400	1.1	15.5	284.50	100.83

[1] For California counties, calculated from road maps as distance from county seat to valley floor of Yosemite, via west entrance; for other states, airline distances.

[2] For California counties, weighted by total population in each county within group; for other states, estimated on basis of common routes of travel and population distribution within states.

[3] Calculated from data in *Yosemite National Park Travel Survey,* National Park Service, California Division of Highways and U.S. Bureau of Public Roads.

[4] Estimated on basis of 1 day per 400 miles of travel plus 1 day in park.

[5] Estimated at average cost of $9.00 per day (reported cost, minus transportation $8.47); plus 10 cents per mile for car for double one-way distance, divided by four on assumption of four passengers per car. These are the visit costs as shown in the original source.

[6] For trips of less than 500 miles the whole cost of the trip is charged to Yosemite; the shared cost is therefore the same as the full cost for these trips. On the assumption that trips of more than 500 miles were undertaken only in part to visit Yosemite, costs of trip were charged 80 per cent to Yosemite for 500–1,000 mile trips, 60 per cent for 1,000–1,500 miles, 50 per cent for 1,500–2,000 miles, 40 per cent for 2,000–2,500

miles, and 33 per cent for 2,500 and more miles. The shared cost figure includes full cost of side trip to Yosemite.

[7] Counties in each group are as follows: Merced; Madera, Stanislaus, Fresno, San Joaquin; Tulare, Monterey, Sacramento, Santa Clara, Alameda; San Francisco, San Mateo, Marin, Kern; San Bernardino, Los Angeles, Orange, San Diego. There are no counties, for which data were reported, that were 250 to 300 miles distant.

[8] States in each group were as follows: Oregon, Nevada, Utah, Arizona; Washington, Idaho, Montana, Wyoming, Colorado, New Mexico; North Dakota, South Dakota, Nebraska, Kansas, Oklahoma, Texas; Minnesota, Wisconsin, Iowa, Illinois, Missouri, Kentucky, Tennessee, Indiana, Arkansas, Mississippi, Louisiana; Michigan, Ohio, West Virginia, Virginia, North Carolina, South Carolina, Georgia, Alabama; Maine, New Hampshire, Vermont, Massachusetts, Connecticut, Rhode Island, New York, New Jersey, Pennsylvania, Delaware, Maryland, Florida.

SOURCE: Based upon Table 1, "Methods of Measuring the Demand for and Value of Outdoor Recreation," by Marion Clawson, RFF Reprint No. 10, February 1959.

limited opportunity for outdoor recreation. While there are some excellent mountain areas available in or near these counties, their recreation capacity is limited. These people are therefore probably led to go northward to Yosemite and other Sierra Nevada areas in larger numbers than would be the case if they were not, to a degree, hemmed in by these geographic features.

A generally similar analysis is made for Grand Canyon, Glacier, and Shenandoah national parks (Table 8 and Figure 12). The relationships between the shared-cost per visit and number of visits per 1,000 base population are quite close and again seem logical. As in the case of Yosemite, the only basis for the sharing of costs is intuitive.

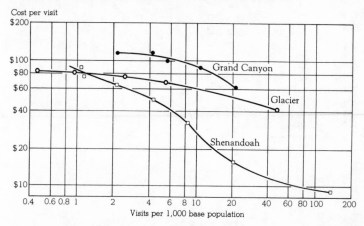

Figure 12. Estimated cost per visit ("shared") related to number of visits per 1,000 base population, Grand Canyon, Glacier, and Shenandoah national parks.

An analysis of a similar nature has been reported by Donald Volk.[9] This study examines the effect of distance and other factors on the intensity of use of various types of recreation areas. Using figures of visits to National Parks by state of origin, he shows a remarkably regular pattern between distance and per capita attendance. But the pattern is not completely regular, indicating the effect of other factors. Other factors that were examined in the study and that proved to have an explanatory effect on attendance were: median family income, degree of urbanization, mobility as measured by per capita automobile ownership, and some indication of alternative substitute recreation areas. A large pro-

[9] Donald J. Volk, "Factors Affecting Recreational Use of National Parks," Paper given at the Annual Convention of the Association of American Geographers, Columbus, Ohio, April 19, 1965.

TABLE 8.
VISITS TO SPECIFIED NATIONAL PARKS PER 1,000 OF BASE POPULATION, AND AVERAGE COSTS PER VISIT

	Grand Canyon			Glacier			Shenandoah		
	Visits per 1,000 base population	Cost per visit		Visits per 1,000 base population	Cost per visit		Visits per 1,000 base population	Cost per visit	
Distance zone		Full cost basis	Shared cost basis		Full cost basis	Shared cost basis		Full cost basis	Shared cost basis
Up to 100 miles	20.8	$63.50	$63.50	46.8	$42.50	$42.50	104.8	$ 9.50	$ 9.50
100 to 300 miles	10.3	116.00	94.60	5.5	80.00	66.60	20.2	15.85	15.85
300 to 500 miles	5.7	168.50	104.70	2.4	117.50	74.10	8.5	32.15	32.15
500 to 1,000 miles	4.0	221.00	115.00	1.0	155.00	82.00	4.3	60.00	49.80
1,000 to 1,500 miles	2.1	273.50	114.80	0.4	192.50	82.40	2.1	99.75	63.45
1,500 to 2,000 miles							1.1	144.00	76.50
2,000 or more miles							1.1	200.20	85.48

SOURCE: Based on Table 2, same source as Table 7. Items have generally the same meaning as in Table 7, including same basis for sharing costs.

portion of the variation in visit rates among the states was accounted for by the factors of distance, income, urbanization, and mobility—75 per cent to 95 per cent, with more than 90 per cent for half of the areas. In every instance the most important factor affecting attendance proved to be the distance of the area from the place of residence of the visitors. We are in agreement with Volk's conclusion that formulations of this sort can be used to make fairly good predictions of the usefulness of potential new recreation areas.

User-Oriented Areas

The major problem in estimating demand curves for user-oriented outdoor recreation areas is the difficulty of assigning cash costs to visits. Children using a neighborhood playground, for instance, incur no cash costs in doing so. Some of them may need bicycles to reach the area, and these mean a past expenditure, at least partly for this purpose, and some recurring cash costs for maintenance. Some children may be brought by parents in the family auto, at some direct cash cost, and only because of some past cash outlay to purchase the family auto. For more distant areas within the user-oriented group, such as picnic areas, tennis courts, golf courses, and swimming beaches, the likelihood of cash costs is greater, but the amount will surely be small. Many, perhaps most, users of these areas would find it difficult to provide basic data from which meaningful estimates of cost per visit could be compiled; and it might be particularly hard to make estimates that would provide reliable differences in money cost for users coming from different distances.

While these problems increase the difficulty of plotting curves relating cost to visits in the straightforward manner of other types of areas, there are discernible patterns of behavior between distance and usage of these user-oriented areas, especially if various socioeconomic factors are taken into consideration.

DEMAND CURVES FOR RECREATION RESOURCES

Thus far we have dealt with the demand for the whole outdoor recreation experience, as defined in Chapter 3. The costs for this whole experience, as we have presented them both in our hypothetical and actual examples, are chiefly for travel, including not only transportation *per se* but also the additional costs, or added outlay, for such things as meals and lodging. If any entrance fees or charges were paid for the privilege of using the recreation area, they were included in the estimated total costs.

As useful as these demand estimates are for understanding various aspects of outdoor recreation, demand curves for the whole recreation experience do not directly measure the demand for the recreation resource. For many types of practical resource and recreation administrative problems and planning, it is necessary to have answers to such questions as: How much are particular resources worth when used for recreation, as compared with their value when used for other purposes? What will be the effect upon the value of recreation resources of more leisure or higher incomes among users? Will proposed investments for more intensive use of a recreation area repay the costs involved? Demand curves for the whole experience are of limited use for such questions, but demand curves for the recreation resource itself would go far toward providing answers.

Wherever it is possible to estimate a demand curve for the whole recreation experience, as we have done for earlier examples, it is possible to estimate one for the recreation resource involved. The procedure uses the information contained in the demand curves for the whole experience to accomplish this. Before illustrating this, a few general points should be made. This procedure in its simplest, most straightforward form assumes that the average of one large group of recreation users will react to costs in the same way as the average of another large group of users. This assumption of rationality or predictability in reaction of consumers to price changes underlies all demand analysis of economics. It seems generally to be borne out by experience with most commercial products. It is not argued that every individual reacts in exactly the same way as does every other individual, but only that fairly large samples of persons, chosen randomly as far as their interest in outdoor recreation is concerned, will react similarly to changes in recreation costs.

Essentially the procedure is to determine, from the curves for the whole experience, the number of visits that would result if the costs were increased by given amounts. The computations are made on the basis of the implied reaction of people to changes in costs to determine how many would visit an area at different increased cost levels.

This procedure implies that if a group of people who had a cost of $5 for the whole experience participated at the rate of 200 per 1,000, and another group had a cost of $10 and a rate of 100 per 1,000, then if the costs to the first group could be assumed to be increased to $10, the same as the second group, then their new rate of attendance would also be the same as this second group. This can perhaps best be shown in a simple hypothetical example.

We can assume a recreation area drawing people from three zones having populations of 1,000, 4,000, and 10,000 people, respectively. The observed demand situation for the entire experience might be as in Table 9.

TABLE 9.
DEMAND SCHEDULE OF WHOLE EXPERIENCE FOR HYPOTHETICAL
RECREATION AREA

Zone	Population	Cost per visit	Number of visits	Visits per 1,000 base population
1	1,000	$1	500	500
2	4,000	$3	1,200	300
3	10,000	$5	1,000	100

The demand curve is plotted in Figure 13. We can now begin to construct the demand schedule for the resource by relating added cost to
total attendance, based on this information. We note first that without
any added cost (or with zero added cost), total attendance is 2,700
visits (Table 10). We may determine next the effect of a rise in cost of
one dollar. The people in zone 1, who had been paying a cost of $1 per
visit, may now be assumed to be faced with the situation of paying $2
per visit. They have been going to the area at the rate of 500 per
thousand, but the demand curve of Figure 13 indicates that for this area
people would attend at the rate of 400 per thousand when faced with
costs of $2 per visit. Thus the number attending from this zone would
be 400 per thousand multiplied by the total population of the zone
(1,000), or 400. The number attending from the second zone is found

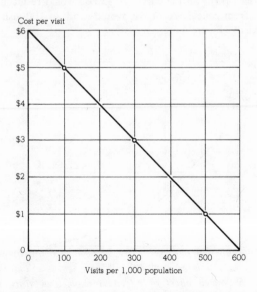

*Figure 13. Demand curve for whole recreation experience for hypothetical
recreation area.*

79

TABLE 10.
EFFECT OF INCREASES IN COST ON NUMBERS OF VISITS
TO HYPOTHETICAL RECREATION AREA

	Number of visits at added cost[1] per visit of:					
Zone	$0	$1	$2	$3	$4	$5
1	500	400	300	200	100	0
2	1,200	800	400	0	0	0
3	1,000	0	0	0	0	0
Total attendance	2,700	1,200	700	200	100	0

[1] In addition to regular travel cost.

in a similar manner. The higher cost attracts people at a rate of 200 per 1,000 instead of the old rate of 300 per 1,000; total attendance would drop from the original 1,200 to 800. An increase of $1 in the cost of attending from the third zone would push the cost to $6 per visit. The demand curve shows that at that cost the rate of attendance would fall to zero; thus no one would be expected to attend from that zone. The total attendance for the increased cost of $1 is 400 from zone 1, plus 800 from zone 2, plus zero from zone 3, or 1,200 visits. This is a second point on the demand curve for the resource.

The effects of a $2 rise in costs would be to further reduce the number of visits, to 300 from zone 1 and 400 from zone 2, or a total of 700. This is a third point on the curve. A $3 rise would result in total visits of 200, all from zone 1. A $4 rise would result in 100 visits, and a $5 rise in no visits (Figure 14).

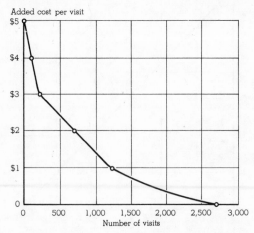

Figure 14. Estimated effect of added cost on total visits, hypothetical recreation area.

We can estimate the demand curve for the recreation resources in and around Lewis and Clark Lake by the same procedure. To do this, it is necessary to first go back to Figure 8, on which the relation between cost per visit and the number of visits was shown. The number of visits per 1,000 base population can be estimated for varying costs directly from the curve, within relatively small margins of error. However, as costs for this area were given by parties of four, we divide the number of visitors by four and deal in party visits. We can thus construct a schedule of demand in the same way as before. (The results are shown in Table 11.) We begin by noting that actual attendance in 1959 was 927,000 persons or 231,000 parties. If the cost of a party visit increases by $1.00, this reduces the attendance rate in zone 1 from 946 parties per 1,000 base population—the rate without increased cost—to 800 parties per 1,000 (these figures are not shown in the Table) which would mean 70,000 party visits in total from this zone. This procedure is repeated for a $1.00 increase in cost for other zones; and then for each zone with other increases up to $20.00 per visit; the total attendance in parties for each increase is given in the last line of the table. This is plotted as the demand curve for the resource in Figure 15. As expected, the number of visitors falls steadily as the added cost rises. At the higher costs, only a small portion of the nearby residents would be expected to visit the area, and virtually none of the more distant ones would do so. Our previous comments about the limitations of these data should be borne in mind here. A different form of the basic demand curve, shown in Figure 8, would lead to considerably different results, but this curve is taken from empirical data which reflect the actual behavior of people toward this recreation area.

A similar demand relationship can be computed from the data previ-

TABLE 11.
ESTIMATED NUMBER OF PARTY VISITS AT DIFFERENT ADDED COST
LEVELS, LEWIS AND CLARK LAKE, SOUTH DAKOTA, 1959

(1,000)

Distance zone	Actual visits, 1959	Estimated party visits at added cost per party of:					
		$1	$3	$5	$10	$15	$20
Less than 50 miles	83	70	51	37	20	13	6
50–100 miles	91	85	69	58	28	12	12
100–150 miles	12	12	11	0	0	0	0
150–200 miles	40	30	5	0	0	0	0
Over 200 miles, in survey area	5	1	0	0	0	0	0
Total	231	198	136	95	48	25	18

SOURCE: Based on Table 4 and Figure 8.

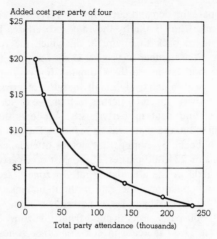

Figure 15. Estimated total party visits under varying added costs, Lewis and Clark Lake.

ously given for the recreation resources of Kerr Reservoir. In this case the following price-visit schedule results:

Level of simulated cost increase	Number of party visits
$ 0	516,699
2.06	149,887
4.13	84,713
8.26	38,629
16.51	10,964
32.02	322

The demand curve for the recreation resource at Yosemite was computed from the demand relationship shown in Table 7 and in Figure 11. Again the number of visitors per 1,000 base population is read from this curve; to this is applied the base population of the areas, and the number of visits is calculated for the new total cost per visit, including added costs in the total. A further assumption or procedure was necessary as to the shape of the curve to the left of the point where observed data help to establish it. In this case, we drew a line extended as necessary in what seemed like a smooth and reasonable extension. The results of this analysis for Yosemite are found in Table 12 and Figure 16.

Similar calculations were made for the recreation resources at Glacier, Grand Canyon, and Shenandoah national parks, and demand curves for these areas are also shown in Figure 16. Because of the rather arbitrary nature of some of the estimates underlying the various

TABLE 12.
ESTIMATED VISITS AT DIFFERENT ADDED COSTS, YOSEMITE NATIONAL PARK

(1,000)

Zone of origin	Actual visits, 1953	Estimated visits at added cost per visit of:					
		$5	$10	$15	$25	$40	$50
California counties:							
Less than 100 miles	35	11	6	5	2	1	1
100–150 miles	114	67	47	33	16	6	3
150–200 miles	143	138	73	46	25	10	6
200–250 miles	119	89	71	58	42	10	5
300 and more miles[1]	245	115	83	57	31	10	5
Subtotal	656	420	280	199	116	37	20
Other states:							
300–500 miles	26	12	9	7	5	3	2
500–1,000 miles	19	20	15	13	8	5	3
1,000–1,500 miles	35	26	20	19	14	12	9
1,500–2,000 miles	66	50	43	39	31	19	12
2,000–2,500 miles	40	36	32	29	23	13	6
2,500 and more miles	51	45	45	40	27	18	9
Subtotal	237	189	164	147	108	70	41
Total	893	609	444	346	224	107	61

[1] There were no counties in the 250-to-300-mile zone.
SOURCE: Based on Table 7 and Figure 11.

demand curves, our lack of knowledge about how to allocate costs of trips when visits to national parks are combined with visits to other areas, and the uncertainty of the shape of the demand curve to the left of the last observed data point, the specific curves presented in this section are more illustrative in character than exact in values. Had the

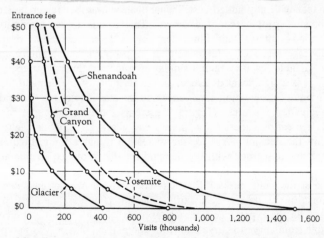

Figure 16. Estimated visits under various entrance fee schedules, Yosemite, Glacier, Grand Canyon, and Shenandoah national parks.

full cost of the whole trip, rather than only part of it, been charged against the recreation experience at the national park, the curves on Figure 16 would have been steeper—i.e., more inelastic than shown there. Conversely, had a smaller portion of the cost been charged against the national park recreation experience, the demand curves would have been flatter, or more elastic. More precise data for the demand curves for the whole recreation experience would have yielded more accurate estimates of the demand for the recreation resource. The method is capable of yielding better answers if better data are available; the conversion from demand for the whole recreation experience to the demand for the recreation resource is relatively simple, and does not introduce errors of its own. In spite of the deficiencies in data, it is probable that the demand curves for the recreation resource presented in Figures 15 and 16 provide estimates of the relative magnitudes involved.

Having derived these estimates for the demand for the recreation resource at various areas we need to take note of several aspects of such estimates. The first is most apparent in Figure 16. The relative position of the demand curves for the recreation resource at these national parks present striking evidence of the role of location relative to population centers on the demand for recreation areas and facilities. Few would hold that Shenandoah is a basically more attractive area than the others dealt with; in fact the curves in Figure 12 showed that this was clearly not the case, for attendance rates per 1,000 base population were lower than for the other parks at nearly all cost levels, and they fell off very quickly with higher costs. But the curves in Figure 16 show that with any added cost Shenandoah will attract far greater total numbers of people than the others. This is due to its proximity to population centers. This illustrates how a given recreation resource within easy reach of a large number of people is potentially a much more valuable resource than a similar area located far from users.

There is a significant difference in the elasticity of the demand for the whole outdoor recreation experience and the elasticity of the demand for the recreation resource. (Figure 8 presents the demand curve for the whole recreation experience at Lewis and Clark Lake, while Figure 15 presents the demand curve for the recreation resource there; Figures 11 and 12 are concerned with the demand for the whole experience at the national parks, while Figure 16 shows the demand for the recreation resource at the same parks.) Elasticity comparisons are not easy because the form of the data is necessarily different. However, the elasticity of demand for the experience generally exceeds 2.0, although it is somewhat variable from curve to curve and from one portion of a curve to another, while the elasticity of demand for the recreation resource generally ranges from 1.0 downward, although this, too, is variable from curve to

84

ask 2,

— ratio of % Δ in quantity / % Δ in price

curve and from one portion of a curve to another. Economists have long known that the elasticity of derived demand is less for a commodity or service which forms only part of a larger commodity or service than it is for the whole commodity or service; comparatively large variations in the price of the component commodity exert relatively small effects on the price of the larger commodity. The methodology for deriving the demand for the recreation resource guarantees that the demand for the resource will be more inelastic than the demand for the whole recreation experience. The significance of this increased inelasticity in demand will be shown, we believe, in later chapters when the matter of fees or charges for admission to recreation areas is discussed.

In Chapter 11, where the value of land and water resources used for outdoor recreation is discussed, we shall return to these demand curves for the recreation resource; their utility for analysis of practical planning problems will be demonstrated there.

In spite of the limitations of the basic data, previously described, it may be both interesting and instructive to contrast the demand curve for the recreation resource of Lewis and Clark Lake with that for Yosemite. In Table 11, we see that, as the added costs rise for Lewis and Clark Lake, the total cost per visit for the distant zones becomes more than anyone is willing to pay, and there are no visitors from over 100 miles away when added costs reach $5.00 or more per party visit. As added costs rise, the number of visitors from nearby areas falls off, but not so drastically. The added costs have the effect of shrinking the potential market area for Lewis and Clark Lake. This is an intermediate type area, it will be recalled; the attractiveness of such areas is often highly localized, and highly responsive to differences in cost.

For Yosemite, a sharply contrasting result arises. As added costs increase, visits from nearby areas fall off far more than do visits from more distant areas. Thus, at an added cost of $25.00 per person visit, visits from the zones within 150 miles are 83 per cent below their level with no added cost, visits from California counties more than 150 miles away are down by 68 per cent, while visits from all areas outside of California are down 54 per cent. In this case, an added cost of a specific sum is a large percentage of the total cost for nearby residents, and their visits to Yosemite fall off rapidly. For these people, this national park is in some respects like an intermediate area. The same amount of added cost for a more distant resident is a much smaller proportion of his total cost; hence, the number of people from such areas shrinks less. In this case, the effect of added costs is to shift the area of origin for visitors relatively *away* from California and from the park. Yosemite's reputation is national—indeed, world-wide—and people will come long distances at great expense to see it.

LIMITATIONS ON THE FOREGOING DEMAND ANALYSIS AS APPLIED TO OUTDOOR RECREATION

This chapter has thus far been concerned with demand analysis as applied to outdoor recreation; we wish at this point to cite some limitations to this approach. If not used carefully and in full knowledge of its limitations, it might result in inaccurate results and lead to false conclusions.

As constructed, the first demand curves such as are shown in Figures 8, 9, 10, 11, and 12 are underestimates of the true demand for the given resources. This stems from the fact that money costs (or the mileage distances as an index to costs), as we have dealt with them, are not the sole constraint on visits to a recreation area. As noted at the beginning of this chapter, costs of outdoor recreation arise in money, time, and travel. These three measures of costs are often, but not invariably, closely correlated. We know that the general total effect of each of these considerations and of any combination of them is negative— fewer people are observed to travel greater distances to recreation areas than shorter distances.

The estimates of demand relationships in the figures listed above have dealt with the number of visits that occur with varying money costs (or with varying distance, when mileage is an index to money cost), without provision for the value of the time given up. Time has value, and to ignore it in the cost of going to a recreation area may seem to invite gross error. However, it would be difficult to put a direct measure on the value of time used for such a purpose. It would of course vary greatly for different individuals, for different times for the same individual, and for going to different places.

The man who had to take time from his job without pay in order to enjoy outdoor recreation would surely value time differently from the man who had a paid vacation; the latter would presumably compare his satisfactions from the total recreation experience, including the time required, with the satisfactions he might get from any alternative use of the same time. In many instances, the decision to undertake a recreation experience is more likely to depend on the availability of free time and the time required than upon the monetary price.

Travel to and from the actual recreation site may have particular significance, aside from any money and time costs involved. If the route is pleasant and other things agreeable, travel may have a positive value; apparently this is often the case, since large numbers of people report travel or sightseeing as one of the main purposes or activities in outdoor recreation. However, in many situations the travel itself is not enjoyable, but only necessary in order to enjoy the on-site experiences. There are various ways in which money expenditures can save on travel time; there are various interactions of money, time, and travel pleasures which affect decisions to visit a recreation area. However, if all other things are equal, more people will visit areas requiring less travel than will visit areas demanding more travel. It is obvious, without attempting to value the time spent in travel, that money alone is not the only constraining force on decisions involving the amount of outdoor recreation to consume.

The demand curves for the resources, as we have drawn them, directly reflect only money costs (including distance as an index of money cost). Thus, they account for only a part of the total cost of the recreation experience. For example in our hypothetical case (Table 9 and Figure 13) we say that people with costs of $1 per visit travel to the area at the rate of 500 per 1,000 population and people with $5 costs have a rate of only 100 per 1,000. The calculation of the demand for the resource then assumes that if $4 were added to the cost of the first group, making their costs $5, they would then visit the area at the rate of 100 per 1,000; and so they probably would, if money costs were the only variable of importance. But time is also a cost. Thus, even if the two groups have the same money cost, the group in the first distance zone will have a lower total cost in terms of money and time; their attendance will fall off, but the rate will still be higher than that for the more distant group. This may perhaps be clearer if we look at the reverse situation, again taking these same two hypothetical groups. If we could somehow reduce the money cost of the distant group from $5 to $1, the number of visits would increase. But it would almost certainly not increase to the rate of the nearby group because the time cost would still be higher. Many of these more distant people could not or would not take the time to travel to the area.

Travel probably has an effect upon outdoor recreation independent of or in addition to the effects of money and time costs. If a travel route is unattractive, or if the mode of travel is uncomfortable, or otherwise tends to be burdensome on travelers, then distance traveled almost surely reduces recreation use of an area beyond the point to which dollar and time costs would have reduced it. Conversely, if the travel route could be made attractive, or if the mode of travel could be made more comfortable and more enjoyable, then the distance traveled might have a positive value, thus offsetting in some degree the dollar and time costs of the recreation visit. Air-conditioned automobiles—to use but one example—might well increase the demand for some outdoor recreation areas, aside from any considerations of money or time cost.

A further limitation on the demand analysis, which acts in the same manner as time and distance, is the presence of intervening recreation opportunities. The number of alternative opportunities would no doubt increase with increasing distances from the recreation site under examination. The effects of the alternatives available to each population group are reflected in their actual visit rate for the whole experience. The attendance rate will be lower for areas with many substitute opportunities than for those with few convenient alternatives. This consideration is taken into account in the data on visit rates to each recreation area. However, when we estimate the demand for the recreation resource, we raise the visit cost for the nearby groups to that of more distant population groups and ascribe the latter's visit rate to the former. To the extent that more alternative recreation areas are in fact available to more distant groups, the visit rate of the less distant group would not go down to that of the more distant group because of money cost increases. Consequently the visit rates will be estimated with a bias similar to that occasioned by the failure to consider travel time. Again, the bias is a downward one; the number of visitors at different price levels is underestimated.

The result of omitting time from our demand curves under varying toll charges, as in Figures 13, 14, 15, and 16, is that we underestimate the number of people who would visit the area from closer zones; in economic jargon, our estimated demand curve for the resource is to the left of the actual curve. At each cost level, more visits would actually occur than our estimated curves show. How many more is, however, unknown; it might be considerable, in some circumstances. The error introduced by including only money costs, and omitting time costs, is a consistent bias toward underestimating the value of the recreation resource.

A further aspect of the curves derived for various areas is that they measure only indirectly what people would pay as the price of the resource. This price is, of course, what is desired in such a demand curve, but the demand for the recreation resource is implicitly determined by the behavior of people rather than directly in a market place. The increased cost per visit may be thought of as an increase in entrance fees, or tolls, although increases in cost might arise in other ways. For some of the uses we shall make of the demand curve, the nature of the increased cost is unimportant. In order to derive the value of given recreation areas, we need only an implicit assertion of how attendance would react. For this purpose, these curves are both objective and operational. For questions of determining actual fee charges, however, such curves are subject to the further limitation that we are not at all sure how people will react to an entrance fee as such. Would they treat it in exactly the same way that they would treat any other increase in costs? The answer might depend upon how well an increased fee were explained to them, and in the use made of revenues raised from fees. This is a subject to which we shall return in Chapter 14. Probably more important, we do not know how much people would shift their attendance to alternative recreation areas which may or may not impose similar fees. Related to this is the implied assumption that people living in the various zones have very similar, if not identical, reactions to outdoor recreation opportunities. This may not be the case, as there may be important differences in various socioeconomic characteristics between different population groups that would cause people to have significantly different propensities to participate in given activities.

At this point, a noneconomist might well exclaim: "If you must so carefully further qualify your already somewhat novel approach to the estimation of demand for outdoor recreation, is not the whole procedure too complicated and too arbitrary to be useful in practice?" While this reaction might be natural enough, it misses the main point. It is not the procedure as such that needs qualification and caution, but rather the basic recreation experience and the available data about it which are complicated and not easily interpreted. Anyone attempting to analyze the same basic experience and same data by any less rigorous or superficially simpler method would encounter the same problems of interpretation and analysis; moreover, he might more easily be led astray by a less adequate method and thus reach less dependable conclusions. Given the necessary data and necessary understanding of the basic recreation experience, we feel that the methods outlined in this chapter will rather readily lead to more accurate results than will any alternative method.

INTERRELATIONSHIPS IN DEMAND

One of the outstanding characteristics of the American economic and social system is that of extreme interdependence. The quantities produced and the values of any good or service are not determined in a vacuum but are directly and indirectly dependent on quantities and prices of nearly all other goods and services; in turn, these are all dependent on preferences and tastes of consumers, which are dependent on a large number of characteristics of people and their environment including the prices and quantities of all goods and services. Outdoor recreation is no exception, and interdependence is abundantly apparent in the complex array of demands, facilities, and activities, and the many things that affect them.

The demand curve for any recreation resource may shift as a result of changes in incomes, leisure, road conditions, or management of the area in question. Although these complications add to our problems, it is important to recognize that they are all part of a system of inter-relationships; useful things can still be said about demand for outdoor recreation in spite of them. This recognition of complex interrelation-ships allows us to explain otherwise puzzling aspects of the demand situation. We must be aware of all the factors that are important to our problem, and we must make allowance for them in such ways as to make our empirical data useful.

When there is more free time or more money available for discretionary spending, more will almost always be spent for outdoor recreation. But just as the decision to use both time and money for recreation means less is available for other activities, so it is that expenditures for one type of recreation activity or on one area means less for other types of recreation and for other areas. All recreation areas or resources are in varying degrees substitutes for one another; attendance at one area is conditioned by the existence and characteristics of others. If the different resources or areas are highly similar, each area is then almost completely competitive with each other area. But if one area has water recreation and another does not, it might be argued that they are independent, that one does not substitute for the other. In practice, the situation is almost always somewhere between these extremes. That is, it is probable that all areas accesssible to a given population are to some extent competitors or rivals, but also to some extent independent of one another. As we have noted previously, under some conditions different areas may be complementary, so that increased use of one promotes increased use of the other. Park and recreation areas of the same kind and those of different kinds form a system, as we noted in Chapter 3; the different units of the system have extensive and rather complex interrelations— they may supplement, complement, compete, or be independent of one another. The degree of substitutability or competition between areas will in large part depend on the inherent attraction of the area and upon its location. Neighborhood parks are generally of importance only to people in fairly close proximity to them, but areas such as Yellowstone Park have an influence throughout the country, and indeed even farther. Practically, the demand for a proposed new national park in a western state would be influenced to some degree by the existence of Yellowstone National Park but not by a city park in Atlanta.

Implicit in each of the demand curves for the whole recreation experience at a specific area, such as we have presented in Figures 8, 9, 10, 11, and 12, is the existence of all other areas to which people might possibly go instead. Also implicit is the present schedule of entrance fees at each of the possible alternative areas. One reason why the demand curve for a specific area is relatively elastic is that persons now going to this area could often go elsewhere if entrance fees were raised. In the calculations of use and of possible revenue under different entrance fees at each area, there is implicit the assumption that present entrance fees will not be changed at alternative use areas. If the latter were changed, the extent of the substitution between parks would be much less. Thus, for instance, if the alternative areas were all parts of the same park system, such as state parks, and if fees were raised at all of them simultaneously, the shift away from each park would be less than our curves suggest. The effect of raising fees at all units of a park system could be studied by logical extensions of our methods.

We have noted, particularly with respect to the four national parks examined earlier, the effect of location of an area relative to population centers. This is of immense importance. But in addition to numbers of people in each attendance zone, their income and other characteristics are also important. Such differences should, if possible, be taken account of in deriving demand estimates. We have assumed in our earlier estimates that the whole population within practical travel distance of any of the given areas, exhibited homogeneous characteristics with regard to their desire to visit an area. More realistic estimates would allow for possible differences in the propensities to visit the area of different people in different tributary groups or zones. For example, if all but one of the areas near a recreation site were rural with low per capita incomes, and the remaining one was principally an urban area with higher incomes, the rate of visits from the latter would, allowing for distance or cost differences, probably be somewhat higher. The final estimate of the demand curve should reflect this difference. A more complete knowledge of the effect of such factors would then allow more accurate and meaningful statements to be made about the demand for the area. Such information would also make possible an appraisal of the effect on demand of imposing or raising an entrance fee.

The demand curves for outdoor recreation implicitly assume the ready availability of such areas. If suitable recreation resources are easily available to a population center, many more visits will be recorded than if the identical population had to travel great distances to participate in outdoor activities at physically identical recreation areas. Potential demand can be satisfied only to the extent that sufficient capacity exists in available recreation areas. While demand may be viewed as wholly dependent upon the supply of recreation areas, it is much more helpful to view the demand situation as related to the presence or lack of facilities.

The upshot of all of this is that demand for outdoor recreation is dependent upon a number of interrelated factors. We are primarily interested in examining the status of recreation resources relative to population distribution, incomes, roads, etc., and determining how the demand situation might work itself out. As further evidence is accumulated, more meaningful generalization can be made about recreation demand. While work proceeds in these directions we need to be aware of the value and limitations of the information available at any time. So long as the limitations noted earlier are kept in mind, our demand curves can be highly useful, and particularly so for certain purposes.

6

Behavior of Some Causal Factors in Demand

In the preceding two chapters we have explored the demand for the whole outdoor recreation experience (as we define it) and for the recreation resource. Our concern there was primarily with the factors affecting the demand for an outdoor recreation area at any given time period, such as a year. The analysis concentrated on two factors—population and costs per visit. The effect of population changes over time or of differences between areas was largely or wholly eliminated by expressing visits in terms of number per 1,000 of base population. The costs per visit were measured by either conventional money costs or mileage traveled. Other factors, such as leisure and per capita real incomes, were considered in a more general way, and primarily as factors causing shifts in the demand curve. Demand was taken as the relation between volume of visits per 1,000 of base population and cost per visit. The emphasis in these two chapters has not been primarily upon factors operating over time to change the demand for outdoor recreation.

Before we turn to the projection of future use of outdoor recreation areas, it seems desirable to explore the probable future trend of some of the socioeconomic factors which are likely to affect the shape and position of the future demand curve for the whole outdoor recreation experience and for recreation resources. We consider here population, income, leisure, and travel, as major factors affecting demand for outdoor recreation, especially shifts in demand over time.

POPULATION

Population, the number of people living in a given area, is clearly one of the most important variables associated with recreation demand,

and one on which we have extensive information over a long period. The population of the United States has increased from less than 4 million persons in 1790, when the first national census was taken, to about 190 million today. The *rate* of growth from year to year declined slowly but rather steadily from about 3 per cent annually in the first half of the nineteenth century to not much over 0.5 per cent annually during the 1930's; it then increased and is about 1.7 per cent annually today.

Every demographer, economist, sociologist, or other student of population changes expects the United States to have a substantially larger total population in the decades ahead. The only questions relate to the extent of such increase. Sensible bases exist for projections that yield different total figures for the future. The consensus of projections lies between 226 and 279 million persons by 1980 and between 268 and 433 million by the year 2000.[1]

Changes in the geographic distribution of population will continue to be as dramatic and as important as changes in total population. The major geographic changes in population have been two: a westward shift, and a country-to-city shift.

The center of total population in the United States in 1790 was 23 miles due *east* of Baltimore. In each decade since then it has moved almost exactly west, at an average rate of just under 40 miles per decade. In 1960, it was about the center of Illinois, approximately 50 miles south of Decatur. The population center will continue to shift westward.

Perhaps more important, socially, economically, and for recreation programs, has been the shift of population from rural to urban areas. In 1790, the United States was a rural nation; only 5 per cent of the total population lived in cities of 2,500 or more, and these cities were relatively small by today's standards. Over the decades, urban population grew faster than rural. By the first World War, the nation was half rural, half urban (by the Census definition which includes within urban all cities and towns of 2,500 or more, plus unincorporated similar areas). Today, it is roughly two-thirds urban, one-third rural; by 2000, it will be 82–85 per cent urban. Moreover, the rural population is changing. At one time it was predominantly farmers; today it includes many people who live in the country and work in a town or city. Total farm population has been declining since it reached its peak about 1920, and further major decreases are in prospect. The influence of the farm on the social, economic, and political life of the nation has been declining at a slower pace, but this is expected to change over the next several

[1] Hans H. Landsberg, Leonard L. Fischman, and Joseph L. Fisher, *Resources in America's Future* (Baltimore: The Johns Hopkins Press, for Resources for the Future, Inc., 1963).

decades. Even our present pattern of school year and school vacation, which so strongly influences seasonal attendance at vacation areas, goes back to the need to have the farm boy work on the farm during the summer.

Changes have taken place within the urban complex itself, which also have an effect on recreation. The suburbs have grown much faster than the city centers. The attractions of suburban life, plus the opportunities opened up by the private auto and the public highway, have drawn an increasing proportion of urban population to the suburbs. In part, this has been an actual flight from the city; in part, it has been because suitable building sites within the older cities were largely or fully occupied. These shifts within the urban complex have had marked socioeconomic characteristics. Settlers in suburbia have been predominantly young white couples with small children. Their demands for education, recreation, and other social services have been markedly influenced by their age and family composition. Will these same couples remain in suburbia, or will they move back to the city center when their children are grown and gone? If they move back, will their places be taken by another wave of young married couples with small children? These questions are full of meaning to recreation people, but they are ones that only time can answer fully.

At the same time that young white couples have moved to the suburbs, the older districts of the city have been increasingly taken over by families of racial, ethnic, or other minorities. The Negroes of the nation are leaving the farms and rural areas and settling in the cities—in northern and western cities as well as in southern ones. Housing and other restrictions often force them to live in older areas within cities—deteriorated areas, which are or often become slums. This, in turn, vastly affects the recreation problems in such areas. The need for adequate recreation facilities is very great, yet these older parts of large cities nearly always lack park and recreation areas, and the opportunities to acquire additional suitable areas are often sharply limited. Such urban districts usually cannot finance the needed programs.

The changes in population have been accompanied by major changes in age distribution. The first declines in death rate are often largest among babies and small children, and hence have the effect of adding to the number of children who survive. A major effect of a declining death rate is the emergence of a much larger population of older persons. In 1900, those 65 years or older made up only 4 per cent of the total population; today they represent nearly 9 per cent. The number of persons in this age group increased from 3 million in 1900 to 16 million today, and may well reach 30 million by 2000. However, the percentage of total population may be no higher than at present; if birth rate stays high and total population grows rapidly, the percentage of old people will be less than if population growth is slower.

As all recreation specialists know, the kinds and amounts of recreation demanded are affected by the age of the person concerned.[2] The small child wants one kind of activity, the youth another, the younger married adult still another, the older married adult something different again, and the older citizen still another lot of activities. Interests and abilities to engage in recreation change with advancing age, as, in many cases, does the economic ability to procure what is desired.

LEISURE

Leisure, discussed in detail in Chapter 2, has clearly an important association with outdoor recreation. The total amount of leisure which is of interest in this commentary is closely dependent upon total number of people, as well as upon the characteristics of leisure time for individuals. The more people we have in an area, or in the nation, the more leisure time is available. In Chapter 2, we suggested that average per capita leisure may rise by 12 per cent by 2000, but this increase will be very unevenly distributed among people of different ages, occupations, and other characteristics. The size of pieces of leisure and their timing may be more important in effect upon various kinds of outdoor recreation than total leisure per person. The patterns of leisure time depend mainly on such things as workweek, vacation, and retirement years. In each of these the trends have clearly been for more leisure time; workweeks are becoming shorter, vacation periods are becoming longer and more generally available, and retirement periods are increasing. The likelihood is that these trends will each continue in these directions in the future.

TRANSPORTATION AND OUTDOOR RECREATION

The enjoyment of almost every kind of outdoor recreation involves some travel; two of the five phases of the whole outdoor recreation experience are travel. Only in the case of backyard activities is the user at the place of the outdoor recreation. Even for the neighborhood playground or park, some travel is involved; most visitors arrive on foot or by bicycle, but some use mechanical transportation—the family auto or public bus. For the intermediate and resource-based areas, studies show that an overwhelming proportion—usually 90 per cent or more—of all visitors arrive by auto.

[2] Eva Mueller and Gerald Gurin, *Participation in Outdoor Recreation,* ORRRC Study Report 20, Washington, D.C., 1962.

Transportation affects the enjoyment of outdoor recreation in three rather distinct ways. First, the kind of transportation facilities available determines travel *time*, and therefore the amount of outdoor recreation that most people can enjoy.

Second, transportation affects outdoor recreation in terms of monetary cost. Studies of visits to various outdoor recreation areas show that a major part of the total monetary cost is associated with travel distance and time. The travel costs themselves are largely correlated with distance; but the lodging, food, and similar costs are more nearly correlated with time, including time spent in travel. Today a very high percentage of all families own one or more cars, for a variety of uses. Once the overhead costs of automobile ownership have been incurred—for any reason—then the marginal or added costs of travel for recreation are relatively low. This has been a powerful factor influencing the use of parks and other outdoor recreation areas.

Third, transportation facilities influence the *character* of the recreation experience. The travel part of the experience has physical and emotional, or interest, aspects. If the road is rough, dusty, or dangerous, or if the meals in restaurants are miserable and rooms uncomfortable, the traveler will not enjoy this part of the trip. But even if the travel is physically comfortable, it may not be interesting or enjoyable. Also, while some people like to travel and take trips primarily for sightseeing purposes, others regard travel to and from the recreation area as something that must be endured in order to obtain the satisfactions at the site itself. Travel may well affect different members of the family in different ways. Making the travel phase of outdoor recreation more pleasurable should be a matter of concern to the recreationist and to the park plannner as well as to the highway specialists.

There have been great changes in the amount of travel per person and in the mode of transportation over the past fifty or more years. Before the First World War, travel by all mechanical means averaged 500 to 800 miles per person per year.[3] Nearly half of that travel was by local public carriers—street cars and electric interurban lines—and almost as much was by steam railroads. Automobiles were still new, and the roads of the day made even a short trip an adventure.[4] Per capita travel rose somewhat during and immediately after the First World War, but it was during the 1920's that Americans really began to travel. By the end of that decade, average travel per capita was up

[3] Marion Clawson, R. Burnell Held, and C. H. Stoddard, *Land for the Future* (Baltimore: The Johns Hopkins Press, for Resources for the Future, Inc., 1960). See pp. 534–536.

[4] Bellamy Partridge, *Fill 'er Up, the Story of Fifty Years of Motoring* (New York: McGraw-Hill Book Co., 1952).

to 3,000 miles. Although it declined during the Second World War, it rose again after the war and since has climbed to more than 5,000 miles per person annually. While travel per person is still increasing, changes in recent years have been less rapid than in earlier periods.

As the total amount of travel rose, its modes changed greatly. Automobiles are now of major importance, accounting for considerably more than half of all passenger travel, and long-distance buses and planes have entered the picture. Local public carriers are far less important than in an earlier day. Railroad passenger travel has declined absolutely and, of course, far more relatively.

At the same time there have been great improvements in comfort and convenience. The early automobiles were open to the weather and dust; and early roads were primitive indeed by modern standards. Trains were much less comfortable than they are today. And all means of travel were much slower. If the United States were measured by rail time in 1912, its relative size is that of a full page in a book; by current jet plane time, its size is smaller than a fingernail.

Not all travel is for recreation, of course. But Census data suggest that travel, especially auto travel, is engaged in by a very large proportion of the total population, for generally recreation purposes. The Outdoor Recreation Resources Review Commission reported that 61 per cent of adults participated in automobile riding for pleasure in 1960.[5] Because such a large proportion of people engage in travel for pleasure, recreation travelers do not fall into sharply defined and easily described groups; rather they include nearly the full gamut of age, occupation, income, family structure, and other characteristics of the total population.

Travel distances are closely related to the kinds of recreation areas and the timing of available leisure. The different kinds of trips are not sharply differentiated. Travel is reported variously in a number of sample studies (one-way distance, total travel, time used, etc.), and the availability of alternative sites varies from study to study. Moreover, there is almost surely great variation among users of different areas; some may actually enjoy a long drive, others may object to it. Season and weather also affect travel time and willingness to travel. With all these variable factors in mind, the following may nevertheless represent typical one-way distances for certain types of outdoor recreation:

After school and during the day for mothers with small children	Less than 1 mile, preferably less than ½ mile

[5] *Outdoor Recreation for America,* A Report to the President and to the Congress by the Outdoor Recreation Resources Review Commission (Washington: U.S. Government Printing Office, 1962).

After work, for adults seeking special opportunities	Up to 5 miles
One-day outing	20 to 50 miles (farther, if traffic is light and attractive areas are unavailable nearer)
Weekend outing	100 to 150 miles
Short vacation (two weeks or less)	400 to 600 miles
Longer vacation (more than two weeks)	1,000 miles or more

As we have noted, revolutionary changes have occurred in the past in the methods, speed, comfort, and ownership of transportation facilities. We have focused attention upon the automobile, for it is the private auto which is the prime means of travel to outdoor recreation areas. But major changes have taken place in other means of travel.

In the future, change may come slowly. A sober, and in our opinion a realistic, appraisal of future transportation patterns and methods has been made by a group of specialists in the transportation field.[6] This group cautions that transportation facilities and methods at any given time are in large part inherited from the past, and that the depreciation time for the large investments in transportation facilities is relatively long. They caution further that there is often a good deal of inertia in the transportation field as elsewhere in the economy and society. Hence, change may come in an evolutionary rather than revolutionary way. Nevertheless, they point to many innovations that may come in power supply, in new forms of transport vehicles, in new systems of control to speed up movement and at the same time increase safety, and in other ways. They particularly stress the possibilities for developing *systems* by integrating the various methods of transportation which have evolved separately.

As real income per capita increases, the average person will be able to afford far more travel than in the past. Car ownership per family will almost surely rise; more families will have more than one car; and a greater proportion of all families will own one car. The anticipated greater leisure will permit more time for driving, either for pleasure or in order to reach outdoor recreation areas. As a result of these and other factors, the average travel per person may well increase from 5,000 at present to perhaps 7,000 miles by 1980 and 9,000 miles

[6] *Conference on Transportation Research,* National Academy of Sciences— National Research Council, Publication 840. Washington, D. C. 1960. (Out of print.)

by 2000; and an increasingly large proportion of this increased travel will be primarily for recreation. The impact of increases of this magnitude upon outdoor recreation areas will be great, with the relatively greatest impact upon the more distant areas, now somewhat inaccessible. Whether we like it or not, the typical American will travel much more in the future than he does today—and this is the most mobile culture the world has ever known up to now.

Although revolutionary methods of general transportation are not probable, or at least not easily foreseen, some new methods of transportation might have serious impact upon certain kinds of outdoor recreation areas. For example, if air platforms, cars riding on airstreams, or other personalized means of transportation not dependent upon roads were to become technically practical and economically usable, the impact upon wilderness and other remote areas might be very great. The jeep, while only a minor factor in the general transportation picture, has already opened up many remote areas, and caused much soil erosion in the process. In some parts of the West, the "Tote Goat" (a special two-wheeled motor scooter, geared for slow travel and equipped with cleated wheels) has permitted mechanized travel on many trails previously accessible only on foot or on horseback. The development of relatively much more powerful outboard motors has revolutionized water sports since the war. Although future changes of these kinds are not predictable, one should not entirely rule out the possibility of new means of transportation that would have a great effect upon outdoor recreation. The use of commercial air lines and rented automobiles might increase so greatly in the future as to be nearly a new means of transportation, at least as far as the impact upon many presently rather remote areas is concerned.

The line of cause and effect does not run entirely from transportation to recreation; some of it runs the opposite way. Historically, an improvement in transportation has led to an increase in recreation use, while an increase in recreation demand has put a major strain on the transportation system. There seem to be three rather general situations in which the effect of recreation demand upon transportation facilities is felt.

First and most obvious, the existence of an attractive outdoor recreation area calls for roads into and out of it. An estimate of the potential use of such an area gives the highway engineer an idea of the traffic volume with which he will have to cope. One of the special problems in designing and building this type of highway is the preservation of the natural scenic beauties which provide the attraction of the area.[7]

[7] Dudley C. Bayliss, "Planning Our National Park Roads and Our National Parkways," *Traffic Quarterly,* July 1957.

Secondly, recreation as a motivation for travel may be an important demand factor on the major highways of a state or region. As we have noted, a substantial part of all auto travel is for recreation in its broadest sense. In many instances, general highways of suitable design for commercial traffic have adequate capacity to accommodate the recreation travel as well. In other instances, the volume of recreation travel will be so large as to require highways of different design and capacity. The recreation traveler wants more than comfort and safety; he wants attractive roads, with waysides and other resting and relaxation points. The kinds of roads he encounters greatly affect the recreation traveler's impression of an area or state, and his willingness to return.[8] In their planning of state highway systems, state highway departments must include recreation as one demand factor, often as a major one.[9]

Thirdly, the demands for outdoor recreation will create serious highway problems leading out of and back into the major urban centers. While the United States is an urban nation, most outdoor recreation opportunities lie outside of the cities. Moreover, people have their leisure at similar times. The result is a rush out of the city on Friday afternoon, Saturday, and even Sunday, especially during the summer; and late Sunday and early Monday there is a rush back in. Weekend traffic peaks often rise above weekday peaks, especially for private autos.[10] Routes leading from large cities to the seashore often have peak volumes double the designed capacity of the highway.[11] This problem of recreation peak travel is likely to grow worse.

The need for making highways more attractive and better suited to the recreationist should also be a factor in planning. Highway planning might well take advantage of the complementary relationships between transportation and recreation. And highways should be designed to avoid infringement upon parks, wherever possible.[12] Also, as two of the five major parts of the whole outdoor recreation experience are spent in

[8] Robert M. Howes, "Recreational Highways of the Tennessee Valley," Conference on the Immediate Highway Program, University of Tennessee, *Record,* July 1946.

[9] The Washington State Council for Highway Research, *The State Interest in Highways, A Report on Highway Classification 1952,* Vol. 1, *Statement of Problems, Policy and Discussion of Methods,* Prepared for the Joint Fact-Finding Committee on Highways, Streets, and Bridges (Olympia, Washington: Washington State Legislation, 1952).

[10] Austin J. Tobin, "The Relation of the Port of New York Authority to Metropolitan Recreation," *New York-New Jersey Metropolitan Region, Recreation for 19,000,000 in 1975,* May 8, 1958.

[11] Dwight R. G. Palmer, "The Role of New Jersey's Highway System in Regional Recreation," *New York-New Jersey Metropolitan Region, op. cit.*

[12] Joseph Prendergast, "The Highway in a Program for Recreation in America," *Seventeenth Short Course on Roadside Development,* Ohio State University and Ohio Department of Highways, October 1958.

travel, one cannot help but think that highways could be designed which would be more interesting and enjoyable to travel on.[13] The traveler's mind and emotions should be catered to, as well as his physical comfort and safety. A study of scenic highways begun in 1964 by the Department of Commerce at the direction of the federal Recreation Advisory Council is expected to lead to the inauguration of a national program to construct or improve such highways. Attention will also be given to improving the attractiveness of the journey on other highways.[14] Since travel to and from an outdoor recreation site may take as much or more time as the experience at the site, it would seem that total satisfactions from the whole experience could as readily be increased from attention to the travel aspects as from attention to the site experience as such.

INCOME AND OUTDOOR RECREATION

The use of income, like the use of time, may be divided into that for existence, that for subsistence, and that which is discretionary. In order to exist—that is, merely to sustain life—and to subsist—that is, to hold a job or otherwise do productive work—a certain level of income and of outlays is necessary. In practice, it is hard to draw a clear line delimiting existence and subsistence income and expenditure; but if one defines these types of income uses strictly, then in the United States today, most income is "discretionary."[15] Actually, the average consumer may feel he has little option in the way he spends his income. Some, perhaps a good deal will be committed over considerable periods—payments on a house, or for a car, etc. His expenditures will be influenced by a large number of factors.[16] In large part, his use of income is socially determined; he wants to do what other people of his social class do, and to avoid being conspicuous or unusual. Some of his income will go for more of the necessities or ones of better quality; he will consider pleasure and comfort as well as existence. But, after all these qualifications have been made, some income, perhaps a good deal for the average citizen in the United States today, is available for discretionary spend-

[13] Marion Clawson, "Implications of Recreational Needs for Highway Improvements," *Impact and Implications of Highway Improvement,* Highway Research Board, Bulletin 311 (Washington: National Academy of Sciences—National Research Council, 1962), pp. 31–37.

[14] *A National Program of Scenic Roads and Parkways,* Recreation Advisory Council Circular No. 4 (Washington: U.S. Government Printing Office, April 9, 1964).

[15] National Industrial Conference Board, *Discretionary Income,* Technical Paper No. 6, New York, 1958.

[16] Ruth P. Mack, "Economics of Consumption," *A Survey of Contemporary Economics,* Vol. 2, ed. Bernard Haley (Homewood, Ill.: Richard D. Irwin, Inc., 1952).

ing. Some have referred to the 1960's as "the decade of the discretionary dollar."[17] To the person whose past enthusiasms have led him to contract larger monthly installment payments than he can conveniently manage, there may seem to be precious little discretion or choice in the way he can spend his income. One can get overcommitted as to money, just as one can get overcommitted as to time.

Much, perhaps most, recreation requires expenditure of some income. Because the whole outdoor recreation experience so often requires travel, specialized equipment in many cases, and other goods or services which the consumer must buy, some expenditure is necessary. Unfortunately, it is difficult to measure expenditures for recreation, whether outdoor or indoor.

There is little agreement as to the definition of recreation as far as expenditures are concerned.[18] The basic difficulty is that recreation is a purpose of expenditure, rather than a kind of expenditure. A few articles, such as fishing rods, are so obviously for recreation they cannot be classed as anything else; the same is true of some services, such as movie admissions. But these are far less than the full expenditures for recreation, although they are sometimes discussed as though they in fact were the total. The trend in such expenditures may accurately reflect the trend in total recreation expenditures. Much of the money spent for housing, for transportation, for clothing, and for the other standard categories of expenditure are in fact primarily for recreation. As we have seen, a major proportion of all private auto use is for recreation. In the discussion which follows, we shall be forced to use expenditures for certain items as indexes of total recreation expenditures; this is possibly not too serious, as long as it is recognized that we are not actually measuring the total.

Most of the discussions of expenditures on recreation are based, to some degree, on Department of Commerce estimates of expenditures. In 1952, this source estimated that about $11.5 billion were spent for "recreation"; of this total, about 23 per cent was for radio, television, and musical instruments, 20 per cent was for sports equipment of various kinds, nearly 19 per cent for reading materials of all kinds, and lesser amounts for other items, including parimutuel and coin machines, billiards and bowling, golf, other sports, organizations and clubs, flowers and plants, and a vast array of miscellaneous items.[19] Dewhurst and

[17] "The Decade of the 'Discretionary' Dollar," *Fortune,* June 1959.

[18] Marion Clawson, "Statistical Data Available for Economic Research on Certain Types of Recreation," *Journal of American Statistical Association,* Vol. 54 (March 1959).

[19] For a comparison of these items for the three sources listed, see Clawson, *op. cit.*

associates use essentially the same definition except that they allocate part of the expenditure for reading materials to recreation and part to education. The editors of *Fortune* accept a somewhat similar classification and generally similar data, but add as major items alcoholic beverages and vacation travel, which have the effect of more than doubling the total expenditures for all recreation. Their vacation and travel item includes some or all of the items we have suggested as frequently omitted —auto and other transportation costs, food and lodging while traveling, vacation homes, special vacation clothing, and others. Their figure is thus much more inclusive, and perhaps nearer to the total recreation expenditure.

As national income has risen, so have expenditures for recreation of all kinds, but not exactly proportionately.[20] On the Commerce definition, total expenditures for all forms of recreation rose from somewhat less than $1 billion annually in the pre-World War I period to more than $10 billion in the early 1950's. A large part of this difference was due to changes in the general price level, but even in terms of 1950 prices the growth was from about $3 billion to $10 billion.

Recreation expenditures have varied from slightly more than 3 per cent to more than 5 per cent of personal disposable income (Figure 17 and Appendix Table 1). Several interesting relationships are shown in the figure. There has been a generally upward sweep of both real personal income per capita and of the percentage of it spent for all recreation. But the timing of changes is different. In the boom period of the late 1920's the percentage of income spent for recreation rose to a peak; while it declined thereafter for several years, the decline lagged considerably behind the lag in real income per capita, and the bottom was reached two years after incomes had turned upward. The proportion of income spent for recreation perhaps returned to a more consistent relationship to real income per capita by the late 1930's; but the abnormal conditions of the war period soon led to lesser expenditures.[21] Many recreational goods and services were unavailable, the means of

[20] J. Frederic Dewhurst, and Associates, *America's Needs and Resources—A New Survey* (New York: The Twentieth Century Fund, 1955), p. 347.

[21] Focusing on the 1929–60 period, George Fisk in *Leisure Spending Behavior* (Philadelphia: University of Pennsylvania Press, 1963) concludes "there is no evidence that 'total measured leisure' expenditures are expanding more rapidly than expenditures on all consumer goods in the U.S." While our analysis would bear out the same conclusion if limited to the same time span, the experience before 1929 suggests that the latter year was exceptional, and that there is in fact a long-term trend toward a larger percentage of expenditures on leisure activities of all kinds. Fisk does conclude that the proportion of expenditures for those categories of leisure goods more directly associated with outdoor recreation has risen relative to total expenditures for leisure; hence his conclusion on this point is in agreement with ours.

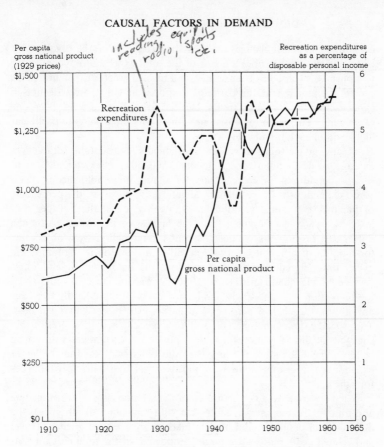

Figure 17. Recreation expenditures as percentage of disposable personal income, in relation to per capita gross national product in constant prices, 1909–60.

travel were restricted, and for other reasons recreation expenditures were down. Immediately after the war, recreation expenditures were very high. The availability of goods and services, plus perhaps the development of television as a major new form of recreation, were factors. Many men had probably been influenced also by organized recreation programs in the Armed Services during the war. One can conclude from these data that there is an irregular upward trend in the proportion of real income spent for recreation—a trend that can be, and has been, interrupted by the force of other economic and social changes.

The division of total recreation expenditures among the component items shows remarkable stability over the years, considering the major economic and social changes that have occurred.[22] With the development of television, a substantial amount of the total expenditure has gone for this purpose. There has been some trend toward greater expenditures for sports equipment and for participant sports, and a relative decline in expenditures for spectator sports. But the over-all picture has been one of stability. This is not inconsistent with considerable shifts in particular items within each broad category.

At any given time, there are undoubtedly considerable differences among people of differing age, income, and other characteristics, as to their expenditures for recreation.[23] As annual household income rises, so do expenditures for recreation. Significantly, however, the percentage of income spent for recreation in 1956 remained at the 5–6 per cent level for every income class, from the highest to the lowest. Although differences in amounts of income spent for recreation were observable for families of different composition, different position in the family life cycle, different educational and employment backgrounds, and other socioeconomic characteristics, in 1956 the percentage of income spent for recreation was amazingly similar for every group—hardly ever, for any group, less than 4 per cent and hardly ever more than 7 per cent. The specific items purchased, and the specific activities presumably engaged in, did vary more than this. For instance, families with young children spent far more for toys than did older families. But the larger expenditures for some items were mostly offset by smaller expenditures for others.

When we come to a consideration of the relationships between income and outdoor recreation (as contrasted with recreation of all types), the difficulties of definition and of data inadequacy are even greater. Travel and related costs represent a larger proportion of the total cost for outdoor recreation than for other recreation. In addition to the other problems for other recreation, a major difficulty for outdoor recreation is that much of the available data relates to purchase of equipment for this purpose, and statistical data on annual expenditures for equipment may poorly reflect current activity.

Money spent for purchases of wheel goods, durable toys, sports equipment, boats and pleasure aircraft (reported as one total item in the published statistics) and for certain specific outdoor activities has risen sharply in relation to available income in the years since the war (Figure 18 and Appendix Tables 1 and 2). In interpreting these data,

[22] U.S. Department of Labor, *How American Buying Habits Change,* Washington, 1959, p. 215.
[23] *Life Study of Consumer Expenditures—A Background for Marketing Decisions,* Vol. 1, made for *Life* by Alfred Politz Research, Inc., published by Time, Inc., 1957.

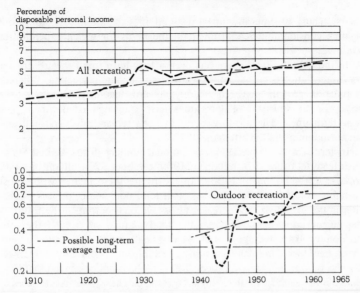

Figure 18.   Percentage of disposable personal income for all recreation and for outdoor recreation, 1909–62.

the changes in the proportion of disposable income spent for all forms of recreation must be borne in mind. During the war, expenditures for outdoor recreation were relatively low; after the war, they rose rapidly, then receded before and immediately after 1950, and have since risen again. On our earlier assumption as to what constitutes reasonably normal periods, some approximations to long-term trend lines can be drawn. These indicate a much steeper rise in percentage of disposable income spent for outdoor recreation than for recreation in general.

Expenditures for selected items of equipment for outdoor recreation show marked upward trends.[24] The annual growth rate in expenditures (uncorrected for changes in the general price level) over the 1947–56 period were 6.3 per cent annually for baseball goods except balls; 9.1 per cent annually for football, basketball, and boxing goods; 9.5 per cent annually for photographic equipment, including film; 25 per cent annually for motor boats; and 25 per cent annually for tents. On the other hand, expenditures for rifles, canoes, sailboats, sails, sleds for children, and a few other items actually declined during these same

[24] Robert E. Snyder, *Trends in the Sporting Goods Market,* published by Robert E. Snyder, Chicago, 1957.

years. Thus, a generally upward trend in expenditures is not proof against considerable readjustment in the items for which expenditures are made.

In the United States there has been a long-term trend toward greater total real national output and toward larger income per capita. Whereas population growth has been steadily upward, income and output have advanced by spurts, and sometimes have stagnated or declined. The long-term upward trend, however, has been remarkably persistent and seems undiminished in strength.

In terms of 1960 prices, gross national product in the United States rose from less than $74 billion in 1900, to about $234 billion in 1940, to over $504 billion in 1960.[25] In the future these figures will almost certainly continue to increase. As with total population, the only question is the extent of the increase. Gross national output in the future is dependent upon many factors—the total number of people, the proportion working, average output per working hour or day, capital investment, new technology and scientific development, availability of markets for the output, and many others. Reasonable variations in estimate are possible for each of these factors. To some extent, errors in estimates of one factor may offset or compensate for errors in others; if they do not, the cumulative effect could be very great.

One set of estimates for gross national product (in billions of 1960 dollars) is as follows:[26]

	1960	1980	2000
	Billion 1960 dollars		
Low estimate	504	965	1,680
Medium estimate	504	1,060	2,200
High estimate	504	1,250	3,290

The lowest of these estimates contemplates an approximate doubling of output by 1980 and a more than trebling by 2000; the highest estimate is for a more than doubling by 1980 and for a sixfold increase by 2000. These are to be contrasted with population increases of from 25–50 per cent by 1980 and 65–100 per cent by 2000. These estimates give a reasonable idea of the probable magnitude of future changes in gross output.

[25] Data for 1940 and 1960 from *Resources in America's Future, op. cit.,* p. 523. Figure for 1900 estimated from data in *Historical Statistics of the United States, Colonial Times to 1957,* U.S. Bureau of the Census, Washington, 1960, p. 139.

[26] *Resources in America's Future, op. cit.*

Disposable personal income is roughly three-fourths of gross national product under present day conditions. The difference is due to various investment and tax deductions. Over a long period of time, the two measures must show generally similar trends because income is available only from output; but from year to year, changes may be considerable, owing to differences in investment and in taxes.

Over a period of years, average per capita income, in terms of constant prices, has risen markedly, although naturally at a slower rate than total national output owing to the increase in total population.

Personal disposable income is now about $2,000 per capita. An increase of 35–55 per cent above the present level may be expected by 1980, and one of 70–120 per cent by 2000 seems likely. Although considerable variation from these projections is possible, a substantial rise in real income per capita seems inherent in the general conditions we noted earlier.

The disparity in annual income between the very poor and the very rich has decreased in the United States in recent decades. There are probably somewhat fewer people today who are very rich in comparison with the average than there were 30 years ago; and there are many fewer very poor ones, also by comparison with the average. There has been some "leveling up" in terms of money income.[27] Possibly more important, many services and satisfactions are available today to essentially all segments of the population, without respect to their money incomes.[28] This is true of many sanitation, school, library, recreational, and other services provided free or essentially so to the public by various units of government or by private nonprofit organizations. Moreover, the general availability of newspapers, magazines, books, radios, TV, movies, and other sources of information, at relatively low costs, has opened up to the low-income consumer means of education and pleasure beyond the scope of even the richest persons a century or more ago.

A further aspect of expenditure patterns of importance to recreation is how people of differing incomes use their income, or how people change the use of their income over time, as average incomes rise. The classic study of this question, which resulted in the "law" which bears his name, was that by Ernest Engel in 1887. Engel's summary of his findings, in his own words, is:

[27] Selma F. Goldsmith, "Relations of Census Income Distribution Statistics to Other Income Data," *An Appraisal of the 1950 Census Income Data,* Studies in Income and Wealth, Vol. 23, National Bureau of Economic Research (Princeton: Princeton University Press, 1958).

[28] *How American Buying Habits Change, op. cit.*

The less the revenues, the greater is the proportion devoted to expenditures for physical and material needs, and the less the remainder for expenditures for religion, for moral and intellectual needs, and in general, for luxury. . . . The smaller the sum essential for the satisfaction of physical and material needs, the greater the proportion which must be used for food alone.[29]

For groups of families, there is a considerable tendency for this law to hold true.[30] For instance, in 1874–75 wage-earner families in Massachusetts with incomes under $450 annually spent 64 per cent for "subsistence," while families with incomes of $1,200 and over spent but 51 per cent for the same items. Again, in 1950, wage-earner and clerical-worker families with average incomes in various groups less than $5,000 annually spent in excess of 30 per cent of their income for food, while families of $10,000 and over spent about 25 per cent of their income for this purpose.

However, this relationship is not invariable at any given time and place; and over a period of time in the United States it has not held closely. A major reason is that food, shelter, clothing, and other "basic necessities" can, and do, take on "luxury" characteristics. That is, the typical American family buys and consumes food not merely to keep alive or even to preserve strength for the job, but because certain types of food consumption are pleasurable. This leads to the buying of a greater variety and higher quality of foods than basic nutrition requires; it also leads to the housewife buying foods into which a large amount of processing and marketing services have been incorporated. The same is true for each of the other "basic" services or commodities. As a result, the difference between basic and luxury commodities and services is no longer to be found *between* groups of commodities or services, but rather *within* each, along grade, quality, and service lines. Largely as a result of this major shift in consumer preferences, the proportion of average consumer income going to broad groups of commodities has been remarkably constant over the decades for which we have information.[31]

[29] Elizabeth E. Hoyt, Margaret G. Reid, et al., American Income and Its Use (New York: Harper and Row, 1954).

[30] For a very interesting and not excessively detailed account of use of income by typical families at different periods in the past, see How American Buying Habits Change, op. cit.

[31] In addition to the sources previously cited, the following are relevant: The Editors of Fortune, The Changing American Market (Garden City, New York: Hanover House, 1955); Ruth P. Mack, "Trends in American Consumption and the Aspiration to Consume," American Economic Review, Vol. 46, No. 2 (May 1956), pp. 55–68; Trends in Consumer Behavior: The Next Ten Years, Report of a seminar conducted by the Foundation for Research on Human Behavior, 1957.

SUMMARY

The future trend in each of the four major factors affecting demand for outdoor recreation, which have been discussed in this chapter, is upward. Total population is increasing at a rate between 1.5 and 1.75 per cent annually. This is a small annual increment, but over a considerable period of years it leads to a large increase, and by 2000 population may be from 1½ to 2 times what it is today. The upward trend in real income per capita may be slightly greater, nearer 2 per cent annually, and this leads to an approximate doubling by 2000. A greater proportion of this higher income will be discretionary, a larger proportion will be spent for recreation of all kinds, and also a larger proportion for outdoor recreation, than is true today. A larger proportion of a doubled real income per capita for twice as many people could easily mean that expenditures for outdoor recreation in 2000 will be eight times those of today.

The trend in leisure per capita is also upward, but only to an extent of perhaps 12 per cent by 2000, the increased leisure is likely to be unequally distributed among people of differing ages and occupations, and also unequally distributed according to vacation, weekend, daily, retirement, or other forms of leisure. The trend toward quicker and more comfortable transportation, probably at lower real costs or at least at costs lower in relation to the higher real incomes per capita, will continue; and much of the increased travel will be for outdoor recreation.

With the trend upward in each of these four underlying factors, the trend in amounts of outdoor recreation demanded can hardly be anything but upward. However, to go from trends in these basic factors to estimates of exact future demands for outdoor recreation is not as simple as might be imagined. There are at least two pitfalls. First, new factors and new relationships—ones that are not apparent, and certainly not measurable at this time—may become significant. For instance, regardless of the amount of data and of study in 1940 or even in 1945, no one could have foreseen the tremendous boom in certain water-based outdoor recreation which has been made possible by more powerful motors at more modest prices, by better boats and better methods of transporting them, by more water bodies created as a result of public water-management programs, by new techniques of water sports, and by other developments. Secondly, some of the present factors and relationships may not work out in the future as a simple extension of past trends would suggest. For instance, total participation in outdoor recreation generally rises as the educational level of the participant rises; however, when the average educational level of the whole population has risen, it may be that the differences between the highly educated and the modestly educated will remain as now, and that the variation will continue around the same general level as now. Some variation in participation in outdoor recreation may be related to the level of the socioeconomic factor involved; others may be related to the relative position of the individual or group in the whole social structure.

Because estimation of future demand for outdoor recreation is both difficult and important, we now turn, in Chapter 7, to a more detailed consideration of alternative approaches to the problem.

7

Alternative Methods of Estimating Future Use

A most important requirement of a rational policy with respect to provision of outdoor recreation opportunities is some forecast of the future demand for recreation. Such predictions are necessary for a number of reasons. A projection of demand may indicate the need for additional recreation areas in the future. If land area and water supplies are to be available for outdoor recreation in the future, they might better be reserved while they are yet available if greatly increased costs and political turmoil are to be avoided. They need to be reserved in advance of urgent needs, before the area is deeply committed to other uses from which it would be expensive or impossible to retrieve it. Otherwise, the areas may be pre-empted for other uses.

Predictions of future use are needed for planning other recreation requirements also. Investments in facilities and improvements must rest upon some idea of the nature of future demand patterns, especially in the immediate years ahead. The level of management operations, even season by season, is dependent upon the estimate of future use for comparable periods. And, for the longer run, the trained manpower needed for recreation area management depends upon future use. If we are to behave at all rationally in planning the provision of outdoor recreation, then some insight into the future becomes a necessity. Provision of public areas requires public decisions primarily by political processes, and facts and estimates of the future can be very helpful to such decisions.

The practical question is thus not whether to make projections but how to make them. Forecasting in the field of social science is at best a hazardous enterprise; but while the uncertainties of projection need to be recognized for themselves, they should also point to the importance of added precision and refinement.

Estimates of the future can be based only on experience, but in the case of recreation, our knowledge of the past and present is most incomplete. We simply do not know about many important factors or the relationship among them. Moreover, our modern experience with outdoor recreation is relatively short and our quantitative data apply to even fewer years. To make the kind of long-range projections for outdoor recreation that are needed by park and recreation executives, we must project for a period in the future that is longer than the one for which we have data on the past. Extrapolation is hazardous at best, but it is doubly so when the base period is so short relative to the future.

But in any case the future may be very different from the past. We have observed major changes in the amount, kind, and role of outdoor recreation in comparatively recent times. Further substantial changes are not unlikely. In view of these facts any projection of future demand for outdoor recreation at best involves some rather sketchy and arbitrary assumptions. Under these circumstances there needs to be an awareness that various types of techniques of projections may be somewhat misleading by implying a degree of accuracy which they do not possess.

This chapter is primarily concerned with public recreation areas. Data on privately owned outdoor recreation areas are too incomplete to justify special analysis of future demand. However, the same general considerations apply to estimating future demand for private areas, and the magnitudes of increase may be similar.

A great deal of the discussion in this chapter centers on aggregate demand analysis, where the emphasis is on the broad general changes in the effective demand exhibited for various kinds of recreation activities by the population taken more or less as a whole. Our concern in this discussion is therefore in the general increase in participation in outdoor activities. This will be based to some extent on the discussion in Chapter 6 about trends in some major socioeconomic factors; it should be distinguished from the demand analysis in Chapters 4 and 5 where the emphasis was on recreation demand in a local community or for an individual recreation site or activity. While the aggregate demand for outdoor recreation is really nothing more than the sum of the demand for individual sites or locations by activities, it is useful to distinguish between them. The kind of analysis required by the two types of relationships and the uses to be made of the information differ. Our main interest in the changes in total or aggregate demand for outdoor recreation is therefore in policy decisions on broad regional or national levels, and it centers on the types of things underlying the gradual or general increases in demand for recreation.

DEMAND AND CONSUMPTION

Discussion of outdoor recreation demand customarily uses the term "demand" in a somewhat special way. Two ambiguities, in particular, have detracted from its usefulness as a guide to planning. As we have seen in earlier discussion, the demand for goods and services refers to the quantity or number of units of the good or service demanded at specific levels of prices. Substantial changes in price can result in far different quantities demanded. Although the whole recreation experience entails costs, which influence the numbers of visits to recreation areas, the outdoor recreation resources or facilities themselves are customarily available at zero or nominal prices or charges. The "demand" that is often cited for outdoor recreation refers, then, to the demand at such prices. The millions of days of outdoor recreation currently being consumed are those demanded at the prevailing zero or near zero prices for these resources. If prices were raised substantially by the imposition of entrance fees or by some other means, a very different quantity would be demanded, or consumed.

A second difficulty involving the use of the word "demand" as commonly applied to outdoor recreation, stems from its incorrect application as a description of use or consumption. Usually what is called "demand" is gross attendance at facilities rather than demand. The number of visits in a given year is not the demand for these facilities in that year, but rather the total attendance or use made of the facilities. It refers to the quantities taken at the prevailing recreation opportunity conditions, for consumption depends both on demand and the availability of supply. That is, the data are use or attendance figures for existing facilities. Such statements do not separate demand and supply conceptually or statistically.[1]

Raw attendance figures reflect demand, to be sure, but they also reflect opportunity or supply as well. It should not surprise us, for example, that people in Knoxville, Tennessee, located in the midst of a half dozen large reservoirs with adequate access and public facilities, water ski in greater numbers than people in Washington, D.C., which is deficient in suitable water. These differences do not by themselves indicate differences in demand for water skiing anymore than gross visitation figures to parks represent statements of demand alone. The figures in both cases are the result of the interaction between demand and supply factors and are the measurement of consequent consumption, or quantities taken by recreationists, given these supplies and demands.

[1] S. V. Ciriacy-Wantrup, "Conceptual Problems in Projecting the Demand for Land and Water," in *Modern Land Policy,* Papers of the Land Economics Institute (Urbana: University of Illinois Press, 1960).

This is more than a semantic quibble; it is an ambiguity which can increasingly cause mischief to well-intentioned planning efforts. When use is made of such statements or projections in policy planning, this distinction between demand and consumption must be kept in mind. Attendance or use figures are the net effect of the existing demand and the existing supply, and should be so recognized. Improper accounting of supply considerations leads to the assumption that people will demand increasing quantities of what they now have, and can perpetuate present imbalances. For example, if some areas of the country show far greater participation rates on the part of the population for water skiing, and this were taken as a demand statement without consideration of availability of opportunities, it could lead to decisions to build even more facilities in areas most adequately served rather than to attempts to provide opportunities in deficient areas.

If we picture recreation consumption as a function of both supply and demand, then the changes in use observed over time, as well as between regions, become more meaningful. There is no doubt an increase in demand, or a shifting of demand curves to the right, as a result of the factors normally ascribed to increases in demand, including such things as increase in population, incomes, urbanization, mobility, and leisure time. However, as we noted in Chapter 4, changes are also taking place over time in facility development changing the supply of recreation opportunities as well. Increases in attendance figures reflect both of these changes.

Projections of consumption figures are really then projections of demand with some implied relation of demand to supply. What is implied is that recreation consumption will increase, and that this increase is based on a shift or increase in demand and expanding levels of supply. As long as these relationships are understood, there is considerable merit, for planning and policy guidance, in examining the likely trends of future recreation participation. In so doing we are principally interested in projecting the use rate expected to prevail in the future, given some assumptions about the availability of facilities relative to the growing population and to other circumstances and characteristics of this population.

ALTERNATIVE PROJECTION TECHNIQUES

Because projection of future demand for outdoor recreation is necessarily so uncertain, and because projections have not been made over a long enough period to test the accuracy of different techniques, a number of different approaches have been tried. Here we discuss the application of five of them to total or general recreation demand for outdoor recreation at low or zero prices for the recreation resource:

1. Simple trend extension of past use in the area, or of the activity, or both, as the case may be.

2. Extension of the trend for the basic causal forces underlying demand for outdoor recreation, and then conversion of the trends in these forces to estimates of the demand for outdoor recreation.

3. Application of the satiety principle, which may set ceilings on the increase in future demand for outdoor recreation.

4. Methods based primarily on estimates of the present relationship between various socioeconomic factors, such as personal income, and quantities of recreation demanded.

5. Estimates of the future based upon "judgment," whereby a number of factors are taken into consideration but not in a simple or easily defined way.

Other methods, or variants of these methods, are probably used or could be used; but perhaps these will illustrate the major approaches.

SIMPLE TREND EXTENSION TO MEASURE FUTURE OUTDOOR RECREATION USE

Extrapolation of past and current trends in outdoor recreation attendance is often useful, but it can also be unreliable and misleading. Basically the method consists of extending the discernible trend into the future as far as is necessary. The chief advantage of this method is its simplicity. Where past growth has been relatively stable, it has often been very useful. The rationale behind the method is that some forces must be operative to produce a marked or regular trend, especially if it has been long continued. Even if these forces are not fully known, yet they must exist and presumably will continue to be effective. In the case of recreation, the trend of use has been regularly upward at a relatively steep pace for as long a period as we have reasonably reliable data.

The available basic data on trends in use of several kinds of resource-based and intermediate recreation areas are presented in Figure 2 in Chapter 4. The best available data for user-oriented areas are given in Figure 19. Direct measures of use of the latter areas are poor with real possibility of substantial understatement not only at the level of use but also in trend. On the assumption that leadership personnel and specified facilities were provided only to meet an actually experienced demand, data on these points perhaps provide a more reliable index of use.

The trends in use apparent in Figures 2 and 19 have been extended to 1980 and 2000 in Table 13. The method of determining and extend-

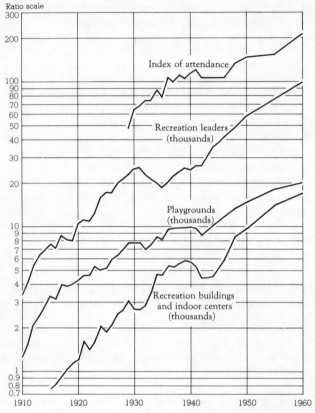

Figure 19. Various measures of user-oriented outdoor recreation activity, 1910–60.

ing these trends was highly informal, which is the usual case with trend analysis. The trend was simply plotted on semilogarithmic graph paper and extended by using a straight edge. With all of the serious questions and the limitations of this procedure in mind, we can examine in more detail the record of past recreation usage and the projections based upon them.

The trend in use of the national park system was upward at an extremely rapid pace in the period before World War II. The park system was expanded significantly in those years; new roads and highways made it easier to get to the parks; and automobiles were greatly improved from year to year. Extension of the trend for this period (with appropriate recognition of the five-year interruption caused by the war)

TABLE 13.
ESTIMATES OF OUTDOOR RECREATION USE IN 1980 AND 2000, BY SIMPLE TREND EXTENSION PROCEDURE

Area or kind of recreation	1955	1960	1980	2000	1960	1980[1]	2000[2]
			........million visits........		....per capita visits....		
National park system	50.0	72.3			0.40		
1910–41 trend			3,000	50,000		12.5	153.5
1946–60 trend			425	2,300		1.77	7.07
1953–60 trend			175	485		.73	1.49
National forests	45.7	92.6			0.51		
1934–41 trend			190	800		.79	2.46
1946–60 trend			750	6,600		3.12	20.3
1953–60 trend			1,700	24,000		7.08	73.7
State parks	183.2	259			1.43		
1942–60 trend[3]			1,200	5,200		5.0	16.0
Corps of Engineers reservoirs	62.3	109			0.60		
1950–60 trend			11,500	800,000		45.7	2,455.0
1954–60 trend			2,000	32,000		8.32	98.3
TVA reservoirs	36.5	52.7			0.29		
1947–60 trend			700	7,400		2.91	22.7
1953–60 trend			360	2,300		1.50	7.07
			....index (1929–55 = 100)....				
User-oriented recreation[4]							
Attendance	154	213					
1929–60 trend			470	1,075			
1936–60 trend			290	470			
			..........thousands..........				
Recreation leaders	77	100					
1910–60 trend			300	950			
1935–60 trend			440	1,800			
Playgrounds	18	20					
1910–60 trend			52	160			
1917–60 trend			49	110			
Recreation buildings and indoor centers	14	17					
1915–60 trend			64	225			

[1] Assuming 240 million total population.
[2] Assuming 325 million total population.
[3] Omitting the war years.
[4] As measured by city and county parks and recreation areas for which information is available.

results in virtually astronomical figures for 1980 and 2000. In the latter year the average citizen would have to visit some unit of the national park system 150 times or more if this estimate were to be realized. Since the war, the use of the national park system has increased only moderately. Few new parks or other units have been added to the system, and the improvements in highways and in autos have been comparatively less than in the earlier period. Between 1953 and 1960 there was some slow-down in growth rates. Moreover, a slow-down in these years compared with the earlier postwar years, even though moderate, raises the possibility for further slow-downs in growth rate in the years ahead.

The difference in projections to 1980 and 2000 on the basis of the clearly identifiable trends is substantial. However, since 1960 the trend has again been more steeply upward.

The trend in recreational use of the national forests is generally similar to the trend in use of the national park system, yet substantial differences appear in the details. In the prewar period, use of the national forests was apparently growing much more slowly. However, there is some question as to the comparability of data in some of the earlier years, and this difference in trend may not be significant. Since the war, use of the national forests has been increasing faster than it did prewar and faster than use of the national park system. Moreover, the rate of increase has been faster in the most recent years than in the earlier postwar years. Thus, there are three rather clearly identifiable trends for the national forests as for the national park system, and the three periods are nearly the same in timing. The results, however, are reversed: projections based on recent years indicate much greater ultimate recreation use of the national forests, but relatively less recreation use of the national park system. If one could be sure of the long-term validity of these recent trends, their significance for the future would be great; but one cannot refrain from doubting the significance of such simple trend extensions in this case.

For state parks, reasonably accurate use data begins only in 1942, and even these data must be adjusted to allow for differences in composition of some state park systems. Although the war years were probably more normal for the state parks than for the national forests and the national parks, it seems wise to exclude the war years in measuring the trend for these parks also. On the basis of the postwar trend, the use of state parks would increase to four to five times the 1960 figure in 1980 and to about twenty times that figure in 2000. This rate of increase is somewhat above the intermediate trend extensions for the national forests and the national park system.

The most explosively rapid increases in recreation use of any group of areas for which data are available have taken place on the reservoirs constructed by the Corps of Engineers. Many new reservoir areas have been added to the system in the comparatively short period of years since the war for which data are available. These years also coincide with the major trend toward use of boats of all types. With better boats, boat trailers, and motors, there has been a great increase in use of nearly all water areas. If the trends for the period from 1950 to 1960 are extended to 1980 and to 2000, truly fantastic figures are obtained. The projection for 2000 would be realized only if every citizen went boating on a Corps reservoir about 2,500 times per year! This example, more than any other, illustrates the inherent danger in extending, or extrapolating, past attendance figures. A relatively slower upward trend is evident from 1954 to 1960 but even it leads to per capita figures in 2000 second only to the very highest estimated for the national park system. A slower upward trend, but still a relatively rapid one, is evident since about 1959. A further slowing down in past growth rates will occur on Corps reservoirs, but when and at what level?

Recreation use of TVA reservoirs has also shown major increases since the war. Behind this increase are the same factors that were responsible for the increase in use of Corps reservoirs. The rate of increase for TVA reservoirs has been less than that for Corps reservoirs, and it also shows some slowing down in growth rates since 1953.

For user-oriented recreation areas, the available measures of use each show a moderately steep trend in use in the past (see Figure 19). On the basis of various measures, projected use in 1980 would be from two to four times what it was in 1960 and in 2000 might be from 3 to 15 times greater than in 1960.

While the simple extrapolation of past attendance figures has some value, it is obvious from the figures presented here that this method cannot be relied on for long-term projections. For shorter periods, up to perhaps 5 years, however, it may yield more accurate estimates than any other method, and its simplicity has much to commend it.

EXTENSION OF TRENDS IN CAUSAL FORCES AS A MEANS OF ESTIMATING FUTURE DEMAND FOR OUTDOOR RECREATION

Since the simple extension of past trends produces diverse and sometimes incredible long-run projections, there is an obvious need for shifting attention to another method of estimating recreation use and considering the possibility of extending past trends in the "causal forces" underlying growth in recreation.

The strongest argument against the simple trend extension is that one does not know what is causing the trend he measures and hence has no assurance that the same relationship will hold in the future. However, an effort to better the situation by the extension of "causal" factors can encounter difficulties of its own. This method assumes that we know what factors are in fact causal and the relative importance of each, that these assumed causal factors can themselves be projected into the future with satisfactory accuracy, and that we know the future relationship which will exist between these factors and increases in recreation demand.

The factors which we discussed in Chapter 6—population, income, leisure, and mobility—are believed to be of major importance in explaining the rapid increase in the demand for outdoor recreation, although no clear proof has yet been established that they are the only determinants of recreation participation. The long-term trends for these four factors are about as follows:

	Average increase per decade (*per cent*)
Population (1900–1960)	15
Per capita real income (1900–1950)	19
Total leisure (1900–1960)	20
Travel per capita (1930–1960)	55

Some variation from decade to decade is evident, although trends in these factors are fairly steady (Figure 20). The increase in travel in earlier decades was relatively greater, but that era has passed.

The comparable trends in use of various kinds of outdoor recreation areas (for the periods for which data are available) are much more steeply upward:

	Decade increase (*per cent*)	Annual increase (*per cent*)
User-oriented areas (average of four measures in Figure 19)	65	about 5
National park system	127	nearly 9
National forests	204	nearly 12
TVA reservoirs	210	12
Corps of Engineer reservoirs	650	23
State parks	108	nearly 8

The difference between these rates of increase and those of the presumed basic causal factors is probably highly significant in both a statistical and an economic sense. The most rapid upward trend in any one of the four causal factors is less than the least rapid trend in recreation use. Use of these various areas reflects their availability as well as the demand; but if the latter had not increased, a greater number and larger acreage of recreation areas would have availed relatively little.

Attempts to examine the basic forces behind the observed increases in outdoor recreation demand are a recognition of the necessity to examine the factors underlying the dynamics of this change. This approach attempts to determine which of the factors present in society are relevant in predicting future demands and which may be discarded as having little or no effect, and also the appropriate magnitude of each. This requires quantitative measurement of past associations between the changes in various causal factors and changes in the use of

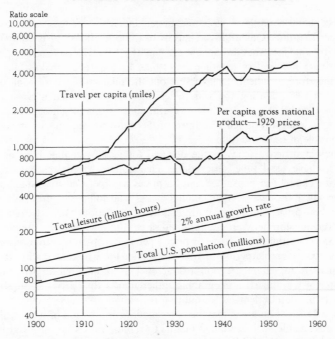

Figure 20. Total population, gross national product per capita in 1929 prices, total leisure, and total travel per capita, 1900–1960.

outdoor recreation facilities. On the basis of these past associations, projections into the future can be made. In this section we illustrate the method by considering trends in total population, per capita income, total leisure, and travel. As noted, these four factors are deemed basic, and we possess reasonable estimates of the trend in each. But other factors could be used, if analysis substantiated their relevance and if adequate data existed.

Projection of outdoor recreation demand on the basis of projections of trends of the basic underlying factors is vastly superior to simple trend extension of recreation itself without any analysis of the underlying causes. We may far better anticipate changes in the demand structure for outdoor recreation facilities if we are aware of the basic demand relationships. However, there remain problems in establishing demand patterns for outdoor recreation. It is particularly difficult, for example, to assess the impact of changes in people's interests and goals which may alter recreation preferences. Serious study will probably reveal that the preferences of individuals are affected by their social and economic conditions. If we knew the relationships between preferences and social

123

and economic conditions, we could better anticipate changes in recreation participation. Quantitative analysis of these relationships is complicated by the fact that broad changes in the basic factors have been occurring more or less together over time, as Figure 20 makes clear. It is therefore a difficult task to sort out the relative effects of each of these variables. During the war, when travel was rationed in various ways and some other restrictions were in effect, visits to national parks and to national forests fell to a third of the prewar level, thus dramatizing the role of transportation.

Many statistical studies of the demand for various commodities and services have used time series data. This approach requires data on quantities bought or consumed and on prices paid per unit for a number of time periods, often on an annual basis. The influence of variables other than price and quantity are estimated in various ways, to retain a net relationship between quantity and price. But for outdoor recreation there are no estimates of cost (or price) per visit or per other unit of use for any considerable period of time, for either the whole recreation experience or for the recreation resource. This is one reason why, in Chapter 5, we utilized a geographic rather than a time series approach to the estimation of demand for outdoor recreation.

Use of recreation areas may be correlated, over a period of time, with some reasonable socioeconomic factor. Correlation does not necessarily mean causation, especially for time series analysis. Nevertheless, a persistent and close correlation of two variables may be useful for making projections of the future.

This approach can be illustrated by data on visits to national parks. One factor probably affecting attendance over a number of years is the size of the total population; the effect of this factor can be eliminated by placing attendance data on a per capita basis. One would expect changes in real income per capita to have some effect on attendance at national parks, since the total cost per visit is often relatively high. In fact, data for the 1929–63 period (excluding the war years) show a close correlation between visits per capita and real income per capita (Figure 21).[2] This relationship seems reasonable, and the unwary might conclude that a causal relationship had been demonstrated, but this is not necessarily the case. For example, for the omitted war years the estimating formula resulted in attendance estimates about three times the actual figures. For these years, some other factor was at work; it seems reasonable to think that the restriction of travel was one factor.

[2] *Prospective Demand for Outdoor Recreation,* A Report to the Outdoor Recreation Resources Review Commission, by Commission Staff, ORRRC Study Report No. 26, Washington, 1962; see pp. 4–10.

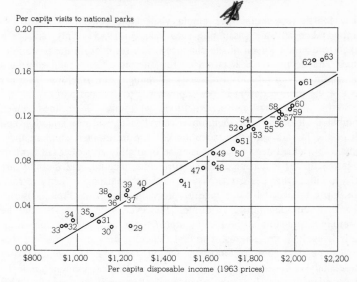

Figure 21. Per capita disposable income and per capita visits to national parks, 1929–41 and 1947–63.

An inspection of Figure 21, which relates per capita disposable income and visits to national parks, should also raise other doubts as to causation. With limited exceptions, the dots representing different years show a chronological progression from left to right; that is, the smaller figures for both variables are in the earlier years, the larger figures for each in the later years, with very little intermingling of years. Strong trend elements are still present in this analysis. In fact, almost any time series with a strong and regular upward trend would show a high correlation with per capita visits to national parks. Per capita consumption of electricity would probably be as highly correlated as was per capita real income, although one would be hard put to find a rational explanation of the apparent relationship.

Some interesting statistics on this matter are presented by the ORRRC report in which visits to national parks in the years 1929 through 1960 were related to different factors. The statistical association was established for each of three factors: per capita income, per capita leisure, and per capita mobility (measured as inter-city automobile travel). In each case the degree of correlation between per capita visits and the presumed causal factor was extremely high. The percentage of the variation in per capita visits to the national parks "explained" or apparently accounted for by these factors taken singly range from 95 to 96 per cent.

In a fourth association, per capita visits were related to a variable simply taken as time (assuming zero value in 1945). This variable is taken to account for all of the changes which result from the passage of time. The degree of association of this factor, which would represent the summation of all causal factors that change over time, was 98.6 per cent of the total variation in per capita visits to national parks.

Statistical associations or equations were also determined which combined all of the aforementioned causal factors in one equation and all of the factors with the exception of time in another. Both of these equations yielded degrees of association of slightly above 99 per cent.

If the theory is accepted that leisure time, income, and mobility are factors influencing per capita visits to the national parks, then the relationship established by this type of procedure has some limited usefulness in forecasting future visit rates. However, such forecasts must be carefully examined and the results interpreted in light of the assumptions underlying such projections. The first difficulty stems from the fact that the independent contribution of the various factors is not established in these analyses because of the high correlations that exist among all of the independent variables as well as between them and the dependent visit rate. As long as causal factors are highly correlated, the most practical planning procedure is to use a single factor, such as per capita income, on which to base projections of future per capita visits, but it must be recognized that the independent variable is only an index of many factors and not a complete explanation. Little is added to the logical or operational validity of the projection by including other highly correlated variables.

There are, however, at least two major difficulties in the way of using this approach to project future demand for outdoor recreation. In the first place, this approach requires a projection of the assumed independent variables—a task which may prove quite as difficult as projection of the future outdoor recreation demand itself, and one which has left many a wreck behind.[3] The possibility of error in population, income, leisure, or mobility projections is very great. In the second place, this approach assumes that past relationships between the independent and dependent variables will continue unchanged. There is good reason to believe that this has not been true in the past and that it will not be true in the future for outdoor recreation. But it may be difficult to estimate just how these relationships will change in the future.

In spite of severe limitations on this approach, it may be useful in

---

[3] Marion Clawson, R. Burnell Held, and C. H. Stoddard, *Land for the Future* (Baltimore: The Johns Hopkins Press, for Resources for the Future, Inc., 1960), see Appendix A.

making short-run projections. The shorter the time period, the less likely that the past relationships between variables will change markedly.

APPLICATION OF THE SATIETY PRINCIPLE

No matter how much income and leisure a person had and no matter how cheap and comfortable and quick transportation facilities were, there is still some limit to the amount of recreation he would seek. Limits probably apply to specific activities, to specific locations, and to recreation in general. At some point each person would have his fill of outdoor recreation, no matter how much income or leisure he had. At this point saturation would put an upper limit to actual increases in the demand.

There is some scattered evidence to suggest that participation in outdoor recreation rises as family income increases up to some middle income level; after this there are no further increases, and decreases often take place. There are also variations in participation in outdoor recreation according to occupation, social status, region, family composition and other social or economic factors. Studies are being made of this subject, but not enough is known to set any general ceilings on the demand for different types of recreation or of recreation areas. Information must be gathered in ways that will throw light on what will happen in the future. Will past and present ceilings or saturation points apply to the future or will major changes occur? These and related questions are difficult to answer yet they are crucial for consideration of future recreation demands.

The availability of time sets one kind of ceiling on participation in outdoor recreation, although possibly such a high one as not to be useful in the next several years. Time will not permit the realization of the kind of projections that result from a simple trend extension of the use of Corps reservoirs; obviously everyone will not spend more than 365 days a year on Corps reservoirs. But much lower, more practical limits on participation might be set in some circumstances by factors other than total time availability. Some outdoor recreation is practical only at some seasons; there may be a limited number of times during the season that even avid devotees will want to go to a particular type of area; and only a certain proportion of the total population may wish to go at all. By making reasonable estimates of upper limits of each of these facts, a ceiling on total participation might be estimated; if trend projection, extension of trends in causal factors, or any other approach resulted in estimates higher than this, especially for a distant future when such methods often yield large figures, then they might well be suspect. Satiety of the general population is unlikely to be a major factor for most areas in the relatively near future, however.

ORRRC PROJECTIONS OF DEMAND FOR SELECTED RECREATION ACTIVITIES

Perhaps the most complete, and in many ways the most sophisticated, approach to examining a large number of individual determinants of demand for recreation of different types was that reported by the Outdoor Recreation Resources Review Commission.[4]

The method used in this report has two main parts. First, the relationship between various socioeconomic factors and the extent of participation in outdoor recreation was established. This was done with thoroughness and imagination. A large number of interviews were taken from a widely representative lot of families, and a great deal of detail was obtained on recreation participation rates for the activities, as well as on various socioeconomic factors including family incomes, education, occupation, place of residence, age, and sex. The net effect of each of a number of variables was thus established, probably with more accuracy than in any previous study.

The second part of this approach consists in projecting the probable future value of the various important socioeconomic factors, and from them estimating the probable participation in outdoor recreation. The problem in projecting these variables, previously discussed, applies to this method also. In addition, the assumption is made that the relationships which existed in 1960 will also exist in 1976 and in 2000.

This approach may be described as part-static, part-dynamic. The static part is the assumption that the relationship of 1960 will continue in the future; the dynamic part is the attempt to take account of the probable changes in socioeconomic factors in the future. The consequences of these two assumptions are considered later in this section.

The basic assumption of projections of future participation rates in outdoor recreation activities was that the associations with socioeconomic factors observed in 1960 would continue into the future. On the basis of estimated future distributions of the population by these social or economic factors, the 1960 activity participation rates of the population may be reweighted to give estimates of the gross effects on these rates to be expected from changes in the social or economic factors. For example, participation rates for swimming and some other activities were found to increase as income increases. The rates here were defined as the number of separate days in which persons 12 years and over participated in the activity.

[4] ORRRC Study Report No. 26, *op. cit.*

128

The participation rates were projected through the use of estimated changes in income distributions of the population at future dates. These could then be applied to projections of population to yield estimates of demand or use of this activity for these future years. While this procedure would perhaps be helpful in explaining the effect of income, it does not as such take account of the other factors influencing the participation rates in outdoor recreation activities. Instead of the income effect alone, we need to consider the effect of each factor on a net basis, or the separate effect of each factor with all other factors held constant.

Through a series of statistical analyses, all of the social and economic factors included in the study were simultaneously considered in explaining changes in per capita participation rates for the various kinds of outdoor recreation.

Additionally, the differences in per capita opportunity to participate—that is, in the availability of facilities—were also incorporated into the analysis because change in the availability of facilities has an important bearing on the estimated participation rate. The measure of recreation opportunity was essentially derived by determining an opportunity rating for different areas in a country and then plotting the relation between average opportunity ratings and per capita daily participation rates for the various kinds of outdoor recreation activities. It was then assumed that changes in opportunity would result in movement of the U.S. average along this line in the direction of the best region or the one providing the most recreation opportunity.

The separate effects of all the socioeconomic factors were compounded to secure the composite participation rates by activities. The composite effect for future years was then multiplied by the 1960 observed rates to secure estimates per person for future years. These rates were then multiplied by the projected number of persons 12 years and over to obtain the number or level of actual recreation activity. This was done for each of seventeen outdoor recreation activities, and projections were made to 1976 and to 2000.[5] The demand differs considerably among the different activities both currently and in the projections for future years.

Participation in most outdoor recreation activities is concentrated in the summer season, but account was taken of activity in other parts of the year to arrive at annual totals. Based on the sample collected in the National Recreation Survey for different seasons of the year, participation rates were calculated for the different activities in 1960–61, and projections were made for participation rates for yearly totals and by seasons for future years. The different participation rates were then ap-

[5] ORRRC Study Report 26, *op. cit.*, p. 17.

plied to total population estimates to arrive at the total number of
recreation occasions during 1960 and projections for the years 1976
and 2000 (Table 14).

The results of this analysis show that the composite effects of socioeconomic factors on estimated participation rates are highly variable
among different types of activities. The projected changes in population
distribution by various socioeconomic factors operate, in combination,
to affect participation rates quite differently for different activities.

The results of this approach agree with the consensus as to the direction of future demands for outdoor recreation. However, even if it is
assumed that the net effect of various socioeconomic variables was correctly estimated and that the future magnitude of these variables was
projected accurately, serious doubt may be raised as to the magnitude of
the future increases shown. Had the data been available to apply this
method immediately after the war, for instance, the subsequent major
increase in water sports and in camping, to take but two illustrations,
would not have been foreseen. Or, were this method of analysis to be
applied backward in time, it would surely result in estimates for some
activities in 1950 vastly higher than actual participation in that year.
Although we lack precise data for earlier years in anything like the detail provided by this study for 1960, experienced recreation administrators all emphasize the dynamic character of popular taste for outdoor
recreation, especially as applied to specific activities. The essentially
static nature of this approach, mentioned previously, would have been
a serious handicap in the past and may well be in the future. On the

TABLE 14.
ACTUAL AND ESTIMATED NUMBER OF OCCASIONS,[1] BY PERSONS
12 YEARS AND OVER IN SELECTED RECREATION ACTIVITIES,
1960, 1976, AND 2000

Period and activity	Number of occasions (million)			Per cent change	
	1960	1976	2000	1960–76	1960–2000
Annual total occasions:					
Driving for pleasure	2,705	4,084	6,674	51	147
Walking for pleasure	2,340	3,454	6,009	48	157
Playing outdoor games or sports	1,659	2,883	5,698	74	244
Sightseeing	771	1,265	2,320	64	201
Bicycling	672	964	1,600	44	138
Fishing	547	736	1,099	35	101
Attending outdoor sports events	489	757	1,300	55	166
Nature walks	352	528	874	50	148
Winter occasions:					
Hunting	200	252	353	26	77
Ice skating	68	130	266	92	291
Sledding or tobogganing	57	88	174	52	203

[1] Number of separate days on which persons 12 years and over engaged in activity.
SOURCE: ORRRC Study Report 26, p. 27.

130

other hand, the analysis is particularly useful in determining and evaluating the importance of different socioeconomic variables. Studies of this kind, if repeated at intervals of a few years, with adequate samples and with equally competent analysis, would do much to increase our understanding of the dynamics of demand for outdoor recreation.

"JUDGMENT" IN PROJECTION OF FUTURE DEMAND FOR OUTDOOR RECREATION

Each of the four different approaches to the estimation of future demand for outdoor recreation discussed above has some merit under some circumstances; but each has major weaknesses. If applied literally and without limitation, they can produce specific projections of future long-run use of outdoor recreation areas which offend common sense. Each of these four approaches, or any other that might be proposed, requires judgment at numerous steps—judgments on which data to use, what conversion factors are most reasonable, how to interpret statistical results, and the like. Nevertheless, we now turn to an approach which, for lack of a better description, we call the "judgment" approach.

It should be observed first, however, that the difficulties of projecting future probable demand for outdoor recreation are due not primarily to the method used, but to the nature of our past experience and to the probabilities of future change. Some methods may be better than others, but no method is infallible when it comes to long-run projections of a highly dynamic phenomena such as outdoor recreation, and especially so when quantitative history is so short. Nevertheless, as was stated at the beginning of this chapter, projections about the future are unavoidable and are implicit in any actions taken today for outdoor recreation administration and organization.

In arriving at a "judgment" estimate, use is made of all data and all analyses available, but the final estimate is based upon subjective estimates of factors not measured and perhaps not measurable quantitatively. The result of this procedure is to come out with a final estimate that bears no exact relation to any single fact or group of facts. The process is subjective in the sense that the personality and experience of the person who employs it affect the result to a large extent. At its best, this approach brings to bear accumulated knowledge of those experienced in outdoor recreation research, planning, or administration.

To arrive at a judgment of future demands for outdoor recreation activities of particular kinds, or for kinds of areas, or in total, the following factors seem relevant: (1) historical and recent past trends in usage of the particular area or activity, and the reasons behind such trends, as far as one can conjecture or measure them; (2) probable future desires of average people for the recreation activity or area, as far as one may guess them; (3) probable future capacity of average people to enjoy the recreation activity or area; in particular, their ability to afford the time and money that such recreation will require for its enjoyment; and (4) the capacity or supply of areas on which the desired activity can be carried on.

It seems highly probable that all observers or operators in the outdoor recreation field would agree on two points: (1) that the trend in demand is now upward, and that it will continue upward for some time and for some distance above present levels; and (2) that the upward trend of the postwar years cannot continue indefinitely, for it leads to absurd figures at some date. The leveling off may well be preceded by a slackening or slowing down in growth. But growth in demand must level off at some date and at some level. Beyond this, it will presumably increase only as fast as does the total population, which is what happens with food consumption. Food consumption in a country rises as higher incomes permit greater consumption per capita, but once some adequate level is reached, as in the United States today, total food consumption increases only as total population grows. Something roughly analogous may take place with outdoor recreation.

Divergence of opinion among recreation specialists and students arises when an attempt is made to translate the foregoing consensus into quantitative terms. When will demand slacken and when will it level off? And how large will the demand for outdoor recreation be when these dates are reached? In some degree, these two questions are but different ways of stating the same point, for if one knew when present trends would slacken off he could calculate the level of recreation activity at that time. Divergence of opinion is likely to grow greater, the more distant is the date under consideration. The uncertainties as to trends in various factors and as to shifts in popular taste are greater the longer is the period under consideration.

Unfortunately, few explicit forecasts of future demand for outdoor recreation have been made in the past, and the bases for such forecasts as were made have not been very clear. Past efforts therefore provide relatively little guidance. There have been a great many implicit forecasts, as a reading of the literature of professional recreation organizations will reveal. Many park and recreation executives in the postwar years commented, often with pained surprise, on the record number of visitors to their area in the year just closed; and frequently said, or implied, that the rapid increases of the last few years could surely not continue. Up until now, all such implied forecasts have been woefully wrong, as park and recreation attendance continue to mount, year after year, with no clear signs of slowing down. This type of talk is much less common today. But the more formal past projections of future demand for outdoor recreation have not been accurate either.

In 1956, in its original Mission 66 plan, the National Park Service projected that total attendance at all units of the national park system would increase from the 1956 figure of 55 million to 80 million by 1966. The projected 1966 figure was actually reached in 1961—in just half of the planning period time. It now appears that the 1966 figure may well be 120 million visits. The actual increase from 1956 to 1966 thus may be 65 million visits, which is about 2½ times the projected 25 million increase for the decade.

Projections of recreation demand on the national forests have also consistently underestimated the actual growth in use. Early in 1957, after a series of unofficial and unpublished estimates of relatively early future recreation demand on national forests, each of which was much too low compared with actual attendance, the Forest Service published *Operation Outdoors*.[6] The projection for 1962, based on data ending with 1955, was for a total of 66 million recreational visits—an increase of 44 per cent above the nearly 46 million visits in 1955. However, what had been estimated to take place in seven years actually took place in three years, and the 66 million visits were recorded in 1958. By 1962, visits had reached a figure of 113 million—nearly 3½ times the estimated increase. In making this estimate for 1962, the Forest Service had explicitly related its increases to those projected by the National Park Service in the Mission 66 plans. The Forest Service estimates turned out to be the less accurate of the two because actual attendance in national forests has risen relatively more rapidly in recent years than has attendance in the national park system.

In 1959, on the basis of data ending in 1958, the Forest Service prepared estimates of anticipated future recreational use of the national forests for the Outdoor Recreation Resources Review Commission. The figures were 250 million visits by 1976 and 630 million by 2000. With an actual attendance record of 145 million in 1964, the increase from the 68 million attendance of 1958 has been 113 per cent in 6 years. These sober and careful projections of future demand for outdoor recreation by competent and experienced persons went astray simply because what actually happened was not what seemed probable but what seemed most improbable. The same thing can happen again; what seems "real" today may prove equally unreal a decade or two from now. Although recent growth trends cannot go on forever, they may last much longer than seems reasonable or even possible today.

[6] *Operation Outdoors—Part 1, National Forest Recreation.* Forest Service, U.S. Department of Agriculture, Washington, D. C., January 1957.

With these general considerations in mind, estimates of future demand can be made for each of the three broad categories of outdoor recreation areas.[7]

For *user-oriented* outdoor recreation areas, we do not know the total volume of present use, and we have only rough measures of past trends. It seems probable that our four factors—population, income, leisure, and travel—have affected use of such areas, income and travel probably to a minor degree, since this type of recreation typically takes but little in the way of either cash or travel. Indoor recreation of various kinds offers keener competition to this type of outdoor recreation than to the other types. One may hazard the guess that the use of this type of outdoor recreation will increase proportionately as total population grows in numbers. Increases in income and improvements in travel may have a negative effect because they make other types of outdoor recreation more readily available to the average person. The effect of leisure will be intermediate, perhaps. The number of persons in certain age groups —particularly the very young and the retired ages—may be important. Supply considerations for this type of outdoor recreation will be very important.

Considering all these factors, we hazard the estimate that by 1980 use of this type of outdoor recreation in the United States may be approximately twice what it was in 1955, that by 2000 it may be three or four times the 1955 figure. This estimate assumes a rate of increase in demand less than half the apparent rate of growth in use since the war.

For *intermediate* outdoor recreation areas, we have fair data on the use of state parks, TVA reservoirs, and Corps of Engineers reservoirs since the war. The upward trend has been particularly steep for the reservoirs, largely as a result of the postwar "boat revolution." The recent slowdown in the explosive rate of growth of the past 15 or 20 years suggests that the revolution may be nearly over. The situation is not unlike the highway revolution of the 1920's when auto travel per

[7] Marion Clawson first calculated estimates of future demand for outdoor recreation for *Land for the Future, op. cit.*; these were rather widely publicized in "The Crisis in Outdoor Recreation," *American Forests,* March and April, 1959. His estimates were then and are yet some of the highest, if not the highest, made by anyone. In the discussions which follow, the highest figure in each range approximately corresponds to the figures previously appearing in these publications. These various figures may indeed prove to be much too high; most students of outdoor recreation would probably so conclude today. Yet they all represent a major slowing down of past trends and all are, in his judgment, possible. Past experience with projections should surely not be ignored. The high projections cannot be realized without a major revolution in the amounts and use of leisure time; but it is precisely the possibility of such a revolution that we must contemplate when dates as distant as 2000 are considered.

capita doubled in a decade. After that, there were improved autos, better highways, and more travel, but the rate of change became more modest. Perhaps the same pattern will be followed by boats in the future.

Projection of past trends undiminished in steepness leads to nonsense results for reservoirs, as we mentioned earlier. Experience of the recent past, while relevant, is thus almost certainly not typical of the longer run.

The desire for intermediate outdoor recreation in the future may be relatively high. Many specific activities common on intermediate outdoor recreation areas are popular with all members of the family, and there is likely to be increasing competition for weekend spare time between this type of outdoor area and other activities at home and in the yard. On the other hand, some people may shift to this type of area for part of their vacation, especially if they take only a day or two at a time. Future capacity of users to engage in this type of outdoor recreation will probably be high. Prospective increases in real income per capita could finance a great deal more of this kind of recreation, and any sizable increase in weekend or day-off leisure would be a major stimulant. The potential exists for a very large increase in demand for this type of outdoor recreation.

Perhaps the biggest question relates to supply and whether there will be major expansion in area and capacity. The land and water resources exist, as we shall show in later chapters. Because intermediate outdoor areas are less demanding in quality of resource than are resource-based types, and less demanding in location than are user-oriented types, there are many more opportunities for expansion.

Balancing up these various forces and factors as best we can, we might estimate that the average person in the United States in 2000 might make as many as 15 visits annually to a state park or federal reservoir. In 1960 the average was 2½—about 1½ visits to state parks and slightly more than 1 to federal reservoirs. However, in some states visits to state parks run to 4 or more annually per capita for state residents, and the total, including visits to federal reservoirs, may be 5 visits for each resident. If this high rate of participation should occur, visits to state parks and federal reservoirs for the whole nation would total 5,000 million in 2000 and 2,000–2,500 million in 1980, each compared with about 465 million in 1960 and with 310 million in 1956. These relatively high figures for 1980 and 2000 involve a substantial slowing down in the postwar growth rate. A further slowing down in that growth rate produces a smaller but still large attendance of perhaps 1,200 million visits in 1980 and 2,000–2,500 million in 2000. The latter totals seem probable at some future date; the major uncertainty concerns the year in which they will be reached. As in the past, most visits to this type of area would be primarily for a single day, with only a small proportion extending to two or more days. However, in absolute numbers the latter might be relatively large, especially if some people chose to spend their vacations in conveniently located and attractive intermediate areas rather than to travel to more distant and possibly more attractive resource-based areas.

In the case of *resource-based* outdoor recreation areas, the best data on use are for the national park system and the national forests; data for federal wildlife refuges are available only since the war. Long-continued, persistent, rather regular trends in increased use are apparent for the two former types of areas. Increases in average income per capita must surely have been one major factor leading to increased usage of these areas, because visits to them are typically comparatively costly. Improvements in travel facilities must also have been a major factor, because such visits typically involve considerable time and money, and sometimes discomfort or boredom. But increases in leisure—particularly the rise in the paid vacation—and increases in total population have also surely been significant factors. It seems highly probable that the *combined* effect of these four factors has been especially strong; that increases in each have reinforced the effect of increases in the others.

The interest of the average citizen in this type of outdoor recreation is expected to be strong. The annual vacation trip is becoming a regular event in the typical American middle-class family. Activities around the home and yard, indoor recreation, and local outdoor recreation are regarded as poor substitutes. Indeed, the demand is rising for two or more vacations per year, at different seasons and for different activities. The future capacity of the average person to engage in this type of outdoor recreation is also likely to be high. Prospective increases in average income per capita, and an increasing proportion of income spent for recreation, will surely permit very large increases in this type of outdoor recreation.

The capacity or supply of resource-based outdoor recreation areas may be the major factor limiting the expansion in their use. Such areas can be found and developed to a degree—but not overdeveloped—and protected from destruction or degradation. But man cannot reproduce them at will. Some expansion in their area is possible. Increased interest in expanding the area of federally-owned resource-based outdoor recreation areas in the East where publicly owned areas of this type are relatively scarce, has been expressed in recent years. If achieved, this could be a major factor facilitating increased use of this type of area. Many proposals for expanding the national park system involved transfer of ownership or jurisdiction of resource-based recreation areas now primarily used for this kind of recreation, and hence are not a net addition to publicly owned land. Increased use of the national park system will also mean more intensive use of presently reserved areas, perhaps of the relatively undeveloped portions of these areas.

Considering all these factors, an expanded national park system might have from 225 to 300 million visits by 1980 and from 500 to 2,000 million visits by 2000, each compared with 66 million in 1960; and with 102 million in 1964; the national forests might have from 300 to 400 million visits in 1980 and from 1,000 to 2,500 million in 2000, each compared with 90 million in 1960 and with 145 million in 1964; and the federal wildlife refuges might have from 30 to 50 million visits in 1980 and from 100 to 300 million in 2000, each compared with 12 million in 1960. Even the larger figure for each kind of area represents a major slowing down in postwar growth rates. On a per capita basis, visits to these three major kinds of federal areas averaged about 1 visit annually in 1960 and about 1½ visits in 1964; if the higher figures are reached, there would be 3 visits per capita in 1980 and nearly 15 by 2000. The latter must approach (some would say, exceed) the practical saturation point. Some people will not care to go at all; others will be physically unable to do so; many will live where such areas will be inconvenient or too costly to visit. But average family incomes of $15,000 or more and average paid vacations of a month or more—each highly probable by 2000—would have tremendous effect. For each kind of area, a considerable part of the increase projected for the 1960–80 period had already been reached by 1964.

These estimates for resource-based areas are obviously rough, with a wide range between lower and higher figures. They are also somewhat arbitrary. They assume that all four of the basic factors are operative and influential, but that the effect of increased real income per capita and of improved travel facilities will be especially strong. They assume also that a considerable part of the increased leisure will be in the form of longer vacation time.

The estimates in this section of probable future increased demand for the various kinds of outdoor recreation are intended to give some orders of magnitude, not to give precise figures. We will make little use of the exact numbers in later discussion, but a great deal of use of the general outlook which these figures illustrate.

DEMAND FOR SPECIFIC RECREATION AREAS AND FACILITIES, OVER TIME

The discussion in this chapter to this point has been concerned with the demand for outdoor recreation on a national scale, or for general kinds of areas widely distributed. One conclusion emerges clearly: large increases in use of outdoor recreation areas have taken place, and the trend toward greater use will continue into the foreseeable future. The total demand for outdoor recreation facilities of each major kind is going to become of ever greater importance as time passes. This conclusion is important, not only to the remainder of this book, but more particularly to recreation planners and administrators.

But a steadily and rather rapidly rising demand for outdoor recreation facilities in general or on a national scale does not necessarily mean that the use of every area, in every year, will rise, much less that it will rise at the same rate as will use on a national scale.[8] Projections on a total basis may be accurate and useful, yet not fully applicable to localities. National projections or forecasts may diverge from projections of local change, for many reasons; this situation is not peculiar to outdoor recreation. For instance, a projection of national automobile sales may correctly indicate a 10 per cent increase in a particular year, but this does not mean that all dealers had increased sales, or that all the dealers selling more cars had increases of 10 per cent. The same general factors enter into projections of future demand or future use of local or regional outdoor recreation areas as enter into such projections for national demand or use; but the magnitude of each factor, and even more the combination of specific factors, may vary greatly. For instance:

(a) The population trend in a state, region, county, or other geographic unit may differ considerably from the national trend. Different areas have increased in population at very different rates in the past; some have lost population—in the decade of the 1950's, while the nation as a whole was increasing by 18 per cent, more than half of all counties lost population. Some states—Florida, Arizona, Nevada, and California —have experienced very rapid rates of increase. Moreover, this increase in population within local areas often exhibits special socioeconomic characteristics; for example, migration may lead to the establishment of communities largely made up of retired persons.

(b) The rise in per capita incomes is more nearly shared nationally, because people tend to move from areas of low income to those of higher income. But divergences in average per capita income have existed for decades and are unlikely to vanish soon. Not only may differences in average incomes persist, but differences in trend of incomes may also exist or arise.

(c) Although trends in leisure are also pervasive, yet differences do

[8] Gordon D. Taylor, "Evaluation of Sites Potential as a Successful Outdoor Recreation Enterprise," a paper presented at the Virginia Outdoor Recreation Symposium, Blacksburg, Va., February 11, 1964.

exist between regions or localities. In particular, some areas attract summer vacationists, others attract winter vacationists, and still others have large numbers of retired persons. The amount and the form of leisure may well differ considerably between one area and another.

(d) Differences in transportation facilities are particularly likely to arise between one area and another. An area previously not served by any road may have a new road built into it, or an area previously served by a dirt road may have a much improved one built; in either case, the use of the recreation area may change dramatically, sometimes literally overnight. But a new airport at the nearest town may affect demand for a vacation area greatly, even when its access roads are unchanged. Other changes in transportation facilities may also affect use of a particular area; or differences in transportation access between areas may greatly affect the level of recreation activity in each.

Differences between states, regions, and localities may also arise in the supply side of outdoor recreation, especially over time. A new reservoir or new reservoirs within an hour's travel time of a city may lead to a vastly increased amount of total outdoor recreation activity in that city, and perhaps to some shift in kinds of activity. The same is true for other investments or programs which open up new areas for use or which improve old areas; the supply increases, and to a large extent this makes its own demand. But developments on the supply side may result in a decrease in the use of a particular area or facility. With the development of a new reservoir or a new park, the old one may no longer seem as attractive, and fewer people may visit it. An increase in alternative intervening opportunities will almost surely lead to reduced attendance at a specific area or facility.

One fruitful line of research in outdoor recreation is to explore the reasons for differences in level and in trend of use at various outdoor recreation areas. For many areas, use has risen over the years; in the economist's terms, volume of output or of consumption has increased. Although accurate data are lacking, it seems probable that average costs per visit (for the whole experience) have risen also, when allowance is made for varying price levels. The larger attendance has nearly always meant more people from distant areas, as well as more people from nearby areas; the market area probably has widened, and thus average costs per visit may have risen. A larger volume at a higher price per unit clearly means a shift in the demand curve; it seems highly probable that this has occurred at many parks and other areas. But it also seems likely, from the available evidence, that such shifts in the demand curve have not been the same for all areas. In addition to differences in trend, there are obvious differences in the intensity of recreation use among areas. Some areas are used very intensively, others much less so. Differences in both level and trend can presumably be related to differences in demand and supply factors described above.

In preparation of this book, we looked briefly at differences in trend in usage of some state park systems and some federal areas. Since the war the trend in attendance at state parks within the Great Plains, for instance, has been much more rapidly and regularly upward than the trend in use of state parks in the group of states from Illinois to Pennsylvania. In this case, it seems probable that supply factors are the ones responsible. These states lack natural bodies of water, but many reservoirs have been constructed since the war, around which have been established state parks. The creation of new bodies of water, just at the time a revolution in water sports was taking place, has produced extremely rapid rates of growth in attendance at these parks. This has been in spite of certain demand factors: these states have experienced slow population growth, income rises have not been unusually large, and neither has there been an unusual rise in leisure as far as we can determine. On the other hand, both state and federal areas in California have experienced great increases in recreation attendance since the war, primarily because of a rapidly growing population, relatively high incomes, and a social climate that has always stressed outdoor living.

There are also great differences among units of the same recreation systems; for instance, several of the major national parks have experienced a long and steady rate of increase in attendance, averaging close to 10 per cent annually, yet Isle Royale National Park has had scarcely any increase in total attendance for many years.

Time and manpower resources available to us did not permit a complete exploration of differences among the hundreds or thousands of individual outdoor recreation areas; and space would not permit a full exposition of the situation, even were the data and the analysis available. We hope that others will pick up this line of inquiry; it is peculiarly well-fitted to study within a state or other geographic area. State park administrators, federal land managers, and others concerned with outdoor recreation should try to find out what is responsible for differences in the level and trend of recreation use of their areas.

One further conclusion emerges from this consideration. In planning a park system for a state or other region, or in planning for a specific facility, it is most unwise to take national trends or national levels of recreation intensity as the chief or sole guide. Both level and trend may be very different regionally or locally than they are nationally. The national trends and levels of use are important as part of the broad environment within which the more localized areas must operate, but local factors may lead to very different results for a particular area.

SUMMARY

In this chapter we have explored various methods of estimating the future demand for outdoor recreation. Each of the methods discussed has some value, but none is wholly satisfactory, especially for estimating demand in the relatively distant future. The methodological problem is admittedly difficult, but a more basic difficulty is the nature of the demand for outdoor recreation. This is dynamic and changing; the future may be very different from the past, and we know relatively little about the past. No methodology can yield wholly satisfactory answers when the problem is so difficult and the data are so poor.

But we think any serious study of outdoor recreation will come to the conclusion that the future demand for outdoor recreation will be very much higher than the present demand. The important question is the exact degree to which it will exceed the present. This, in turn, largely turns on the question of when the present steeply upward trends begin to level off, which also means at what level the leveling off takes place. But we regard it as a settled conclusion that public policy on outdoor recreation must be based on the assumption of much higher future demands than those now experienced.

Further research might well begin to throw more light upon the projection of future demands, as we suggest in Chapter 15. Perhaps no technique can avoid some of the elements of "judgment" which we have discussed in this chapter, but it should be possible to narrow the range within which various methods and investigators would estimate the demand at any future date.

Although current programs in outdoor recreation, especially investment programs, require some estimate of probable future demand if they are to be sound, the opportunity will exist for modifications in programs over the next few years. The decision may have to be made today to acquire a certain tract of land, if it is to be acquired at all; but other tracts could be purchased later if demand is larger than estimated, or the first tract might conceivably be sold if not needed. Plans should be under frequent review, and new studies can be made from time to time.

In this chapter, we have considered various estimates of probable future use of outdoor recreation facilities. It has been more or less implicitly assumed that the supply of outdoor recreation opportunity would be adequate to meet the estimated demand. One purpose of making such estimates of the future is to help guide programs for expansion of park and other recreation programs. But it is by no means certain that supply will in fact expand to meet the increased demand; too seriously restricted a capacity might well mean that some of the potential demand would be choked off by overcrowded and hence unattractive areas.

III

Recreation Resources

In this part, the emphasis shifts from demand to the supply side of outdoor recreation. Outdoor recreation requires the use of areas of land or bodies of water or both for its fulfillment. Sometimes the areas are devoted to recreation alone, and sometimes they are used for other purposes as well. The areas involved are often large, but they need not be.

Major public attention and much planning has been devoted to the matter of the *area* of land and water used for outdoor recreation. The establishment of standards of adequacy or need, requirements as to proper location of recreation areas with respect to users, considerations of acceptable intensity of use of recreation areas, and other subjects arise out of this concern over area. Area is important, but it is not the whole story. It is only one consideration, and sometimes it is not even the major one.

Chapter 8 deals with the many aspects of recreation use—amount, kind, timing—and the interactions between use and supply.

Chapter 9 takes up the matter of recreation quality, a dimension that is often ignored in discussions of recreation use, but one that is highly important to visitor satisfaction. The maintenance of recreation quality is neither easy nor cheap, but it is a problem that must be recognized.

Chapter 10 reviews the existing outdoor recreation areas and their use. Each group of areas—federal, state, and local—is appraised in terms of acreage, both total and regional distribution, and in terms of per capita expenditures.

8

Use of Resources for Recreation

A natural resource for recreation is land, water, or other natural features actually used for recreation. It may be an area of land, with or without tree cover; it may be a body of water or a flowing stream; or it may be other natural features, such as caves which extend far below the surface. The natural features may or may not have been modified or improved by man. The probability of use within the foreseeable future may make an area a potential resource for recreation.

In any event, it is *use* or the possibility of early use which determines that natural features are actual or potential recreation resources, not any physical characteristics of the land or water area itself. Some physical features or characteristics are, it is true, better adapted to outdoor recreation than are others, and will be preferred when choice is possible. For swimming, nearly everyone will prefer a sandy beach to one with sharp rocks, and moderately tempered water to very cold water. Some characteristics of nature, such as water temperature, are easily measured, quantifiable, and probably subject to general agreement among all or most users. Most people have preferences as to the type of scenery or landscape they prefer for outdoor recreation, including the type of trees or forest, or of topography, or of beauty in the natural scene. These features or characteristics are more difficult to define, less easily measured in quantitative terms, and probably are subject to more differences of opinion among users. Yet, no matter how difficult it is to measure or to define the natural qualities that are prized most highly for outdoor recreation, it is the willingness of some people to use the area for outdoor recreation which makes a recreation resource out of what otherwise would be rocks, trees, and water. When one inventories, or describes, or attempts to measure resource availability for outdoor recreation, it is really human attitudes and actions he is measuring.

There are often many and complex interrelations between the area, the user, and the use. The attitudes of the user, generally arising out of his past recreation experience, strongly condition what he looks for in an outdoor recreation area. He is likely to prefer what he knows best and has enjoyed in the past. If he has had a past experience with certain kinds of outdoor recreation, he is likely to seek to continue that kind of experience, and to do so will accept areas perhaps physically not well suited to it. Members of the American expedition to Antarctica were reported to have played baseball on the ice one sunny but cold day—not because ice is the best baseball field, or because the day was ideal, but because they were tired of confinement and sought a familiar form of recreation under the best circumstances available to them.

As use is a necessary component of recreation resources, inventories of recreation resources have rather serious limits. One can find which areas of land and bodies of water are presently used for outdoor recreation, and to what extent. But present use of one area may reflect the absence or unavailability of physically better areas as much as it does any characteristic of the particular area.

It is particularly hard to identify potential outdoor recreation areas because it is not the observable natural qualities that make an area suitable or desirable for outdoor recreation, but the presence or absence of users and the availability or lack of better alternative areas. Hundreds of millions of acres of farm and other land in the United States are physically well suited to user-oriented outdoor recreation, but their distance from urban populations precludes their use for this purpose. Even for intermediate-type recreation areas, the number of suitable sites is probably far beyond any financial capacity to develop them, and, perhaps, in excess of any need for their output. While resource-based areas are by definition more limited in occurrence, many of them have capacity for some activities, such as camping, that so far outruns any foreseeable future demand as to render meaningless any estimate of the extent of physically suitable areas. Inventories may well include physically suitable areas which may be needed in the future, but only within some reasonable range of possible future demand, not in complete disregard of potential use.

STANDARDS OF ADEQUACY FOR RECREATION AREAS

Legislators, general planners, administrators, conservationists, and citizen groups generally want answers to such questions as: How much park and recreation areas is "enough" to meet the needs of our people? What is a reasonable goal? How does our city or state compare with others?

Standards of areal adequacy can help answer such questions, *if* they are taken as general guides and not as explicit directives. The location of an area, its physical characteristics, its design, its administration, and other factors are often as important as the actual areal extent. Moreover, "standards" can never be rigid; each community must determine what its citizens want, and what role they assign to recreation. What can the community afford, and what is it willing to pay for? How does the demand for outdoor recreation compare with the demand or need for other public services which may compete for the same (usually limited) public investment funds? Parks and recreation are considered necessities by some but luxuries by others; willingness and ability to pay may be more critical than "need," and hence standards can be only general guides.

Recreation area standards are meaningful only with respect to the type of areas. The kinds of standards that have been established, and their degree of explicitness, differ considerably between user-oriented, intermediate, and resource-based areas.

By far the most attention has been directed toward the establishment of area standards for user-oriented areas. There, the early work of the National Recreation Association and of George D. Butler is classic.[1] In response to many requests, but rather reluctantly, he proposed a standard of 10 acres of park and open space per 1,000 of population within each city, and an equal area in parkways, larger parks, forests, and the like either within or adjacent to the city. Butler went further to suggest standards for small play lots, units of 2,000 to 5,000 square feet, primarily for housing projects and other residential areas lacking private backyards; neighborhood playgrounds, of 4 to 7 acres each, within half or a fourth mile of where children live, with 1 acre per 800 total population; large parks, not less than 100 acres each in size, at least one for every city, and one for each 40,000 total population in larger cities; natural reservations, 1,000 or more acres each, often outside the city, perhaps not needed if equivalent state or federal areas are available; special recreation areas; neighborhood parks, etc.

The NRA standard of 10 acres per 1,000 population has been widely quoted and applied as a standard for city parks. Butler's reluctance to suggest a standard arose because he foresaw that his standard, or any other, would likely be used indiscriminately; he was fully aware of location and other factors. Moreover, he realized that such a standard would often be unattainable.

A careful study in California, which considered climatic conditions

[1] George D. Butler, *Introduction to Community Recreation* (3d ed.; New York: McGraw-Hill Book Co., 1959).

and hence recreational patterns in different parts of the state, proposed neighborhood recreation centers of 3 acres per 1,000 population if adjoining an elementary school, and 6 acres if separate; community recreation parks of 1 acre per 1,000 population if adjoining a high school (junior or senior) and double this if separate; and city-wide recreation facilities of 10 acres per 1,000 population.[2]

In 1940, of the cities reporting parks to the National Recreation Association, 25 per cent had 10 acres or more of parks for each 1,000 total population.[3] This would suggest that the NRA standards were not completely unattainable.

For a large urban area, the NRA standard of 10 acres per 1,000 may be useful as a *general* guide, but it is a standard that cannot be met in most of our larger cities. In Manhattan, for example, it would require more land than there is in the whole borough. The average gross density for the five cities of a million or more inhabitants in 1950 was over 14,000 per square mile.[4] For these cities, the NRA standard would mean that nearly a fourth of the total area would have to be in park or recreation areas; for the most intensively used residential areas of these cities, the proportion would be much higher. Providing these areas would be even more difficult if density should reach the figure that Ludlow suggested as an average acceptable density per square mile of total developed urban area (including commercial, transportation, and other service areas)—22,400 persons per square mile when people are housed in 13-story apartments.[5]

Considerations of this kind led the Regional Plan Association of New York to propose different standards for local recreation areas in different parts of the New York metropolitan region.[6] For the extremely high-density apartment area of Manhattan, the proposed standard was 1.8 acres per 1,000 of total population; for the very high-density apartment area of the Bronx, 4.8 acres; for a high-density apartment area, such as Queens or Newark, 5.6 acres; for low-density apartment areas, such as

[2] California Committee on Planning for Recreation, Park Areas and Facilities, *Guide for Planning Recreation Parks in California* (Sacramento: Documents Section, Printing Division, 1956).

[3] George D. Butler, *Municipal and County Parks in the United States, 1940*, National Recreation Association, New York, 1942.

[4] Marion Clawson, R. Burnell Held, and Charles H. Stoddard, *Land for the Future* (Baltimore: The Johns Hopkins Press, for Resources for the Future, Inc., 1960), p. 85.

[5] William H. Ludlow, "Urban Densities and Their Costs: An Exploration into the Economics of Population Densities and Urban Patterns," Part II, in Coleman Woodbury (ed.), *Urban Redevelopment: Problems and Practices* (Chicago: University of Chicago Press, 1953).

[6] Regional Plan Association, *The Race for Open Space*, RPA Bulletin No. 96, New York, 1960.

Fort Lee and Tuckahoe, 5 to 6 acres; for high-density one-family districts, 8 to 9 acres; and for low-density residential areas (lots one half acre or larger), 11½ to 12½ acres; or, for the whole New York metropolitan region, 7.2 to 7.8 acres of *local* recreation acreage per 1,000 total population. The Association also proposed that these local areas be supplemented by county and state parks roughly three times the acreage of the local areas and located within ½ to 2 hours traveling time of metropolitan residents.

The Regional Plan Association's standards can be attacked on the grounds that the need for public recreation areas is likely to be most critical in those places where they will be scarcest. However, the unreality of uniform standards has already been pointed out. Moreover, in intensively used areas of our largest cities, every land use must be intensive—residential, trade, transportation, and recreation. One cannot have the advantages of downtown location and of sweeping open suburban lawns; they simply are incompatible. The Regional Plan proposals are admittedly something of a compromise, and yet they represent a distinct improvement over present conditions in the New York metropolitan region.

Park standards are only beginning to be applied to *intermediate-type areas,* and, so far, more attention has been given to location than to area. Proposals have been made to establish such areas within 40 miles of urban residents in California, and within 25 miles in Massachusetts and Pennsylvania.[7] These states did not establish specific area standards, but the acreage in each case is to be adequate for the kinds of activities most common in such parks; presumably, the total number of such parks would be great enough to accommodate all or nearly all visitors even on peak days. The Detroit metropolitan region proposed sufficient "regional" parks (generally similar to intermediate parks) to accommodate at one time as many as 15 per cent of the total regional population —a number that various studies suggested might seek such parks on a pleasant Sunday afternoon.[8] In an earlier RFF study, we proposed one or more state parks within two hours driving time of 90 per cent of the total population of a state.[9]

The Outdoor Recreation Resources Review Commission, in its report, stressed the key role of states in the provision of outdoor recreation, and recommended that each state prepare a long-range plan and undertake

[7] *California Public Outdoor Recreation Plan, Part II* (Sacramento: Documents Section, Printing Division, 1960). *Report of An Inventory and Plan for Development of the Natural Resources of Massachusetts,* Commonwealth of Massachusetts.
[8] "Park Users Survey," *Recreation in the Detroit Region, Part II,* Detroit Metropolitan Area Regional Planning Commission, April 1959.
[9] *Land for the Future, op. cit.*

a program of land acquisition and development.[10] Such parks would be, in general, intermediate areas. However, the Commission did not attempt to establish acreage standards for these or other intermediate-type areas.

As far as we know, no acreage standards have been established for *resource-based* outdoor recreation areas, and perhaps none should be. Boards and commissions now apply informal standards to areas proposed for inclusion in national and state park systems, and periodic surveys are made to define possible additions to such systems. Since the distinguishing characteristic of such areas is their unique quality, not their area or location, it may be that all areas which meet strict quality standards should be reserved for outdoor recreation, usually in public ownership. The practicability of such a proposal depends on how carefully and strictly the standards of excellence for such areas are stated. If the standards are tightly drawn, presumably only prime areas would qualify, and all could be reserved; but, if they are drawn more loosely, it would be difficult to resist the inclusion of mediocre areas.

ROLE OF LOCATION IN RECREATION AREA ADEQUACY

The relative importance of location depends upon the kind of outdoor recreation area. Location is critical for user-oriented areas; it is highly important but subject to much greater flexibility for intermediate type areas; and it is of least importance, though still significant, for resource-based areas.

By definition, user-oriented outdoor recreation areas must be close to their users. Also, when the areas are used mostly by children or by elderly people, the travel routes must be simple and fairly safe. A playground, for example, must be within a half-mile of where children live, and there must be no major arterial street or highway to cross at grade level. The total area of land required for playgrounds and "rest parks" is relatively small; but, unless the plots are located within the distance constraints mentioned, such areas are useless to those who need them.

For the larger city park, the golf course, the zoo, and many other kinds of user-oriented outdoor recreation areas, the locational factor is not quite so restrictive. However, these areas must still be within the city or at least within the total urban complex. And when distances exceed perhaps a half mile, access by public transport is desirable. While automobile ownership is very widespread in the United States, there are important groups who do not own or cannot operate an auto— the young, the old, and those who cannot afford one.

[10] *Outdoor Recreation for America,* a Report to the President and to the Congress by the Outdoor Recreation Resources Review Commission (Washington: U.S. Government Printing Office, 1962).

For a great many cities, the over-all statistics on acreage and numbers of parks and recreation areas, in relation to total city population, look satisfactory. But a closer examination of maps for such cities will often show that the distribution is far from satisfactory. Extensive areas of the city, very often lived in by large numbers of lower-income people, have seriously inadequate park and recreation areas. These are usually the older parts of cities, built in a day when the need for parks and playgrounds was not so generally recognized. In these areas, the children typically play in the streets because neighborhood playgrounds do not exist.

In a great many American cities, park and playground acreage is more unevenly distributed than is personal income. The lowest income parts of the city have an even smaller share of recreation area than they have of personal income, while the higher income sections have relatively generous park and recreation areas. The poorest people, who most need easily accessible parks and playgrounds, often have them least. This situation is made still worse by the racial pattern of urban living. The low-income central city areas so deficient in recreation space are likely to be Negro; the suburban and outer city ring areas, generously supplied with recreation, are likely to be white. One of the great myths of the outdoor recreation field is that free public parks are a boon to "poor" people; actually, it is the poor who frequently lack them.

Intermediate-type outdoor recreation areas—frequently state or metropolitan regional parks—have much greater latitude in location. Even when the distance standard is set at one hour's travel time, there are usually many possible alternative sites. Since few of these areas are served by public transportation, their use is usually restricted to those who can afford a car and who are able to drive it. Location with respect to transportation arterials is likely to be more important than actual distance. The park or recreation area probably should not border a major transportation arterial, because this would introduce sights and sounds undesirable for such areas and could possibly cause other complications; but perhaps most of the travel distance from home to the recreation area should be on an arterial or other relatively rapid transit route.

Fewer traffic peaks and bottlenecks, as well as variety in the recreation experience itself, are among the advantages of having several intermediate recreation areas of adequate size rather than one very large area. Also cross-city travel will be reduced if the areas are spotted around a large city or metropolitan complex, so that travel is not all in a single direction. Economies in land acquisition and in park management may suggest fewer and larger areas, yet the advantages to the public of more areas of a modest size should be kept in mind. Of course,

151

for the kinds of activities typical of this kind of area, 100 to several hundred acres is often necessary. For water skiing and some of the other relatively new water sports, lakes (natural or artificial) of a few hundred acres are desirable. However, in 1955, a third of all state parks had less than 50 acres each and well over half had less than 250 acres each.[11]

Within the time and distance restrictions of intermediate park and recreation areas, there are often several excellent sites, some of which are not highly valuable for other land uses. A valley bottom subject to moderately frequent overflowing, perhaps with relatively steep side slopes, may have limited value for agriculture, forestry, residential, industrial, or other use; yet these same characteristics may make it a good park and recreation site. A body of water need not be a natural one to be highly valuable for recreation; relatively small dams with fixed overflow height can often, in a few years, create a lake almost indistinguishable from a natural one. Moreover, the choice need not be limited to sites that are presently readily accessible by arterial or other major highway; the latter can often be built to available and desirable intermediate type areas. In short, the flexibilities of time and distance on the one hand and of natural character on the other combine to provide a great many alternative sites of good to excellent character.

The resource-based outdoor recreation areas, by definition, are located where one finds them, and people must travel to them as necessary. In the United States, most mountain, seashore, and lake areas of high natural suitability for outdoor recreation are located at some distance from most of the larger cities. Likewise, most of the national parks, national forests, and other publicly-owned parks of this type are relatively distant from most urban people. The Outdoor Recreation Resources Review Commission has called attention to the serious imbalance between such federally-owned areas and population in the West and East. This divergence between geography and population may be largely unavoidable and irremediable. But this calls for closer examination.

In recent years it has become evident that no resource-based area, no matter how large or how remote, can go completely unmanaged; Man has already intervened so heavily in every area that Nature is no longer free. Man has modified the operation of natural forces in many ways: by controlling predators in some national parks and forests; by trying to prevent and control forest fires, which were once part of the natural environment; by trying to control insect and disease outbreaks

---

[11] Marion Clawson, *Statistics on Outdoor Recreation* (Washington: Resources for the Future, Inc., 1958).

which menace forest or other vegetation. Above all, by his very presence, in the form of roads and trails, and by the introduction of domestic livestock, Man has intruded into the primeval scene. Along many lake and seashore areas, attempts have been made to prevent or reduce wave and other erosion. Thus, in many ways the resource-based outdoor recreation area has been modified and brought under Man's control, and will be increasingly so in the future.

At a different part of the spectrum of "naturalness" and management, are tracts of land of high natural resource value which often lie within 100 miles or less of our larger cities, and which can be greatly enhanced by skillful management. These areas include a few "virgin" or uncut woods, some swamps that are still largely untouched, and, more commonly, forests which though once cut have regrown to a very pleasing "wilderness" appearance—even if the purist recognizes them as less than virgin. With long-continued and skillful management, many areas could take on very high natural resource values. In a future with increasing population and little opportunity to escape to relatively untouched areas, such developed or managed natural areas might have great appeal. To some, there may seem an incongruity in talking of managed natural areas; yet we argue that unmanaged natural areas are, or soon will be, a thing of the past; that management might be used for restoring areas and not only for protecting them.

CONCENTRATIONS OF RECREATION ACTIVITY WITHIN RECREATION AREAS

The usual statistics and discussion about recreation activity deal with total use for some designated area, such as a park. Such information is valuable, especially as it provides a contrast between different areas or different time periods. But treating each designated area as a unit conceals enormous variations *within* it. There is very little specific data on this matter, yet nearly every park and recreation area administrator will agree that use is extremely uneven in different parts of his park.

Recreation use tends to be highly concentrated within any recreation area, the degree of concentration depending on the kind of area (see Figure 22).[12] Concentration is probably most extreme in a large national park, such as Yellowstone, where a few easily accessible, highly popular spots attract hundreds of thousands of visitors during the relatively short summer season, while a vast back country, accessible only by trail, and

[12] See Robert C. Lucas, *Recreational Use of the Quetico-Superior Area,* U.S. Forest Service Research Paper LS–8, Lake States Forest Experiment Station, St. Paul, Minnesota, 1964. This paper includes a chart that is similar to Figure 23 but indicates a still more uneven distribution of use.

by horseback or walking, has almost no use. Perhaps as much as 95 per cent or more of total use occurs on as little as 5 per cent or less of total area. There is a vast area with no "use." When we say, "no use," we mean no human foot is set on or near it; there is no no hiking, no hunting, no fishing, etc. But much of this area has use, in the sense that it provides background scenery for those who actually set foot on the more popular areas. Some of the back country of Yellowstone and other large areas does not do this, for it is not visible from the popular spots; it may, however, serve the same function for those relatively few people who do travel the back trails.

In a smaller state park that is more intensively developed and used, especially if located where use is possible during a large part or all of the year, total use will be more evenly spread over total area; but, even here, use will be concentrated to a considerable degree. Some spots will be heavily used, perhaps literally trampled to death, while others will be lightly used or scarcely visited. Even in a very intensively used and developed city park or playground, use will be concentrated more in some spots than others.

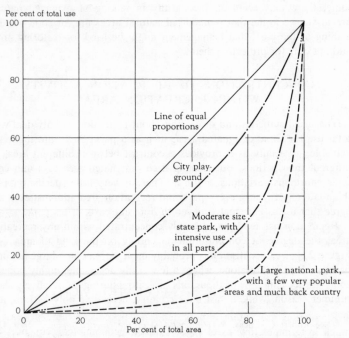

Figure 22. Recreation use in relation to area of land and water within an established park (hypothetical data).

Recreation use tends to concentrate along travel routes—highways, parking areas, ramps, sidewalks, paths, portages, and other travel routes or intersections. It also tends to concentrate around special recreation features, such as geysers, waterfalls, natural swimming beaches, historic spots, and the like. Almost all man-made improvements tend to concentrate use—service facilities, campgrounds, play equipment, etc. If skillfully designed, these may divert some use from a previous concentration point to new areas, but they can rarely disperse use widely and evenly over large areas.

Extremely heavy recreation use can create many special problems. Most obvious is the actual physical damage to the area; people, if there are enough of them, can do as much damage as a bulldozer to young vegetation, and by packing down the soil they can even damage large, mature trees. Soil compaction may easily lead to accelerated runoff and increased erosion. The park manager may sometimes reflect that people are more difficult to control than the cattle who concentrate around watering spots on the range, trampling out the vegetation for a goodly distance in all directions. Concentrations in popular spots are responsible for overcrowding.

Although large parts of many outdoor recreation and park areas are the scene of little activity, they are nevertheless highly valuable and sometimes indispensable to the heavily used areas, by serving as a buffer zone. As such, they keep out nonconforming or differing uses, and also often the sights and sounds of activities carried on outside the recreation area. Perhaps even more important than these physical effects, they play a critical psychological role—a campground on a city block would never provide the same experience as a campground in a forest, even though the sites were physically identical and the user never left the small site in the forest. No one familiar with our larger national parks would be content to reduce Yellowstone to Old Faithful and a dozen other major spots, or Grand Canyon to a few vista spots along each rim. On the contrary, one common criticism of many state parks and private areas is that the surrounding buffer zones are too small. Buffer zones may in time come to absorb some of the increased future use of the whole area; but, even if they remain simply as buffer zones, they are often indispensable to the whole area.

TIME PATTERNS OF RECREATION ACTIVITY

Recreation use within a park tends to be concentrated at least as much in terms of time as of space, and the economic consequences are probably even more serious.

Typically, an outdoor recreation area is used intensively during a brief period of time, moderately at other times, and wholly unused for much greater periods of time. A school play yard, for example, is a beehive of activity at recess time, it receives some use after school and over the weekend, but it sits completely unused during most of each day and all during the night. The situation is similar, though perhaps not quite so extreme, for most user-oriented outdoor recreation areas. Nearly all playgrounds and sports fields are heavily used for a few hours during some or all days of the week, lightly used for some other hours, and unused most of the hours during the week. City parks, zoos, museums, and many other kinds of user-oriented areas have generally similar time patterns of use.

The same situation prevails for many of the intermediate areas. The campground in a popular state park may have to turn people away on the July 4th and Labor Day weekends; it may operate at capacity for a few other summer weekends, have modest use during the rest of the summer, light use at intervals during the spring and fall, and no use at all during half or more of all the days in the year.

Our larger national parks will have more than a million visitors during three months or less of the summer season, or an average of more than 10,000 visitors per day. Because so many people live too far from these parks for weekend visits, attendance is relatively even throughout the week. Some national parks are closed during the winter, and none has many visitors during much of the spring and fall.

Published data on park and recreation area usage generally do not reveal the extreme variations in time pattern of use. Data showing total attendance by months give some idea of seasonal variation in use, but they generally seriously understate the daily variations in use. At the extreme, some areas or parks may get half their annual use in as few as ten selected days during the year—holidays and a few weekends—and very little, if any, use during half to three-fourths of the whole year. Such a situation exists not only for public areas but for many private ones as well. Resort areas in Maine, for example, may be full during the summer season, but closed from Labor Day to Memorial Day. Even a calculation on divergences in attendance based on daily attendance data may understate the extreme variation in time of use. Not only may half the week's use occur on Sunday, for instance, but much of this may be during the afternoon hours.

The time pattern of use depends in part upon the climate. Where the climate is moderate enough to permit winter use, or where winter sports are possible, use may be distributed throughout the year in a way that is impossible, or at least unpracticed, in many areas. But, under the most favorable circumstances, probably more than 50 per cent of the use of intermediate and resource-based areas is had on less than

20 per cent of the days of the year. It would be helpful if we had more detailed and dependable data on this point.

Extreme time-peaking of use always means high costs, or poor service, or both. For some services, the public has demanded that suppliers provide adequate capacity to meet all peaks. This is true for electricity for household consumption, telephone service, domestic water supply, and others. For other common services, the public has tolerated inadequate capacity and resulting poor service at the extreme peaks of demand. This is notably the case with nearly all forms of transportation. During the peak-hour traffic, jams and delays arise on streets and highways because capacity is simply not adequate. But jams and delays arise with airlines on holidays also.

The cost of meeting extreme peaks can be very high. When the cost of the last units of capacity are charged against the relatively few units of service provided to meet the extreme peaks of demand, the cost per unit is often many times the average costs on an annual basis. A large part of costs are associated with investment and maintenance, not with service as such. The costs of providing peak service are usually concealed by pricing systems which are based upon average annual costs—this may be true of electricity or telephone, for instance. But there are costs associated with extremes in peak demand even when no capacity is provided for meeting them. Workers in a city, for example, bear a real cost from the delays, inconveniences, and discomforts of sharply peaked traffic flows.

Time concentration of use seems to offer no compensating benefit like the buffer zone which results from space concentration. The person who cannot find a picnic table when he wants it Sunday afternoon gets little comfort from knowing that the area will be half deserted Monday afternoon. It is true that some areas can recuperate during the periods of light use, but if use were more evenly distributed, the need for recuperation would be less.

The extreme time-peaking of demand for nearly all types of outdoor recreation and park areas is one of the most serious economic and management problems in the whole outdoor recreation field. It has not yet had the attention it deserves, and the suggestions for improvement have not yet resulted in much improvement.

SUBSTITUTION OF CAPITAL, LABOR, AND MANAGEMENT FOR NATURAL RESOURCES

In outdoor recreation activity, as in other uses of natural resources, the resource alone has little or no productivity unless it is combined with capital, labor, and management. The amount and proportions of these other inputs can vary, sometimes over a wide range, with a consequent effect upon volume and sometimes on quality of output. Within limits—sometimes wide, sometimes narrow—one input can substitute for another to maintain the same volume and kind of output. These are well-accepted principles for most resource uses; they have not been so generally applied to outdoor recreation in the past, and may not seem so obvious here, yet they are fully applicable.

In a park or other outdoor recreation area, desired kinds of vegetation can be protected or established by investment of labor, capital, and management. A good grass sod, which is desirable for many sports areas, can often be established or improved by such means as cultivation, seeding, and fertilization. Where screening or background shrubs and trees are desired, these, too, can be established and protected. In the more humid parts of the United States, establishment and protection of vegetation is relatively easy; in the drier parts, it may be necessary to provide irrigation, protection from wind until the trees are established, and other measures which add to the cost. In extreme cases, topsoil or better soil materials may have to be imported to the site.

For many kinds of outdoor recreation, a body of water is desirable if not essential. Some areas are fortunate in having a satisfactory body of water that needs only to be kept free from pollution or other damage, and that is easily maintained. In other areas, a water area must be built or improved by impoundment, water regulation, and other actions, all of which cost money. Shorelines and stream banks may require protection from erosion, and sometimes the cost is considerable. For some water bodies, sand must be brought in for swimming beaches. What appear to be quite unlikely areas can sometimes be made over into attractive park and recreation areas. An abandoned stone or gravel quarry, for instance, can sometimes be made into an attractive lake suitable for a variety of water sports. Or a marsh or frequently overflowed bottom area can be converted into an attractive lake by stream impoundment and regulation, with the same result.

Any outdoor recreation area, if it is to be generally used, requires access. It may be necessary to build a road, or to improve an existing one to provide adequate access for all who seek to use the area. Roads, trails, and parking area must be provided within the park or recreation area. Sometimes special access facilities, such as boat launching ramps, are needed for some kinds of areas. All of these facilities require investment and planning for their establishment and maintenance.

Water supply, sanitary, and other personal service facilities are almost always required for an outdoor recreation area. Someone has commented that the most welcome sight in a park may be a sign which says "Men." The character of the needed facilities will depend largely upon the kinds of activities planned for the area, the number of visitors, and location. A local playground may have no more than a drinking fountain. Wilderness areas can no longer get by without facilities of some kind; in areas where use is increasing, outdoor toilets and garbage pits are preferable to surface wastes. In recreation areas where use is intensive, even more is needed in the way of facilities. The cost depends in part upon the ready availability of central water and sewer services, or on the availability of ground water or of soil conditions which permit safe use of septic tanks, and of course in considerable part upon the volume of use which must be accommodated. In a great many circumstances, the initial cost of providing such services is considerable, and this is often a factor tending toward relatively large installations and use areas, as in camping areas. Under all circumstances, the facilities established must be maintained, both to prevent deterioration of the investment and to provide continuous acceptable service.

Under a great many circumstances, grass or other natural vegetation or bare soil cannot withstand the intensive use of the area. Gravel, asphalt, or other surfacing is often necessary, especially for school playyards, and sometimes for other playgrounds. But, even within areas which are prized for their "naturalness," asphalt may be necessary for roadways, parking lots, parking pads beside the picnic table or campground, and elsewhere. If well located, these may take much or nearly all of the traffic, and the natural areas may be further guarded from too intensive use by thorny or spiny plantings.

Park and other extensive recreation use areas are often thought of as areas set aside by Nature for our use, yet in fact substantial management of the vegetation may be necessary. Fertilization and irrigation of shrubs, trees, and grass may be necessary in parks even though not common on home lawns or on farms. An unobtrusive sprinkler irrigation system in a campground or picnic area may be less objectionable than bedraggled shrubs and beat-out grass.

A trend toward more intensive management of park and recreation areas seems evident in recent years, although precise and fully applicable data are lacking. Since the war, the state park systems of the country have spent about twice as much in capital investments to improve existing areas as they have spent in the acquisition of new areas.[13] A similar relationship between outlays to improve existing areas and expenditures to acquire new areas probably exists for city parks, federal areas, and other kinds of areas, although detailed data are lacking. Improvement of available areas is often the quickest, and sometimes the cheapest, way to acquire additional recreation capacity. It has other advantages also.

[13] *Statistics on Outdoor Recreation, op. cit.*

When areas are used more intensively, they are less vulnerable to invasion by highways, commercial developments, or other uses. Moreover, acquisition of new areas may involve not only large money costs but also substantial "turmoil" costs—disruption of existing uses, condemnation proceedings to acquire part of the area, adverse publicity and political opposition, etc. However, improvements of existing areas cannot be substituted for acquisition of new areas indefinitely or completely without creating serious problems in the future.

For the future, the trend will almost surely be toward more intensive use of outdoor recreation areas than is typical today, even if the acreage of such areas expands relatively generously. Recreation planners and administrators must find new ways to substitute capital, labor, and management for land and water area, in order to provide more recreation capacity of equal or better quality than at present from any given area. For this, research, experimentation, and experience should help provide some answers.

MULTIPLE USE MANAGEMENT AND RECREATION

There has been a great deal of discussion of multiple use management of forest and other relatively natural lands; and although not usually in the same terms, the same general ideas have been extensively applied to the management of artificial bodies of water. Multiple use management is an important idea, with many possibilities for increasing the output of given areas of land and water; but there has also been some exaggeration and fuzziness of discussion.

Multiple use is partly a matter of the size of the area under consideration. The national forests, some other federal lands, many state forests, and much private forest and grazing land can be said to produce more than one product or service or to be used for several purposes, when the whole of each tract or body of land is considered as a unit. But often the recreation activity is largely confined to one smaller area within the larger whole, the forest harvest takes place on localized areas, the grazing is restricted to other areas, and so on. This interweaving of different uses calls for the most careful planning and management of the whole area; this is multiple use management, on this scale and in this sense.

In other cases, the same acreage or tract of land is used for two or more purposes either at different times during the year or simultaneously; this, too, is multiple use management. This latter system will become, undoubtedly, the more common practice as the demands for the various uses of the resources increase. Accomplishing this will require a thorough study and analysis of the resources and their potential and of the demand. The result will be the establishment of levels of use of the resources on various areas that represent optimum combinations of uses and not maximum production of any single use.

The economic rationale of multiple use is that the sum total of the values thus created is greater than the value from any single use—and enough greater to more than offset the added costs. Under many circumstances, this is probably true. Under any multiple use program, each user group must accept the fact that other users have an interest in the area also; and that the area is not being managed for his interest only.

The same general relationships apply to water areas. Some natural and artificial lakes are used wholly for recreation; but even here there are divergent interests among swimmers, fishermen, canoeists, power boat operators, etc. Other water bodies are used primarily for flood protection, power generation, irrigation, or other purposes, yet may provide significant amounts of outdoor recreation. In the future, outdoor recreation is likely to be increasingly included as an equal partner in the management of multiple use water bodies.[14]

A great many kinds of outdoor recreation take place on specialized outdoor recreation areas. This is true of almost all organized sports, such as tennis, golf, baseball, etc. But it is also true of intensively used park areas, such as play areas, picnic areas, and areas used for hiking, swimming, boating, and other activities. Even camping areas are likely to be specialized areas. These various activity areas may lie within, or constitute, a specialized outdoor recreation area such as a country club, playground, park, etc.; or they may be the specialized parts of a generalized resource management area such as a national forest or state forest. The same relationship generally prevails for privately owned and managed areas providing similar kinds of services. Privately owned campgrounds, for instance, are nearly always operated as specialized tracts or as specialized parts of farms or other larger land management units.

In contrast, some kinds of outdoor recreation require a relatively large area of land, but not exclusive use of it. Hunting is a prime example of this kind of recreation. The hunter wants freedom to move where he thinks his chances of a kill are greatest without having to bother about property lines. The landowner often wants a reasonably adequate harvest of the annual crop of game animals so that their numbers do not build up to a destructive point. But he is also often rightly concerned over the possibility of damage to livestock, to fences, to machinery, to roads.

[14] Jack L. Knetsch, "Economics of Including Recreation as a Purpose of Water Resources Projects," *Journal of Farm Economics,* Vol. 46, No. 5 (December 1964).

Damages, even if caused by only a small minority of hunters, can be serious to the landowner. Large forest and other landowners are often sensitive to general public relations and dislike the adverse publicity that often accompanies the closing of their lands to hunting. Landowners are thus caught between opposing or conflicting forces, and sometimes they are not sure how to treat hunting on their land. In any case, some problems of equity arise in pricing. Hunting privileges represent a valuable service which the hunter hardly has a right to expect free. Costs may be imposed on the landowner, but often there are offsetting advantages.

Specialized land uses other than recreation, in a large tract managed for multiple uses, may be especially valuable in providing desirable buffer strips. This assumes that forestry, under which timber would be cut from a particular tract only at relatively long intervals, is a far better buffer zone than would be a major through highway, as far as campground use is concerned. Special management methods may greatly reduce the adverse impact on the specialized recreation area, thus making the buffer zone function more usefully.

By research and experimentation, it should be possible to devise more and better ways to permit the recreation use of land primarily used for other purposes, especially for forestry and grazing. The problem is more difficult for privately owned land, but it exists for the publicly owned land also.

LAND AND WATER FOR OUTDOOR RECREATION IN THE FUTURE

It is extremely difficult to project the future need for land areas and water bodies for outdoor recreation use with any accuracy. The difficulties of such projections arise from two major considerations: the long-run future demand for outdoor recreation cannot be accurately known now for reasons discussed in Chapter 7; and the intensity of recreation use per unit of area will almost surely be higher in the future, but the degree of change is not known precisely. Reasonable variations in these two major factors, when combined, can lead to widely varying estimates of future recreation area.

But some kind of projection of future area is unavoidable. Decisions taken now as to recreation areas will have long-run effects and areas must be reserved if they are to be available for future needs. If a city or state decides to buy land for park and other recreation areas, it has implicitly made a projection as to future need; and similarly, if it decides *not* to buy land or develop water today for future use, it has made a projection of future area needs. As noted earlier, the problem is not merely the cash cost of the land desired, but its availability for recreation use when needed for this purpose. When suburbs are in the expansion period, land may be set aside for parks at no more cost than the purchase price of the land; later, if the area is built on, land can be secured with great difficulty, if at all. Both "turmoil" cost and money cost rise greatly, the longer is purchase postponed.

Both public agencies and private organizations interested in outdoor recreation must make long-range plans, and move to acquire land relatively early in relation to need. Timing is especially acute for user-oriented areas, where location is so extremely important. For intermediate-type areas, there is somewhat more latitude because location is more flexible; but, even here, early acquisition may pay rich dividends. For resource-based areas, the location factor is even more flexible, but the quality factor becomes dominant. If truly unique areas are not set aside while still available, there may be no substitute later. The intensive efforts of recent years to secure ocean, Great Lakes, and other waterfront acreage is evidence of recognition of this point.

9

Preservation of Recreation Quality

Statistics of outdoor recreation use are mostly available in terms of visits to recreation areas or of factors associated with use. The emphasis is on quantity, and there is an almost implicit assumption that the quality of the outdoor recreation remains constant. However, quality is neither constant nor unchanging. An increase in the number of visits to an area does not necessarily mean that the output of the area is increased, if output is measured in terms of total satisfaction, i.e., if it is regarded as the product of the number of visits and quality per visit. An increase in visits may be accompanied by crowding and therefore by a reduction in quality. In that case, total satisfaction might increase, but not in the same proportion as use, or it could even decline.

Quality, as applied to outdoor recreation, is hard to define and to measure; yet everyone with any experience, as consumer or as manager of a recreation area, will agree that it exists. Some outdoor recreation experiences are inspirational, or educational, or simply enjoyable, in high degree. Others are mediocre in one or more respects, and still others are inferior, some to the point of negative value or dissatisfaction. Not everyone would rate particular areas or activities in the same way, or agree on the factors that make them good or poor. Yet some consensus exists. Park managers and recreation workers have fairly well agreed-upon standards or values. The fact that large numbers of people seem to prefer some kinds of areas or systems of management to others suggests that they, too, have fairly well defined if not explicitly stated standards.

Quality is a dimension that applies to resource-based, intermediate, and user-oriented types of recreation areas. Resource-based outdoor

164

recreation areas, such as national parks, are chosen for their unusual qualities. Their superb features could be destroyed through careless use or bad management—by fire, or improper road building or other unsuitable "improvements," or through such crowding that many people could no longer enjoy the features which had led to selection of the area in the first place. But intermediate type areas can be attractive, too. The basis of selection of such areas is the best available site within the distance limitations. The natural quality of the areas available depends in part upon the region of the country, its climate, vegetation, and other environmental characteristics. Intermediate areas will reflect Man's activities to a greater degree than will resource-based areas; quality can be built, as well as found. User-oriented areas may have some innate quality, but frequently they embody Man's developmental programs to a very large extent. A well-designed small local park can have high quality—quality measured in different terms than the quality of a national park but quality nonetheless. A local rest-park can be beautiful or it can be drab; a playground can be exciting to its users, or it can be dull and uninteresting.

Some measure of public attitudes—but only some measure—may be secured from the matters which outdoor recreationists, when interviewed, complain about. When surveys are made of usage of recreation areas, it is common to ask those interviewed in what respects they considered the area deficient or in what ways it could be improved. A fairly common complaint is that the area is not adequately maintained; another complaint is lack of facilities.[1]

Perhaps a better measure of how recreationists view quality is what they do, rather than what they say. Most people probably prefer a clean campground or picnic area to one littered with papers, but there may well be great variation among individuals. In numerous instances, campers or picnickers will congregate in one part of an area when there is unused capacity and more room in other parts. Some seem to seek out people, while others try to avoid them. Observations made in the canoe area of northern Minnesota revealed quite different preferences and perceptions of quality between motor-boaters and canoeists.[2]

This matter of quality in recreation areas, activities, and experiences is

[1] Many surveys have contained information of this type. See, for example, Marvin Taves, William Hathaway, and Gordon Bultena, *Canoe Country Vacationers*, Miscellaneous Report 39, Agricultural Experiment Station, University of Minnesota, June 1960; and H. Clifton Hutchins and Edgar W. Trecker, Jr., *The State Park Visitor*, Technical Bulletin 22, Wisconsin Conservation Department, Madison, Wisconsin, 1961.

[2] Robert C. Lucas, *Recreational Use of the Quetico-Superior Area,* U.S. Forest Service Research Paper LS–8, Lake States Forest Experiment Station, St. Paul, Minnesota, 1964.

closely similar to the matter of quality in art, architecture, literature, and music. Individual tastes vary greatly, yet there is some consensus as to what is good and what is fair; and there would often be general agreement as to what is poor. For these other fields, as for outdoor recreation, some people are willing to acknowledge that what they personally prefer is not necessarily the best. In each case, considerable weight is given to popular preference, yet popularity is rejected as the sole measure of worth. As long as efforts to measure and to define quality do not take the form of condemnation of kinds not generally valued highly, or of restriction on the right to enjoy other forms, it seems highly desirable to seek such definition and to recognize superior quality.

When we come to the matter of quality in outdoor recreation, there may be a difference between the views of the expert or specialist and those of the general public. This has been found to be true in the case of foods, for example. The public has traditionally valued red apples more highly than other apples which the experts would rate of equal quality; white eggs sell for a premium over brown eggs in some markets, brown eggs for a premium over white ones in others, without relation to what the expert considers quality differences. Nevertheless, some objective standards for quality in outdoor recreation areas can be set up that would have nearly universal acceptance, at least for some activities or kinds of areas. For instance, ocean beaches, lake shores, streams, and other natural swimming areas should have certain characteristics: tides or currents should not be dangerous, sand shores and bottoms are highly preferable to mud or rocks, temperatures beyond some range will render the water unfit for use by most people, and the like. These characteristics affect the enjoyment of swimming, as well as its safety. Fishing and hunting areas require some minimum level of success to be used at all; some areas are famed for their sporting fish or trophy heads. Many sports require essentially level topography and are best carried out where good grass turf exists. Other physical attributes could be cited for other kinds of activities, that would involve a high degree of consensus as to quality. In each case, areas with high quality features will be preferred over areas of low quality, all other factors being equal.

It seems highly probable that people can be taught to appreciate quality in outdoor recreation just as they can be taught to appreciate good music, good art, good literature, as contrasted with poor. Not everyone, of course, will have the same tastes, nor will everyone acquire sensitivity to the same degree. Familiarity with the good, and explanation of why those with more experience rate it as good, can do much to build appreciation.

The designers, constructors, and managers of outdoor recreation areas have a responsibility they cannot escape, if they would. People use what they can; if good opportunities are available, they use these; but if only poor ones are available they use these too. If parks and recreation areas are well maintained, the average person will probably treat them better than if they are dirty and ill-kept. Examples may not be enough; education, to which we shall return later, and even regulation may be necessary, at least for some. In sports, the need for rules and for umpires is universally recognized. Quality must be a concern of everyone interested in outdoor recreation. Often, but not invariably, provision of good quality outdoor recreation costs more than provision of poor quality; recreation management cannot escape the necessity of deciding what levels of quality are most economic, given the nature of the area, the financial resources available, and the demands of users.

QUALITY AND INTENSITY OF USE

Few people like to be the only ones on the beach or the only family in a campground, and for some kinds of activities, notably sports, some minimum number is necessary for the activity to proceed at all. Some people are more concerned with privacy and place a higher value on solitude than do others, of course. But for everyone, no matter how gregarious, there comes a degree of intensity of use which he will agree is undesirable crowding, where his satisfactions from the area or activity decline. In fact, crowding may become so extreme that some people will consider the experience no longer worth having—they will go home in disgust, or at least not come again.

The point that coincides with crowding will not be the same for all areas and kinds of recreation use. Figure 23 illustrates how satisfaction may vary with different levels or intensities of use for wilderness, unimproved campground, and highly developed campground areas. A wilderness area is valued, by those who take advantage of the opportunities it offers, for "Nature," not for Man and his works. It is the opportunity to see and enjoy a relatively untouched and relatively primitive environment which gives such areas their greatest appeal. It might be argued that satisfaction per user here is highest at the very lowest intensity of use (but scarcely at zero use, because "no user" would mean "no satisfaction") and that it falls steadily as intensity rises. But even here, almost every user values maps, simple trails, and portage routes—all evidences of past usage of the area by someone, and almost certain to portend some degree of present use. Even the opportunity to meet an occasional fellow traveler, with similar standards and interests, may create satisfactions. But satisfaction per visitor reaches a peak at a very low intensity of use—something on the order of a relatively few visitor days per million acres of land. After that, if intensity of use continues

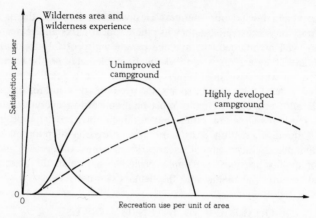

Figure 23. User satisfaction in relation to intensity of recreation area use (hypothetical example).

to rise, satisfaction per visitor falls rapidly, and reaches zero at a still relatively low intensity of use. After that, the area is no longer a wilderness, no matter what it is called or what its physical resources are. The Forest Service regards the encountering of two other parties per day as an informal standard for a tolerable level of intensity of use within wilderness areas. Whatever may be the actual limits, there would be general agreement that the tolerable intensity of use must be relatively very low if the wilderness experience is still to be maintained.[3]

The same area might be converted into an unimproved camping area—access over dirt roads only, minimum facilities in the campground, such as no flush toilet, only natural water supply, and the like. Users of such an area would value it largely for its natural conditions, for the feeling of privacy which would be available. But, even here, most users would neither expect nor want to be entirely alone. Their satisfactions would begin to rise at a higher level of use, reach a peak at a greater use intensity, and fall to zero at still greater intensities, than for the wilderness areas and the wilderness experience (the horizontal scale on Figure 23 is relative, not exact). This same area might be converted into a highly developed campground—accessible by oiled road, with flush toilets, hot water and showers, electricity in the wash room and possibly even at trailer sites, many more camp sites on the same physical area, all much closer together, etc. Now, the satisfactions per user would continue to rise to a much greater intensity of use, and probably would

[3] Robert C. Lucas, *Visitor Reaction to Timber Harvesting in the Boundary Waters Canoe Area,* U.S. Forest Service, Res. Note LS–2, Lake States Forest Experiment Station, St. Paul, Minnesota, 1963.

decline more slowly from that peak. The recreation experience under the latter circumstances would simply be different from the former—the area is identical, and each experience is camping, yet the emotional and intellectual content of the experience has changed greatly.

These same general relationships are even more marked for most kinds of sports. A minimum of two people is necessary to play tennis, yet four are the most that can be accommodated on one court at the same time. On a golf course, players can be required to join up into foursomes, and one party can be allowed to tee off after the preceding party has played its second shot, if the course is very crowded; yet this is about the limit of intensity of use. Children will play some variant of baseball with a good many less and with somewhat more than the eighteen required for two full teams, yet there are obvious lower and upper limits beyond which no game is possible. Longer hours or a longer season can intensify use of a sports area. Yet there are limits here also.

Even quiet sitting and resting in a park is subject to similar use-intensity relations. One values the privacy and the quiet, yet an opportunity to talk or merely to see a friend or congenial companion may increase satisfactions; but too many people, even if relative quiet still prevails, can diminish the satisfactions obtained by each.

"Overcrowding" of outdoor recreation areas must be viewed in light of the above considerations. It begins to occur when intensity of recreation use rises above the optimum satisfactions per user. Overcrowding is sometimes primarily psychological, rather than physical, although the latter enters also. Daniel Boone is reputed to have felt that an area was too crowded when he could see the smoke from a neighbor's cabin. In many parks today, people camp very close to one another, with tables and tents only a few feet apart. Yet there is no visible evidence that most of these campers find such crowding unsatisfactory or that their satisfactions are reduced thereby. A common wisecrack is that a campground is full when you can use the other fellow's tent pegs.

Many outdoor recreationists tolerate or seem to prefer an intensity of recreation use which others would regard as unsatisfactory or intolerable. In busy seasons and popular areas, many people will be turned away because the administrators feel that the campgrounds are "full," yet in relatively few cases will these or other people refuse to camp under such conditions because they think the areas too crowded. Recreation specialists may well have conscious or unconscious standards of use intensity which many if not most users are willing to exceed. One might take the position: if this is what people want, let them have it; why worry? But the problem is not quite so simple. People want, to a very large extent, what they know, and that in turn depends largely upon what public recreation administrators have given them. And one cannot ignore health, safety, and other problems which might arise from overcrowding.

While our knowledge of the relation between intensity of use and satisfaction per user is most incomplete, it is entirely possible that intensity of use could vary considerably without much if any loss in satisfactions, but that extremes of intensity would mean losses in satisfactions to the users at such times.

MEASURES TO IMPROVE RECREATION QUALITY

The quality of the recreation experience is affected by the design, the investment, and the management of outdoor recreation areas.[4] In this respect, outdoor recreation is similar to many other social services, and to many productive processes of a physical character. In the case of outdoor recreation there are means of improving the satisfactions or pleasures received by the average user or of maintaining them while increasing the number of users.

In Chapter 8, we pointed out that nearly all outdoor recreation is subject to extreme peaks of use at certain times and to a very low level of use at other times. One consequence of this extreme peaking of demand is that natural resources, capital investment, and, to a large extent, management and other personnel are most inefficiently utilized. The result is a high average cost per unit of output, however the latter be measured. If the costs of meeting the peak demand were charged to those comparatively few users who create the peak, then the cost per unit of this peak use would be very high indeed.

Development of use at off-peak times is one of the most promising means of maintaining recreation quality and at the same time increasing output. Some areas have developed winter sports in districts previously chiefly noted as summer resorts. Florida has used off-season rates to

[4] Standards of design and construction in outdoor recreation areas, notably in national parks, have been the subject of lively, not to say acrimonious, discussion in recent years. A serious professional description and defense of existing practice is found in Conrad Wirth, "The Landscape Architect in National Park Work—His Projects, Opportunities, Problems, and Obligations," *Landscape Architecture* (October 1955). Critical discussions appear in Devereaux Butcher, "Resorts or Wilderness?", *The Atlantic Monthly* (February 1961); and in Charles Stevenson, "Shocking Truth about National Parks," *Reader's Digest* (January 1955). A defense of current National Park Service practice and objectives appears in a long letter to the Secretary of the Interior from the Director of the National Park Service, and a reply from the Secretary, each attached to a Department of the Interior Press Release of April 2, 1961, "Secretary Udall Approves Basic Wilderness Preservation Policies of National Park Service." Other critical discussions of national park programs of this kind have appeared in recent years in publications of the Sierra Club. The same general issue has arisen for national forests, state parks, and other public recreation areas.

attract tourists in summer as well as in winter. A few private operators have developed businesses catering to summer vacationists in one area and to winter vacationists—possibly the same individuals—in another area. By and large, most of this type of effort has come from the private side of the outdoor recreation business. Public agencies have done much less. For one thing, they have sometimes not been averse to quiet periods when both the camping area and the staff might recuperate from the crowds. But there are still times when use could be increased. Differential charges, with perhaps relatively high entrance fees at naturally popular times and much lower ones, perhaps none, at other times, could do a lot to spread demand into other time periods.

This matter of peaking of recreation demand is also closely related to the timing of the available leisure. Peaking could be reduced by changes in vacation times. Many families take their vacations in the summer, when children are out of school. Some adjustments might be made at school to permit family vacations at other seasons. An increasing proportion of workers, now that life expectancy has increased, will not have children of school age. If such people could be induced to take their vacations in other seasons, they could often be well accommodated in outdoor recreation areas that are overcrowded in the summer. It would not be necessary to go so far as to shift vacation from summer to winter; and extension of the summer vacation season a month earlier and a month later would exert a marked effect. Perhaps additional vacation days could be extended to those workers not going at the peak season; to a business which must keep operating in the summer, this would have advantages. The use of outdoor recreation areas by retired people could also be off-season to a larger extent. Many summer vacation areas are very attractive in the fall and spring, for instance.[5] Schools could be used during off-seasons for education on outdoor recreation.

Another, and perhaps more direct, attack on peaking is to discourage or restrain use at the peak season or time. The use of charges for this purpose has been mentioned. Another device might be to require advance registration. One might be allowed in a particular national park in summer only on the day he had reserved long in advance, and only as many persons might be admitted as the park would accommodate satisfactorily, for instance. A somewhat similar, but different, basis of allocation of limited recreation facilities is to require people to line up and wait for their turn. This can be very wasteful of limited leisure time, and on the whole seems less desirable than a system of reserva-

[5] There apparently has been some trend toward greater use of off-peak vacations. *Redbook Magazine* has made travel surveys in various years, and reports that the following proportions of its respondents took off-season vacations: 10 per cent in 1947, 44 per cent in 1957, and 54 per cent in 1958.

tions—it should be no simpler for the administrative agency to operate than reservations, for instance.

A combination of effective restraints on use at peak times and of inducements to use at off-peak times might, over a period of time, considerably modify the pattern of use of some outdoor recreation areas. To the extent that this was accomplished, more people could be taken care of on the same area and by the same facilities, without reduction in the quality of the recreation experience and possibly at higher levels of satisfaction per visit, and probably at lower average cost per visit.

Another major problem in maintenance of quality in outdoor recreation is the tendency of people to crowd into the popular areas. Every park or recreation manager has had direct experience with severe crowding of well-known, popular spots, and sometimes with very light usage of relatively nearby areas that to him seemed equally attractive or nearly so. Why do people crowd up in certain areas? Sometimes, of course, the main attraction of their visit is highly localized: Old Faithful geyser, some historic spot, a swimming beach, or a particular kind of playground equipment.[6] But also, as we noted above, there are people who *want* crowding, at least up to some point.

With due consideration for such factors, it still seems possible that recreation usage could be spread more evenly than it now is in some areas without lowering the quality of the average visit. Actually, the quality of the visit might even be improved, and at the same time the number of visits to the area might be increased. Again, as in the manipulation of the timing of demand, it may be necessary to promote the use of lightly used areas and to develop some restrictions on the use of the more popular areas.

There is another problem—one of misuse—which is not easily expressed without danger of misunderstanding. Many people who visit or use certain types of outdoor recreation areas do not fully appreciate what they see or do; for them, the qualities of the area or of the experience are largely wasted. Some people regard the finest national parks as simply a pleasant bit of outdoors, not significantly different from any other piece of woods and water; or they regard the tennis court as a good place to roller skate or the golf course as a good place to go bicycling; or they are willing to play ball in a quiet rest-park, with consequent adverse effect upon the flower beds; or, in countless other ways, people use recreation resources in ways that do not take full advantage of their best qualities or for purposes that could be served

[6] In the letter from the Director of the National Park Service to the Secretary of the Interior cited in note 4, above, the statement is made: "In most parks, about 99 per cent of park travel is accommodated on from 1 to 5 per cent of the total lands within their boundaries."

by some less unusual lot of resources. Through education, discussed later, many people can be taught to appreciate the unusual values of any outdoor recreation resource.

It may be necessary to make some minimum level of knowledge or skill a requirement for admittance to certain types of outdoor recreation areas. There is already a good deal of this type of selection practiced. Inexperienced persons are not now allowed to attempt difficult mountain climbing in national parks; some public golf courses are open at peak periods only to golfers who have been able to achieve a particular level of scoring; tennis courts are open only to adults at peak periods; inexperienced persons are discouraged from canoeing on certain streams and not allowed on others; and so on. Most of the restrictions now in force are designed to protect the users themselves, but some are for the convenience of others. Might the requirement for use be a knowledge of the area and of its characteristics instead of proficiency in a particular activity? Might some sort of "literacy test" be applied to would-be users of outdoor recreation areas where there is limited capacity and excessive demand?

This type of restriction could best be applied to scientific or historical areas that have strictly limited capacity and that cannot be duplicated. If the demand for such areas should exceed their capacity, then someone would be forced to forego the experience. Should this be a person to whom the experience was a casual one, or should it be a person to whom it was a major and significant experience? How would one compare the satisfactions of another visit by one who knows and loves the area with those obtained from the first visit by one who was deeply impressed though perhaps not so well informed? Would rationing on the basis of knowledge and interest be fairer than rationing on the basis of financial ability to pay higher entrance fees? These are obviously difficult and slippery questions; but they cannot be avoided today, and even less in the future, in many areas and for many types of outdoor recreation experience. Arguing that such questions are unanswerable is scant help to the recreation administrator who is forced to ration limited recreation opportunities among too many would-be users.

We hasten to add that any program for limiting access to important areas to those persons with some knowledge and appreciation of the unique character of such areas—however unavoidable it might be— would be acceptable only if accompanied by educational and other programs which would make it possible for people to acquire the necessary level of knowledge to use areas in which they had a deep interest.

If the demand for resource-based outdoor recreation areas mounts over the next generation to anything like the degree we indicated in Chapter 7, many areas may have to be restricted. Modest entrance fees will have some effect, but these may have to be supplemented by some form of rationing based upon knowledge and interest.

ROLE OF EDUCATION

As suggested above, it should be possible to teach average people to appreciate quality in outdoor recreation experience, and to gain greater satisfaction with less wear and tear on the environment. Every park or recreation area manager knows of destructive acts that do not seem to provide unusual satisfactions to their perpetrators.[7] Elimination of the more destructive forms of use would be a major gain. To the extent that people can be taught to behave so that more people can use the same area without loss in quality, the result is the same as if the area had been enlarged.[8]

The major problem with education in this regard is, who should do it? One hesitates to suggest the schools, for most of them are overloaded now, and many people would regard the subject as inappropriate for the public schools. Yet the young people are likely to be the ones most willing to learn. A great deal has been done in the past decade or so in the campaign against litterbugging; people have been taught not to throw paper and other waste materials along the highways and in parks. The Advertising Council of America has put on education campaigns, especially in bus advertisements and over radio and television, to make people conscious of the evils of litterbugging. True, their preachments against litterbugging along highways, and to a limited extent in parks, have been backed up by laws and penalties and by vigorous enforcement. Progress has also been made in teaching campers, picnickers, and others how to handle campfires. Smokey Bear has become a part of American folklore; some may scorn this approach, yet it seems to have been highly effective.

Perhaps some means could be devised whereby recreation area administrators, school people, officials of boys' and girls' clubs such as Boy and Girl Scouts, parents organizations, and others could devise

[7] Some damage or destruction of outdoor recreation areas or their properties is inevitable if use is heavy. For instance, mere walking or trampling will reduce or eliminate grass cover, and often lead to erosion. Unavoidable damage is serious enough, but wanton damage or destruction is far worse, largely because it is difficult to believe that it really adds significantly to the enjoyment of those who practice it. For an interesting discussion of this problem in national parks, see Richard J. Hartesveldt, "Can We Save The Parks for The People?", *Westways* (April 1960).

[8] For an interesting discussion of this problem as applied to wildlife, see J. V. K. Wagar, "Can Weak-kneed Public Education Retain Rare Wildlife Values?", *Transactions of the Twenty-Third North American Wildlife Conference*, Wildlife Management Institute, Washington, 1958.

more comprehensive and inclusive programs of recreation manners and constructive outdoor enjoyment than they now have. Various kinds of user groups have undertaken instruction of novices to a limited extent, and perhaps much more could be done. A canoe association might undertake to teach beginners more about canoeing, or a sportsman's group could teach novice hunters, or a fisherman's group could teach fly-tieing and fly-casting, etc. This type of educational work would be interesting and satisfying to many active participants in such fields; it would often help to arouse public interest in their type of outdoor activity. While this might lead to excessive use of available facilities, it might also help to build public support for various kinds of public programs.

Improvement of attitudes of some park and recreation personnel toward users might also be possible. While most people in the outdoor recreation field probably like to work with people, some unfortunately regard the recreation user as a nuisance, much as some librarians regard book-borrowers as nuisances. Some recreation users, unfortunately, must be restrained from anti-social or destructive acts; but the co-operation and help of most people can be enlisted, when they can see the purpose of the action for which their co-operation is sought.

POTENTIALITIES OF DESIGN

Design of park and other outdoor recreation areas is an extremely important matter. Good design can increase the satisfactions that most users obtain from an outdoor recreation area. It can also increase the recreation capacity of an area without loss in the quality of the recreation experience. Internal traffic through the whole recreation area can be reduced, thus minimizing wear and tear on the environment and reducing the points of friction between users. Vegetation can be used to screen the activities of one group from those of other groups, thus adding to a feeling of distance and privacy and, in effect, substituting design for area. Good design can reduce the psychological aspects of crowding by creating a feeling of spaciousness. Design offers great opportunities, but it cannot work miracles; no amount of design can overcome a basically inadequate area.

Good design of parks and other outdoor recreation areas can also affect the attitudes and actions of their users, and thus reduce the maintenance and management problems. Again, design cannot work miracles; some users will commit careless, damaging, or unsocial acts no matter what the design, but the average user will respond to a well-designed outdoor recreation area. Good design must be matched by good management and good maintenance, in order to be most effective in this direction. There is little to be gained by designing and building a good playground or campground, and then not maintaining it properly. Personal observations suggest that a great many outdoor recreation areas are not maintained as well as they have been designed and built.

ESTABLISHMENT AND MAINTENANCE OF USE CEILINGS

No matter how well an outdoor recreation area is planned and managed, and no matter how well people behave, there is nonetheless some limit beyond which recreation use of a given area cannot be increased without direct loss of recreation quality. Once loss of quality begins, further deterioration often follows swiftly and severely. It seems almost inescapable that popular areas must have use ceilings established and enforced.

In many other types of natural resource use, the concept of maximum allowable use has long since been accepted. If too many livestock graze on an area, they consume nearly all the growth of palatable material, the plants are weakened, and in time the productive capacity of the area is lessened. If an attempt is made to harvest too much timber from an area, the volume of growing stock is reduced, and in time the productive capacity of the forest is lowered. In both grazing and forestry, various intensive practices are possible, which increase output from a given area and hence raise the maximum allowable annual harvest; yet in each case there is some limit, depending upon soil, climate, and other factors, beyond which annual output cannot be increased and below which annual harvest must be kept if productivity is to be maintained.

We see no reason to think that recreation use differs from grazing and timber harvest in this respect. Some amount of recreation is often possible with no improvements or with very simple ones; recreation output can often be increased without serious sacrifice of quality by more investment and by more intensive management. But, as in the case of grazing and forestry, there is some limit beyond which use cannot increase without serious deterioration in quality of the recreation experience—and frequently, serious physical deterioration of the area as well.

Unless the trend toward heavier and heavier use of some areas can be modified, and even in some cases the present degree of intensity of use reduced, then many present recreation areas will suffer severe physical deterioration. In a great many popular areas, trees and shrubs cannot reproduce while use continues at the present intensive level. Soil erosion is advanced in some highly popular spots. "Sore spots" exist in national parks, national forests, state parks, and elsewhere, wherever use has been excessive.

Some park administrators and users have been exploiting virgin mature forest stands and associated ecology as completely as have forest industries which cut timber without thought of regeneration or as have ranchers who seriously overgrazed their land. Park users and nature lovers have regarded themselves, and have generally been accepted uncritically, as conservationists, even though their actions were seriously downgrading the areas in which they were most interested. "Recreation conservation" may be as necessary as soil conservation, sustained yield forestry, or good range management.

Under some circumstances, recreation use of areas could be rotated over a period of years, much as timber harvest or grazing is now rotated for these uses. Thus, a campground could be developed, used rather intensively for some years, and then closed, to be replaced by another in a generally similar location. This would be economically more feasible if improvements were not too costly, or if they could be rather fully worn out during the period of use of the campground; and, of course, this assumes that satisfactory additional areas exist, to which use could be shifted. This type of rotation might be synchronized with timber management and harvest, at least under some circumstances; the area could be used for recreation during the growing period for immature timber, but taken out of recreation use during the timber harvest and early reproduction parts of the cycle. The costs and benefits of permitting relatively heavy recreation use of an area and then shifting use elsewhere during the cycle would have to be weighed against the costs and benefits of much lighter but continuous use throughout. Recreation rotation would not be practical for intensively developed user-oriented areas, nor would recreationists probably be willing to forego use of the most valuable resource-based areas during any part of a cycle. Management of recreation areas, to conserve not only the physical resources but also the quality of the experience, will become more important and more difficult in the future, as total recreation use increases.

The most serious problems arise over *how* recreation use may be limited in some areas, not over *whether* it should be limited. Steadily mounting demand may bump so hard against limited capacity as to make the answer to the latter question inescapable. As a matter of general social policy, we suggest the co-ordinated use of three general approaches, in the following order of priority.[9]

[9] These are the same ideas, and the same order of priorities, as expressed by Marion Clawson in "Our National Parks in the Year 2000," *National Parks Magazine,* July 1959.

1. Provision of other areas, of the same quality if possible, or of lower quality if unavoidable, so that people excluded from one area will have other places to go. In fact, if places can be provided that are more convenient, even if somewhat lower in quality, many people may choose them. This has special significance in the problem of protecting the national parks against overuse.[10] If intermediate recreation areas, perhaps state parks, can be supplied in sufficient number and extent, many people will choose them for their greater convenience of location; for such people, location advantage will more than offset differences in quality. If this takes place on a large enough scale, the overuse problem of the higher quality areas is thereby reduced. But even if the shift in use is less than this, it is easier to refuse people access to one area when there are plenty of other areas available.

2. Employ more positive inducements to shift use. Entrance fees, especially differential fees, can be a major inducement to shift use from one time period to another, and from one area to another. Not everyone will shift, of course; but that is unnecessary. But perhaps enough shifts in use will occur to cure the overuse of favored spots and times.

3. As a last resort, establish absolute restrictions on entry, using one or more of the devices discussed earlier in this chapter.

Until the present, the American people have not really had to face the problem of how best to ration scarce recreation resources, but we shall probably have to deal with this problem more and more in the future.

SPECIAL PROBLEMS OF QUALITY IN PRIVATE OUTDOOR RECREATION

Many of the points discussed above apply to privately owned areas as well as to public outdoor recreation areas. In addition, there are some special considerations for private areas. Here we briefly consider two of the several kinds of situation that exist for private recreation areas: (1) where the enterprise is operated for a profit, by provision of recreation opportunity to the public; and (2) where a nonprofit organization undertakes to supply recreation to its own members.

Private enterprises which provide outdoor recreation to members of the public on a price or payment basis, in the expectation of a profit, are under constant pressure to increase the intensity of recreation use of their area. Such businesses often have relatively high fixed costs; a little more use may mean a much higher net income, in the short run.

[10] As long ago as 1946, Harold L. Ickes stated the case for ample local recreation areas as a protection against overuse of national parks, in his usual outspoken way, in "Space for Play," *Holiday* (May 1946).

But a "little more" use may well mean a long-run deterioration of the area, physically or in terms of satisfactions per unit of use or both. Quality in private outdoor recreation areas is often a fragile commodity; it depends in large part upon how people regard the area. Among a great many people, there is a bias against private campgrounds, for instance, because some such areas are badly overcrowded and poorly maintained. People seem to regard the chances of an acceptable quality to be better on public areas. Some resort areas have acquired a reputation for high quality, others just the opposite. Some associations set a high standard for their members, and this may be a significant feature of these enterprises.

The nonprofit organization maintaining a summer camp or other outdoor recreation opportunity for its own members faces some of the same considerations. It, too, is likely to have relatively high fixed costs, and be constantly tempted to take in more members or otherwise to use its area more intensively. But the long-run result may be a deterioration in the quality of the recreation experience, and a consequent decreased willingness to share in costs or, at the extreme, a withdrawal from membership.

In each case, the situation is somewhat like that of a farmer considering soil conservation practices. Adoption of these latter may mean reduced income in the immediate future, or increased expenses, or possibly both; but neglect is likely to mean long-run losses in productive capacity of the land. Present and future costs and benefits must be balanced, as well as advantages and disadvantages of intensive as compared with extensive use of the resources. In the case of private outdoor recreation, the problem is made more difficult by the fact that losses in quality may be small and gradual, yet cumulative over periods of years until they can be overwhelming and nearly irreversible.

Another problem which faces private areas is the hasty onset of obsolescence. A physically attractive area, with forest and water, may retain its usefulness even under changing conditions, since use can be shifted from one activity to another. But facilities may become obsolete before their investment can be repaid. A motel may be only a couple of years old and still be considerably downgraded in value if a newer motel is built in the immediate vicinity. Motels in this country started out as very plain, often family-operated affairs; today, most motels are comparable to hotels in class of service and are operated by large business concerns. Will the same thing happen to the small private campgrounds and other outdoor recreation facilities now being constructed? In this connection, it should be noted that an outmoded outdoor recreation facility has little value, although the area may be usable for other purposes.

179

SPECIAL PROBLEMS OF WILDERNESS AREAS

The special problems of wilderness areas have been much in the forefront of discussion about outdoor recreation in recent years.[11] Our concern at this point is how to preserve the quality of the wilderness recreation experience. Fortunately, there is coming to be some objective research on wilderness use and on attitudes of wilderness users, to supplement some of the more emotional discussion about such areas.[12] Among those who support the idea of the wilderness areas are many who have never been there and perhaps many who never expect or wish to go there. The idea of a wilderness, "unspoiled" by man, has great emotional appeal to many. Some people seem to regard any patch of dense woods as a wilderness. But there are surely many thousands, if not millions, of people who understand what a wilderness is, and what there is about it they wish to preserve.

The essential character of a wilderness, as contrasted with any piece of attractive outdoors, seems to be the feeling of being alone, or at most with a few chosen companions, in largely untouched natural surroundings. One may tolerate a few other users of his wilderness, but not many; when use exceeds some undefined yet subjectively significant point, the wilderness disappears. Optimum satisfaction per user is achieved at a very low intensity of use; thereafter, satisfaction per user falls rapidly as intensity rises.

The chief wilderness areas involving uncut timber in the United States today are in national forests, national parks, Indian reservations, and other public ownership. Their extent depends in part upon the definition of wilderness area. Some wilderness areas have commercial timber, or mineral prospects, or other exploitable products. But many wilderness areas do not have such products, at least under the demand and supply and transportation conditions of today. One reason why some of them still exist is because there has been little or no effective demand for their products in the past. Some may well be threatened now by commercial exploitation, and others may be threatened in the

---

[11] For a fairly complete statement of contrasting and conflicting views about wilderness areas, see *Hearings Before the Committee on Interior and Insular Affairs,* United States Senate, 86th Congress, First Session, on S. 1123, March 30 and 31, 1959 and April 2, 1959. Also later hearings on the same and similar legislation. See also ORRRC Study Report 3, *Wilderness and Recreation—A Report on Resources, Values, and Problems,* prepared by The Wildland Research Center, University of California. The passage of the Wilderness Act in 1964 represents a conclusion as to values of wilderness area.

[12] Lucas, *op. cit.,* and references cited therein. Also, J. Allan Wagar, "The Carrying Capacity of Wild Lands for Recreation," Forest Science Monograph 7 (Washington: Society of American Foresters, 1964).

future. But a constant threat, now and in the future, is overuse by recreationists; and "overuse" begins at a very low level of use.

Previously logged, grazed, mined, or farmed areas may acquire many characteristics of "wilderness" after extended periods of nonuse. Sometimes something approaching the original ecosystem may be restored; more frequently, the new "wilderness" differs significantly from the original one, at least in the eyes of one who is fully informed. But many people would not know the difference, if use today is essentially at wilderness levels. Extensive areas in New York and New England, once cut or even farmed, today are accepted as "wilderness" by most people.

The quality of the recreation experience must be maintained, or the wilderness will be destroyed as surely as if it were logged. Too many people in a wilderness area means it is no longer a wilderness. Topography and other natural conditions often conspire to concentrate such use as does occur, so that there is likely to be serious overuse of some areas and no use at all of much larger areas. In some way, wilderness areas must be managed for recreation as well as against fire and commercial exploitation, if they are to be preserved. The only real question is how. Since, by definition, wilderness areas cannot be reproduced at will, it appears that more direct measures than provision of substitute areas will be needed. All of the troublesome questions raised earlier about restricting recreation use to capacity arise in heightened fashion for wilderness areas.

One of the most troublesome questions about wilderness areas is: how does one measure the value of a wilderness area, in contrast with the value of the same area if used for other purposes? In other chapters, we present some means whereby the monetary value of outdoor recreation might be measured. The only sensible measures depend upon the extent of the use of the area. In wilderness areas, where use may have to be severely restricted to prevent destruction of the wilderness itself, direct economic values based on use may also be held down. In this case, values to nonusers of the area seem to loom large, and we would judge legitimately so. The alternative use value of the wilderness area (which may, in fact, be low or high) represents a cost to society of reserving the area as wilderness. The choice might be to retain some area as wilderness, even though its direct economic value would be higher in other uses. The justification for wilderness areas does not rest primarily on maximization of direct economic values to users, but on benefits to nonusers and preservation of a certain type of value or experience. Moreover, a public decision to preserve wilderness areas can always be reversed by permitting their exploitation for commercial use, whereas a decision to use them for other purposes is likely to be irreversible.

10

Existing Areas and Their Use

The purpose of this chapter is to bring together some of the relevant facts on the different areas presently available for outdoor recreation.[1] Outdoor recreation areas are as diverse as the activities they encompass. They differ in size, type, and location; serve numerous purposes; are used with highly variable intensities; and are administered by a large number of different public and private agencies. At the federal level alone there are more than twenty agencies with programs that include some aspect of outdoor recreation. A similar multiplicity of agency programs is found at the state level throughout the country.[2] And the situation is much the same for county and city governments.

There are approximately 2.3 billion acres of land and water in the United States as a whole, including Alaska, which has 375 million

---

[1] In addition to the general references cited in the Foreword and at the beginning of Chapter 3 and to the specific references at various points, the interested reader is referred to: Freeman Tilden, *The National Parks: What They Mean to You and Me* (1951) and *The State Parks: Their Meaning in American Life* (1962), both from Alfred A. Knopf, New York; Devereux Butcher, *Exploring Our National Wildlife Refuges* (Boston: Houghton Mifflin, 1963); John Ise, *Our National Park Policy: A Critical History* (Baltimore: The Johns Hopkins Press, for Resources for the Future, Inc., 1961); reports of the Outdoor Recreation Resources Review Commission including *Outdoor Recreation for America, A Report to the President and to the Congress* (Washington: U.S. Government Printing Office, 1962) and the individual Study Reports; National Park Service, *Parks for America—A Survey of Park and Related Resources in the Fifty States, and a Preliminary Plan* (Washington: U.S. Government Printing Office, 1964); and Marion Clawson, *Statistics on Outdoor Recreation* (Washington: Resources for the Future, Inc., 1958).

[2] *Outdoor Recreation for America, A Report to the President and to the Congress, op. cit.*

acres. In 1960, according to the ORRRC report, about one eighth of the nation's total land and water area was included in nonurban, publicly owned land and water management projects upon which some form of outdoor recreation is a specifically recognized use. These include federal, state, and county or other local nonurban parks, forests, wildlife refuges, recreation areas, reservoirs, lakes, and highway wayside areas.[3] The ORRRC figures do not include the considerable acreage in urban recreation use, or the large, ill-defined acreage of private recreation areas.

The wide diversity of size of public recreation areas is indicated by the fact that over two-thirds of all of the public nonurban recreation areas were under 40 acres in size, but altogether these small areas contain less than one-tenth of 1 per cent of the total recreation acreage in the country.[4] In contrast, slightly over 1 per cent of the areas were greater than 100,000 acres, but together these totaled 88 per cent of the total area.

Although the administration of recreation areas falls under a multiplicity of different agencies and organizations, it is useful to group the different kinds and types of areas by the level of government administrating them—federal, state, and local. To some extent, a grouping according to level of government administration is also a grouping according to kind of recreation area. Federal areas are largely resource based, though some are intermediate; state areas are largely intermediate, but some are resource based, and a few are close to being user oriented; city and other local government areas are primarily user oriented. The federal government, encompassing a number of different land and water agencies, administers 84 per cent of the total acreage of all types of nonurban public recreation areas.[5] Approximately 14 per cent of the total acreage is administered by state agencies, and the rest is administered by county and other local agencies, which are involved more with urban recreation.

Any discussion of the use of outdoor recreation facilities must recognize the clear limitations in the available data. The various reports of the ORRRC have added immeasurably to our knowledge of recreation facilities and their use. However, serious gaps remain. Owing to the work of the Commission, the information on publicly administered areas is in relatively good condition. Although considerable information on numbers of areas and acreage of privately available recreation facilities has been compiled, much less is known on their use. Studies currently

[3] ORRRC Study Report No. 2, *List of Public Outdoor Recreation Areas 1960*, p. 1.

[4] *Outdoor Recreation for America, op. cit.* See also ORRRC Study Report No. 1, *Public Outdoor Recreation Areas—Acreage, Use, Potential.*

[5] *Outdoor Recreation for America, op. cit.*, p. 51.

under way by the Bureau of Outdoor Recreation should provide still better data on numbers and acreage of public and private areas, both existing and potential.

Use data on all facilities tend to be far less than adequate. The multiplicity of different kinds of recreation areas and activities and the multiplicity of agencies have added to this problem. Traditionally, there has been little demand for statistics on outdoor recreation, and even less for any meaningful economic analysis, in connection with planning decisions. The data collected in the past have been, in practice, a compromise between those that were desirable and those that were comparatively easy administratively to collect, with perhaps more weight given to ease than to usefulness. The administrative needs of the agencies involved have also been given major emphasis. The individual agencies may have regarded the results as satisfactory, but the data as a whole are hard to analyze meaningfully. It may be a relatively simple matter to collect data on number of visits at areas where there is an entrance gate, but for the most part the data are collected in a much more informal manner and are often suspected of being highly inaccurate. Some caution should therefore be exercised in interpreting the existing statistics. The general picture of outdoor recreation in this country can be determined from existing information, but the gaps in our knowledge loom increasingly large as the individual problems become more particularized.

AREAS ADMINISTERED BY THE FEDERAL GOVERNMENT

The federal government today owns one-third of our national area when Alaska is included or a fifth if Alaska is excluded. At one time or another, the federal government has owned more than two-thirds of the nation's land. The major part of this land was sold, given away, or granted to individuals, states, railroad companies, and others.[6]

A movement developed, particularly during the last quarter of the nineteenth century, to keep part of these federal lands permanently in public ownership. The first major reservation was that of Yellowstone National Park in 1872; the first major system of permanent federal landownership was that of federal forest reserves, now called national forests, which began in 1891. These were expanded to almost their present extent by 1910 (Figure 24). National parks have been added periodically ever since the first one. Federal wildlife refuges have been

---

[6] For a brief historical account but relatively full statistical information, see Marion Clawson and Burnell Held, *The Federal Lands: Their Use and Management* (Baltimore: The Johns Hopkins Press, for Resources for the Future, Inc., 1957). See also references cited therein.

established to protect wildlife and migratory waterfowl, and the grazing districts have been organized since 1934 to bring the remaining federal lands into definite management units. Recreation of the types most common at intermediate and user-oriented areas is not the primary purpose, or indeed any purpose, of these federal lands. Preservation of outstanding natural, scenic, and historic areas for use by present and future generations is the purpose of the national park system. For the national forests and many other management units, recreation is one major

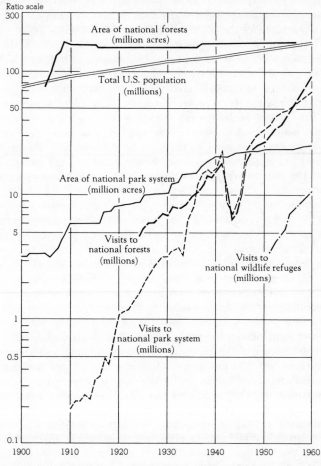

Figure 24. Growth in visits to the national parks system, national forests, and national wildlife refuges, compared with growth in acreage and in national population, 1900–1960.

purpose in a program of multiple-use management. When first established, many of these areas of federal land and water were comparatively isolated from population centers and were difficult and relatively expensive to visit. Moreover, these were decades when all forms of outdoor recreation were severely limited by income, leisure, travel, and other considerations. With the passing years, however, the various kinds of federal land have become increasingly popular for outdoor recreation purposes.

The best known and most distinctive types of outdoor recreation areas are the units of the national park system, administered by the U.S. Department of the Interior's National Park Service. Today, there are 32 national parks with a total area of 13.6 million acres. In addition to a large number of other units included in the national park system, such as national battlefields and monuments, there are national lakeshores and seashores, and other national recreation areas.

The fundamental purpose for which the national park system was established as set out by the act of 1916 was "to conserve the scenery and the natural and historic objects and the wildlife therein, and to provide for the enjoyment of the same in such manner and by such means as will leave them unimpaired for the enjoyment of future generations." The National Park Service has attempted to adhere to this policy over the years but has experienced increasing difficulty as the use pressure has mounted in recent years. The national recreation areas are subject to fewer restrictions than the parks, and grazing, mining, hunting, and occupancy of summer homes, for example, may be permitted under certain circumstances.

The trend in the use of the national park system is strongly upward. By 1963, the monuments attracted over 11 million people, national parks over 33 million people; and other areas administered by the National Park Service, a total of over 49 million.

A second group of national areas important for recreation are the national forests administered by the U.S. Forest Service. These areas are administered for multiple purposes; recreation, though only one use, is an increasingly important one. Additionally they are important sources of timber, forage, and water.

The lands of the national forests are in part physically similar to the national park lands; and, like national parks, the forests are heavily concentrated in areas far removed from large population centers. Of the approximately 160 million acres of national forest land within the 48 states about 85 per cent is in the eleven western states; the remaining acreage is chiefly in the Lake States and across the South with only a minimum acreage in the central part of the country and in the Northeast.

After the passage of the Forest Reserve Act of 1891, the area in-

186

creased rather slowly to reach 40 million acres in 1900. Between 1900 and 1910 the rate of growth was very rapid, the additions coming entirely from the public domain. In 1911 the Weeks Act provided for the federal purchase of lands for inclusion in national forests, but additions were comparatively small until 1933. In the ten following years relatively larger purchases plus some small withdrawals of public domain brought the total area to about 180 million acres. Since then, there has been little change.

The official policy of the Forest Service is, and has been for some time, to encourage recreational use of national forests. In one sense the total area of the forests is available and is used for recreation. Some hunting, fishing, and general enjoyment of the forest environment takes place through a very wide area. However, as part of its program of encouragement of recreation use, the Forest Service has developed some specialized recreation areas. On these it installs and administers public use facilities necessary to meet public needs, but for the most part strives to keep them simple and appropriate to the environment.

One special type of recreation area in the national forests is the wilderness area. Included under this general term are areas more exactly known as primitive, wilderness, wild, and roadless. The acreage of all the broadly termed wilderness areas reached 14 million acres by 1937 and has since remained roughly constant, although changes and designations of specific areas have taken place.

The number of visits to the national forests for recreation purposes increased from approximately 5 million in 1925 to 16 million in 1940 to 27 million in 1950, 92 million in 1960, 147 million in 1965. The almost phenomenal postwar increase in visits has created problems of use pressure on many of the facilities in the national forests. Recreation and other facilities were constructed during the 1930's as part of the public works programs of that period; in many cases, capacity was constructed to meet future demand. After that, there was, in general, far less of an increase in facilities until about 1960. Since then, there has been a major increase in capacity.

The national wildlife refuges are another federal resource available for recreation. The primary purpose of these refuges is to provide a suitable habitat for various species of wildlife, including waterfowl. However, they also provide a large and important kind of recreation. Many of the areas have qualities that would make them desirable solely for recreation, and the presence of the wildlife adds greatly to their attractiveness. Some areas permit hunting, many permit fishing, and camping is possible at several, in addition to wildlife viewing. The first wildlife refuges were established in 1903. The area in all such refuges was small for many years, being under one million acres as late as 1932.

A very rapid increase then occurred which brought the area in refuges in the 48 states to 9 million acres by 1939. Since then there have been only minor changes in total area. When Alaska and Hawaii are included, total acreage is nearly 29 million acres.

Wildlife refuges are distributed over the United States somewhat more widely than either national parks or national forests, 42 of the states having some refuge lands within their borders. But in terms of area they, too, tend to be concentrated in the West and in Alaska, chiefly because these are the regions in which large-game refuges are located. However, migratory waterfowl raised or wintered on one refuge may provide scenic enjoyment or hunting at many other areas along the flyways.

The recreational use of national wildlife refuges has increased rapidly. In 1960 recreationists made over 10.7 million visits to these areas, more than double that number in 1954, and, by 1964, use was up to 14 million visits. This recreational use in 1956 was classified as follows: 6 per cent for the purpose of hunting; 37 per cent for fishing; and 57 per cent for other purposes including picnicking, swimming, and wildlife observation. The refuges are by and large inadequately equipped with either facilities or personnel to accommodate the large and rapidly increasing number of visitors.

The grazing districts, O&C lands, and other public land under the administration of the Bureau of Land Management have not had large-scale recreation use in the past, but they may become more important for recreation in the future. The Multiple Use Act of 1964 and the creation of the Public Land Law Review Commission almost surely presage programs to make these lands more generally available to outdoor recreation use.

Federal water areas also have an important bearing on the resources available for recreation in the nation (Figure 25). By and large the federal water areas available for recreation are of the intermediate type; their use is predominantly on a daylong basis. The most important of the federal agencies, from the standpoint of facilities and resources available for recreation, is the Corps of Engineers of the U.S. Department of the Army. This agency, which is the nation's largest and oldest public construction agency, is responsible for the federal program for the improvement and maintenance of rivers and other waterways in the interests of navigation and flood control. Responsibility for flood control was definitely assigned to the Corps and spelled out in the Flood Control Act of 1936. Subsequent flood control acts generally broadened the interest of the Corps to include power, recreation, fish and wildlife conservation, domestic water supply, and pollution abatement. Later authorization extended the interests of the Corps to include beach and

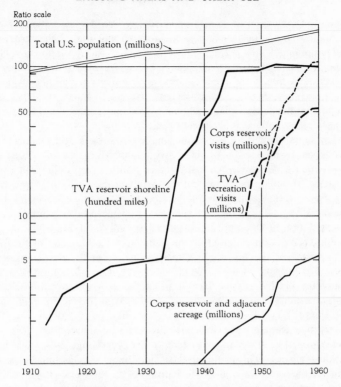

Figure 25. Area or shoreline of reservoirs built by Corps of Engineers and TVA, and visits to such reservoirs, in relation to total population, 1910–60.

shoreline erosion control. The objective of the multiple-use management is to maximize the benefits of the water resource. The Corps of Engineers normally provides basic facilities for recreationists on most of its projects, and state and local agencies and commercial enterprises provide additional facilities on and near some of these water projects.

Total attendance at Corps reservoir projects has mounted rapidly in recent years. Visits to Corps projects rose from about 5 million in 1946 to 70 million in 1956, and 156 million in 1964.

Another federal agency having important resources available for recreation purposes is the Tennessee Valley Authority. TVA was created in 1933 as a regional resource development agency; it controls approximately 30 dams which are planned, constructed, and operated for multiple purposes. The primary goals of the reservoir control system are flood control, navigation, and electric power production. TVA, while not having any direct responsibility for administration of the recreation sites, does encourage the recreational use of the reservoirs and adjoining land. The region is well suited for recreation activities from the standpoint of geography, scenery, climate, and proximity to population centers, and the recreation potential was seriously considered by the agency in its planning activity. Access to all of the lakes was insured by the project plans, and suitable sites were set apart for parks, boat harbors, bathing beaches, and camps.

The lakes created by the TVA dams cover some half a million acres and have a shoreline totaling well over 10,000 miles. Visits to the TVA reservoirs for recreation purposes totaled a little over 7 million in 1947, grew to 30 million in 1956, and to 48 million in 1964. The growth of the use in these facilities for recreation purposes is also evidenced by the increase in the number of boats used on these lakes from approximately 9,600 in 1947, to 38,600 in 1956, and 52,700 in 1964.

The reclamation program of the Bureau of Reclamation of the U.S. Department of the Interior is aimed primarily at the development of water for irrigation and for hydroelectric power production, but the reservoirs which form the basic part of the program are also suitable for recreation use. In some areas, they provide the major recreation opportunity. The Bureau of Reclamation, like other federal water resource management agencies, turns over the administration of recreation on most reservoir areas to some other federal agency or to a state or local agency. The National Park Service acts as administrator for some of the larger units, the U.S. Forest Service for areas within national forests, and state park and recreation agencies as well as local agencies in many other cases.[7]

By 1960 the Bureau of Reclamation was operating 178 reservoirs with approximately 7,000 miles of shoreline. Recreation use of the Bureau's facilities has increased rapidly in the past 10 or 15 years. In 1950, 6.5 million visitors were registered at Bureau of Reclamation reservoirs; by 1955 the number had increased to 10.7 million, and by 1960 was well over 24 million.

Acreage and number of areas are not the only indications of the magnitude of federal involvement in outdoor recreation. An additional indication is the *direct* outlay for outdoor recreation purposes on the part of these agencies. In the case of relatively specialized recreation agencies such as the National Park Service and Bureau of Sport Fisheries

---

[7] It must be realized that double reporting is likely when recreation facilities are administered by an agency other than the one that is in charge of managing the resource. Much of the use of the Bureau of Reclamation reservoir areas is included in statistics for recreation reported by other agencies as well. However, our estimates of total use eliminate these duplications as far as possible.

and Wildlife, such outlays probably made up the greater part of their total expenditures. These two agencies account for over 70 per cent of the total reported federal expenditures for outdoor recreation for 1951–60 (see Table 15). In contrast, an agency with numerous programs, such as the Forest Service, may make many expenditures that benefit recreation indirectly but spend little directly for this purpose, hence their reported expenditures on recreation seem low. In total, all the agencies spent approximately $70 million in 1951 and $194 million in 1960, with a decade total of $1.1 billion. The regional imbalance in these reported federal expenditures is also striking: well over half was spent in the South Atlantic, Mountain, and Pacific regions; and only about 10 per cent was spent in the New England and Middle Atlantic regions, which in 1960 had 25 per cent of the total population.

OUTDOOR RECREATION FACILITIES PROVIDED BY STATE AGENCIES

The public recreation areas administered by the various states in state parks and related areas form a second major class. Although a few of these areas are resource based, most are of the intermediate type. Just under 4 per cent of the nation's land area is owned by state agencies

TABLE 15.
FEDERAL DIRECT OUTLAYS FOR RECREATION 1951–60,
BY REGION AND AGENCY

(Million dollars)

Region	Bureau of Sport Fisheries and Wildlife	Corps of Engineers	Forest Service	Public Health Service[1]	National Park Service	Total[2]
New England	12.8	0.1	0.9	19.9	5.0	38.7
Middle Atlantic	22.2	1.2	0.3	29.8	26.6	80.3
East North Central	43.3	1.1	1.8	34.1	4.9	85.1
West North Central	48.2	4.4	3.5	28.2	19.4	103.6
South Atlantic	41.3	3.1	3.3	36.6	128.0	216.0
East South Central	21.1	3.2	1.3	22.6	47.0	95.7
West South Central	33.2	9.4	1.6	22.9	10.7	77.8
Mountain	62.4	1.0	18.3	21.6	118.8	222.2
Pacific	48.3	2.0	16.3	22.0	82.6	171.6
U.S. total[3]	333.0	25.7	47.9	250.0	472.7	[4] 1,167.3

[1] Water pollution construction grants directly beneficial to providing outdoor recreation opportunities.

[2] Totals also include 0.3 for Bureau of Land Management, 6.1 for National Capital Planning Commission, 0.2 for St. Lawrence Seaway Development Commission, 0.7 for Tennessee Valley Authority, as well as other lesser amounts.

[3] U.S. totals include outlays in territories in some cases.

[4] This total figure includes all federal agency spending in U.S. and territories.

SOURCE: ORRRC Study Report 25.

of various sorts. The percentage of land in state ownership is about 12 per cent in Arizona, close to 12 per cent in some other western states, about 10 per cent in New York and Pennsylvania in the Northeast, but only about 2 per cent for the South as a region. Considerable acreage within these areas provides resources useful for recreation purposes, although most state-owned land is used primarily for grazing, mineral leasing, transportation, and other non-recreation uses.

Many of the state parks and related areas possess features of scenic, scientific, historical, archeological, and other recreational interest of statewide significance. However, many of the other state parks and recreation areas have been selected primarily for their proximity to concentrations of population, and they have been developed largely to meet the need for nonurban recreation.

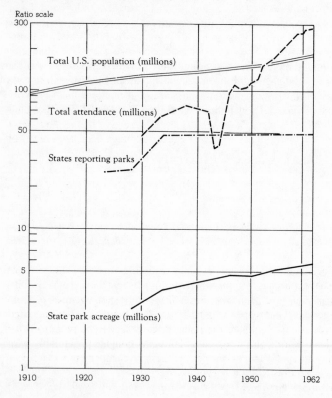

Figure 26. Acreage and usage of state parks, in relation to total population, 1910–62.

The acreage in state parks has grown steadily, but rather slowly, from 2.7 million acres in 1928, to 4.6 million acres in 1946 and 5.8 million acres in 1962 (Figure 26). The growth in numbers of state parks has been quite different. Just under 200 areas were reported in 1928, 1,500 in 1946, and 2,500 in 1962. The much more rapid growth in number of areas illustrates rather clearly the great diversity in the size of parks within the state system.

The state parks took on many of their present characteristics during the 1930's. Various federal programs were undertaken to provide employment. Some of the more important for outdoor recreation were the Civilian Conservation Corps, under which specific work programs employed thousands of young men; the Public Works Administration under which major public works were undertaken; and the Works Project Administration under which smaller scale hand labor programs were carried out. Funds for these programs came from the federal government, but were either dispersed within the states or transferred to the states for specific agreed-upon projects. States often embarked on major park and recreation projects because these were often well-suited to the use of the labor available under these programs. State projects of this type also provided important amounts of local employment. Roads were built into the new parks, sometimes dams were built to establish lakes, camp and picnic areas were developed, and other improvements were made. By 1940 almost all states had some form of state parks system. The area outside the big New York reserves increased fourfold between 1930 and 1940.

The federal programs of this period gave major assistance to state parks in two other ways. Some grant funds were provided for state park and recreation planning which enabled many states to develop planning for the first time. Federal funds were also used to buy marginal and submarginal farmlands which were later turned over to the states for parks.

Of total acquisitions for state parks since the war only 38 per cent have been by purchase, approximately 24 per cent have been by gift, and 30 per cent have been by transfer from other state agencies or from federal agencies. One reason why park land purchases have not increased more in recent years may be the rising price of land. The price paid for land declined during the war as less land was bought; presumably with less money to spend the park agencies bought cheaper land but prices paid have risen drastically if irregularly since 1945.[8]

The regional distribution of the various kinds of state-owned land

[8] Marion Clawson, *Statistics on Outdoor Recreation, op. cit.,* p. 67.

designated for outdoor recreation, while somewhat uneven for various kinds of land, tends to be much more nearly in proportion to total numbers of people than was true for the federal land.

All indicators of activity of state recreation agencies show a rapidly rising trend in recent years. Total expenditures for state park agencies rose from just over $10 million in 1941 to approximately $109 million in 1962. Even when allowance is made for differences in price levels, this is still a major increase. Revenues from state park operations in the same period rose from $3 million to over $26 million, and the number of year-round employees rose from 2,600 to over 7,000 and total employees from 5,500 to over 10,000.

The states differ enormously in the amounts they spend directly for outdoor recreation and in the percentage of state expenditures that they allocate to this purpose. At the top, in terms of total outlays from 1951 to 1960, are California, New York, and Pennsylvania, each with over $100 million. In terms of percentages of total state expenditures for outdoor recreation, some of the smaller western and eastern states lead: Wyoming, New Hampshire, Idaho, South Dakota, Utah, in that order, with several others close behind.[9] In some of these latter states, expenditures by fish and game commissions make up the predominant part of the total; this money is often obtained from sale of fishing and hunting licenses. As in the case of the federal agencies, these are direct outlays for outdoor recreation; they do not include expenditures on programs that benefit recreation indirectly. However, it seems probable that the latter are relatively less important for state than for federal programs.

The most significant and at the same time the most spectacular indication of the greatly expanded activity in the state park systems has been the attendance totals. In 1947, 97 million visits were recorded for such areas; by 1962, the total was 285 million. Because the growth in acreage of state parks has been much less rapid than the increase in attendance, use has gradually become more intensive per unit of area.

In 1962, visits to the state parks averaged about 1.5 per capita, but the rate varies considerably among the different states. Some states have more adequate state park systems than do others. In some states—South Dakota, for example—the proportion of out-of-state visitors is high, while in many other states the parks are used almost wholly by state residents. Among the states with higher per capita visitation rates are some of the most populous industrial states. Some of these states also have high acreages of parks per capita, which indicates that it is not necessarily impossible to provide adequate parks in highly urbanized areas.

[9] ORRRC Study Report 25, p. 14.

PUBLIC OUTDOOR RECREATION RESOURCES PROVIDED
BY LOCAL AGENCIES

The third large class of public recreation areas are those provided by cities, counties, special recreation districts, and other local agencies. With comparatively few exceptions, these are user-oriented areas. Public parks in cities in the United States are only about 100 years old. The early New England town had a publicly owned area in its center, which started as a common pasture but gradually developed into a public park. Philadelphia purchased a plot of 24 acres in 1828 specifically for a park, and in 1853 New York City made the first purchase of land for Central Park. These actions were exceptional until well after the Civil War. Sixty-six out of the 103 cities with a 1950 population of 100,000 or over had by 1880 one or more parks. Many of the parks were small; and they were not developed as they are today. Nevertheless a good beginning had been made, and open unimproved space was available for walking and informal sports.

Supervised public playgrounds began to appear at about the turn of the century. By that time the idea of city parks had begun to have much wider acceptance. As nearly as our imperfect knowledge permits us to estimate, it seems that the areas of city parks expanded relatively faster from 1880 to perhaps 1940 than did the populations for the same cities.[10] At the same time, privately owned vacant land, often consisting of a few open lots in a settled area, was gradually disappearing, and this may have given rise to the common impression that play and recreation areas in cities were decreasing during those decades. The increase in publicly available improved areas may have been offset by the decrease in privately owned open, unimproved areas.

Within the legal boundaries of the larger cities, park area has expanded at about the same rate as population, but the failure of many suburban areas to add land to meet their needs has caused a serious lag in park acreage for many metropolitan areas since the war.

Information on local municipal and county recreation areas, their use and management, has been collected for many years by the National Recreation Association either alone or jointly with various public agencies.[11]

[10] *Statistics on Outdoor Recreation, op. cit.,* p. 88.

[11] The Association and others have asked the park departments and other units of local government in all cities of 2,500 population or over and similar officials in counties where such parks were believed to exist to supply information concerning the areas under their jurisdiction. Response has been entirely voluntary. Repeated requests have been made to non-respondents thus reducing the amount of non-response. At the best, however, the kind of data collected in this way is limited by the information the agencies concerned may have, and this in turn depends upon their manpower and interest as well as their continuity in park management.

The data in the NRA surveys relate to parks and other non-school recreation areas owned by local government units, including cities, towns, boroughs, counties, and districts, whether located inside or outside of the municipality. The NRA relies on voluntary replies to mailed questionnaires. Its published reports simply include the results provided by the cities, and make no allowance for underreporting.

In spite of the serious problems of underreporting and the fact that the degree of underreporting may not have been constant from year to year, several interesting trends show up from an examination of the data through the period for which data are available.[12] Between 1925 and 1960 the acreage of parks increased nearly three times. The increase in the number of recreation facilities provided in these areas was even greater. Softball diamonds increased more than ten times; baseball diamonds more than quadrupled; golf courses and bathing beaches more than tripled; and ice skating areas and tennis courts more than doubled. It seems fairly clear that the intensity of use has been rising rather considerably in these areas. A further indication of this trend, and of the increased intensity of park land use, lies in the number of recreation leaders over the years. The increase is rather steady from 1910, when information was first available, until 1931 when it was nearly eight times the former. During the 1930's the number of regularly paid leaders declined considerably. By about 1941 the number of workers had increased to about the 1931 level. Numbers rose slowly during the war but have increased very rapidly since then, by 1960 reaching four times the prewar figure.

It is perhaps more difficult to get reasonably accurate data on attendance at parks and on the use of park facilities than on any other aspect of park administration. Getting attendance figures for city and county parks is especially difficult because they usually have neither an entrance gate nor an entrance fee. Nevertheless it is important to have some idea of attendance if park management and elected officials are properly to appraise the role of parks in local life.

Examination of data for six selected facilities reveals that playgrounds are by far the most popular, receiving over half the total reported use. The next most popular is bathing beaches in some years and indoor centers and buildings in others. The total of all attendance reported at all facilities, without regard to the differences between different kinds of activities, provides at least an index of use. With all the shortcomings of the data, this index may still give us a reasonable idea of the growth of the use of municipal park areas. From 1929 to 1955 this index

[12] See *Statistics on Outdoor Recreation, op. cit.,* Table 23, pp. 82–83.

increased about three times; although data for 1960 are not fully comparable, further large increases had occurred by 1960.

Total reported visits in cities reporting all types of facilities exceeded 900 million in 1955 and were about 1,100 million in 1960. These data are serious underestimates of true totals, for only about 30,000 of the roughly 87,000 special outdoor facilities reported attendance in 1955. However, even the number of visits reported is large in comparison with visits to other kinds of outdoor recreation facilities.

Another important bit of evidence as to the relative importance of local recreation in the total picture of outdoor recreation is given by expenditure figures. Here, again, the data are incomplete, but the Outdoor Recreation Resources Review Commission has made estimates of the expenditures on parks and recreation by cities and other units of local government, using various Bureau of the Census publications. The ORRRC figures indicate that estimated expenditure for local outdoor recreation is considerably greater than the direct outlay for outdoor recreation by all state and federal agencies combined.[13] However, the limitations of direct recreation expenditure data, previously discussed, should be borne in mind here also. The ORRRC figures for the decade 1951–60 indicate that direct outlays were $1.2 billion for federal agencies, $1.5 billion for state agencies, and $5.8 billion, or a little over 68 per cent of the total, for local agencies. While there are undoubtedly a number of expenditure items included in the local outlays which are not directly comparable to the direct outlays of the federal and state agencies, the importance of this class of recreation facilities is most obvious. The NRA survey of 1955, which included information on expenditures for outdoor recreation comparable to the ORRRC series, reported local expenditures of $378 million, which represents 61 per cent of the total for federal, state, and local. By either measure the expenditures of local government for outdoor recreation are a large part of the total expenditures made for this purpose in this country.

The foregoing discussion about outdoor recreation areas provided by local government uses data obtained by the National Recreation Association, primarily from cities but also to some extent from counties, and primarily from park or recreation departments; most of the areas, expenditures, and uses relate to parks within cities. The Outdoor Recreation Resources Review Commission, in accordance with the terms of its enabling legislation, did not obtain data about parks and other recreation areas lying within cities. It did, however, get a considerable amount of data about *nonurban* outdoor recreation areas under the

---

[13] *Public Expenditures for Outdoor Recreation,* ORRRC Study Report 25, p. 18.

TABLE 16.
MUNICIPAL AND COUNTY PARKS: NUMBER, ACREAGE, AND PAID
WORKERS, 1960, BY REGIONS, TOTAL AND PER MILLION
OF URBAN POPULATION

		Parks					
		Total		Per million urban population		Paid workers	
Region	Urban population (1,000)	Number	Acres	Number	Acres	Total number	Numbers per million urban pop.
New England	8,033	2,152	52,389	268	6,522	13,448	1,674
Middle Atlantic	27,810	4,235	127,246	152	4,576	43,257	1,555
East North Central	26,439	5,205	282,108	197	10,670	43,924	1,661
West North Central	9,047	1,884	70,591	208	7,803	14,491	1,602
South Atlantic	14,853	3,752	101,382	253	6,826	19,165	1,290
East South Central	5,834	917	31,906	157	5,469	6,726	1,153
West South Central	11,479	1,740	62,572	152	5,451	7,732	674
Mountain	4,600	1,021	119,937	222	26,073	5,933	1,290
Pacific	17,190	3,459	167,330	201	9,734	31,303	1,821
Total, U.S.	125,285	24,365	1,015,461	195	8,105	185,979	1,485

SOURCE: *Recreation and Park Yearbook 1961*, George D. Butler, editor, National Recreation Association, 1961.

control of local government. The regional distribution of the various kinds of local areas is most uneven. The North Central region shows up with three-fourths of the total acreage; even when the large acreage of forest agencies under local government is excluded, this region still has 29 per cent of the total nonurban recreation acreage under local government, in the whole country.

When consideration is limited to municipal and county *parks,* using NRA data, a different regional distribution pattern arises (Table 16). Although there are still considerable differences among regions, the disparity is relatively much less. On the whole, the southern regions make a poor showing in number of parks, acreage, and paid workers per million urban population; and in some ways the older regions of the northeast are also somewhat below average. But the sharp regional disparity of federal and state park acreage is not apparent in these data for city and county parks.

♦

COMPARISONS OF FEDERAL, STATE, AND LOCAL RECREATION ACREAGES

The West, with only 15 per cent of the population of the 48 states, has 72 per cent of the acreage in nonurban public recreation areas; the

Northeast, in contrast, with 25 per cent of the people, has only 4 per cent of the acreage. Nearly half of the national acreage is represented by federal land within the Mountain states (Table 17).

On a national basis, the total public nonurban recreation acreage is dominated by the very large area of federal forest lands—about 70 per cent of the national total falls in this category. The national forests, which make up most of the federal forest lands, are open to outdoor recreation, but only relatively small parts of these forests are managed primarily for recreation. Even at the state level, more than half of the recreation land is managed by forest agencies. Local government shows up with very little acreage, in part because urban parks and other areas are excluded from these data. Any comparisons limited to acreage alone have serious limitations, for reasons previously discussed, but these data do make clear the fact that most public land available for recreation is not under the administration of park agencies.

These comparisons of acreage and of numbers of areas cannot include consideration of the location factor, except in the most general way, nor of the amount and kinds of improvements to the land area. In spite of these limitations, however, striking differences between regions in the role of different levels of government are evident.

REGIONAL DISTRIBUTION OF RECREATION AREAS

In terms of gross acreage of publicly owned nonurban recreation land the West dominates the national statistics. The dominance is even greater in terms of recreational area per capita. The acreage of publicly owned land available for nonurban outdoor recreation per capita varies from a low of 0.16 acre in New England to a high of nearly 16 acres in the Mountain states.

The acreage of publicly owned land available for recreation use in each region is obviously not based upon "need"—however "need" may be defined; instead, it largely represents historical accidents of land-ownership, plus some influence by local leaders and some reflection of regional concepts as to proper kind of public action. By the time that provision of outdoor recreation was generally recognized as a desirable public undertaking, there was little federal land left except in the West, and acreages of state-owned land were limited in most states. City and other locally owned land and state lands have been acquired in more recent years, but acquisition has often been expensive and difficult, and the acreages concerned have been limited. In every region and in most localities the acreage of city and state park lands reflects to a large extent the interest and drive of a relatively few leading citizens. In some

TABLE 17.
NUMBER AND ACREAGE OF NONURBAN PUBLIC DESIGNATED RECREATION AREAS, BY REGION AND LEVEL OF GOVERNMENT, 48 CONTIGUOUS STATES, 1960

Region	Number of areas				Acreage (1,000)				Percentage of regional total acreage		
	Federal	State	Local	Total	Federal	State	Local	Total	Federal	State	Local
New England	42	316	19	377	1,058	643	115	1,816	58	36	6
Middle Atlantic	35	378	64	477	541	6,707	41	7,289	7	92	1
East North Central	43	651	117	811	5,564	5,854	2,395	13,813	40	42	18
West North Central	94	1,094	36	1,224	9,821	4,634	22	14,477	68	32	(¹)
South Atlantic	111	290	12	413	9,491	1,794	8	11,293	84	16	(¹)
East South Central	55	150	30	235	3,800	954	8	4,762	80	20	(¹)
West South Central	66	158	15	239	6,058	1,008	79	7,145	85	14	1
Mountain	206	246	39	491	106,555	2,959	89	109,603	97	3	(¹)
Pacific	124	375	122	621	51,188	4,334	113	55,635	92	8	(¹)
Total, 48 States	776	3,658	454	4,888	194,076	28,887	2,870	225,833	86	13	1

¹ Less than 0.5 per cent.
SOURCE: ORRRC Study Report 1, Tables 11 and 12, pp. 16–17. This table includes only areas of 41 acres or more, hence it includes only 20 per cent of the areas but about 97 per cent of the total acreage.

regions—the South, perhaps—a general conservatism about the role of public action in providing services for people has probably also served to limit the acreage of recreation land locally available.

A review of geographical differences in acreages of publicly owned land available for outdoor recreation may be useful for some purposes, but it can also be misleading unless the results are interpreted with care. Acreage is only one indicator of recreation opportunities. While no single set of data can perhaps measure precisely the availability of recreation opportunities to the public, the expenditures by agencies at different levels over a series of years may provide one good index. To a considerable degree agencies can offset acreage limitations or deficiencies by larger expenditures, and hence the latter may provide a more accurate index of felt need. Expenditures on outdoor recreation are only one factor, but they are an important one, and one that may be a better guide to the extent to which recreation opportunities are made available. The total decade outlays by government at all levels of outdoor recreation in each of the nine Census regions, together with population for each region in 1960, are shown in Table 18.

Regional expenditures by the federal agencies directly for outdoor recreation are loosely related to the total federal land acreage in the several regions. There is essentially no relationship between decade regional federal expenditures for recreation and regional population; the correlation coefficient measuring the degree of association between population and expenditure is 0.16, indicating a statistically insignificant correlation.

Examination of direct expenditures for recreation by the states indicates that there is a somewhat closer correspondence between regional population and the sum of federal and state expenditures during the decade. The correlation coefficient is 0.58, indicating considerable but not a strong correlation between the two series, and the relationship seems reasonable.

The association between regional population and expenditures for recreation becomes strong only when expenditures by local agencies are taken into account. When estimates of expenditures by local units of government (based on the incomplete survey of the National Recreation Association) are added to the federal and state figures, there is a close association between total regional expenditure for recreation and regional population, the correlation coefficient being 0.92.

The same conclusion is demonstrated by the decade figures of recreation expenditures per capita (Table 18). While the region of highest expenditure per capita spent more than three times as much as the region of lowest expenditures, yet the variation in per capita expenditures is far less than the variation in acreage per capita. Expenditures

TABLE 18.
EXPENDITURES ON RECREATION 1951-60 BY FEDERAL, STATE, AND LOCAL GOVERNMENTS, AND ACREAGE OF STATE AND FEDERAL LAND, BY CENSUS REGIONS

Census region	Total population 1960 (millions)	Outlays for recreation 1951-60 (million dollars)					Outlay for recreation per capita (dollars)	Acreage in state and federal areas[3] (million)
		States[1]	Federal[1]	State and federal[1]	Local[2]	Total		
New England	10.5	80	39	119	192	311	30	1.7
Middle Atlantic	34.2	318	80	398	884	1,282	37	7.2
East North Central	36.2	246	75	321	1,078	1,399	39	11.4
West North Central	15.4	118	94	212	232	444	29	14.4
South Atlantic	26.0	148	216	364	418	782	30	11.3
East South Central	12.0	67	96	163	92	255	21	4.8
West South Central	17.0	45	78	123	189	311	18	7.1
Mountain	6.9	101	223	323	77	400	58	109.5
Pacific	21.2	248	172	420	613	1,032	49	[4]55.5
United States	179.3	1,371	1,072	2,443	3,774	6,217	35	[4]230.4

NOTE: Totals may not add, due to rounding.
[1] Direct outlays on recreation only; data from ORRRC Study Report 25.
[2] Total outlays, calculated by multiplying reported outlay in 1955 by ten; data from *Recreation and Park Yearbook, 1955*, National Recreation Association.
[3] Data from ORRRC Study Report 1.
[4] Acreage excludes Alaska and Hawaii.

per capita are highest in the West and lowest in the South, but elsewhere fall closely about the national average.

The regional distribution of recreational opportunities is one, then, of some ambiguity. In terms of recreation acreage, there is a vast disparity between different regions of the country. However, in terms of per capita expenditures for recreation by all levels of government there is a great similarity between the different regions.

There is some correspondence between the expenditures of different levels of government and the general type of recreation area administered. For the most part the federal government manages large resource-based recreation areas, and its expenditures tend to be channeled into the areas with large federal land acreages, which also are areas of small population concentration. State agencies very often administer the intermediate-type areas, and there is a greater regional correspondence between expenditures and population. The local units of government provide for recreation resources which are for the most part user-oriented; their expenditures are made much more closely in accord with the size of the regional population. One of the consequences of this regional pattern of expenditure is that in areas of high population concentration (notably the mid-Atlantic, East North Central, and New England) the public recreation opportunities available are disproportionately user-oriented types, while in areas of low population concentration (predominantly in the West) the recreation opportunities are disproportionately resource-based.

A further indication of the existing recreation opportunities in the various regions of the country is provided by information collected by the Outdoor Recreation Resources Review Commission on the use of various types of facilities. The Commission study asked supervisors or administrators of various recreation facilities to rate certain types of facilities in their area as to the amount of use they received relative to their design capacity. The responses are not based on any generally accepted standard for, as this report points out, no such standard or yardstick exists; they simply reflect the respondent's observation as to the ratio between use and capacity. Five kinds of facilities were rated: parking areas, overnight facilities, designated campgrounds, designated picnic grounds, and water access points. For each type of facility the respondent was asked to rate the degree of use as "light" if its use was below 75 per cent of its design capacity; "moderate" if up to 25 per cent more people could use the facility; "heavy" if current use was at the designed capacity level; and "very heavy" if more people tried to use the facility than could be accommodated. This survey therefore generally only rated the degree of crowding in the judgment of the respondent. It was concerned with the adequacy of the facility

RECREATION RESOURCES

relative to the demand for its use, and not the number of people using any facility.

The first two categories, "light" and "moderate," can be lumped together as under capacity, and the second two, "heavy" and "very heavy," can be rated at or above capacity. The responses are summarized in Table 19. While it is admittedly difficult to make any general statements on use pressures from these data alone, it is apparent that overnight facilities and campgrounds are generally heavily used, with well over half of the areas having heavy or very heavy use pressures in all regions of the country. A high proportion of picnic grounds are also rated as being used at or above design capacity.

In each of the five kinds of facilities surveyed, the Northeast had a

TABLE 19.
USE OF FACILITIES IN PUBLIC DESIGNATED AREAS BY DEGREE
OF USE AND REGION, 1960

Census region and kind of area	Total reporting	Percentage of areas reported	
		Light-moderate use	Heavy-very heavy use
Parking:			
Northeast	497	56	44
North Central	1,593	78	22
South	672	60	40
West	841	60	40
U.S.	3,603	68	32
Overnight:			
Northeast	189	31	69
North Central	511	46	54
South	344	44	56
West	423	38	62
U.S.	1,465	41	59
Campgrounds:			
Northeast	208	33	67
North Central	544	46	54
South	349	48	52
West	464	36	64
U.S.	1,565	32	58
Picnic grounds:			
Northeast	434	35	65
North Central	866	48	52
South	570	42	58
West	598	43	57
U.S.	2,468	43	57
Access points:			
Northeast	283	66	34
North Central	887	77	23
South	420	63	37
West	487	63	37
U.S.	2,077	70	30

SOURCE: ORRRC Study Report 1, pp. 52–61.

higher proportion reported as receiving heavy or very heavy use than the average for the United States. This perhaps might have been expected in view of the population concentrations relative to facilities provided. However, in the North Central region the proportion of areas reporting heavy and very heavy use was lower than the United States average for all five of the types of facilities, and in the West it was higher than the national average for all five facilities. While there are some consistencies, there are also inconsistencies with the generally held notion that the West is far better supplied with recreation facilities than the rest of the country.

DATA ON PRIVATELY OWNED AREAS AVAILABLE FOR OUTDOOR RECREATION

This chapter has dealt primarily with publicly owned land available for outdoor recreation, because so little is available on the use of privately owned land for this purpose. The Census of Agriculture for many decades has obtained much detailed information about crop acreages and yields and other information about land in farms; the Department of Agriculture has for 100 years obtained annual estimates of crop acreages and yields, and other information about agriculture; the Department of Commerce has compiled estimates of national income for several decades; and other illustrations of national data series could be cited. While the National Park Service, Forest Service, and other recreation-administering agencies have annual attendance data, there is nothing remotely comparable, as yet, for data about privately owned areas used for outdoor recreation. With their growing importance, some form of meaningful annual data will become increasingly necessary, although the difficulties of collecting such information will be considerable.

Studies during the past decade have added considerable information. Several commercial firms have published campground directories, for instance; some of them list as many as 3,000 private campgrounds in addition to the public areas. Information acquired by the Forest Service under its research program indicates that private campgrounds have increased tenfold in the past decade.[14] The New Hampshire State Planning Project estimates that private campground capacity in that state is four times public campground capacity.[15] This generally agrees with

[14] Letter from Edward P. Cliff, Chief, Forest Service, May 1965.
[15] State of New Hampshire State Planning Project, *The Privately-Owned Campgrounds of New Hampshire,* Report No. 7, Concord, New Hampshire, March 1965.

Forest Service estimates for Northeastern states. The Bureau of Sport Fisheries and Wildlife has called attention to the role played by private ponds and by private duck clubs, in the provision of nesting and other areas and as places for hunting.[16] Several specific studies of privately owned resources used for outdoor recreation have added to our knowledge.[17] However, without exception, these have been one-shot studies, not ones that lead to continuous data series. They have mostly focused on numbers and acreage of areas. Some of them have included additional information on investment, employment, and users. But what has been most notably lacking is information on numbers of visitors, their origin, costs of visits, and similar data.

In the absence of complete and reliable data on recreation use of private land, speculation and generalization based upon limited personal experience are inevitable. It has often been asserted that recreation use of private land exceeds recreation use of public land; we know of no objective quantitative data to support this statement. It is clearly true that the *area* of *all* privately owned land far exceeds the area of all publicly owned land; but we do not know that the areas of privately owned land used for outdoor recreation—however "used" may be defined—exceeds the area of publicly owned land so used; and far less do we know how the number of visits, days of use, or any other measure of recreation activity compares between private and public land.

The recreation use of private land has not been measured on a national scale. The task is a difficult one. Before useful data can be collected it is necessary to formulate clear and meaningful concepts of what is to be measured, to prepare careful definitions, and to enumerate the items desired.

In this connection, it is useful to recall some of the major kinds of situations under which privately owned land is used for outdoor recreation. Some groups or organizations own their own land, and use it for their recreation. A Boy Scout troop may have its own campground, a church group its own summer conference grounds, or a conservation organization its own land. In another broad group of cases, private owners make their land and facilities available to other users, often at a fee and for profit but sometimes without charge. Those who operate campgrounds, summer resorts, and the dude ranches hope to make a profit, while farmers, ranchers, and forest landowners often permit hunting by others on their land at no charge or on payment of a small

[16] Joseph P. Linduska (ed.), *Waterfowl Tomorrow* (Washington: U.S. Government Printing Office, 1964).

[17] Ronald Bird and Buis T. Inman, *Income Opportunities for Rural Families from Outdoor Recreation Enterprises,* Agricultural Economic Report No. 68, United States Department of Agriculture, Washington, 1965. See its bibliography.

fee. It should be possible to formulate questions and obtain information about these kinds of outdoor recreation on private land.

A much less easily defined situation can exist when a person owns land for his own recreation. A summer cottage on a lake or in the mountains usually presents no problem, as it is clearly for recreation. But many farms, ranches, and forest properties are bought for recreational use but managed for other purposes.

In New York, more than a million acres of farm land have reverted to some kind of forest within the past decade or so; most of this is now owned and used by people who do not regard their landownership as primarily an income-raising proposition. In a large proportion of cases, the dwellings on this land are second, or even third, homes for the people involved. Yet it may be true that some forestry output is produced from this land. In California, it has been estimated that about a million acres of commercial forest land in smaller ownerships is owned primarily for recreation or other non-income reasons.

It would be very hard to get meaningful data on this latter kind of recreation use of private land, but not impossible to do so. The most difficult part would be to define clearly the difference between recreation and other uses of land. We noted in Chapter 3 that recreation was often an attitude toward activity; it would be difficult to measure attitudes but perhaps actions indicative of attitude could be measured.

Until we get comprehensive, reliable, and pertinent data on recreation use of private land, we can only speculate as to its role. The total recreation situation may, in fact, be very different than it appears when only the data on public areas is considered. Earlier in this chapter we discussed the marked regional imbalance in outdoor recreation when only federal and state areas are considered; the Outdoor Recreation Resources Review Commission discovered this situation and stressed it a good deal. But when local recreation areas were added to the total picture, and particularly when consideration was given to expenditures rather than to area, the regional balance changed greatly, toward more regional equality. It is possible that addition of data on recreation use of private land would reveal a still different picture of regional variations. In planning to meet future demand for outdoor recreation, it is essential that account be taken of the availability of private lands, and of the kinds of uses made of them.

IV

Some Economic Considerations

To this point we have developed some general concepts of demand as applied to outdoor recreation, indicated the shape of future demands, and explored some of the supply aspects of outdoor recreation. We now begin a series of four chapters on some of the economic consequences of the interplay between supply and demand factors. Building upon the demand analysis previously presented, these chapters deal with the value of land and water resources when used for outdoor recreation, particularly when used for publicly-provided recreation; with the economic effects of outdoor recreation on local areas; with costs and investment decisions; and with the matter of pricing and paying for public outdoor recreation facilities. They emphasize the need for more explicit evaluation of the benefits and costs of outdoor recreation and the value of clearcut alternatives as a guide to decisions.

11

The Value of Land and Water Resources
When Used for Recreation

The growing demand for recreation increases the value of the natural resources that can be used to provide it. These changes in values call for continuing adjustments in resource allocations to better satisfy varying wants and preferences of consumers. In the case of privately-owned property used primarily to provide recreation for the owner or other private persons, the increasing worth of the resources for outdoor recreation finds expression in higher prices bid and paid for such properties. But the market cannot, or does not, operate in this way for public outdoor recreation areas. Land and water resources generally are constantly being re-evaluated in terms of needs for their products and services. This perhaps comes into sharpest focus in current public issues and public decisions regarding such things as the establishment of national recreation areas; the setting aside or preserving of areas for parks and open spaces in and near our expanding urban areas; and in questions of justification, location, and operation of water development projects.

With this growth in the values attached to outdoor recreation has come an awareness of the increasing competition for land and water resources for all uses. The nation is therefore inevitably faced with the problem of choosing between alternative uses of resources, each of which may offer desirable results. Satisfaction of wants and desires for outdoor recreation may well mean sacrifice of other goods and services also in demand.

While there are other determinants of resource allocation, the values associated with the various alternatives are of great importance. As we have noted earlier, under many circumstances consumers are able to evidence their preferences for different uses of resources through market

211

behavior. Even when a formal market does not exist, their choices, as backed up by their willingness to spend part of their income, may serve as a basis for estimating what the results of a freely functioning market would have been. A more explicit evaluation of the economic benefits and costs of recreational use of land and water would allow a much more positive approach to questions not only of quantities of resources, but also of kinds, of location, and of timing of acquisition and development.

RECREATION RESOURCE VALUES FOR PUBLIC DECISION MAKING

In recent years public agencies at all levels, not only in this country but in others as well, have turned increasingly to more quantitative or objective analysis of the consequences of alternative policies and projects that are open to them.[1] Benefit-cost analysis has been used—and probably developed to the greatest extent—in evaluating the relative desirability of water resources development projects. Here, the beneficial effects of such things as water navigation, hydropower, flood control, and irrigation are explicitly recognized in value terms and comparisons are made with the cost of providing them.

This type of analysis can be applied to other types of investment. It is particularly useful where there is a fairly easily recognizable product or service produced by the contemplated project. Analysis of alternative benefits and costs is no panacea for resolving all problems of resource development or all conflicts among potential users, but it provides a basis for comparing alternatives, and it can lead to the realization of a far greater product from given resource availabilities.

There are obvious advantages in evaluating recreation in the same manner as its most important competitors for natural resources. However, such an application has been hampered in the past by a lack of agreement on the measurement of meaningful values which might be imputed to resources used for recreation purposes. While there has been a growing recognition that recreation has an important economic value, planners have been ill prepared to include its values in the social or public calculus in ways that lead to better allocations and management of our resources, particularly of land and water.

In advocating future investment in recreation facilities, some groups have taken the position that there is no need to measure values, that any recreation development is good. A related approach in recreation

[1] Roland N. McKean, *Efficiency in Government through Systems Analysis* (New York: John Wiley and Sons, 1958). See especially Ch. I–III.

planning holds that no matter what is developed or built, it will shortly
be overwhelmed with use. Although there is truth to both views, neither
is helpful in making choices among individual possibilities. If the
greatest value is to be obtained from an investment, it is necessary to
know and be able to compare the values that would be added by the
various alternatives.

There are a number of reasons why research into these areas has not
been noted particularly for its abundance or its imagination.[2] One is
that public outdoor recreation has by and large developed as a non-
market good, and there has been very little attempt to charge prices
that in any way reflect the value to users. Related to this has been a
great deal of discussion of the merits of outdoor recreation in terms of
its social or personal values. Statements are frequently made to the
general effect that outdoor recreation fills some profoundly felt need;
that it has personal, unique, and highly variable values for individuals;
that outdoor recreation defies any kind of measurement; or simply that
it is priceless. But there are those who hold, as we do, that such values
are directly reflected in economic values and that there is no irrecon-
cilable conflict between the social values and the more specific economic
values. Assertion of personal and wide social values do not provide as
useful a basis for determining such public issues as how much more
outdoor recreation area or capacity should be provided, where facilities
should be established, what kinds are more valuable or more important
than others, and what priorities should be established. Indeed, many
who assert the social values most strongly recognize that financial and
other limitations may force choices based upon other grounds. Yet it is
these kinds of questions the nation continually faces in dealing with
outdoor recreation. Legislators, administrators, and others necessarily
must make practical operating decisions on just such issues.

The only value that has relevance for a specific decision is the value
of a contemplated addition or increment of recreational development.
The decision should be based on the desirability of the specific opportunity under consideration, not on the general desirability of recreation.
Little is gained, and no doubt a great deal has been lost, by devoting
so much discussion and attention to the importance of outdoor recreation as such or its total supply. The focus should be on the values of
specific additions to our present opportunities.

It is also the case that no goods or services are priceless in the sense
of an infinite price. There is an individual and collective limit to how

[2] Marion Clawson and Jack L. Knetsch. "Outdoor Recreation Research: Some
Concepts and Suggested Areas of Study," *Natural Resources Journal* (October
1964).

much wealth we will sacrifice or give up in order to enjoy the services of any outdoor recreation facility development or to preserve any scenic resource.[3] This limit is defined by how much we are willing to give up in order to obtain such services. It would be pointless to continue expenditures in a recreation development if the funds could produce greater satisfaction if invested in other things.

In seeking the most beneficial or efficient investment patterns and operational choices, the objective is to increase the satisfaction obtained from our resources or, in other terms, to increase the value of benefits over costs. The primary problem faced in dealing with recreation as a valuable output of resource employment is a measurement problem. We do not have clear expressions of economically meaningful values which might be imputed to resources used for recreational purposes.

Outdoor recreation for various reasons is centered largely on publicly owned and controlled areas and has developed largely outside the market mechanism. However, the absence of ready-made market prices does not mean that there are no values created by this use of resources. Economic values which are relevant to allocation decisions and directly comparable to the values imputed to other uses of resources are indeed produced. It is precisely such measures of value which best express the intensity of desire for these services and amenities. The problem lies not in an absence of values but in the absence of a direct measure of value.

Economic values are measured basically by what people are willing to give up; a relevant economic measure of recreation values is, therefore, the willingness on the part of consumers to pay for outdoor recreation services. This set of values is the same as the economic values which are established for other commodities, but in the case of recreation there is no price to serve as a measure. The supposed dichotomy between economic values and the kinds of values afforded by recreation opportunity is a false one. Economic values are created only as people desire things, and are but a reflection of these desires. This is not to deny human emotions and wants. The notion of demand, on which economic values largely rest, has intensely human reactions and choices underlying it.

It is sometimes asserted that economic worth implies commercial returns, and that the real values of outdoor recreation are not necessarily consistent with such commercialization. This is in large measure incorrect. Economic values can serve as guides to social choice even though they are not registered in the commerce of the area or of the

[3] Robert K. Davis, "Recreation Planning as an Economic Problem," *Natural Resources Journal* (October 1963), pp. 239–49.

nation. The value of recreation afforded at a particular facility or site is not what consumers spend each year on travel and on recreation equipment. Rather, it is what the recreation provided by that site adds to our total stock of value or welfare.

There are also expressions that resource development projects and recreation development projects particularly should somehow be exempt from economic analysis. There is somehow believed to be something peculiar about this type of activity that warrants that it not come under the same rules as other types of decisions. This seems incongruous. There is no reason to believe that we should not want to see the same kind of efficient use of resources made, in terms of satisfactions or values gained, in this field as we do in any other. The same reasons and methods of allocation apply equally well to each, and are beneficial to each.

NATURE OF RECREATION RESOURCES VALUES

The primary values or direct benefits from recreation areas are those realized by the users of the area. Such enjoyment has economic value to the extent that, again, people express a willingness to pay for the opportunity to engage in such activities. In the case of privately-owned areas, their willingness to pay finds expression in the prices paid for the land and improvements. Users of public outdoor recreation areas may not be required to pay an entrance fee or other direct use charge, but they do incur costs for the whole outdoor recreation experience, as we have shown in earlier chapters. Although "free" in one sense, use of the public recreation opportunity is far from free when one considers the travel and other costs necessary to take advantage of it.

Monetary values assigned or attributed to natural resources used for public recreation—by whatever process seems most appropriate—need have little or nothing to do with prices or fees charged for such recreation opportunity. In the natural resource field, many kinds of resources are developed or made available through public action on either a free or nominal cost basis. For instance, the federal government annually spends many millions of dollars to reduce flood hazards in various parts of the nation, yet the beneficiaries of these programs pay only a small fraction of the costs or none at all. There are many other public programs where costs are borne out of general public revenues and little or no charge is levied against the prime beneficiaries. This is not to suggest that beneficiaries of public services should not pay for them, but only that services may well have value without charges being paid.

To argue that these recreation benefits to users are measurable and that such measures should be taken into account in decisions affecting the allocation and use of resources, does not necessarily exclude the existence of other benefits to non-users. Nor does it ignore the fact that investment is sometimes made as a public good. Such considerations may be more important where great scenic or historic values are attached to areas used for outdoor recreation. They are much less important in the use of resources for recreation as such, and for areas which are used for recreation alone. This is distinct from other non-user benefits which may also arise to some extent from provision of parks owing to such things as keeping people off the streets and reducing noise levels, and from maintaining the option for people to go to an area even if they never actually make such a visit.[4] Values not measured by the willingness of users to pay for them do exist, but their magnitude at the margin where decisions must focus has in many cases doubtless been subject to gross exaggeration. We return to this issue in later discussions of pricing policy.

Aside from the primary recreation values which accrue to users and to some extent to non-users, there are other economic benefits of recreation areas which are also of interest. Foremost among these are the local economic aspects of many recreation developments to communities in the vicinity of such areas. This impact on the local area is in the form of such things as the increased sales of retail business establishments, the increased number of certain types of commercial enterprises catering to the users of the park, changes in tax structures, better markets for commodities produced locally, and increases in employment opportunities. These values are discussed in the following chapter. Our concern in this chapter is with the direct benefits that are produced by resources when used for outdoor recreation.

ESTIMATING USER BENEFITS FROM PUBLIC OUTDOOR RECREATION AREAS

The method of estimating the value of natural resources used for public outdoor recreation areas flows directly out of the demand analysis presented in Chapter 5. The relevant figure is the value to the users, which in turn depends upon the willingness of the users to incur costs in order to enjoy the recreation experience. Demand curves conceptually link such willingness to pay with the estimated value of the resources when used for this purpose. Demand curves, as we noted previously, reflect human choices and aspirations, as consumers weigh one good against another, with incomes inadequate to buy everything that they might desire.

[4] Burton A. Weisbrod, "Collective-Consumption Services of Individual-Consumption Goals," *The Quarterly Journal of Economics,* Vol. 78 (August 1964).

In Chapter 5, we showed, first, how the demand for the whole recreation experience can be estimated from data on numbers of visitors according to costs of visitation by distance zones, and, then, how a demand curve for the recreation resource itself can be derived from the demand curve for the whole experience. These curves were derived for all types of areas.

While this approach is not without difficulties—in part alluded to in the earlier discussion—it has the merit of measuring the net values produced by public use of the area. That is, it is correct in principle; and the estimates can be improved by extending the analysis to include more comprehensive factors affecting values, such as site and population characteristics. The estimate of the demand curve for the resource and its value is dependent on the ability to estimate a demand curve for the whole experience.

To illustrate, we go back to Tables 9 and 10 and to Figures 13 and 14 of Chapter 5, where we developed these curves for a hypothetical area. The demand curve for the whole experience shows what recreationists were observed to pay for the opportunity to enjoy that kind of recreation. As costs rose, numbers of visits per 1,000 base population declined rapidly, and were estimated to reach zero at a total cost per visit of $6.00. By assuming added costs or tolls for each population group, we can calculate the total number of visitors to the area under varying added costs, yielding an approximation to the appropriate demand schedule for the recreation resource itself.

Primary recreation benefits are here viewed as the value of the output of the project to those who use it; the best estimate of recreation benefits, or the total worth of this increased supply of recreation services, may be measured directly from the demand curves, which indicate what consumers would pay for the various units of recreation output, rather than go without them. Some users could and would pay a great deal, rather than forego this recreation experience; others could and would pay much more modest sums; and still others could or would pay very little—perhaps because they prefer to use their income in other ways. Those who could afford to pay relatively large sums, if necessary, might be willing to do so only for a limited amount of recreation; for a larger degree of participation, they would insist upon a lower cost. Thus, total numbers of visits at varying assumed added costs per visit reflect participation by different groups of people and by the same people to different degrees.

The measure of the total user benefit is the sum of the maximum prices which various users would pay for the various units of output from the area or project. This is equivalent to the total area under the demand curve in Figure 14 (and in similar figures for the actual areas considered in Chapter 5). This measures the total economic worth to society of the recreation services provided by this project or area.[5]

This method can be illustrated by the data in our hypothetical example given in Table 10. The first 100 visits were valued by those who made them at from $5 to $4, giving a value for these visits of 100 times $4.50, or $450. Another 100 were valued at between $4 and $3 for $350; 500 at between $3 and $2 for $1,250; 500 at between $2 and $1 for $750; and the remaining 1,500 were valued at less than $1 for $750. The sum of these values is $3,550, which is taken to be the appropriate measure of the economic value of the recreation opportunities provided in this hypothetical situation.

If significant investment or annual operating costs are incurred in the provision of outdoor recreation opportunity on these public land or water areas, these added costs should be subtracted from the total benefits to arrive at the estimated net benefit accruing to the resource itself. These added costs might vary with numbers of visits. Moreover, the area might be managed extensively or intensively, with consequent differences in cost, demand, and net benefits. Estimation of the level of management which would yield the largest net benefits to the recreation resource would be an important management study in itself.

We have noted previously that the quantities taken at a given price, as shown by a demand curve, always apply to a specified interval of time. For much analysis of outdoor recreation resource values, the time interval is likely to be a year. The net benefits accruing to the recreation resources for this year, or other time period, are only a part of the time stream of benefits produced by this area and this activity. There might be good reasons for anticipating that over time the net benefits would increase, be constant, or even decline. A time stream of benefits— whether increasing, constant, or decreasing—can be converted into present capital values by appropriate capitalization procedures. If the time stream is a constant one, simply dividing the interest rate into the annual amount yields the total present value. Choice of the most appropriate interest rate is, in itself, a difficult and important matter— but one that is constantly faced in estimating values of natural resources under different programs of public development.

The procedure outlined for outdoor recreation whereby the total area under the demand curve is used to measure the total economic benefit is generally the same as that now widely accepted for all public resource development programs. But it is a different use of the demand curve

[5] Roland N. McKean, op. cit., Ch. 10; and J. W. Milliman, "Land Values as Measures of Primary Irrigation Benefits," Journal of Farm Economics, Vol. 41, No. 2 (May 1959), pp. 234–43.

than is common for privately produced goods and services. For them, the total value is typically a single value or price per unit multiplied by the total number of units. We need to consider briefly why this procedure is consistent with private values and appropriate for public resource activities.

In the case of wheat, for example, the production increases that can be brought about by a single farmer are inconsequential to the total national output; his added production has no influence on price, and each unit can be valued at the market price. The total value of wheat produced in any year on any farm is determined, therefore, by multiplying the price per bushel by the total number of bushels produced.

So long as the additional output is small relative to the existing total amount, as in the case of wheat, the entire willingness to pay is measured adequately by a single price multiplied by the number of units supplied. This procedure is consistent with measurement of social value created by the wheat production.

If the additional recreation produced by a project is small relative to the total amount of all recreation available, then as in the case of wheat, the entire willingness to pay is adequately measured by a single price multiplied by the number of units supplied. The needed condition for this to hold is that the increment supplied be so small as not to have an influence on the market price which is charged for all units of the added output.

The "production" of outdoor recreation areas, however, usually occurs in "large lumps"—a park, or a reservoir, for example. Were it not for the immobility factor, the lumpiness would cause little difficulty because the number of visits added by any single facility is usually not large relative to the total visits to all recreation facilities in the nation. The number of visits added, however, may be large relative to the market served. Each separate recreation area provides an economically distinctive service owing to the fact that it may have few competitors for the market that it serves. We therefore are faced with the lumpiness or nonmarginal question in the form of a demand curve telling us that different users have a different willingness to pay for use of the area. To the extent that there are readily available areas which can be substituted, the demand curve for the area in question will become flatter, indicating that we are approaching more closely the case of most other goods and services which can be appropriately valued at a single price for each unit.

Most natural resource developments present the twin aspects of lumpiness and immobility which characterize outdoor recreation facilities; most serve a local or regional market, and locational characteristics are often highly important. The method of estimating benefits of federal resource development programs therefore provides, in effect, for estimation of the total area under the demand curve.[6] It is applied to irrigation, flood protection, and hydroelectric power development, for instance. The procedure we have outlined for estimating the total value of public recreation projects, by estimating the value under the demand curve, is consistent with the benefit calculations that would ordinarily be made for other uses of these same natural resources.

For example, in the case of irrigation use of water from a water development project, the economic value of the water, or the irrigation benefits, are the worth to the farmers, measured by their increased net incomes attributable to the water. This is their willingness to pay. This, too, is the area under the demand curve for water.

A further point that needs to be made involves the bias in this derived demand curve for the recreation resource. The procedure used to derive the demand curve from travel cost information results in a consistent underestimate of the number of visits that would be made under the varying assumed added cost or toll levels of the demand schedule. This unresolved difficulty, discussed in Chapter 5, stems from the fact that money cost, on which the calculations focus, is not the sole constraint to such visits. Time is certainly another. While time for the whole experience is an important decision consideration, it is travel time that is of most concern here. The demand curve constructed earlier is a relation between money costs and numbers of visits, as it should be, but by ignoring these other factors, it underestimates the actual demand for the given resources.

The value imputed to the natural resource used for recreation is therefore also underestimated, for our measure of value is the area under the demand curve. While the error may be considerable, it is consistent in direction and it results in conservative estimates of resource value. These considerations preserve much of the value of the analysis.

These general ideas can be illustrated with two specific examples— Lewis and Clark Lake, and Kerr reservoir, demand curves for which were estimated in Chapter 5. These are both intermediate-type areas, but the methods are, of course, not limited to such areas.

The estimated demand curve for the recreation resources of Lewis and Clark Lake was presented in Figure 15. This curve indicates over 230,000 party visits at zero toll, just under 100,000 at $5, and continues to fall at successively higher added cost levels. The total annual benefits of the recreation produced by this project, viewed as equal to the

---

[6] *Policies, Standards and Procedures in the Formulation, Evaluation and Review of Plans for Use in Development of Water and Related Land Resources,* 87th Congress, Second Session, Senate Document 97, approved May 1962.

whole area under the curve shown in Figure 15, is approximately $1.4 million.

For the other example, Kerr reservoir, the demand curve for the total recreation experience was presented in Figure 10 in Chapter 5. From it, another demand curve for the recreation resource can be derived, in a manner similar to that used for other areas. There are estimated to be about 500,000 visits annually with no entrance fee or added toll; this number falls off rapidly to about 150,000 at a $2.06 entrance fee, to about 85,000 at twice this fee, and so on. Use of this reservoir is sensitive to costs; or, in other words, its demand is highly price elastic. The total economic value of the recreation at this site, as shown by the total area under the demand curve, for the July 1, 1963–June 30, 1964 year, was about $1.6 million.

These are both gross benefit figures—that is, no amortization or other costs arising out of investment in recreation facilities nor any costs for annual maintenance and management have been deducted. Data were not available to us whereby this could have been done. However, the gross benefits so estimated are generally comparable with the gross benefits as they would ordinarily be estimated for flood protection or other project purposes.

Owing to the incomplete accounting of the effects of time, of intervening opportunities, and other constraints to visits in addition to money cost, these benefit estimates also have a downward bias. However, even with this restriction, the estimates are (1) economically meaningful and (2) consistent with and comparable to the benefit estimates for other project services.

The estimated average annual project benefits for the Kerr Project, calculated as the yearly average of the discounted benefit stream are $0.8 million for flood control and $5.2 million for power. Although comparable, the recreation benefit estimate of $1.6 million is an estimate for a single year rather than an average of a discounted stream of future benefits. As such, it is likely to be a further relative understatement, as the evidence points to more rapid expansion in demand for recreation services than in demand for the other products.

This estimate is for one reservoir, but it quite clearly indicates that, first, recreation benefits can be a substantial portion of total returns from multipurpose water projects of this kind and, second, the magnitude of recreation benefits will be dependent upon a project's individual circumstances, including such things as location relative to population centers, design and development characteristics, and location relative to other recreation opportunities.

Another and interesting application of the same general approach has been made in evaluating the primary or net economic value of the

Oregon salmon and steelhead sport fishery.[7] A demand curve was derived from survey information in which the number of fishing days sought by fishermen was estimated with different levels of assumed increases in costs. Computation of the area under the curve, or willingness to pay on the part of fishermen, showed that in 1962 the yearly value was approximately $5.7 million. By taking account of projected changes in incomes and population it was estimated that the values were likely to increase approximately 50 per cent by 1972. In this case, the values measured were those resulting from preservation of an existing recreation resource, rather than from creation of a new one. The methodology is applicable to each.

CAPITALIZATION OF RECREATION BENEFITS ARISING OUT OF PUBLIC RESOURCE PROJECTS INTO PRIVATE LAND VALUES

Owing to the immobility of a recreation area and the nature of the distance gradient, some users may desire to purchase proximity or access to a recreation area. As the preference for closeness to parks increases, the value of land near the area would be expected to increase. An increment to the value of land resulting from this preference should, for most decision purposes, be credited to the economic worth of the recreation area. Such land increments are particularly evident in the case of lakeshore property, and they often occur near urban open areas.

It is, of course, possible that heavy recreation use of a local park might actually depress values of neighboring residential property, if noise, parking, and other aspects of visitation interfered with comfort of local residents. The method herein outlined could deal with negative as well as with positive value effects of recreation areas.

Full evaluation of the economic worth or value of the product of recreation areas needs to take account of not only the user benefits of visitors, but also the possible increment in land values resulting from the influence of such areas. The measurement problem centers on determining the consistencies or patterns of land value and how these are dependent upon proximity to recreation areas.

In a study of the TVA system, which in many ways is not unlike the case of parks or other recreation areas,[8] the contribution of the

---

[7] William G. Brown, Ajmer Singh, and Emery N. Castle, *An Economic Evaluation of the Oregon Salmon and Steelhead Sport Fishery*, Technical Bulletin 78 (Corvallis: Agricultural Experiment Station, Oregon State University, 1964).

[8] Jack L. Knetsch, "The Influence of Reservoir Projects on Land Values," *Journal of Farm Economics* (February 1964), pp. 231–43.

multipurpose reservoirs to the value of land in the vicinity was isolated in a manner which enabled estimates to be made of the increase in land values that would result from construction of a proposed new reservoir project.[9]

The value of land, as determined by sales data, was found to be influenced by location relative to population centers, alternative lake opportunities available to the people in the area, characteristics of the reservoir, road access, site characteristics of the individual tracts, and distance of the tract from the reservoir. While these factors did not account for all of the determinants of value or the many idiosyncrasies of individual buyers and sellers of individual parcels of land, together they provided significant information about how reservoirs directly affect the value of land.

The results of this particular study indicated that the land immediately surrounding a proposed reservoir would increase in value from about $2.3 million to about $4.3 million on completion of the project, and that the increased worth of the land would be due almost entirely to the recreation opportunities afforded by the project.

The findings showed that in this case the increased sale prices of land established in the real estate market reflected values due entirely to location on or near reservoir projects. These increased prices represent the capitalization of values derived from such locational advantage. The dollar amounts of capitalized value are substantial and are an important consequence of this type of investment. Further, these values vary greatly depending upon particular circumstances of locational and site characteristics. It seems likely that similar studies would be feasible and highly useful for the economic evaluations of other types of recreation areas.

The total direct economic value of public recreation areas is the sum of two sets of values: (1) the user benefit or the values which people receive from visits that involve travel to the area, and (2) the values capitalized in land near the recreation area. The relative size of these two components depends on individual circumstances, particularly freedom of access, and can vary greatly between areas. The land value portion may be relatively large for lakes with few or no points for public access and for some urban parks, but small for more remote areas with few access restrictions. In the case of large public areas where no private

[9] For this purpose two sets of estimates were made, one relating prices of reservoir land to a number of factors, and one involving lands without reservoir influences. The first relationship was used to estimate the land values under the assumption that the project is constructed and the second assuming that it is not. The difference was taken to represent the contribution of the reservoir. Estimates were obtained for a period of future years by including certain factors to account for growth of the relative demand for this type of land.

lands are near the primary recreation attraction, the increase in land values would probably be negligible or absent.

Care must be taken to avoid double counting. Benefits will be overstated to the extent that the landowners are counted as visitors and revenues from sales to park visitors are distributed to the value of the land. The value of the revenues derived from visitor expenditures is already counted, at least in part, in the tabulations of user benefits, which are based on their expenses. The larger the portion of the expenditures made in the vicinity of the park, the larger the element of double counting.

OTHER MEASUREMENT METHODS

In recent years a number of other methods have been proposed for evaluating recreation benefits. Some measures are clearly incorrect; others attempt to measure appropriate values but fall short on empirical grounds. Part of the confusion and difficulty encountered by some of the methods stems from failure to identify the relevant product. For purposes of benefit analysis the product having value is the recreation service produced by the project or by the investment. If the recreation activity is fishing, the product is fishing and not the fish that may or may not be caught.

Gross Expenditure Method. This method attempts to measure the value of recreation to the recreationist in terms of the total amount spent on recreation by the recreationist. Estimates of gross recreation expenditures are very popular in many quarters. For one thing, such estimates are likely to yield large figures, which give the impression of a large and profitable tourist-recreation business. Indeed, this is often one of their chief purposes.

Such gross expenditure estimates have at times been used to indicate the importance of the recreation opportunity afforded by a multiple purpose project. If, for example, the gross value of recreation was X millions of dollars and the gross value of electric power produced was Y millions of dollars, then the ratio of X to Y somehow suggests the relative importance of the two.

This method has been used by a number of agencies, particularly state fish and game departments, and by travel departments and tourist promotion agencies. The contention of most is that the value of a day's recreation is worth at least the amount of money spent by a person for that purpose. These expenditures include travel expenses; expenses for equipment such as boats, motors, and tackle; and expenses incurred while in the recreation area. The 1960 National Survey of Fishing and Hunting indicated that the median yearly expenditure of sport fishermen was $27.09 and the median time spent fishing was 9.0 days; an expenditure of about $3.00 per angler-day.[10]

These values are of some use in indicating the amount of money spent on a particular type of outdoor recreation, although it must be recognized that they represent expenditures for many goods and services, some in the year under study but some in previous years. The figures also have some utility in establishing the income effects of recreation on residents in the area, and therefore in determining the effects of local investments for this purpose. But they are of little or no consequence for justifying public expenditure on recreation, or for determining the worth or benefit of recreation opportunities afforded.

What is needed is not some gross value but the value added by a particular recreation opportunity. It is the net increase in the value of the recreation opportunities produced that is crucial; this represents a true net yield that can be compared with what the resource would yield if it were used to produce other services. It is the margin above the cost of taking advantage of the recreation opportunity which measures the real monetary value that would be lost if the recreation opportunity were not available. The gross expenditure figures in themselves do not measure this. They tell us the magnitude of the industry, in one sense, but they do not indicate the value of the losses that would be sustained if the particular recreation opportunity were to disappear, or the value of the net gain from an increase in a particular recreation opportunity.

The gross expenditure method bears a superficial resemblance to the method of estimating user benefits we have outlined. Each approach depends on information on expenditures by recreationists—money spent for travel, meals, lodging, equipment, etc. But the gross expenditure method assumes that somehow these total outlays measure the economic value of the recreation opportunity. The user benefit method we employ requires the estimation of the demand curve for the whole recreation experience, using user expenditure data; and from this, a demand curve for the recreation resource is estimated.

Market Value of Fish Method. A method proposed to estimate the recreation benefits afforded by fishing imputes to sport fishing the market value of fish caught, calculated at the dockside price of commercially caught fish. This procedure implies that the primary objective is the catch and not the activity. This is most certainly not the case.

Cost Method. This method, used by some agencies, and particularly in the early 1950's, assumes that the value of outdoor recreation resource use is equal to the cost of generating it or, in some extreme

[10] Bureau of Sport Fisheries and Wildlife, *1960 National Survey of Fishing and Hunting,* U.S. Department of the Interior Circular 120, Washington, 1961.

applications, to a multiple of that cost. Any recreation project which is contemplated can therefore be automatically justified on grounds of "intangible considerations." However, this method offers no guide to evaluating a contemplated loss of recreation opportunities, and it allows very little discrimination between the relative values of alternative investment opportunities.[11]

Market Value Method. No doubt the most common method for measuring recreation benefits at public recreation areas is the market value method, which uses a schedule of charges to represent the market value of the recreation services produced. Attendance is multiplied by the appropriate charge to arrive at a recreation value for the services produced by a project. The market value chosen is normally related to prices charged at privately owned recreation areas. A judgment is usually made of the merits of the individual project, and then some adjustment is made in prices.

This method forms the basis of benefit estimates made by various federal agencies concerned with use and development of water and related land resources.[12] The schedule of market values currently in use and the rationale for their selection is contained in a supplement to the general policy guide for water resources development, which states "In evaluating outdoor recreation as a project purpose it is necessary that it be viewed as producing an economic product in the sense that a recreation opportunity has value and is something for which people are willing to pay."[13]

The standard unit of measurement is a recreation day. Estimates of the number of recreation days of use are developed, and each recreation day is assigned either a "general" or a "specialized" value. The general recreation day includes primarily activities that are attractive to the majority of outdoor recreationists and that generally require the development and maintenance of convenient access and adequate facilities. The range of these unit-day values is from $0.50 to $1.50 per day. The specialized recreation day includes activities for which opportunities are generally limited, intensity of use is low, and personal expenses are often large. The range of values for such days is $2.00 to $6.00. These

[11] James A. Crutchfield, "Valuation of Fishery Resources," *Land Economics* (May 1962), and Lionel Lerner, "Quantitative Indices of Recreation Values," *Economics in Outdoor Recreation Policy,* Report No. 11, Committee on Water Resources and the Economic Development of the West, Western Agricultural Economics Research Council, 1962.

[12] *Policies, Standards, and Procedures in the Formulation, Evaluation, and Review of Plans for Use and Development of Water and Related Land Resources,* 87th Congress, Second Session, Senate Document 97, approved May 1962; *Evaluation Standards for Primary Outdoor Recreation Benefits,* Supplement No. 1, Ad Hoc Water Resources Council, Washington, D. C., June 1964.

[13] Supplement No. 1; *op. cit.,* p. 1.

unit values are intended to measure the amount that the users would be willing to pay if payment were required.

The values set forth in the schedule are offered as interim statements of recreation benefit analysis "pending the development of improved pricing and benefit evaluation techniques."[14]

This method has both advantages and disadvantages. It is on sound ground in its emphasis on willingness of users to incur expenses—to make choices and back them up with money. However, it seems inappropriate to use charges at private areas to measure the value of recreation at public areas, as the market for all outdoor recreation is not a commercial one, and private outdoor recreation areas are affected by the existence of virtually free public areas. The charges that users are willing to pay at private areas may largely reflect payments for benefits in excess of those available at public areas—better natural resources, better improvements, better management, less crowding, for example. It is precisely because private areas are not fully comparable with public areas that users are willing to pay fees or charges.

Even if the value figure for a day's recreation were the correct one, there is still the problem of establishing the number of visitor days. The number at a zero charge will be considerably larger than the number at the entrance fee which would maximize revenue. Multiplying the value per visit by the number of visitors at a zero charge will therefore result in an overestimate, perhaps a serious one, of the benefits or values produced.

Multiplication of any single price per day's recreation by any single estimated volume of recreation use would never produce, except by occasional accident, the same estimates of total economic value to users as those produced by our calculations of the area under the demand curve.

It should be evident that a single value figure based on broad regional averages will be inappropriate for many recreation areas. The value of any good or service is affected, for example, by location. This is particularly true for outdoor recreation. A recreation area close to a city will draw many more visitors than an equally attractive one, in a physical sense, located much further away. Moreover, differences in quality and attractiveness of recreation areas should be recognized. In the federal procedure the basic figures are varied somewhat for facilities provided but are invariant for many of the factors important to value determination. This means that they largely fail to take account of determinants expressed by willingness to pay and are consequently less sensitive to variations in recreation values which determine the relative

[14] *Ibid.,* p. 5.

efficiency of alternative investments, or alternative design and operating procedures.

Direct Interview Method. Another means of arriving at the sought-after estimate of the net economic yield of resources used for recreation purposes is a direct sample survey of users in which reactions to varying fees would be recorded. This method has been used with success in imputing a schedule of user-days at alternative prices of the resources.[15] It is a direct means of assessing the willingness to pay, and if care is taken it can produce economically meaningful results. There are obvious problems of bias in stating reactions to hypothetical purchases, but this may be reduced with skillful interviewing. There are also disadvantages from the standpoint of generalizing the results to wider and proposed new areas, and costs of obtaining the needed information are high.

DEVELOPMENT OF RULE-OF-THUMB STANDARDS FOR VALUE OF RECREATION OPPORTUNITY

In this chapter, we have outlined a procedure for estimating the value of recreation opportunity, one that will yield sums comparable with value estimates if the same resources are used for other purposes. But, admittedly, this procedure is not easy to apply. It requires an estimate of the demand curve for the recreation experience. Moreover, one must estimate the whole demand curve in advance of actual experience, if one is trying to estimate the value of recreation opportunity in a park not yet established or on a reservoir not yet built. For planning purposes, it is always the estimated future values which are significant, and there are always problems of estimating probable future relationships. To do this, one must rely on experience elsewhere, and make adjustments appropriate to the situation under study. However, in this latter respect, recreation is no different than irrigation, power production, navigation improvement, or any other result of resource improvement and management programs. This problem has received much attention from economists and market specialists for many goods and services, and there appears to be little reason why recreation cannot be treated in an analogous manner.

Rules of thumb are useful in all types of resource management and improvement situations. A rule of thumb is a rough average relationship that will apply in general but not necessarily in every individual case; it can be refined by corrections or adjustments to meet common variations of the general relationship. A rule of thumb should not take

---

[15] Robert K. Davis, "The Value of Outdoor Recreation: An Economic Study of the Maine Woods" (unpublished dissertation, Harvard University, 1963).

the place of a careful, detailed study for each specific situation. But it does have utility in various ways: as a rough preliminary estimate, as a rough check on detailed studies (which have been known to yield erroneous results), and as a substitute for a careful estimate if the latter is, for some reason, impossible.

By careful research as to the value of outdoor recreation in a number of areas of differing characteristics, it should be possible to develop some useful rule-of-thumb guides. These might be formulated in terms of alternative values for alternative areas of given attractiveness and accessibility. In practice, it might be possible to introduce other factors. A table could be set up showing a general range of values, but a specific value would have to be established for a specific case in order to be meaningful. The figures might vary in different regions of the country. In all of these, and perhaps in other ways, the rules of thumb could take account of actual situations to produce more nearly accurate and relevant estimates. Great improvement is possible, if we are willing to undertake a number of specific research projects and then to generalize from their findings.

12

Economic Impacts of Outdoor Recreation on Local Areas

The economic impact resulting from the development of outdoor recreation facilities in a given area or locality is increasingly becoming a matter of more than passing interest. Many communities virtually live on the business of tourists and vacationists. Seacoast, lake, and mountain vacation areas with little other basic economic activity are often heavily dependent on such business.

Tourism and recreation development are often regarded as particularly attractive investments for a region because of the export characteristics of the business, goods and services being marketed, in large part, to nonresident consumers. Many towns and localities want more tourists or vacation business as a means of economic support for the community. And outdoor recreation has been suggested as a way of providing economic support to depressed rural areas. At times there seems almost an assumption that an area with no other values or source of income must surely be well suited for outdoor recreation. Investments are proposed or undertaken in the hope or belief that large recreational use will thereby follow and that this will bring a measure of economic well-being to the area.

There is also much discussion of the economic impact of recreational development in connection with the establishment of new parks or recreational areas. Testimony before committees of the Congress considering the establishment of new national parks or national recreational areas reflects the intense interest in the impact that the area will have on the local economy. The economic effect may indeed be substantial, and the concern of the local people is understandable, but it is by no means clear that there is complete understanding of what recreation expenditures mean in terms of the local economy, and what relationship they have to public investment decisions, particularly on the part of the federal government.

As we have repeatedly emphasized, the economic effects or values of outdoor recreation are substantial and are important. But it needs to be understood that there are two kinds of benefits. A failure to separate them can result only in a confused discussion, improper recognition of relevant and legitimate economic interests, and inferior planning and policy choices.

One class of values includes the primary benefits, largely expressed as the willingness to pay on the part of consumers of recreation services. Those who use the recreation opportunity receive a direct benefit whose value is largely measured by their willingness to spend available income. These values may or may not register in the commerce of the region or even in the commerce of the nation, but this does not make them any less real, as we have indicated in the discussion of Chapter 11. These are the values that, when appropriately measured, provide the basis for calculating the economic worth of natural resources when used for outdoor recreation.

A second class of benefits includes the gains in the area where the expenditures are made. What is expense to the recreationist is income to the supplier of his goods and services. This is particularly the case for travel, equipment, lodging expenses, and other items paid for by the recreationist. Although the recreation opportunity is generally not marketed as such, there are substantial commercial impact effects from the expenditures necessarily involved in use of the available areas.

This distinction of classes, or types of economic values or gains, has relevance for the decision-making body or unit as it weighs the values of recreation area proposals. The decision-making unit for establishment of a new national park is the Nation—the President, the Congress, and associated units of national government; the decision-making unit for a state park must be the State, with its governor, legislature, park department, and other units. These decision-making bodies must be concerned with the primary benefits from the proposed park—how many people will use it, where will they come from, how much will they spend, and the like. But they are likely also to consider, to some extent, the regional or geographic impact of the park. The federal government may wish to stimulate recreation in an economically depressed region such as Appalachia, for instance. The welfare of different parts or districts of its total geographic area is the proper concern of any unit of government.

The recipients of the impact benefits have a natural concern about the economic benefits of the proposed park or recreation area. After all, this may well be their livelihood, or an important part of it. The recipients may be "local," in the sense that they are located near the park; but they may also be located at a considerable distance from the park, if visitors travel a long way. Much summer travel through the western half of the United States is motivated by a desire to visit one or more of the national parks located there, for instance, and expenditures from this travel may be significant for hundreds of miles away from the parks themselves. Recipients of impact benefits may seek a particular type of public recreation development, just as recipients of the benefits of flood protection or irrigation may seek a particular type of public investment.

The amount of money spent in connection with outdoor recreation and tourism is large and growing. This makes outdoor recreation expenditures of concern to localities and regions that stand to gain from them.

We have, then, not a single interest, but a cluster of economic interests surrounding recreation development proposals. It is not at all surprising that all interests may not be served to the same degree or even in the same direction by any plan. Conflicts can occur over the legitimate issue of what kind of park or reservoir or highway development is consistent with both the national and local interest.

EXPENDITURES ON A TYPICAL VACATION[1]

Notions as to what happens to the recreationist's dollar are often sketchy. For a better understanding it is important to know: how much of the expenditure stays in the local area, however that is defined; who in the area receives it and who benefits most from recreation expenditures; the relationship of recreation-vacation business to the local tax burden; and, probably of most concern, the employment and wages that are generated by these expenditures.

It may be useful, at the outset, to discuss the expenditures made by a typical family on a recreation visit to an intermediate or resource-based outdoor recreation area—that is, one involving travel.

Of most interest are the total, the type, and the place of travel and recreational expenditures. Some expenditures will be made in the home town or city of the recreationist, some in or near the recreation site itself, and some en route.

A visit to either a resource-based outdoor recreation area or an

[1] The discussion in this section draws on Marion Clawson, "Private and Public Provision of Outdoor Recreation Opportunity," *Economic Studies of Outdoor Recreation,* ORRRC Study Report 24, Washington, 1962. The results are illustrative of general methodology and provide estimates of general magnitudes and general relationships. Table 20 includes a few items that were not available in 1960 when the original study was made.

intermediate class area nearly always involves travel by private auto-mobile. Sometimes this may mean a major cash outlay for transportation equipment, or for more specialized travel and recreation equipment. The family may have, or may buy, luggage, boats, boat trailers, fishing and hunting equipment, camping equipment, water skis or any one of many other kinds of specialized equipment of varying quality and cost. Most of this equipment would probably be purchased in the home community, though some may be bought en route or at the recreation area itself. To the ardent fisherman there is always a pressing need for just a few more flies or just a little more tackle, and similarly for many another enthusiast.

The family will incur significant travel expenditures. They must buy gas and oil for the car, and may need tires and repairs at intervals. They must have a place to sleep, if the trip is longer than one day, and food to eat. If the trip is short, they may take the food with them from home. If they can afford it or if their tastes run that way, they may buy special clothing for the trip, and perhaps cameras and film. All of these items may be bought at home, en route, or at the destination. Some special expenses such as boat rental are likely to be at the site. The family may well consume valuable services provided by some public agencies such as park or recreational opportunities free or at nominal cost. The expenditures for the return trip will be in many respects similar to the trip to the site.

Since our concern is with the economic impact of these expenditures, we use the total expenditures made. To the family making the trip, a more relevant figure is the difference between what is spent for the trip and what would have been spent at home. That is, the family would have to buy groceries if it stayed home; its expenditures for groceries on the recreation trip may be little more than they would have been at home, hence in deciding that it could afford to make the trip, only the added cost of the groceries may have been considered. From the view-point of all grocery stores everywhere in the United States, it may have made little difference whether the family made this vacation trip or not; but from the viewpoint of the grocery store where it habitually traded as well as from the viewpoint of the grocery stores along its travel route, the trip does make a difference.

A considerable number of tourist or recreationist travel surveys have been made since the war. Some of them are summarized in Table 20. Such surveys generally did not provide careful definitions of "expendi-tures." Presumably only current cash outlays, excluding purchase of major items of equipment, were included. Although it is not clear, it seems probable that only cash expenditures made while actually on the trip were included. Thus food, gasoline, and other expenditures made at home before the trip started but necessary for the recreation experience may well not have been included. Some of the surveys, particularly those relating to national parks, specifically included expenditures only in the vicinity of the park studied.

Actual dollar outlays per day varied in some part because these were years of changing general price levels. However, a high degree of consistency in percentage distribution of the expenditures among items is evident in the table. Food, including restaurant and grocery store expenditures, accounted for about one-third of the total; lodging for about one-fourth; transportation, which probably means primarily gas for the family automobile, about one-fifth; and "other," undoubtedly made up a wide variety of items, for the remainder, roughly a fifth.

While differences appear from area to area, the general similarities are far more striking than the differences. Data of this type would be immensely more useful if (1) the various studies employed comparable known definitions of expenditures, and more detail were included as to specific items of expenditure instead of broad categories, (2) the expenditures included all items, including either cash-cost or estimated depreciation charges for equipment, and (3) data were included on expenditures at home preparatory to the trip, and expenditures en route to the recreation area were separated from those at or near the site. Data to these specifications would obviously be somewhat more difficult to get, particularly because most vacationists have only a vague idea as to how much they spent for what and where. But it might be possible to devise some means of estimating these items.

Based on the surveys reported in Table 20, and on other sources, a rough estimate of average daily expenditure per visitor at different kinds of areas is presented in Table 21. The estimate for 1960 is that the average visit to a national park, including travel to and from the park, cost the visitor $15.50 per day, for instance. Roughly two-thirds of this was cash cost, the remainder a charge for use of the equipment, particularly the automobile. The percentage breakdown of cost among items is about that shown in Table 20.

In contrast, the daily expenditures at other units in the national park system is estimated at $9.50. The typical trip of this kind is much shorter, thus much less frequently requiring an outlay for lodging, meals will be less, and travel and equipment charges lower. The estimate for the average day at the national forest is intermediate because such trips are often longer than to national museums or historical areas on the one hand yet shorter than typical trips to national parks, on the other. The typical visit to a state park is a one-day affair requiring little for lodging, less for food because more meals will be eaten at home before or after the trip, and less for travel because of the shorter distance,

TABLE 20.
DIVISION OF VISITOR EXPENDITURES ON TRIPS, SELECTED AREAS AND STATES

Survey[1]	Date	Percentage distribution of expenditures			
		Food	Lodg-ing	Trans-porta-tion	Other
Crater Lake National Park	1950	29.3	31.3	17.8	21.6
Yellowstone National Park	1950	34.4	30.6	24.6	10.4
Shenandoah National Park	1952	36.9	23.8	21.0	18.3
Yosemite National Park	1953	41.1	24.2	19.6	15.1
Grand Canyon National Park	1954	35.6	25.5	22.2	16.7
Great Smoky Mountain National Park	1956	35.2	27.2	14.5	23.0
Average—National Parks		35.4	27.1	20.0	17.5
Arkansas	1949–50	34.0	19.0	23.0	24.0
Washington State	1950	32.0	23.0	20.0	25.0
Kansas	1952	35.5	14.6	37.0	12.9
Colorado	1953	30.8	25.8	25.3	18.1
Pennsylvania	1954	28.0	17.0	23.0	32.0
Virginia	1955	30.4	20.8	23.3	25.5
Arkansas	1956	35.0	20.1	23.3	21.6
Connecticut	1956	36.0	36.0	10.0	18.0
Montana	1958	31.1	23.9	25.4	19.6
Minnesota	1958–59	27.1	36.3	10.6	26.0
Wisconsin	1958	41.0	17.0	14.0	28.0
Missouri	1959	25.0	19.0	28.0	28.0
Wyoming	1960	25.1	25.3	32.9	16.7
Average—State travel surveys		31.6	22.9	22.8	22.7
Average—All surveys		33.5	25.0	22.8	22.7
American Automobile Association	1950	47.0		20.0	33.0
American Automobile Association	1956	28.0	22.0	22.0	28.0
American Automobile Association	1960	36.0	33.0	24.0	7.0

[1] Each of the surveys indicated the number of interviews.

SOURCES:

The national park surveys were conducted by the various State Highway or Public Works Commissions in co-operation with U.S. Bureau of Public Roads and National Park Service.

Lewis C. Copeland, *Travelers and Arkansas Business, 1948–1956*, Arkansas Publicity and Parks Commission, Arkansas State Highway Commission, U.S. Bureau of Public Roads, and the University of Arkansas.

The Washington Tourist Survey, State College of Washington, School of Economics and Business, and the Bureau of Economic and Business Research, Bulletin No. 17, 1950.

The Kansas Tourist Survey, Bureau of Business Research, and University of Kansas, School of Business, Lawrence, Kansas, 1953.

1953 Statewide Colorado Summer Tourist Survey, Bureau of Business Research and University of Colorado.

The 1954 Tourist Survey, Out of State Motorists, Pennsylvania Department of Highways and the U.S. Bureau of Public Roads.

Out of State Passenger Car Travel on Virginia's Primary Highways, Virginia Department of Highways, 1955.

Survey of Out of State Motorists, Connecticut State Development Commission, 1956.

Tourist Travel and Expenditures in Montana, Montana State Highway Commission and the U.S. Bureau of Public Roads, 1958.

Vacation Travel Survey, 1958–1959, Minnesota Arrowhead Association and The Iron Range Resources and Rehabilitation Department.

H. Clifton Hutchins and Edgar W. Trecker, Jr., *The State Park Visitor, A Report of the Wisconsin Park and Forest Travel Study*, Wisconsin Conservation Department, 1961.

Ronald Bird and Frank Miller, "Contributions of Tourist Trade to Incomes of People in Missouri Ozarks," Missouri Experiment Station, Research Bulletin 799, 1962.

Richard E. Lund, *A Study of Wyoming's Out-of-State Highway Travelers*, University of Wyoming, 1961.

Various surveys and estimates made by the American Automobile Association.

TABLE 21.
ESTIMATED EXPENDITURE PER PERSON PER DAY, FOR VISITORS TO
SPECIFIED KINDS OF PUBLIC RECREATION AREAS, 1960

Item of expense	National parks	Other units of national park system	National forests	State parks	Federal reservoirs
1. Cash outlay during or immediately preceding visit:					
Food:					
In restaurants	$ 2.00	$ 1.50	$ 1.75	$ 1.00	$ 1.00
Groceries	1.50	1.00	1.75	1.00	1.00
Lodging	2.70	1.00	1.50	.50	.50
Transportation:					
Gas and oil	1.50	1.20	1.50	1.00	1.00
Other	.50	.30	.50	.25	.25
Miscellaneous ("other")	1.80	1.00	1.50	.75	1.50
Subtotal	10.00	6.00	8.50	4.50	5.25
2. Reasonable charge for use of equipment:					
Auto	4.00	3.00	3.50	2.50	2.50
Other	1.50	.50	1.50	1.00	2.00
Total, all items	$15.50	$ 9.50	$13.50	$ 8.00	$ 9.75

SOURCE: ORRRC Study Report No. 24.

and so on. Federal reservoirs are similar to state parks, except that it has been assumed that the cost of other equipment would be higher because of the more frequent use of boats and other water equipment. At best, the data in Table 21 can be only broadly accurate; large differences will exist between different areas in each of the systems.

The geographic distribution of expenditures is shown more explicitly in Table 22. The place where expenditures are made depends in part upon the kind of expenditure and in part upon the length of the trip. Food will be purchased in restaurants largely at the recreation site if the trip is short, and largely en route if the trip is long. Food will be bought from grocery stores largely in the home community if the trip is short; more will be purchased en route and at or near the recreation site if the trip is long. The geographic distribution of gas and oil expenditures is somewhat like that for food from grocery stores; outlays for travel and other equipment are nearly always made in the recreationist's home community. It should be emphasized that these estimates are based on the general nature of the recreation experience and the length of the trip; specific data on these points is lacking.

A further major expenditure consideration is the recipient. The expenses of a family in a recreation experience are the gross revenues or gross receipts of the businesses which service them. When the family drives into the service station to buy a tank full of gas for, say, $5.00, the service station operator may keep 60 cents of it as his margin.

TABLE 22.

DIVISION OF VARIOUS KINDS OF RECREATION EXPENDITURES, ACCORDING TO TYPE OF RECREATION AREA AND LOCATION OF EXPENDITURE

Per cent

Item	National parks			Other units in National Park System			National forests			State parks			Federal reservoirs		
	In or near park	En route	In home community	In or near park	En route	In home community	In or near park	En route	In home community	In or near park	En route	In home community	In or near park	En route	In home community
1. Cash outlays:															
Food:															
In restaurants	40	60	0	50	50	0	50	50	0	65	35	0	65	35	0
Groceries	35	50	15	25	25	50	25	15	60	10	5	85	10	5	85
Lodging	45	55	0	75	25	0	65	35	0	60	40	0	60	40	0
Transportation:															
Gas and oil	30	60	10	30	40	30	30	40	30	20	10	70	25	15	60
Other	30	60	10	30	40	30	30	40	30	20	10	70	25	15	60
Miscellaneous	50	40	10	60	20	20	20	40	40	50	15	35	50	15	35
2. Equipment charge:															
Auto	2	3	95	2	3	95	2	3	95	2	3	95	2	3	95
Other	15	5	80	5	10	85	5	20	75	10	20	70	20	20	60

SOURCE: ORRRC Study Report No. 24.

237

Perhaps $1.50 is required to pay the state and federal gasoline taxes out of which in turn the roads are built and maintained, and the rest buys the gasoline at wholesale. Of the service operator's 60 cents, 30 cents may be paid as wages to his employees, 10 cents may be needed to maintain his station, pay the taxes, buy electricity and water, and meet a myriad of small but necessary expenditures, and possibly 20 cents is left to pay for his own labor and as a return to his managerial ability and capital.

Roughly similar comparisons could be made for the money spent at the motel or in a restaurant or at the grocery store or any other place. The expenses of the recreationist for gasoline, food, shelter, and the many other items he buys are thus in part apportioned in the community as wages and salaries, interest, profits, and taxes. However, a considerable part of what the family spends is sent out of the local community to pay for necessary supplies of goods and services available only from outside.

A breakdown of various kinds of recreation expenditures according to recipients is shown in Table 23. The estimates were made largely from service industry reports published by Dun and Bradstreet and other organizations. Most goods purchased probably came from outside the local area where the recreation expenditure was made, but not all goods came from outside and even for those that did, some local servicing may have been performed. Thus the gasoline a service station sells is ordinarily made by a refinery outside the local community. But the gasoline wholesaler will have performed some services in making it

TABLE 23.
DIVISION OF VARIOUS KINDS OF RECREATION EXPENDITURES
ACCORDING TO RECIPIENT OF MONEY

Item	Percentage distribution of expenditure[1]				
	For goods purchased	Owner's compensation	Wages	Other	Total
1. Cash outlays:					
Food:					
In restaurants	52	8	20	20	100
Groceries	85	5	5	5	100
Lodging	25	15	30	30	100
Transportation:					
Gas and oil	75	8	8	9	100
Other	65	10	10	15	100
Miscellaneous	60	15	7	18	100
2. Equipment charge:					
Auto	85	3	5	7	100
Other	70	10	5	15	100

[1] These are rough approximations, based on judgment and by reference to trade publications such as Dun and Bradstreet, *Operating Ratios for Forty-One Lines of Retail Trade.*
SOURCE: ORRRC Study Report No. 24.

available to the service station. The other categories of owner's compensation, wages, and "other" probably accrued primarily to persons in the local community, although this is not necessarily always the case.

The amount spent for goods purchased outside the immediate area varied from about 85 per cent for groceries and autos down to only about 25 per cent for lodging. By and large, owner's compensation, wages, and "other" varied in the same general direction—all three inversely to the percentage paid for goods purchased. A particularly unsatisfactory part of this classification is the "other" column. It probably included a very wide range of items, including taxes.

IMPACT ON LOCAL AREAS

The characteristics of recreation expenditures have a number of implications for the economic impact on individual areas located near facilities. One of the more important consequences in the local communities is that by no means all of the total expenditures made by recreationists take place in the community located in proximity to the recreation area. Another is that the type of expenditures that are made in these local communities are of rather specific kinds. Food, lodging, and automobile service comprise the bulk of the expenditure items that take place en route and near recreation areas. Further, there is a variation in type of expenditures that take place in local areas depending upon the type of recreational area or development and upon its location with respect to visitors. For example, if the visitors are within a few hours' drive there will be little demand for lodging.

Also apparent is the fact that total expenditures, however they may be defined or measured, are not all net income to the locality. Much of the gross income must go outside the area to buy the goods and products necessary to service travelers, and to provide facilities. But some of the income is used to buy goods and products produced locally, and some of it is used to pay wages, salaries, profits, interest, and rents to members of the local community. While a good portion of the money leaves the community more or less directly, a portion of it does remain in the local community.

The economic impact on the economy of local areas cannot be measured by total expenditures. But income, the number of jobs or employment, sales, and value added (which is the gross expenditures made in the area less the cost of the goods and services purchased by the firm making the sales to the recreationist) are all units which might be appropriate for one purpose or another. A saving fact is that these different measures of the local economy tend to move together. That is, as sales rise, value added and employment generated also tend to rise.

Sometimes, of course, these measures do not move in the same proportion, and sometimes when the changes are small they may even move in opposite directions. While these problems exist and should be borne in mind, it is still possible to use these measures to assess the changes in the economy that are likely to occur with the development of recreational facilities.

Whichever method or measure is chosen, the chief economic consideration for the local community is the impact on the economy of a dollar expenditure stemming from the facility or recreation area. These dollars stem in large part from the recreationist, but also to a significant degree from expenditures of the park agency on wages, and on goods and services purchased locally. Fundy National Park, for example, is the largest single employer in Albert County, New Brunswick.

It is the initial expenditures which generate whatever impact is felt in the community. A portion of what is received is sent immediately out of the area to pay for imports to the area, but a portion is also paid to local suppliers of goods and services. Then, a portion of the expenditure that remains in the local community is spent by those who receive it for other goods and services which are in part produced locally and in part imported into the community.

The second-round recipients—those who receive money directly from recipients of the original expenditures—have less to spend than the total that was spent by the original recreationist, and the third-round recipients have less again. The service station operator buys groceries and the grocery worker buys gasoline, but since the community is not and could not be self-contained, a major part of the expenditure at each round escapes from the community.

The result of these expenditure patterns is a multiplier process. At each successive round a smaller amount of the original expenditure accrues as local income because of the need to spend outside the community. The effect becomes insignificant after the first few rounds. The multiplier effect will vary from community to community, and will vary also with the type of consumer or recreation expenditures. The more self-contained the local economy is, the greater will be the proportion of the expenditures resulting in increases in local income, because less will have to be spent outside the community. By the same token, the greater the proportion of expenditures made for goods and services produced in the community, the greater will be the increases in local income. For example, gasoline station sales will result in less income produced locally per dollar of expenditures on the part of tourists, than will lodging facilities, owing to the fact that service station sales are made up in large part of supplies from wholesale or other sources outside the local community, whereas lodging sales are largely in the form of labor and other services which would be supplied locally.

Although the input of recreation spending is spread over a number of rounds and varies among expenditures it is, fortunately, not necessary to trace out each round of spending to determine the local income created. A multiplier formula has been devised which will give us the answer to this more simply.[2]

The first factor is the extent of the increase in local income resulting from tourist expenditures. This is equal to the expenditures minus the payment for goods and services bought from outside the community. On a per dollar basis, it is the proportion that remains to be spent within the community. (Since this enters the estimate in a multiplicative manner, the type or nature of recreation expenditures with respect to local sources of supply has an extremely important effect.) This factor is then multiplied by 1 over 1 minus the proportion of their income which local people spend on local goods and services, which we can call propensity to consume locally, times the proportion of such expenditures that accrues as local income. Writing this out we have:

$$\text{Total income increase} = A \times \frac{1}{1 - BC}$$

where A = proportion remaining in area,
  B = proportion of income that local people spend in local goods and services, i.e. propensity to spend locally, and
  C = proportion of expenditures of local people that accrues as local income.

This expression in this form gives us an estimate of how much local income results from each dollar of expenditure in the region.

This equation may be illustrated by using some simple hypothetical but perhaps not unreasonable numbers. We might assume first that for every dollar of expenditure made in the community one half is for goods and services produced locally (the other half dollar going for goods and services produced outside the local economy). The first term on the right of the equation is then 0.5. We may assume that the propensity to consume locally is 0.4 for the community, and that the income created, in the form of wages, salaries, etc. per dollar of local sales, is 0.6. We have, then, by substitution:

$$\text{Total income increase} = 0.5 \times \frac{1}{1 - (0.4 \times 0.6)} = 0.66$$

[2] This discussion draws heavily on Charles M. Tiebout, *The Community Economic Base Study,* Supplemental Paper 16, Committee for Economic Development, 1962.

Under these assumptions we find that for every dollar received from recreation expenditures, the increase in local income which results is $0.66.

We know that these numbers vary with the kinds of expenditures made and the nature of the economy of the community. With more detailed information it should be possible to assess, in at least generalities, the impact of recreation-tourism expenditures on the economy. Some information of the kind necessary has been provided by studies of particular areas.

A study of tourist expenditure in Hawaii found that about 95 cents of personal income was created for every dollar of expenditure. This estimate allowed first for outside purchases and the subsequent spending rounds of the income.[3] A similar type of estimate reported in the ORRRC studies placed the figure closer to 75 cents of local income per dollar expenditure.

Further information on the order of magnitude of the numbers and their variation among expenditure categories can be gained from a study of expenditures by fishermen and their families in New Mexico.[4] The percentages of sales resulting in value added for the state were as follows:

	Per cent
Vehicles	12.0
Boats and motors	25.0
Camping equipment	28.4
Transportation	18.3
Food	45.9
Lodging	69.0
Fishing tackle	28.4
Special clothing	24.5
Horses, etc.	31.5
Fees	100.0

Again, the local income produced per dollar of sales is much higher for lodging than for other items, particularly transportation.

Another interesting study reports the impact on community income from expenditures on outdoor recreation in Sullivan, Pennsylvania, a predominantly rural county located adjacent to the Pocono Mountain

---

[3] Reported in Bank of America, *Community Action for Balanced Development, Tourist-Recreation Industry*, San Francisco, 1964.

[4] Nathaniel Wollman *et al.*, *The Value of Water in Alternative Uses* (Albuquerque: University of New Mexico Press, 1962), pp. 241–52.

resort area.[5] The recreation expenditures of three classes of recreationists were surveyed—tourists, hunters and fishermen, and summer vacation home owners—using a method of analysis which systematically examines the flow of expenditure funds through the economy of the county. For every dollar spent in the county by these recreationists, the total economic activity generated was found to be $1.56 for the hunter-fishermen, $1.58 for the tourists, and $1.62 for the summer home owners. The multiplier was also found to vary by type of expenditures from $1.31 for gas station sales, $1.93 for food and beverage sales, to $2.19 for local taxes paid by the hunting camp or summer home owner.

Residual county incomes, which were taken as the sum of the direct and indirect returns to households, local governments, and nonprofit organizations of the county, were also calculated for each of the three types of recreationists. These figures more accurately reflect the benefits accruing to the local people. These returns on each dollar of expenditure were estimated to be $0.35 for tourists, $0.48 for hunter-fishermen, and $0.50 for summer home owners. These differences reflect the differences in the expenditure pattern of the groups and the differences of local income generation that stem from the various types of expenditures.

In assessing the potential of recreation and tourism as a means of economic support, it must be remembered that a recreation business can be a hazardous undertaking. Among the difficulties are the extreme seasonal patterns of demand, the susceptibility of this kind of expenditure to fluctuations in the business cycle, the hazards of weather, and the somewhat unusual types of business skills called for in this type of industry.

If recreation is to improve the economic well-being of a community, it is important to consider the extent to which the area will attract visitors. Not all areas attract large numbers of people, and a realistic appraisal of the demand potential is of prime importance. A further consideration is how long visitors are likely to remain in the area, where they come from, their income level, and other factors which influence the expenditures that are likely to be made in the area.

In many parts of the industry the pay scales rank among the lowest of major industries in the total economy. There is also the problem of employment, and particularly its seasonal nature. Also, of the total returns that might be available for various kinds of recreational enterprises, to what extent can returns be made to accrue to the local people, and to what extent do they leave the local area not only for payment for

[5] Hays B. Gamble, "Community Income from Outdoor Recreation," a paper presented to the Maryland Governor's Recreation Conference, Ocean City, Maryland, May 1965.

goods and services which are imported but as returns to outside capital and management? Again, this is not to say that recreational developments cannot play a role in the betterment of local economic conditions. But it is important to recognize that there are problems connected with the recreation business itself and that the recreation business potential of an area is affected by specific characteristics of area, location, and economic structure, as well as other conditions. Realistic appraisals must be made in each case.

RECREATION AND TRAVEL EXPENDITURE SURVEYS

The great local and national interest in expenditures by tourists and recreationists has led to many surveys. Some of these have dealt explicitly with hunting and fishing.[6] The earlier of such surveys were often very sketchy, with inadequate procedures and methods, leading to inaccurate and often highly exaggerated results. Some state promotional agencies reported expenditures by out-of-state visitors which were three times as high as the figures reported by careful surveys as representing the expenditures by residents as well as visitors.[7] This type of inaccurate data has tended to discredit this type of survey.

To meet the need for accurate data about tourism and travel generally, a Western Council for Travel Research was formed in 1959.[8] This unofficial organization includes individuals and organizations affiliated with "universities, state travel promotion and recreation agencies, state economic development organizations, state highway planning and research departments, federal bureaus, chambers of commerce, advertising agencies, media and firms furnishing travel services such as railroads, shipping lines, airlines, buses, etc., as well as other private agencies and associations connected with the travel industry." One of its purposes has been to stimulate more accurate surveys of travel, including more uniform and dependable methodology for conducting surveys. Its emphasis has been upon survey design, sampling, interviewing, and data processing. While the Council is primarily western, it does have some members from other parts of the country, and its ideas on survey methodology will almost surely have national impact.

This effort to bring uniformity and accuracy into travel surveys is highly commendable. "Travel," as used in such surveys, is not equivalent

[6] Bureau of Sport Fisheries and Wildlife, U.S. Department of the Interior, *1960 National Survey of Fishing and Hunting*, Circular 120, Washington, 1961.
[7] Committee on Research Methods, Western Council for Travel Research, *Standards for Traveller Studies* (Salt Lake City: Bureau of Economic and Business Research, University of Utah, 1963).
[8] *Ibid.*

to "recreation," as we have been using the term, but perhaps could be made so. Information on purposes of the trip is to be obtained, under the methodology recommended; "pleasure or vacation" is one purpose, "combined business and pleasure" is another; perhaps these two combined may be somewhat similar to "recreation," at least according to some definitions of the latter.

These studies, even when using the recommended methodology, are subject to some deficiencies.

1. They obtain expenditures (cash and credit) only within the sample area, which is often the state or a region of the state. They do not include cash expenditures in preparation for the trip; this omits a large part of the cash expenditure occasioned by the trip. Since the concern of these studies is with the local impact of the travel, it is proper that they should obtain data on expenditures within the study area; but these data may seriously underestimate the total expenditures motivated by this activity. Since the inquiry deals with cash expenditures in the study area, it does not include an allowance for use of equipment purchased earlier, often before the visitor entered the study area. Moreover, it is by no means clear that such studies include equipment purchases within the study area. They typically ask for "all auto expense"; but would this include the purchase of a new car or of a better used one by some traveler whose old jalopy gave up the ghost? They also ask for expenditures on "all other goods and services"; would this include purchase of boats, guns, or other relatively expensive and relatively durable recreation equipment? It is not clear, from the published instructions, how these matters would be handled in a specific survey.

2. The data obtained will show the area of origin (usually on a state basis only) of the visitor; but these data are not usually related to the base population within such area of origin, to get numbers of visitors per unit of base population. While data on expenditures within the study area are obtained, neither these nor any estimate of total expenditures per trip are typically related to the numbers of visitors per unit of base population.

3. Such studies do not explore the impact of the reported expenditures on the local economy. They do get expenditures by type of good or service purchased, usually in about six broad categories. But these data could readily be misinterpreted, especially by those who wish to magnify the importance of travel, if the expenditures were taken to represent value added within the study area. Such surveys do not obtain data on employment stimulated or resulting from the expenditures, nor on the investment stimulated by or necessary for this type of business, nor on the taxes paid and government services required for it. Measurement of economic and social impact of the travel would call for addi-

tional inquiries; data on gross expenditures have limited value without such measurement of impact.

THE EFFECT OF ENTRANCE FEES ON EXPENDITURES

Entrance fees are another factor that should be considered in attempts to estimate the effects of a recreation development on the local economy. Fees have a bearing on total visitors and also on the number from different distance zones. They will therefore have an effect on total expenditures and on the nature of the expenditures.

People who live close to the recreation area make all their expenditures in that area. Those in more distant areas spend most of their money in their home areas if trips are primarily one-day visits, and visitors from the more distant areas spend some money at home and some in locations nearer the recreation area.

If an entrance fee were imposed, the number of visits would fall off. Total expenditures would therefore decline. The pattern of expenditures might also shift, with expenditures falling off more sharply for visitors from some areas than for others.

The decrease in expenditures from different areas would be affected by the concentration of population in a particular zone, as this would greatly affect the number of visitors under any change in fee. It might be found that elasticity was not the same for different zones. A small increase in fees might seriously curtail the number of visitors from the closer zones, and have little effect on the number of visitors from the more distant zones where people are already spending a comparatively large sum. If length of the average trip were considerably different, there would be a corresponding difference in the cost per visit, and the effect of specific entrance fees would be very different.

An increased park entrance fee may affect different local businesses in quite different ways. If visitors from more distant areas typically stay overnight near the park, and if higher entrance fees disproportionately reduce visits from these areas, the gross income of hotels and motels will decline relatively most. Conversely, if the demand by nearby residents is highly elastic and a small increase in entrance fees results in very large decreases in their attendance, the burden will fall more heavily on some other types of suppliers. The interests of persons and firms providing goods and services to recreationists is best served by low entrance fees, for these produce the greatest volume of business. With accurate data on origins of visitors, average cost per visit, etc., it should be possible to make rather specific estimates of the impact of increased entrance fees on the various parties involved.

EFFECT OF RECREATION DEVELOPMENT ON TAXES AND ON COSTS OF LOCAL GOVERNMENT

Another question to be considered is whether recreation development can provide a local tax base sufficient to meet, or more than meet, the added costs of local government arising out of that recreation activity. There is no simple answer to this question; like so many in economics, the short answer must be, "it all depends." A number of factors are logically involved, and, again, there is a serious lack of specific information.

In a summer vacation or resort area, outdoor recreation may provide a substantial tax base. Taxes are paid primarily by summer residents of the area out of income earned elsewhere. Property owners who are summer residents only may require relatively few local governmental services. Their children will go to school elsewhere, roads to their homes need not be cleared of snow in the winter, a dispersed pattern of settlement may require no sewers because individuals provide their own septic tanks, and in other ways services of local government are kept to a low level. Something like this may exist today in the Poconos of Pennsylvania or in some areas of Vermont or Maine, as well as elsewhere.

However, even in this situation, some or most of the people who service the summer recreationists may live in the area on a year-round basis. In that case, it will be necessary to provide schools and other services, and fewer economies in costs of local government will be possible. Moreover, many summer vacation areas are beginning to get more use at other seasons, for winter sports, for vacations of people who are not tied to the summer school vacation, or even as retirement areas. Broadened seasonal use makes a more economic use of investments and provides more employment for those who service recreationists, but it does reduce the possibility of economies in local government cost.

The situation of summer vacation areas repeats itself to some extent in winter vacation areas where the users are largely retired or elderly people who do not bring children with them, and do not add to local school costs. However, investment for winter vacations often leads people to use the areas on a year-round basis or at least for a longer season, especially after retirement, so that the initial saving in local government costs may be lost.

Many areas that attract a substantial number of visitors may find that the taxes generated by the recreation business do not cover the costs of local government that are also generated by such activity. The recreation use of the area generates local business, and these businesses and their employees pay local taxes. But they also demand and require services which may cost fully as much as the taxes. Residences and small business create the need for schools and other relatively costly local services. Heavy industry is frequently the large taxpayer in relation to the direct government costs it creates; but outdoor recreation is not heavy industry.

A local area seeking to promote outdoor recreation and tourism as an economic support can only estimate, as best it can, the probable additional tax revenue and the probable additional costs of local government; the balance may be either positive or negative. An area may seek such business even when costs exceed taxes, as the best means of employing its local people. But there should not be an easy presumption that increased recreation or tourist business will naturally lead to an improved local revenue situation.

13

Cost and Investment Considerations in Providing Public Recreation Facilities

To this point, we have been primarily concerned with the values or benefits of outdoor recreation. We now turn to costs, for costs as well as benefits must be considered in reaching reasonable planning decisions. This applies to outdoor recreation facilities as it does to any other product. And it applies regardless of the nature of the decision—whether it be judging the feasibility of a facility, the merits of alternative locations, or alternative types of facilities, or the timing of acquisition of different areas.

This chapter examines the related considerations of cost and investment criteria primarily for public recreation areas. The analysis is in principle equally applicable to resource-based, intermediate, and user-oriented kinds of outdoor recreation areas. It can be used to provide some of the basic ingredients for decision making on the establishment of a national recreation area, a state park, or a city one; or for the inclusion of recreation as one of the outputs from a multiple-purpose federal water development project, or from multiple-use management of federal forest lands. Since management programs for recreation areas nearly always require some investment, an analysis of costs and returns is directly useful in terms of park and other recreation area management and administration. Considerations other than measurable benefits and costs may enter into all of these decisions, but intangible benefits or costs can hardly be accepted as governing for decisions without some consideration of the more tangible results.

Some of the same considerations outlined in this chapter also apply to privately owned and developed outdoor recreation areas. In many ways, the investment problem is simpler for private recreation areas than for public areas. The measures of costs and benefits which are relevant to

249

the private supplier's decisions are more easily measurable. He can rather readily ascertain the prices he has to pay for necessary inputs of goods and services, and the income he receives from his customers measures the benefits to him. But he has some of the same problems of trying to estimate the demand for the service he provides, some of the same uncertainties of possible competition from other public or private areas, and some of the same difficulties in estimating probable future costs and returns.

In this chapter, we first deal with some of the aspects of cost, subsequently take up the relationship between costs and benefits, and finally consider investment criteria useful for making public planning decisions.

COST CONSIDERATIONS

Resources including the myriad of inputs useful to recreation such as land, water, beaches, buildings, parks, forests, personnel, and budgets at all levels of decision making, are in no sense really free. The nature of the world is such that the amounts of the various kinds of resources are limited, relative to total wants and desires. The result is varying degrees of competition for use of resources. If more are to be devoted to recreation or diverted or reallocated to different recreation uses, something must necessarily be given up. This is the meaning of cost–giving up or foregoing something of value in an alternative use. This is clear in a direct money charge for the services of different resources, but it is no less the case when resources are withdrawn from one use and channeled into another.

While it may seem obvious that certain costs must be borne in order to divert resources into expansion or improvement of recreation facilities, it is worth while to note the nature of cost. This is helpful not only in improving understanding of the relevant costs to be considered in planning, but in subsequent discussions of investment criteria and of pricing various services produced by recreational use of resources.

We may perhaps best look at the matter of cost by first noting some of the underlying fundamentals of a market economy. While an oversimplification, it is nevertheless useful to think of this marketing economy as consumers spending their incomes on various goods and services and individual producers supplying these same goods and services.

The individual consumers in this oversimplified economy are each faced by a number of allocation decisions: First, each has a limited amount of time available to be allocated between work and leisure; second, and more important for our present purpose, each has a limited amount of income available to him. This income is distributed over all of the available goods and services in a way that maximizes each consumer's total satisfaction within his level of income. He is faced with a range of goods and services which have varying prices and yield varying amounts of satisfaction or utility. He makes his purchases on the basis of their prices and the relative satisfactions gained by their purchase.

If the consumer finds one good priced lower than another and yielding equal satisfaction to him, he will shift more of his income away from the higher-priced good to the lower-priced one. He will continue doing this until the relative satisfactions derived from the added or incremental purchases of each correspond to their relative prices. If a large number of consumers behave in a similar way, the price of the higher priced good will drop and/or the price of the lower priced good will rise as the demand is shifted to it. When all of the adjustments are made in consumer spending habits, the prices of the two goods will be in proper relationship to one another in accordance with their relative desirability to all consumers. No consumer will find it to his advantage to shift purchases from one good to another. Therefore no possible gains remain for any improvement in the reallocations of consumer expenditures. Thus, when the economy is in this type of adjustment, relative prices of goods and services reflect their relative desirability on the part of consumers.

The producers of these goods and services behave in an analagous manner. They are faced with two sets of market conditions. The first is with respect to the factors of production. These may consist of land, labor, machinery, and other capital items. These items will have varying prices, or in this case costs, attached to them. Also, the products of their enterprise, the goods and services produced, will have the prices established by the market. Producers will allocate their expenditures in such a way as to align the relative productivity of the various input factors with their cost. Thus if the price of machinery is low, relative to the wages of a given class of labor used in the production of a single commodity, the producer will shift more of his expenditure to this kind of machinery and away from this class of labor input. Similarly, other producers will also make adjustments in the relative rates in which they use the various factors of production. This imposes various demand conditions on these factors of production until their relative prices or earnings are adjusted for their relative contributions to output.

The relative costs of the input factors are related to the prices of the goods and services by the market mechanism. If consumers demand relatively more of products requiring higher rates of capital inputs than, say, land inputs, the price of the capital inputs will rise relative to that of land inputs. Price, then, is an appropriate measure of the worth to the economy of another unit of some good or service, and also of the various factors in production. Prices established by consumers determine which goods and services producers are to supply; this in turn through technical conditions of production leads to a demand for various factors of production. These are supplied in relative quantities depending upon the prices that are offered and the willingness of the owners of these production factors to supply them.

These market forces, in an economy composed of individual consumers and individual producers supplying large numbers of individual goods and services, establish one price for each kind of good or service produced and one price for each factor of production. Furthermore, by taking account of complex interrelationships between consumers' preferences, technical conditions of production, and the willingness of suppliers to supply productive factors, this system makes the best use of the available factors of production and best satisfies the desires and preferences of individuals within the limited amount of resources which are available.

In such an economy the cost of a given item of input is ultimately measured by what has to be given up. If the economy is in perfect adjustment, a dollar's worth of any input, whether it be labor, land, or capital expenditure, is producing a dollar's worth of output. Consequently, altering the adjustment by taking out a dollar to invest in recreational facilities means in fact taking a dollar's worth of production out of the economy. If the dollar's worth of land or labor, or whatever is required to improve a park or to establish a seashore or otherwise invest in recreational facilities, is diverted to other uses, this means that the economy will now be unable to produce a dollar's worth of some other goods or service elsewhere in the economy.

If a park is developed from an otherwise unproductive parcel of land, for example, its purchase price or cost would be very low. If its cost were very high we know that the parcel of land was producing goods and services in the alternative use which were valued highly by the economy or by society. It is for this reason that costs differ so greatly for alternative investments or improvements in recreation facilities. The costs of establishing a remote picnic area, for example, are far less than those for establishing an urban playground because the land in the remote area produces less of value.

Although this pricing and allocation process does not work as smoothly and perfectly as the simplified description implies, there is a constant force toward adjustment. This force is often powerful, and over some period of time it will bring about large changes in production and consumption. The market mechanism described permits each of the thousands of producers and millions of consumers in the economy to exercise his ingenuity toward maximizing his profit from production or his satisfactions from consumption. Because of this harnessing of individual initiative and ordering of widely divergent tastes and demands of individuals, the market price system is in many circumstances a very efficient one. It can achieve many results which would be impossible under any alternative. Moreover, it permits the individual a wide range of choice in consumption and many opportunities to achieve profits in production. In both of these ways, a market price system conforms to many widely held standards or goals of the American society. But there are some kinds of economic and social problems that require a kind of over-all planning which the market does not do.

The economics of outdoor recreation are really little different from the economics of other of man's activities. As a general proposition, the market prices of land, capital, labor, and other inputs are a good measure of cost in investment considerations for outdoor recreation. There are, however, situations where the market price might be inappropriate, and, depending on the consideration and type of decision, it may be desirable to alter the calculation of the costs involved. One such example occurs in the case of land prices, particularly in rural areas where the price is affected, probably materially, by the national agricultural programs. There may be good reasons in such cases for not considering the market price as a true cost to the economy. The latter is no doubt lower because agricultural land prices reflect the interference with the market mechanism for agricultural products. The appropriateness of the interference is quite beside the point for our present purpose. The consideration here is that this price is not an appropriate measure of the cost to the economy of diverting land from agricultural use to recreational use.

In another situation, there may be locally unemployed labor; if used to develop recreation areas or to build facilities, this would entail small cost to the nation. This may be true in labor surplus areas, such as the Appalachian region, for example. This was the case before the Second World War, and many state parks and other recreation areas were built or developed then with labor that otherwise would have been unemployed and producing little or nothing. While these are cases in which market prices differ from real costs, by and large one can reasonably take market prices as reflecting the true value of resources, and the true costs of recreation development.

THE NEED FOR INVESTMENT CRITERIA

As there are simply not unlimited quantities of all kinds of resources, decisions must be made as to how to allocate them. In some cases the choice is between recreation and other uses. In deciding how much area is to be put in wilderness, or in national parks, or in state parks, it is important to keep in mind the cost in timber harvest foregone or in potential hydropower sites undeveloped. The problem of resource allocation among recreation uses also arises. For example, each of two proposals for recreation areas may have great site value and both might well be made part of a recreation system, but priorities must be established. In these cases there is a great deal to be gained from putting evaluations in the most useful terms possible and making investment decisions on the basis of criteria that take account of both the costs and the benefits.

The absence of market guides makes it difficult to formulate public investment criteria, and many workers have turned to the requirements or standards approach. An appraisal is made of outdoor recreation for a given area such as a local community or region, or of some special aspect of outdoor recreation such as local playgrounds, or of the amount of water-based outdoor recreation. Specified requirements are then stated, usually in terms of the number of acres needed, or the number of units of playground equipment per unit of population. The investment criteria are then established in terms of how much is needed to reach this standard. This approach really states that outdoor recreation is good and that more is needed. It gives no explicit consideration to the cost, or what has to be sacrificed in order to obtain this requirement.

Choices are most usefully made not in terms of either the cost or the gain of the proposed expenditure project, but rather in terms of *both* the cost and the gain of various alternative programs or projects.

There is a limit to what users will give up to have or to enjoy outdoor recreation facilities. In this sense "wants" are more meaningful than "requirements." No doubt a great want exists for recreation, but how much does society really desire a particular recreation facility, compared with its wants for an alternative? Natural resource development projects and more particularly outdoor recreation development should not be exempt from these principles of resource allocation; the greatest possible recreation opportunity should be provided with the limited budget available.

The probable greatly higher future demand for outdoor recreation, which we discussed in Chapter 7, will undoubtedly mean that large investments in outdoor recreation will be made in the next few decades, thereby calling for even greater emphasis on the need for the best possible investment criteria. In the past half dozen years voters have approved state bond issues for parks and recreation to the amount of $600 million to $800 million, and most of this money has been spent or is committed. Additional large state bond issues will probably be approved in the next several years. The Land and Water Conservation Fund is projected to yield about $180 million annually over the next decade; this is to be spent in grants-in-aid to states and for federal projects in parks and recreation. Federal grants-in-aid for urban and suburban open space may be far in excess of $100 million over the next decade. And these are but a few examples of the more or less clearly visible sums contemplated for direct recreation investment.

In addition, the allocation of part of the costs of federal multiple-purpose water projects to outdoor recreation purposes will involve further large investments. In California alone, federal and state water development projects are likely to mean $250 million or more allocated to recreation over the next decade. With total federal water development programs running well over $1 billion annually, the allocations to recreation could readily become very large. These figures underline the importance of sound criteria for judging recreation investments.

BENEFIT-COST ANALYSIS

Alternative opportunities for investment in outdoor recreation areas and facilities require that choices be made. Investment criteria based on a rather explicit analysis of the costs and the benefits that might be expected from the various alternatives are likely to lead to wiser choices.[1] Benefit-cost analysis provides a means for being more rational in decision making about outdoor recreation investments and consequently for making better investments of scarce resources. This is not to say that perfect investment decisions can be made in outdoor recreation, or in any other field of public expenditure for that matter. All of the costs and ultimately all of the benefits cannot be known with precision. However, this does not abolish the need for making choices.

This type of analysis has been used for years in the field of water resources development to estimate the benefits and the costs associated with each individual water resource development project. Procedures have been evolved for estimating the cost of various kinds of water control structures, irrigation ditches, hydroelectric power generators, flood control structures, and the like. Similarly, calculations are made of the expected value of the outputs or benefits of each project. Increasingly, analogous kinds of consideration and analysis are being ex-

[1] There is a large and growing literature on benefit-cost analysis, particularly as applied to water resource development investments. See: John V. Krutilla and Otto Eckstein, *Multiple Purpose River Development* (Baltimore: The Johns Hopkins Press, for Resources for the Future, Inc., 1958); Otto Eckstein, *Water Resources Development* (Cambridge: Harvard University Press, 1961; Jack Hirshleifer, James C. DeHaven, and Jerome W. Milliman, *Water Supply: Economics, Technology and Policy* (Chicago: University of Chicago Press, 1960); Arthur Maass, Maynard M. Hufschmidt, *et al., Design of Water-Resource Systems* (Cambridge: Harvard University Press, 1962); Roland McKean, *Efficiency in Government through Systems Design* (New York: Wiley and Sons, 1958).

tended to other fields—road construction and highway improvement, urban renewal, defense systems analysis, for example. Analysis of this kind is often inexact, but it is meant to be only a guide to decisions and not the final determinant of choice. Its use in consideration of public investment opportunities is increasing. As choices must be made, it is far better to make them with the best possible information than it is to forego such possibilities.

The essential feature of benefit-cost analysis is the comparison of the cost of an investment possibility with as explicit a measure as possible of the benefits or the gains to be realized. The general notion of benefit-cost analysis is applicable to any level of decision making. In different cases quite different items of costs and benefits may be of interest. For example, a local community may consider only its own costs, costs borne by others being irrelevant to the community's decision. If a national or state park or a federal water development project is established in a particular locality, the local community may be required to provide little or none of the first investment costs or even of the annual operating costs. As local people have an interest in local economic or commercial impact, items other than primary recreation benefits will loom large to them. These will include, particularly, expenditures of nonresident recreationists, which, as we have seen, do not represent increases in economic product from a national viewpoint, but are the source of a great deal of income in local communities. Even though such new economic activities in a region are generally not "net" for the nation, they are still "net" gain for the area.

A benefit-cost analysis should be made for each investment opportunity. A comparison of the costs and gains of different alternatives will aid in determining which investments are to be undertaken and which are to be foregone. This, too, is a purpose of a benefit-cost analysis—to serve as a decision tool to help in making choices among alternative investment opportunities. It is an aid not only in ascertaining if an investment ought to be made but also in establishing the priorities among alternatives.

Because most recreation management decisions require expenditures of various sorts, benefit-cost analysis can also aid management decisions. For instance, it should help ascertain the relative merits of intensively developing a given reservoir for outdoor recreation, with many boat launching ramps, campgrounds, or even resort and other facilities, as opposed to an extensively managed development with only the minimum roads and sanitary facilities.

If a project or investment is economically worthwhile, the total benefits must exceed the cost. In the literature and discussions of benefit-cost analysis there is frequent mention of the ratio test. This is merely another means of expressing the essential test that benefits must exceed cost. The ratio of the value of the benefits to the value of the cost must be greater than one for the investment to be economically sound.

In spite of a number of practical difficulties in establishing the appropriate numbers to go into the benefit-cost analysis, the framework remains an immensely useful one for deciding among alternative investments in the field of outdoor recreation. The major practical difficulties stem from the difficulty of quantifying in precise ways the values which we attach to different kinds of project outputs. As we become more proficient in value determination for such project services or output and increase our accuracy in estimating the costs and benefits associated with all such investment opportunities, the usefulness and the precision of benefit-cost analysis will be increased. Lacking precision it still provides a useful decision tool for investment criteria.

The calculation of cost estimates for an investment specifically for outdoor recreation is relatively straightforward. With limited exceptions, market prices are generally a good indication of the economic worth of the resources in alternative uses and provide a proper measure for evaluating cost. When recreation is part of a multiple purpose water development project or a multiple use land management project, the cost situation is more complicated. Direct costs required for recreation, which would not have been incurred if recreation had been omitted as a project activity, should obviously be charged against recreation. But, if the multiple purpose project includes outdoor recreation as one of its explicit purposes, then some part of the general or overhead costs of the whole project should also ordinarily be charged against this purpose. There is an extensive literature on cost allocation, reflecting the long experience with this difficult and rather slippery problem.[2] Although most of the attention has been focused upon multiple purpose water projects, some of the same considerations also apply to multiple use land management. Part of the costs for roads, fire protection, forest disease protection, general administration, and other management activities benefit recreation as well as many other purposes of the land management.

The benefit calculations are unavoidably less straightforward. In most cases there are no readily available market values for outdoor recreation as there are for most other goods and services. Consequently, imputed values are needed. In the previous chapters we discussed the problems of the simulation of the market and also outlined some possible measurement tools that might prove useful for various classes

[2] See, for example, Eckstein, *op. cit.*, and *Proposed Practices for Economic Analysis of River Basin Projects*, a report to the Interagency Committee on Water Resources (Washington: U.S. Government Printing Office, 1958).

257

of outdoor recreation. We feel that this type of calculation would markedly improve recreation planning decisions, even with their present shortcomings. For example, we estimated that the annual benefits to the recreation resource for the Lewis and Clark reservoir were $1.4 million and for the Kerr reservoir were $1.6 million. They are for benefits accruing to the resource under the methods of management actually in use at these areas. These figures are illustrative of the uses that could be made of such measures. If we make the unreal assumption that investments and annual operating costs were equal and that no other benefits flowed from either project, then Kerr reservoir is a better investment than Lewis and Clark Lake. For a more nearly complete analysis, operating and other direct costs should certainly be deducted from these estimates of gross benefits in order to get net benefit figures. Since each of these projects included other functions in addition to outdoor recreation, account should be taken of the whole investment and of all the benefits flowing from each. Perhaps, if these factors were considered, the relative standing of these two projects would be reversed; and for a truly complete resource program, other projects would have to be considered also.

We do not mean to underestimate the problems of getting reliable data for analysis of costs and benefits; they are real and difficult. But we believe that they are solvable, and that the methodology exists for meaningful analysis of the relative costs and benefits of investments in outdoor recreation.

A chief difficulty with present methods of benefit estimation, as outlined earlier, is their exclusive concern with benefits accruing to users or potential users of recreation sites. This largely ignores any benefits which may accrue to non-users.

Another factor complicating investment decisions is the typically uneven distribution of costs and returns over time. In most cases, an investment involves a present or near-future cost, while benefits come later, sometimes extending over very long periods. As even perfectly certain future income is less highly valued than present income, the calculations of the value of future costs and benefits must be discounted back to a present worth equivalent, thereby making them comparable. The choice of the most appropriate interest or discount rate for this purpose is a difficult one.[3] The difference between a three per cent and a five per cent interest rate can be very great in terms of presently justifiable investment.

[3] In addition to citations in footnotes 1 and 2, this chapter, see Otto Eckstein, "A Survey of the Theory of Public Expenditure Criteria," and "Comments" by Jack Hirshleifer (p. 495), in National Bureau of Economic Research, *Public Finances: Needs, Sources and Utilization* (Princeton: University Press, 1961).

Uncertainties about the accuracy of benefit-cost analysis derive largely from uncertainties about the future, not from the analytical process itself. What assurance is there that tastes will not change to some other type of recreation or to some other area? If the investment under consideration has a long physical life, can we be reasonably sure that it will be useful throughout this time? This type of problem is not peculiar to outdoor recreation; it applies to all resource development programs. What seem to be the best estimates of future demand may turn out to be wrong; this has happened many times in the past. It is axiomatic that the future is unknown and often unknowable. But these uncertainties would exist, no matter how decisions are made about investments or other actions with long-run consequences. Analysis of costs and returns for different investments may help to pinpoint the nature and possible magnitude of uncertainties about the future, and thus help to minimize the hazards; but, like other procedures, it cannot completely remove the effect of such uncertainties.

Estimates of future costs and benefits are bound to be hazardous, yet they must be made. The discounting of future benefits removes the discrepancy between present and future income. But it does not wholly overcome the problem of not knowing the future. Analysis and planning should aid greatly in the timing of development so that units or increments are constructed when needed, but are not built too early to meet large but distant demands. There is an important need to recognize that pre-emption of sites for other uses may occur where recreation development is postponed. Open space for recreation in growing urban areas is particularly susceptible to this danger. But, at least in principle, appropriate analysis of costs and benefits should provide insight into selection of reservation possibilities as well.[4]

A further factor of some importance in investment decisions, especially in public decisions, is who gets the benefits and who pays the costs. Calculations showing the final incidence of benefits and costs can be very useful in arriving at a choice among repayment policies, as well as investment alternatives. We properly speak of the nation or of society making decisions to invest or not to invest, for example; yet society is made up of many individuals, not all of whom share equally in either the costs or the benefits. There may be great differences between groups, and differences in political attitudes may arise largely out of these differences.

The benefit-cost approach can be used to some degree even when all

[4] See Maynard M. Hufschmidt, John Krutilla, and Julius Margolis, *Standards and Criteria for Formulating and Evaluating Federal Water Resources Development,* Report of Panel of Consultants to the Bureau of the Budget (Washington: Bureau of the Budget, June 30, 1961).

the costs and benefits cannot be completely quantified. For instance, two projects might have approximately equal comparisons of benefits and costs for the quantifiable factors, but observers might agree that one of the projects had more intangible benefits than the other, even though they could not put value figures on either. To take another example, the direct benefits to users might be approximately equal for two projects, but one might be in a depressed area where the local economic impact would be of more importance. Or one might be able to say that the unquantifiable benefits from a particular project would have a certain cost, and then leave to the judgment of others whether or not these intangible benefits were worth the costs. The rationale and the approach of benefit-cost analysis are often more important than the specific figures, although every effort should be made to make the latter accurate and to keep bias out.

Certainly there are shortcomings to this, but decisions must and will be made, and there is great utility to increasing their rationality. Further, the calculations need not be exact to be useful. Implicit judgments will be necessary under any circumstances. What we are calling for here is to make more of these implicit judgments as explicit as careful analysis will permit. The results of this will be better investments in outdoor recreation and a better distribution of resources between outdoor recreation and other uses.

FINANCIAL AND ECONOMIC APPRAISALS

As we noted in Chapter 11, there is usually a distinction between an economic appraisal and a financial appraisal of the same public investment opportunity. The benefit-cost analysis is an economic appraisal of the economic consequences of a project in terms of the costs and the returns.

The financial point of view is concerned with how the budget is organized. It is concerned with such things as raising taxes or selling bonds in order to pay for the project; it is concerned with how the project is actually paid for. It is also concerned with the returns in terms of possible entrance fees.

The chief reasons for varying outcomes of the two appraisals is that much of the return credited in the economic appraisal cannot usually be captured in the financial sense through any feasible pricing scheme. This is somewhat analogous to the case of education where the economic benefits of the school system greatly exceed the sum of tuition payments. While pricing practice has a bearing on benefits, the magnitudes of financial and economic returns may differ greatly.

This difference between economic and financial feasibility may be extremely important to a local area which tries to develop recreation and tourism as a local economic support. A park or other area may draw many thousands of visitors, yet benefits to the local community may not be captured in actual dollar accumulations and be less than the dollar costs. Financial feasibility is especially important when revenue bonds are issued, or when the investment is large in relation to the financial capacity of the unit of government which makes it.

RESEARCH AND RULES OF THUMB FOR INVESTMENT DECISIONS

At the end of Chapter 11, we discussed the usefulness of rules of thumb for estimating the value of land and water resources when used for outdoor recreation. We pointed out that rough standards, adjustable to the major differences in situations, can be developed from research; these can be highly useful in practice, although the estimates so provided should be tested and refined, if possible, by specific inquiry for each particular situation.

The same general concepts apply to investment decisions. It should be possible by analyzing the costs and benefits of some alternatives to devise some sensible general investment standards, adjustable to various circumstances. These would have great utility. For instance, one might say that investments per campsite of a given type in a campground should ordinarily be within a range of so many dollars; or that investments per unit of playground capacity should ordinarily not exceed some figure. For this approach to be workable, it would often be necessary to establish measures of recreation capacity. But it seems possible to do this with tolerable accuracy.

Permissible investments for outdoor recreation would depend, in general, on the same factors which affect value of resources when used for outdoor recreation. Location with respect to probable users, capacity of the area, innate attractiveness, travel costs and difficulties in reaching the area, and related factors would affect the value of the resources and, therefore, maximum permissible investments. While a careful and detailed benefit-cost analysis is highly desirable in each case, useful approximations could be made by the development of rules of thumb based upon careful research.

14

*Pricing and Paying for Public Outdoor
Recreation Facilities*

Provision of outdoor recreation is not without costs. It may often appear to be free because no direct charge is levied upon users. This means simply that someone else has borne the costs. In this chapter, we consider some of the analytical problems involved in pricing and paying for outdoor recreation, and in Chapter 16 we discuss the policy issues.

Costs in provision of outdoor recreation opportunity can take several forms. Capital costs are involved, to buy or to hire the necessary land, water, and other resources from other competing uses. These costs are "real" in the sense that when resources are used for recreation they are not available for other uses, or at least not to the same extent. Capital costs are also involved in provision of necessary improvements such as access roads, water supply, sanitary facilities, campgrounds, play equipment, and many others. In addition, substantial annual outlays are required to manage and maintain the areas and to replace or restore the improvements.

The costs of providing outdoor recreation opportunity may be expected to be higher in the future than they are today. The demand for outdoor recreation will almost certainly rise a great deal, requiring more areas and more facilities, and hence greater costs. In addition, several factors are likely to make for a higher cost per unit of recreation, or at least for higher costs per unit of additional recreation. Where recreation is secondary to other major uses of the resources, or when its level is low, or both, the costs chargeable to recreation may be small. But the competition for use of natural resources will almost certainly become sharper in the future, and it will cost more to bid resources away from other possible uses.

For these reasons, the matter of paying for the provision of outdoor recreation has important equity, economic, administrative, and political aspects. Decisions can rarely be reached on the basis of partial consideration without creating serious problems of other kinds.

Resource-based, intermediate, and user-oriented types of outdoor recreation areas must all be paid for, and pricing problems arise for each. Since publicly-owned resource-based areas are often federal, decisions about paying for them must be made by this level of government; some intermediate areas are federal and some are state, with decisions made at these levels; and most user-oriented areas are owned by local government, with consequent decision making about prices at this level. Sometimes local groups act as if the federal Treasury were an inexhaustible fountain, but pricing and paying problems arise for federal areas also, for raising revenue is only one of the functions of fees and charges. Imposing charges can have results that affect all levels of government.

HOW PRIVATE AND PUBLIC COSTS ARE MET

The costs incurred by private persons and groups for recreation opportunity are unlikely to exceed their estimate of the value of that opportunity, or they would be paying more than they gain. For public agencies, costs should not exceed value, to avoid waste of public funds. Private costs or outlays for outdoor recreation may be of different kinds. Persons or groups owning outdoor recreation areas pay the capital and annual operating costs involved. Those who use the areas and facilities provided by other private persons or groups pay a fee; they are charged largely for personal and management services, but also for use of the natural resources involved. In most cases the recreation user must incur a substantial travel cost in order to use either a publicly or a privately owned area.

In the case of publicly provided outdoor recreation areas and facilities, decisions have been based more upon popular appeals and political pressures than upon careful economic analysis. A more explicit balancing of costs and values is probable in the future, but the traditional appeals will surely continue.

The costs of providing public outdoor recreation opportunity in the United States can be met in any one or more of the following ways.

1. *From general tax revenues* of the nation, state, county, city, or other unit of government. Some political scientists will defend this method of meeting the costs of outdoor recreation acquisition, construction, and operation because it forces the legislative body and the executive to make definite decisions periodically on how much to spend for

this purpose and how to raise the necessary revenues, etc., and because the legislative body retains continuous control of the program. As there is a strong tendency for every budget decision to reflect last year's decision, some doubts may be raised as to the extent of current control. From the viewpoint of those interested in more public outdoor recreation opportunity, the major weakness of this approach is that funds are very hard to come by; there are many other demands for public funds, and outdoor recreation, as a relative newcomer on a large scale, may be poorly dealt with. Also, payment of cost by means of taxes is not related to individual participation in the recreation opportunities provided, and probably is not proportionate to general social values arising out of the availability of recreation to others.

2. *By bond issue* specifically for outdoor recreation. This device has been resorted to in several states in recent years, and several hundred million dollars have been raised in this way. This approach does not solve the issue of how to pay for outdoor recreation; it merely postpones it. Interest and principal of the bonds must be paid for in some way—out of general tax revenues, if general bonds are issued, or from revenues from the recreation facility if revenue bonds are issued. The latter method requires some form of charges or fees, high enough to pay the interest and retire the principal. Many recreation specialists do not support revenue bonds because they may require, for financial reasons, a type of park management that would be rejected on other grounds. The bond issue approach does have the advantage from the recreationists' viewpoint that it oftens makes easier the rallying of sufficient political power to get desired action; it is much easier to make one large effort for public support than it is to fight an annual budget battle. The legislator can defend it as a means of ascertaining the strength of public sentiment for using public funds for this purpose.

3. *By special taxes* earmarked for outdoor recreation. At the federal level, there are taxes on guns, ammunition, fishing tackle, and other sports equipment which are used directly for provision of outdoor recreation. In Minnesota and in Wisconsin, a special tax of 1 cent per pack of cigarettes is put into a fund earmarked for outdoor recreation; in at least one state, a special millage levy is added to the general real estate tax, earmarked for state park purposes. The special tax approach has the great advantage, from the recreationist's point of view, that a definite source and often a predictable amount of public money can be counted upon, and programs built on this basis. Many political scientists decry the earmarking of taxes for special purposes, on the grounds that this takes control of the program out of the hands of the legislative body concerned. However, in such cases as hunting and fishing, it does

mean that the beneficiaries of the program are directly paying for it, at least in part. In such cases it provides a measure of the real, rather than the vocal, level of political demand for the recreation opportunity provided.

4. *By grants-in-aid* from higher to lower levels of government, specifically for outdoor recreation purposes. The federal government has made grants to cities to aid in the acquisition of open spaces primarily in and around cities, and primarily for park and other recreation purposes; under the Land and Water Conservation Fund program, grants are being made to states for acquisition and development of state parks and for grants-in-aid to counties, cities, and special districts. Where state bond issues for outdoor recreation have been approved by the voters, typically a part of the funds has been earmarked for grants to cities and other units of local government. A grant-in-aid may solve, or help to solve, the payment problem for the recipient government; but, for the granting government, it merely postpones the issue of who pays and how—in this respect, it is like the bond issues. As long as many users of public outdoor recreation areas are neither residents nor taxpayers in the political unit which provides the area, and as long as costs are not met by levying user charges, then there is much justification for grants-in-aid. The local unit of government thus recoups at least some of the costs it incurs to provide outdoor recreation opportunity to nonresidents.

5. *By charges levied directly on users* of public outdoor recreation areas. Although this method has been used relatively little in the past, its use is growing. Charges can be levied in a number of ways, depending in part upon administrative convenience; entrance or admission fees are one major form, and charges for specific services are another. The essence of this method is the attempt to make the actual users pay some or all of the costs involved. Because of its growing importance, as well as because of differences of opinion about it, we consider it at more length in this and in following chapters.

RATIONALE FOR PUBLIC PROVISION OF OUTDOOR RECREATION

A number of arguments, not always consistent, have been advanced at one time or another for public provision of outdoor recreation facilities. One class of arguments pertains to the nature of the recreation commodity. For private provision of outdoor recreation to be profitable and feasible, there must be a market and a marketable product. Sellers must be in a position to withhold the product or service, so that buyers are forced to pay a price to make use of the facilities. National defense, for example, is not marketed, since it is impossible to withhold protection from those people who do not pay. There are many recreation areas which have some of the same characteristics; where it would be too costly to withhold use, a seller does not have a marketable commodity.

Many private landowners find it difficult to withhold recreation use of their areas from the public. Large private forest industry firms, for example, have opened their lands to hunting, as a result of the pressure of public opinion and in spite of lack of a direct economic advantage in doing so. All in all, the market structure of the outdoor recreation "industry" does not favor private suppliers of recreation opportunity.

Another case of market imperfection that is put forward for public ownership occurs in certain kinds of development where a single private developer may not be able to collect for some of the beneficial effects, or does not need to pay for the adverse ones. In such cases a gross waste would result from development which did not in effect convert these external factors into internal considerations, with all of the beneficial effects considered. It might be argued that large-scale, perhaps cooperative, private endeavor could make just as good use of the recreational output, but it is seldom practical to organize a private enterprise of the requisite scale, especially since profit prospects would often be dark. The situation occurs on large areas of natural forest land in the United States. By political decisions, reaffirmed many times, the nation has decided to retain in public ownership many millions of acres of forest land. Much of this land has high potential for recreation, and theoretically this activity could be managed by private business. But the necessity of integrating recreation with timber production and other activities has in practice meant that provision of the recreation opportunity was primarily a public undertaking.

Another argument in support of public development concerns the question of scale economies. In many cases, the scale of development is unavoidably large relative to existing capacity and demand. A major federal reservoir, for instance, may provide a recreation capacity far in excess of the immediate demand for this type of recreation; yet the reservoir must often be managed as a unit for recreation purposes. The time factor may be important here also; the enterprise may have to operate for some years at a scale where costs per unit are relatively high, before volume builds up to the larger and more efficient operating level.

Under conditions where scale economies exist, the profit prospects for a private firm or an association of firms which might undertake such development are often poor, even if managerial and financial capacity to undertake the project could be found. Not only will the usual type of pricing not cover the full cost of development in such cases, but the firm would supply only part of the whole recreation experience—the part which has in the past not been the most profitable part. These considerations of scale and lack of profitability are often found in natural resource development activities and form a primary justification for public provision of such services.

An important further reason for public support for, or provision of, outdoor recreation stems from the existence of what might be termed social externalities in consumption. This is what a recreation or park specialist would probably call the general public benefit argument. It is widely argued by the latter group that outdoor recreation is essential to a full and well-balanced personal life; that those who participate in outdoor recreation tend to become better adjusted socially and better and more productive citizens; and thus the welfare of the whole nation is enhanced. According to this argument, everyone benefits in some way, and even those who do not partake of outdoor recreation have an interest in its ready availability, and should be willing to help pay for it.

The public benefit argument has been used to support universal free public schools and certain kinds of public health services. Many objections were raised at one time or another against such provisions on grounds, for example, that it was immoral for one man to pay for the education of another man's children or that public health services are the responsibility of an individual rather than the public at large. In these two cases the electorate, and economists, have long since decided that the general public benefits were so great as to far outweigh any inequalities that might arise from using general tax revenues for such purposes.

This belief in general social benefits arising out of outdoor recreation is widely held by many able people in this field. There is surely something to this argument; the unresolved question is, how much? A person may wish to live in a city with adequate and attractive parks, just as he may wish to live in a city with good art galleries, even if he never patronizes either. Moreover, most people are probably willing to pay some modest amount to make such opportunities available. However, the direct evidence as to the social values of outdoor recreation is weak. There has been little empirical research to test this assertion, and some research has failed to substantiate the claims made. Some of the more extreme claims for the beneficial effects of outdoor recreation have surely been exaggerated in the past. There may well be differences among kinds of outdoor recreation in this regard. There may be considerable external effect from visits to various kinds of historical sites or major scenic or scientific areas, for example, or from interpretive programs carried on by some park and recreation agencies. But use of picnic areas, beaches, campgrounds, and other such facilities is less likely to benefit any but the immediate users.

The belief in the social benefits of outdoor recreation is not as widely accepted politically as is the comparable belief in public schools. While there is substantial popular support for publicly provided outdoor recreation, and while many legislators and general administrators support it too, there are some who doubt its appropriateness and many who are unwilling to give it the degree of public financial support which park and recreation administrators think is essential.

Another factor of importance for recreation development is a large element of uncertainty which accompanies recreation development as an economic undertaking. Demand for specific facilities is often unsure, particularly over their physically useful lives. Acting together, individuals are able to pool the uncertainties of such enterprises. While it might be possible for large private groups to work together to spread the risk, the difficulties of assembling and governing such a large grouping would usually make government activity of some kind more feasible. Government might conceivably develop some kind of risk insurance for outdoor recreation, as it has in other fields, but so far this has not been seriously proposed, as far as we know. A public agency has greater manpower and financial capacity than a private organization, is probably in a better position to use land and water areas for other purposes if they are not needed for recreation, and by its control over highway development and other public services can often influence demand for recreation at specific sites.

Public development also offers a means of obtaining a better balance of recreational facilities and areas than could be achieved by individuals undertaking recreational development as a private business venture.

Even when the market functions properly in a technical sense, society may still prefer a nonmarket provision of outdoor recreation because the community rejects the outcome of private market decisions. In many instances, society desires to maintain a quality or a condition which the private market might destroy. The impetus for public acquisition of some historical, scenic, and scientific sites has come because the areas were so obviously being abused in private ownership. Definition of quality is often difficult, yet there may be a clear indication that mass popular use, which the private recreation operator is usually under pressure to increase in order to increase his profit, would destroy the qualities which now make an area valuable.[1] The community may also

---

[1] See William J. Hart, "Factors in Park Building Design," *Trends in Parks and Recreation* (April 1965).

choose to make an area available primarily to school children or youth groups even when it would have a higher return used by some other age or income groups.

A properly functioning commercial market response to consumer preferences may also not insure that various special types of recreation developments are adequately represented in the choice open to individuals making up the community. The community might recognize, for example, that many people do not appreciate quality in outdoor recreation opportunities and might consciously adopt policies which include more recreation for this type of development than individuals are willing to pay for or for which they express such willingness to pay. In the outdoor recreation field, various kinds of private recreation developments take place which are undesirable from a number of viewpoints. In an effort to extract the largest commercial return, private developments often neglect various aesthetic or cultural aspects of an environment. This is not a condemnation of private developers as such; the economics of private recreation development are such as to bring forth a kind of development which is often rejected by the community at large. This kind of development occurs, at least in part, because private property rules often do not make all of the costs and returns focus on the decision makers. For these and other reasons, public provision of outdoor recreation may be advocated and chosen.

Public agencies, particularly those which operate over a rather large city or on a statewide basis, may also have the advantage of being able to afford skilled planning and management personnel. This is particularly true for certain types of specialists. The National Park Service, for example, can afford an archeologist to help explore and restore a historical site, but a small city park department or a private developer cannot.

On the other hand, it must also be recognized that public activities often tend toward a level of uniformity, or even mediocrity; this is less likely to produce adverse political criticism than would unusual undertakings. Public recreation agencies might well use standardized designs, these being economical as well as generally publicly acceptable. A few private suppliers might be willing to cater to special segments of the general recreation public.

If recreation had had the kind of publicly-supported research and education programs that have characterized agriculture for many decades, expertise in the problems of outdoor recreation could have been made available to local units of government and to private organizations. A little work of this kind has been done in some states, but there has been nothing on a national scale at all comparable to the large efforts in agriculture.

RATIONALE FOR FREE ENTRANCE TO PUBLIC
OUTDOOR RECREATION AREAS

The foregoing arguments for public provision of outdoor recreation areas have all been used at one time or another to favor free or nearly free entrance fees; but most of them are really inapplicable to that issue. The only one of any real force, in our judgment, is what the economist calls the externality effects.

The externality argument really says that recreation benefits everyone —some directly and others indirectly—and that all should share the costs. As we have noted, the American people long ago accepted this viewpoint for basic education; the conviction that there are important social, political, and economic advantages in having a literate population led to the establishment of free public schools. To the extent that there are external benefits from outdoor recreation, the case for public provision of free outdoor recreation facilities is stronger.

There are, however, at least two reasons to doubt the strength of the externality argument as grounds for free outdoor recreation. In the first place, as we have noted, the value of outdoor recreation in producing an intellectually and emotionally healthy populace is not firmly and clearly established. We suspect there are as many emotionally ill-adjusted wandering through the woods or lying on the beaches as there are cooped up in apartments before TV sets; and, conversely, there may well be as many well-adjusted who never go near the outdoors as who do. In the second place, participation in outdoor recreation is highly variable among the population. Every survey of a cross section of the whole population has shown a substantial number of people who never go to public parks or recreation areas, others who go very infrequently, still others who go moderately often, and only a few who go frequently. The exact numbers in each category vary with the kinds of areas in question and the income level of the group concerned. The majority of Americans do not visit a national park each year. Probably most people visit a city park each year, although we have no comprehensive estimate on this point; others go frequently, and some go very often. In this regard, outdoor recreation differs sharply from education. Every normal child is compelled to go to school; thus the social benefits of free public education are widely distributed.

Many park and recreation people are deeply convinced of the social wisdom of free public parks and recreation areas. Their "help the poor people" argument is a form of the externality argument, but it has an additional weakness. By and large, the supply of free public parks in the United States is less adequate in crowded city areas where people are poor than it is in suburban and higher income residential areas, where the people concerned are more nearly able to pay for their own outdoor recreation. On a state or national basis, the discrepancy is even worse; the really poor people do not own the private automobiles which are necessary to get to most state parks and to all national parks and na.ional forests, nor can they, in most cases, afford the other travel costs of such visits. The argument that free public parks help the poor is almost wholly myth.

There are other defenses for free entrance to public parks and recreation areas that are seldom made explicitly but may underlie some of the discussion. One of these is that free provision of outdoor recreation is a form of income redistribution, as are free schools, free public libraries, free art or scientific museums, and many other cultural and economic facilities publicly provided. Many tax systems, notably most income taxes, are also income redistributing, since those with high incomes pay more. One may argue, on social or humanitarian grounds, in favor of more income redistribution; but in this case, one must go further and argue that provision of free public outdoor recreation is an efficient and socially desirable way of redistributing income.

ROLE OF GOVERNMENT IN PROVIDING OUTDOOR RECREATION

Any level of government, whether federal, state, city, or other, may play more than one role in the provision of outdoor recreation. It acts as the entrepreneur, planning the area or project, acquiring the necessary land, making the improvements, managing the area later, and so on. In most public outdoor recreation it also plays the role of financier, raising the necessary funds, usually by taxation or by bonds, paying the necessary cost, and either collecting fees or deciding not to collect any. Most park and recreation people have assumed, perhaps unconsciously, that these functions were necessary and inseparable in government provision of outdoor recreation.

But, in fact, any level of government may assume the entrepreneurial function of providing outdoor recreation without at the same time committing itself to being the financial angel. It may, if it wishes, make those who use the area pay all the costs involved. To be sure, it would often be necessary to advance some funds for the initial acquisition and construction. But these funds could be raised by borrowing, as they are for private undertakings, and the annual income from fees could be used to pay the interest costs and perhaps repay the principal as well.

There are important issues of public policy in the question of how high the charges for publicly provided recreation should be. We are trying to demonstrate here that the range of choices is wider than is usually assumed to be the case; we are not necessarily committed to free public recreation areas.

VALUE AND PRICE ARE NOT IDENTICAL

We emphasize again the point made earlier, to the effect that the value of natural resources used for outdoor recreation and the prices charged for their use are not identical, and in fact may differ greatly. In Chapter 11 we developed a basis for estimating the social value of natural resources used for recreation, but, in practice, it would be impossible in many cases to recapture this value.

The price or admission charge to a public recreation area could be administratively set at nearly any level. Unless entry were restricted in some other way, people would use the area at this entry price until the value of the whole recreation experience equalled its costs to them. Since entrance fees are often only a small part of total costs, differences in entrance fees might make little difference in total use of the area. If revenue were the guiding consideration, then no management agency would set the entrance fees higher than those which would produce the maximum revenue. As we shall point out later, prices serve other functions than raising revenue, hence entrance fees might be set at different levels for other reasons.

For any one or more of several reasons, the entrance toll might be set administratively below the maximum revenue point, ranging downward toward zero. One objective might be to raise sufficient revenue to meet the current management costs of the area; this could be defended in popular terms by stating that users should pay the costs they placed upon the management agency. An efficient and appropriate variant of this would be to place fees at the point where they met the marginal, or incrementally added, costs of caring for additional visitors, where those costs are more inclusive than simply operational costs. Our purpose at this point is again to suggest that many alternatives of policy and of action are open.

ROLE OF PRICES IN RESOURCE MANAGEMENT

Prices—whether for recreation or for other goods or services—play many roles, and a better understanding of these roles would eliminate much of the confusion about prices for outdoor recreation.

Prices serve to allocate natural resources, capital, labor, and management among various activities or uses. In the case of outdoor recreation, prices could aid the allocation of forests to the provision of recreation instead of to the production of sawlogs (to the extent the two were incompatible), or the allocation of water resources to recreation instead of to irrigation or hydropower production. The situation need not be all or none; frequently, the use of a resource for recreation will mean reductions or restrictions but not the elimination of other uses.

Prices also play a role in helping consumers choose among alternative ways of using their available incomes to their own ends. Very few people have such large incomes that they can afford everything they want; their purchases are made on the basis of price as well as personal preferences. In the case of outdoor recreation, the choice must be outdoor recreation as against indoor recreation or against still other items of consumption; and within outdoor recreation, among the various kinds of activities which are possible. Here, the concept of the total recreation experience and its costs is highly relevant. If total costs are high, relatively few people can afford them or will choose to give up the comparatively large amounts of other goods and services that could be bought with the same money; if costs of the whole recreation experience are lower, time and other factors will be more important restraints than cost.

The foregoing is the traditional or customary exposition of the role of prices as a mechanism of choice. If prices are to play this role, there must be an approximation to a market, where consumers can exercise their choices, and through which their choices can be communicated to the suppliers of the goods and services concerned. The more smoothly this market works, the better the choices for both consumers and producers. A market of this type is an extremely powerful tool for making effective the economic decisions of both producers and consumers; under exceptional circumstances there may be good reasons to interfere with the operation of such a market, or to try to set it aside completely, but its advantages are great indeed. In a highly developed economy and society such as we have in the United States, economic and social decisions are made on the margins of production and consumption. An increase in the quantity taken by consumers, or in the prices they pay, tells producers that the demand for the good or service has risen; conversely, larger volumes of goods on the market, or lower prices, tell consumers that they can now consume more of the good or service at the same total outlay. Over a period of time such communications can be extremely effective in redirecting consumption and production. In addition to its economic effectiveness, such a system conforms to our democratic ideals of individual choice and individual freedom.

Total welfare is maximized when such choices are possible; the users of resources or the consumers of the commodities pay in accordance with their use. If prices of goods and services bear no relation to the cost of their production, consumers will look upon the goods or services as free and will use them in greater quantities than they would if they had to bear the cost. This introduces waste into the system. For example, if consumers are charged a flat service fee for water, they have no incentive to use only what they need; in effect, they are urged to waste water. A similar situation exists for much of outdoor recreation. The facilities are produced at anything but a zero cost, but they are in many cases consumed as if they were a free good.

The notion of having beneficiaries pay the costs of providing services involves very important equity and efficiency arguments. It is in a real sense proper that those who enjoy the benefits that give rise to costs should, in the absence of countervailing reasons, pay these costs.

Charges can be used to discourage excessive use and thus preserve efficiency, in terms of the amount of recreation satisfaction provided by our scarce resources. Overcrowding and congestion impose a real cost on all users of the area, for beyond a certain intensity of use each user suffers a decrease in satisfaction or value. As individual decisions are based only on the added private cost to the individual, which may be less than the real cost which includes the added cost imposed on other individuals, an optimum level of utilization can be achieved only by the use of prices.

Prices can be used as a management tool to bring about a more efficient management of recreation areas. The way in which fees or charges are levied may well be as important as their amount. Entrance fees might be charged on weekends but not on weekdays, for example. Concentration of fee collection on days or hours of heavy use would both reduce the cost of collection, which is sometimes high relative to the money collected, and provide an incentive for users to shift to off-peak hours and days when use would otherwise be below capacity. Or parking or camping charges might be imposed in heavily used areas but not in lightly used ones; or charges might be imposed for campground use beyond the first week in order to discourage longer stays. Many other programs of differential charges can be imagined. The objective of each would be to bring about better use of the resources by influencing visitors to choose certain areas, times, and activities, and to adopt certain modes of conduct. Such charges could not be expected to be effective unless they were high enough to represent a real burden to the user who paid them and a real saving to the one who avoided them. The precise charge that would fulfill these requirements would no doubt need to be determined in each individual case. However, it seems clear that differential charges offer real possibilities for increasing the efficiency of use of outdoor recreation facilities.

There is a further efficiency argument for pricing of outdoor recreation facilities in the common instance where the benefits derived from some of the visits to a recreation area are exceeded by the capital and operational cost of supplying the facilities and the congestion costs imposed on other users. We have seen in earlier discussions that the value derived from visits to a recreation area decreases as the number of visits to the area increases; that is, demand curves slope downward to the right. This implies that some visits to the area have little more than zero value to the actual users. However, costs are often incurred which are significantly above zero on a per visit basis. The important implication for price policy is that if significant costs are incurred and a zero price nevertheless used, then all visits beyond the point where the costs exceed the indicated value cost more than they are worth. Efficiency would suggest that in such cases visits be rationed to the more efficient level through some sort of user charges. If this is not done, then in effect a subsidy is given to the marginal users. We may prefer to do this but it might well be made more explicit in our planning procedures. These added costs which are incurred are likely to be quite significant, particularly when long-term resource depreciation or depletion is considered. In many outdoor recreation areas the use rates which result partly as a function of zero charges are such as to cause rapid erosion of the value of the resources itself. Under the guise of meeting the demand we are in fact allowing overcrowding and deterioration of the resource. In such instances we are under pressure to impose some sort of pricing scheme, or to ration use by some sort of administrative action.

Pricing is a factor in investment decisions also. Both the design capacity and choice of projects may well depend on reimbursement policies. If the use is limited by price so that the incremental benefit corresponds to the incremental cost, the design called for may be very different from the one required if no charges are imposed and marginal costs exceed the value or benefits.[2]

Free public outdoor recreation can also have a negative or adverse effect on the development of private facilities for recreation. More efficient development of total recreation facilities depends on much more realistic pricing of public facilities. A general policy of zero or near zero prices for public areas will severely limit the development of private facilities. However, if users of public developments bear the cost of their development there would probably be a more efficient total development of facilities; private development may be able to compete in some cases by being able to offer wider choices of types and locations of facilities.

[2] John V. Krutilla, "Is Public Intervention in Water Resources Development Conducive to Economic Efficiency?" *Natural Resources Journal* (January 1966).

Finally, charging for public outdoor recreation is one way of collecting revenues to provide the recreation opportunity demanded. Aside from the very practical advantage of raising the necessary funds, costs are paid by the beneficiaries.

We have tried to show the important function that economically relevant prices can play in planning and provision of outdoor recreation. These should not be confused with administratively determined prices which bear no relation to costs and which try to ignore demand; these are false friends, and may convey a misleading message. Instead of helping users make choices which are economically rational to them and to the whole of society, administratively determined prices may encourage wasteful and excessive use of available recreation opportunity. Some part, perhaps a large part, of the apparent rising demand for outdoor recreation in recent years has been due to users paying less than the full costs of their use. Legislators and others responsible for decisions about public expenditures have naturally tended to underestimate the value of outdoor recreation when it produced no revenue. Highway departments, private groups, and others have tried to use park and recreation lands for other purposes, again in part because the values were not evident in the absence of user charges. In these and in other ways, administratively fixed prices for outdoor recreation which do not reflect what users are willing to pay are false and misleading signals for individual and group decisions.

In Chapter 16, we shall examine some of the issues of public policy with respect to the imposition of user charges for public outdoor recreation areas.

EXPERIENCE WITH PRICING

Most public recreation projects in the past have been financed out of funds raised by general taxes. However, the trend has been toward consideration of other alternatives for financing new recreational development. Systems of admission charges, entrance fees, user rentals, and license or permit fees have been used in parks and other kinds of recreation areas for many years, particularly to pay for special services such as boat launching. Money secured from these sources has often been used to pay part of the costs for operation and expansion of the recreation systems. The trend of more recent vintage toward use of entrance fees to finance bond issues for area acquisition and development is an acceleration of the earlier trend.

The indications are that fees will be used increasingly in the future to support outdoor recreation programs. For example, it has been estimated that over 1,500 city and county agencies levied charges at their parks in 1960. This was an increase of about 30 per cent from the count in 1950.[3]

In the spring of 1962 the State of Ohio, Division of Parks, made a mail survey of the use of fees and charges on state administered park areas. Of the 45 states replying to the questionnaire, 17, or 38 per cent, reported some charge for use of parks.[4] This ranged from a $10 annual entrance fee to a 25¢ daily parking fee. The survey further revealed the great diversity in the kinds of fees and charges made in state parks. For example, six states charge an annual or seasonal fee and a daily use fee when no annual or season permit is purchased. Three states charge a parking fee in addition to an entrance fee, while four charge parking fees only. Three states make daily admission charges only, and four have an extra charge for parking boat trailers or buses. Even with respect to camping, which is generally conceded to be an activity for which charges are appropriate, there was a wide range in the type of fee arrangements reported. Seven states, for example, reported no charge for camping; one state charged at only one of its parks; one state had a provision that it would charge only if the area became crowded. Camping fees ranged from 25¢ to $12 per week, averaging about $1.00 to $1.50 per night. Nine states made no separate charge for electricity. Eleven states charged for electricity where available.

A 1960 study by the National Park Service, "State Parks: Areas, Acreage, and Accommodations," noting trends in the state parks, found that the total expenditures in state park operations had increased about 5½ times for 1959 over 1946. Total revenues from operations increased just about 5 times. However, the increase in revenues from entrance and parking fees increased over 10½ times. The general increase in the use of such charges is particularly evident when it is also noted in the same study that total attendance increased about 275 per cent over the period. In 1956, 23 per cent of total expenditures by state park agencies, or 39 per cent of operation and maintenance expenditures, were offset by total revenue collections in that year.[5] More than half of the latter was from facilities (including resorts) operated by the park agency; only about 20 per cent was from entrance and parking fees.

The National Association of Counties at its 1964 meeting adopted a statement regarding the role of counties in the provision of outdoor recreation.[6] Among other things, this statement endorsed the idea that

[3] Wall Street Journal, December 27, 1963.

[4] State Park Survey, Fees and Charges, Division of Parks, Department of Natural Resources, State of Ohio, Columbus, 1962.

[5] Marion Clawson, Statistics on Outdoor Recreation (Washington: Resources for the Future, Inc. 1958).

[6] National Policy for County Parks and Recreation, National Association of Counties, Washington, 1964.

SOME ECONOMIC CONSIDERATIONS

a substantial part of the total costs of providing outdoor recreation by counties should be raised by the imposition of user charges. While this is not direct experience with charges, it does reflect the attitude of this group of local officials that user charges are both administratively feasible and politically acceptable.

The National Park Service has long collected entrance fees at some major national parks; but less than 10 per cent of total expenditures on the national park system came from this source up to 1956; receipts per visit (for all visits to all areas) averaged about 10¢, and car entrance fees for the whole system averaged less than $1.00 per car.[7] In recent years, entrance fees to the national park system have covered 5 per cent or less of total expenditures.[8] The Forest Service had made some charges, but rather low ones, for some campgrounds and other areas; its receipts from this source were too small to have been shown separately until after 1956.[9] Other federal agencies, in general, made no charges for recreational use of land and water properties under their management.

The situation changed in 1964 with the passage of the Land and Water Conservation Fund Act. User or admission fees to federal areas were permitted and encouraged when all four of the following conditions were met: (1) the areas have been designated and posted as ones where fees are collected; (2) the areas are administered by a federal agency (this excludes federal areas leased to state, local, or private agencies); (3) the areas contain recreation facilities or offer recreation services provided at federal expense; and (4) the areas are administered primarily for scenic, scientific, historical, cultural, or other recreational purposes. No fees may be charged under this program as a hunting and fishing license, but imposition of admission fees does not preclude charging for services within the areas, such as a camping or boat launching fee.

The funds raised from fees at federal recreation areas, plus certain funds from taxes on motor boat fuel, plus certain other revenues from sale of surplus real property, are placed in the Land and Water Conservation Fund. Subject to Congressional appropriation, these funds are available for grants-in-aid to states, as described previously, and also for acquisition of additional land for inclusion in federal areas for recreation purposes. The federal agencies will be under considerable internal and external pressures to raise money by these recreation charges in order to increase the Land and Water Conservation Fund.

[7] Marion Clawson and R. Burnell Held, *The Federal Lands—Their Use and Management* (Baltimore: The Johns Hopkins Press, for Resources for the Future, Inc., 1957).

[8] Unpublished data provided by National Park Service.

[9] Clawson and Held, *op. cit.*

Although our prime concern at this point is with public recreation, the experience of some of the larger private forest landowners is instructive. Most such companies make their lands available for public use for recreation, at least of some kinds; generally with a motivation of building good public relations and cultivating a good public image, rather than profiting from leasing for recreation use. In many cases there is no charge for hunting or fishing, or even for the use of improved campgrounds. However, some companies have started to charge for hunting, fishing, and other uses, and others are interested in the possibilities for the future. Most companies have found that public resistance to the payment of recreation fees is not a serious factor, especially if management services are provided.[10]

There is also a growing market for camping at private campgrounds. Several directories of campgrounds list private areas, more than 3,000 campgrounds are listed for the whole country. These campgrounds differ greatly in size, attractiveness of area, location, degree of improvement, capital investment, skill of management, and in other ways. All were begun in the hope and expectation of making a profit, or at least of earning wages for labor and management; these hopes will probably not be realized in all cases, yet many such enterprises seem quite successful. The fees charged vary considerably; a common fee is from $2 to $3 per party per night, with varying discounts for longer stays. These private campgrounds are gradually establishing a market for this type of outdoor recreation service. The fees which they can charge are certainly influenced by the fees charged at public areas, which in general are much lower.

While the imposition of user charges for public recreation areas is far from universal, and as a major source of revenue is still the exception, experience to date indicates that it is operationally practical. The trend in the future will almost surely be toward greater use of such charges, as the demand for outdoor recreation grows and as the need for funds becomes more acute.

Many park administrators have rather reluctantly agreed to increased reliance on entrance fees and other charges as a means of raising revenue. Some of them seem to have been afraid of adverse public reaction—an attitude which experience to date has not supported. Others had convictions that outdoor recreation should be "free." Only when they realized that appropriations from general tax revenues would probably be inadequate to deal with the recreation problem they faced, were they willing to accept the idea of user charges. These charges seem

[10] *Proceedings of Sixth Conference on Southern Industrial Forest Management,* School of Forestry, Duke University, Durham, North Carolina, 1964.

to be a lesser evil than mounting demands from the public and inadequate funds.

ADMINISTRATIVE ASPECTS OF RAISING REVENUES FOR OUTDOOR RECREATION

In establishing a system for raising revenues to provide public outdoor recreation, consideration should be given to administrative feasibility. Raising funds by general or special taxes, or through bond sales, creates no special problem for park and recreation administrators. Such general public revenue programs are normally in the hands of specialized financial branches of the federal, state, or local governmental units, and the necessary procedures are well developed. In the United States, there may be active political struggle over the imposition of taxes or their modification; but, once voted, taxes are paid with only a minimum of evasion and contention. Administrative problems do arise, however, when a user charge is levied. Park and recreation administrators have often opposed such charges on the grounds that they are administratively difficult to collect.

The argument that it is administratively unfeasible to collect recreation user charges has validity in many situations. The typical city park, for instance, is open all day the year around, and usually has no gate or control point. Under these circumstances it would indeed be difficult to collect an entrance charge. A different difficulty exists at many more remote parks; there, the level of use is so low most of the time that fees would do no more than cover the cost of collection. In contrast, a great many state parks, national forests, national parks, and other areas can readily collect user charges when entrance roads have been constructed so that entry is largely restricted to a very few points. Where this is true and where there are enough visitors to make fee collection worthwhile, user charges seem to be entirely practical from an administrative standpoint.

The Forest Service has carried out some interesting experiments in which the recreationist pays his fees on a self-service or honor system basis.[11] Under one variant, the camper puts 50 cents (or some other amount) into a device from which he then pulls a ticket that he puts on the windshield of his car or on his tent at the campsite. Coin-operated entrance gates have also been tried. The results have been gratifying when the devices were well adapted to the area. Some states have experimented with similar devices.

[11] *Collecting User Fees on National Forest Recreation Facilities, An Administrative Study,* Forest Service, California Region, San Francisco, 1963.

In many instances such types of aids would seem to overcome many of the administrative objections to collection of fees. Most people want to pay their way, and, if fees are reasonable, policing could probably be limited to spot checks. Experience with fishing licenses offers a commentary on the feasibility of such fee schemes. Nearly everyone purchases a license, even though the probability of being checked sometime during the season is very low. It is altogether likely that people would feel much the same about paying a park entrance or service fee in an area which is not constantly patrolled by some enforcement officer.

In a similar vein it is also often argued that the cost of collection often exceeds the amount collected, and therefore the proposition is unfeasible. There is obviously something to this argument if the primary objective is to raise money. However, as we have pointed out, an important part of the gains that can be derived from charge systems lies in their contribution to the efficient allocation of resources and the efficient administration of recreation areas. While the annual revenue collected may in some cases be rather small when administrative cost is accounted for, the gains may nevertheless be substantial.

The imposition of user charges raises questions as to who is to be charged, for what, and how much. Perhaps the simplest system is to charge each person for admittance to an area or for the provision of a service. A variant of this is a charge per party, including charges per car. The latter obviously benefits large families or large parties. A different approach is to permit free entry into the recreation area but to charge for many activities ranging from parking cars to swimming, to boat launching. Such an approach may have some advantage in that the recipient knows what he is paying for. It does, however, fail somewhat in associating the cost of the recreation area itself with the beneficiary. Another variant is to sell a windshield sticker which permits unlimited use for some limited period or for the whole season. This scheme has the administrative advantage of reducing the cost of fee collection. However, because this type of charge has a zero incremental cost, it has the disadvantage of being much less efficient as an allocator of recreation resources. We are left with a disassociation of cost and benefits of the actual services consumed; once the sticker is purchased, the use that is made of various services provided is no longer determined by the price of the actual service.

Of obvious concern in the whole matter of price policy is the level of charges. The use of outdoor recreation areas and facilities is always priced, even when the price is zero. A decision lies behind the setting of a zero price just as it does for any other price. We have argued that for a good number of reasons the absence of positive fees and charges is inconsistent with the efficient use of recreation resources. The present policies will become even more defective in the future as the pressures for economizing increase. It is clear that the present policies should be at least re-examined in the light of oncoming recreation problems.

The most relevant consideration in determining rates is the added cost, and not the original cost of providing the recreation facilities or the average cost of services. While there are a number of complications which are apparent in the decision to base user charges on incremental cost, the principle remains a valid one. If there is to be a more efficient use of our recreation resources, there must be a closer association between the actual costs which are imposed by the user of the resource and the price he pays to receive this benefit. As pointed out earlier, these added costs include more than the added costs for operation and maintenance of the recreation facilities themselves. They include the cost imposed on other users in the form of decreased enjoyment as a result of the crowding brought about by the added visitor rate, and also the cost of resource erosion and depletion.

While a good many arbitrary decisions may need to be made in connection with the administration of some sort of pricing principle that approaches the incremental cost, it seems possible to devise some practical approximations of this cost which would be relatively easy to administer and would also produce substantial efficiency gains in allocation of recreation resources. User charges need not be completely arbitrarily assigned but can be devised to bear some relationship to the added costs imposed by the added visits.

A major consideration in administrative feasibility is the attitude of the general public toward the user fees imposed. If the fees are regarded as reasonable, they will surely be paid more readily than if they are regarded as exorbitant. The need for some public education, if user charges are instituted, is obvious. Moreover, many people would probably resent recreation user charges which they regarded as an attempt to raise general revenue, but would be more willing to pay charges which they thought were related to the provision of the recreation area and service. If funds raised from recreation user charges were employed to provide better management and servicing of the park or recreation area, or to acquire or develop new areas, then people might be more willing to pay such charges.

EFFECT OF RECREATION USER CHARGES ON DIFFERENT AREAS AND GROUPS

User charges for public recreation areas would have varying effects upon users from different areas of origin and upon different groups of users and on those with whom they do business. We should expect different effects for different levels of prices or entrance fees, depending upon the demand characteristics of the area. Attendance for different kinds of recreation areas will be differently affected by different price policies.

The shape of the demand curve gives an indication of the effect of an increased price on the expected use or attendance for the given area. We would expect, for example, to find demand schedules or demand curves indicating very little drop-off in attendance over wide ranges of prices charged for areas which are highly unique and offer outstanding scenic or recreation opportunities. Some of our national parks undoubtedly fall into this category. Because the added entrance charge is such a small per cent of the total cost of visiting such areas, relatively large percentage increases in fees would have very little effect on attendance. The case with areas of much more modest types of attraction and those perhaps located closer to population centers would very likely be the opposite. Here we would expect relatively minor increases in fees to lead to a substantial decrease in attendance because user charges would be a large percentage of the total cost of visits to such areas.

The imposition of fees at one area will also have an effect on the various alternative areas because, as we have seen earlier, there is often a competitive relationship between attendance at different recreation areas located within the same region. The imposition of a fee at one area will reduce attendance at that area and in most cases result in an increase in the use of various alternative parks. The extent of the increase will depend, first, on the size of the fee and consequent reductions in use at the area where the fee is charged, and, secondly, upon the nature of the interrelationship between the areas. If two areas are located close together and have similar recreation opportunities, diversion might be expected to be large. But if the areas are unrelated in position and in character, the effect would probably be small.

Not only would the actual visitors to recreation areas be affected by the imposition of user charges, but also those businesses which supply them. If the imposition of user charges should reduce total attendance at an area, it would also reduce the total volume of business, and, to the extent that such business was profitable, the imposition of a fee would work against the local suppliers concerned. However, the adverse effect of increased user charges upon local business might not be as serious as it would seem at first glance. We have suggested that increased fees would have the least effect upon resource-based types of recreation areas because such areas are often unique and because the fees would be only a small part of the total cost of visiting them. It is in just such areas that the business of supplying visitors is most important. In contrast, in the more run-of-the-mill intermediate type areas, where imposition of user fees would have more effect upon attendance, the local business in supplying visitors is less important, in large part because such recreationists buy most of their supplies in their home towns. Nevertheless, it is a mistake to assume that all the adjustments to higher recreation use fees are made by the recreationists themselves.

SOME PRINCIPLES FOR LEVYING USER CHARGES

Because there is now so much interest in the possibilities of levying greater charges upon recreation users, because the issue is likely to become more important in the future than it is now, and because there are many differences of opinion on the matter, the discussion thus far in this chapter may perhaps appropriately be summarized into a few guiding principles for the levying of recreation user charges, as follows:

1. Avoid user charges which are administratively unworkable or unsound. If costs would be out of proportion to results, if widespread evasion is probable, or if collection would present unusual administrative difficulties or have undesired other effects, user charges should not be levied.

2. Define carefully the purpose to be achieved by collection of user charges. Is it to raise revenue, to increase efficiency in allocation of resources as between recreation and other resource uses, to change user attitudes toward the resource, to accomplish certain management goals, or for other reasons?

3. Choose the method or methods of levying charges which are appropriate to the goal. If the objective is to shift use from one area to another, the difference in charge is perhaps more important than the level of either charge; if the objective is to raise maximum revenue, then the maximum revenue fee as estimated from the demand curve for the resource is the proper criterion; if the objective is to raise revenues sufficient to meet annual management costs, then the necessary fee can be estimated from the demand curve; and so on.

4. Tell the recreation users, frankly and fully, why a charge is imposed and what will be done with the funds; management must certainly work with recreationists, not against them.

5. Consider carefully the equity considerations in any proposed fee schedule; try to anticipate the side effects, and eliminate the undesired ones.

The establishment and administration of a system of recreation user charges is not a simple matter; but neither is it so difficult as to be unworkable. Careful advance consideration can go far toward reducing problems to the practical minimum.

EFFECT OF RECREATION BENEFITS ON LAND VALUES AND REPAYMENT POSSIBILITIES

We have found in earlier discussion that the economic value of recreation facilities may be determined by measuring what consumers are willing to pay for these products and services. In addition to the values created by visitors, it is quite likely that some users of the area may desire to purchase proximity to the park, thereby increasing the value of nearby land. The previous owners are thus able to sell it at an enhanced price. The relative size of this component of a value would vary greatly depending upon individual circumstances. While we might expect this land value increment to be relatively large in the case of lakes and urban parks, it is likely to be small in more remote areas.

In many cases, certain beneficiaries obtain substantial gains in the form of increased land values. These are obtained as a result of public investment; little or no payment is usually made by such individuals. Because of this fairly explicit capital gain derived by the owners of land on or near recreation projects, there are important implications with respect to repayment policy. Just as there are important efficiency and equity arguments for charging users of recreation areas for such use, there are also analogous arguments for capturing the land value increments that result from proximity to recreation facilities created by public investment. There are a number of ways in which this might be accomplished: one way is through the use of various taxes, another is for the public to acquire the surrounding land before the recreation facility is created and then sell the land afterward. There are also various possibilities within this general framework, stemming from such operations as concessions. Although many units of government would hesitate to buy land around recreation projects with the expectation of its later resale at a profit—or would lack either the legal power or the funds or both—yet, at the least, the unit of government which builds a dam with a reservoir suitable for recreation or which acquires land for a park should acquire ample land for its own needs at the beginning stages of the project. Otherwise, it may be in the unhappy position of later having to buy land it needs, at prices inflated by reason of its own action.

V

Outdoor Recreation for the Future

To this point we have dealt mainly with the present situation and the underlying changes in economic and social factors having a bearing on outdoor recreation. We have noted the rapidly increasing demands for recreation, the greater competition for resources, and our need for a better knowledge of the many aspects of outdoor recreation.

We turn now to two chapters dealing with subjects growing out of the earlier discussions. As we look ahead, issues of research and policy choices loom increasingly important. As demands and investments increase, research and policy become critical.

15

Research for Outdoor Recreation

The steadily mounting demand for outdoor recreation cannot be satisfied without large new areas of land and water for outdoor recreation, much capital investment for this purpose, more manpower for managing the areas, and a much larger total output of recreation services and values. The problems of providing adequate outdoor recreation are going to grow increasingly difficult. Uncertainties are going to remain a problem; the cost of various resources is going to increase, and budgets will remain limited. Unco-ordinated, intuitive approaches that lean heavily but uncritically on past experience cannot provide adequate solutions. Research is going to play an increasingly important role. Wise, timely, and economic expansion of recreation facilities and efficient administration of existing areas will require a great deal more in the way of both planning and research.

FRAGMENTATION OF PLANNING AND RESEARCH

Planning and research in outdoor recreation lag far behind current needs. Lack of funds has been a limiting factor. But lack of co-ordination among the efforts of different levels of government and among the many agencies at each level has also stood in the way of progress.

The federal agencies have probably done most in the way of planning for their own lands, although until a decade ago much of this work was on a rather superficial basis. The National Park Service has done some general planning in co-operation with state agencies for about 25 years; its efforts have been only moderately effective, in part because of lack of funds. The Forest Service is engaged in recreation research, but its output was small until recently, lack of funds being a factor here, too. However, a few years ago the Forest Service expanded its program, and in 1963 and 1964 it published over sixty papers and reports dealing with the results of its research into a wide range of recreation problems. It is noteworthy that about half of its research staff are social scientists. Other agencies in the Department of Agriculture have done some research in outdoor recreation, particularly on private activities, but their efforts have been rather small until recently.

The federal government entered the planning and research phase of outdoor recreation on a more comprehensive scale when the Outdoor Recreation Resources Review Commission was established by special legislation in 1959. The work of the Commission led, in turn, to the establishment of the Bureau of Outdoor Recreation in the U.S. Department of the Interior. The Bureau's functions include collecting information, conducting research, doing general recreation planning, and coordinating recreation activities among federal agencies.

States have been woefully weak in recreation planning, and much of what they have done has been in response to impetus provided by federal agencies. During the 1930's, federal grants made park and recreation planning possible for the first time in many states. The state park agencies have until recently typically not developed long-range plans even for their own programs and most certainly not for all recreation in their state. Within the past several years a few states have made notable advances in this regard, and further progress is expected to result from the provisions of the Land and Water Fund bill under which the states are to conduct statewide plans covering a broad range of outdoor recreation.

Research in outdoor recreation at the state level has been almost nonexistent. Agencies administrating outdoor recreation and parks have not been authorized, staffed, or financed to do research. The result is a serious lack of facts and understanding that is probably costing heavily even now.

State park systems collect some information regarding the areas they administer, and such information has been published by the National Park Service, the Bureau of Outdoor Recreation, and by private organizations. But even this information is rather limited. Many state agencies publicize estimates of numbers of tourists or recreationists and of expenditures by them. Unfortunately, these estimates generally rest on a very slender factual basis and are often based upon fuzzy and ill-defined concepts, as we pointed out in Chapter 12. Efforts are under way to improve such estimates.

Recreation planning is even weaker at the city level. General city planners must take recreation needs or demands and opportunities into account in any well-rounded plans that may be developed. However, there has been an unfortunate gap between the recreation specialist and the general city planners in many cities.

Recreation research is almost unknown at the city level. City departments are unequipped to do research. As a rule they are not given the responsibility for research. And they must frequently strain their budgets to handle administrative and management problems alone. As with the states, the results are unfortunate. Research in this field would almost certainly yield handsome dividends to society.

In general, legislative and appropriating bodies have not encouraged outdoor recreation managing agencies to look ahead and often they have not provided the funds for making such plans. There has also been a serious lack of agreed-upon factual information and measures of the value of recreation. The agencies concerned have had to present plans and proposals which often rested primarily on personal judgments and personal standards of value.

What is needed is not just more research, but more productive research. Ways must be found to co-ordinate the activities of the various agencies.

COLLECTION AND PUBLICATION OF FACTS

Most public agencies administering outdoor recreation areas collect some facts about their operations. They often have data on number of areas, acreage, personnel, and expenditure data that are more descriptive than analytical and that are collected primarily to meet the administrative needs of the respective agencies. The data may be suitable for that purpose, although one cannot but wonder at times if major improvements could not be made even for this purpose. Comparability between kinds of areas is difficult or impossible, owing to the wide variety of definition. There has not been in the past any well-formulated plan of data collections and analysis for outdoor recreation areas, so one cannot fairly blame the various agencies for pursuing their own methods. But the over-all results are poor.

Bad as it is, the collection of data about outdoor recreation is better than its publication. Typically, a park or recreation administering agency issues a mimeographed press release giving information about the season or year just ended. Such press releases seldom contain much data about earlier years, so that historical comparisons, especially beyond one year, are very difficult. The physical form of these press releases is such that no librarian can or does save them, and it would be difficult for any organization to preserve them from year to year. Some of these data are quoted in various professional or trade magazines or journals, but usually in such form as to make comparisons between years or areas difficult or impossible. The National Recreation Association has collected some data for many years, now on a five-year interval basis, which is very helpful. But their effort depends on return of mailed questionnaires, and the results are always incomplete to an unknown degree. Some of the more meaningful data are not collected, and perhaps could not be in this way. Formerly the National Park Service prepared annual summaries of data relating to state park systems. But these, too, are perishable mimeographed releases, not easily preserved.

Efforts should be directed to assembling and publishing really relevant data in a usable form. It is altogether possible that sufficient effort is being directed—or misdirected—to the collection of data about outdoor recreation. The results are very poor, but the greatest lack is not effort. In some cases, often very significant ones, far more useful data were collected than were ever used in any meaningful way. The program direction and analysis of data have often been far weaker than the data collection itself. The Bureau of Outdoor Recreation is in a position to provide some real leadership here; we can only hope that it rises to the challenge.

SOME GENERAL CONSIDERATIONS[1]

An absence of facts actually encourages speculation as to the true situation. Individual generalization can be based upon insufficient experience, opinion, or dogma. Legislators, administrators, and much of the general public have naturally been skeptical of the needs and problems of outdoor recreation when the factual basis was so obviously deficient. No amount of data will solve all practical administrative and policy questions, of course, but if good data are available, discussion and debate can be confined to significant issues and not wasted on argument about missing facts. Provision of really adequate facts and their general understanding would probably do more to achieve sound coordination among the many and diverse public agencies and private groups than could possibly be accomplished by any amount of administrative coercion.

Research is organized search for new knowledge, including a new understanding that comes from a rearrangement of old facts and old ideas. The emphasis in research is on understanding, especially of the basic relationships. Research requires facts but fact-gathering and fact-summarizing alone is not research.

---

[1] The remainder of this chapter draws heavily upon Marion Clawson and Jack L. Knetsch, "Outdoor Recreation Research: Some Concepts and Suggested Areas of Study," *National Resources Journal* (October 1963), pp. 250–275.

So defined, research must be carefully distinguished from planning and from the accumulated knowledge that comes out of management experience. Planning is primarily a means for putting known facts together, evaluating them, and coming up with a proposed line or lines of action. It may draw on research and may use some of the same basic data, but the moving purpose and the scheme of analysis are different.

Resource management, including outdoor recreation, leads to a body of experience and in the hands of an observant practitioner to an accumulation of knowledge. The experienced manager often knows a great deal, but he may generalize too widely and freely from too limited experience. His knowledge is conditioned by his history, and he may not know what would occur under markedly different circumstances. The researcher, in contrast, has or should have tested concepts, ideas, and hypotheses in controlled circumstances or within known bounds. What he gains by rigorous logic and analytical procedures should more than compensate for what he unavoidably loses by lack of involvement in the processes he studies. One should be careful about concluding that a researcher has a "better" understanding. He merely approaches part of life from a different viewpoint and with a different purpose.

There are several reasons why there has been so little organized research into the problems of outdoor recreation. Recreation simply has not been recognized by many professions as a respectable field for scientific inquiry. Many persons equate recreation with "fun"; they do not consider it a subject for serious study. Emotional and sentimental attitudes toward outdoor recreation have also discouraged research. Many persons have asserted values and considerations not easily subject to analytical research. Some have advocated reservation or establishment of outdoor areas or proposed other actions that they did not care to subject to critical research.

The need for research may not have been so apparent in an earlier period when the competition for use of natural resources was less severe, and the problems of recreation use of resources were not so serious. The fact that outdoor recreation is an activity with a general absence of market transactions and for the most part provided by public bodies has clearly also inhibited research. Further, no institution was organized specifically for outdoor recreation research. There has been nothing remotely comparable to the USDA-Land Grant College system for research in agriculture. Any one of these factors may have been serious. The combination has been almost overwhelming. Not only has there been comparatively little research in the problems of outdoor recreation, but much of it has been incidental to research in other uses of natural resources and some of it has not been especially imaginative.

Certain recognized principles and methods of scientific research are as applicable to research on outdoor recreation as they are for inquiry into any other field. For example, a way of generalizing from specific experiences to a broader range of occurrences is to construct hypotheses and theories and to test them empirically. This usually requires quantitative measurement and specific tests designed to test particular theories. This may involve certain types of organized experimentation where it is possible to establish controls or to determine conditions. Close observation and measurement of various events or phenomena in a typical analysis of data may be an appropriate approach under many circumstances and indeed may be the only practical approach for many economic and social problems where controlled experimentation is impossible or undesirable. The specific problems and the relationships that occur in outdoor recreation differ from those in other resource fields, but the scientific approach is as applicable.

As a general comment, it can be said that outdoor recreation is not a separate field of human knowledge, but a kind of human activity. Many problems are related to this activity, and they can be studied in an organized way by applying the theory, logic, and methods of many of the established fields of special knowledge either singly or in combination. Outdoor recreation research has a unifying theme, a kind of activity, and a range of problems, but it is not a special field of knowledge as such.

Although each phase of outdoor recreation is closely related to others and although each outdoor recreation area is related in some way to other areas, as a matter of practical fact it is necessary to subdivide the field of outdoor recreation research into manageable "chunks." One man or one group cannot possibly study everything at one time. Some problems will loom as more important than others; some fields of specialty will condition the individual researcher's approach, and some physical areas will require more specific attention. Administrative considerations in research agencies will require a project approach or at least delineation of some specific research attempts. For all of these reasons, subdivision of the broad field of outdoor recreation research is necessary.

At the same time it must be recognized that any subdivision of the field is arbitrary in some degree and that various segments of research are related just as various groups of problems are related. Specific research projects may properly have two or more specific aims, or two or more kinds of problems may be studied at one time. In fact, joint undertakings which deliberately cross boundary lines often may be highly productive. The organization of specific research projects may be affected by administrative convenience, and by the interest and abilities of the researchers in each of the problems. The researcher should have a broad understanding of recreation as ₠ whole and an appreciation of the fact that he is studying only a part of this whole. Research in outdoor recreation will be advanced by individuals and groups working on different aspects of problems but conscious of the relations between them. Each may conduct a project in his field of interest, but each project is related in some way, and contributes to a furthering of the field.

RESEARCH ON DEMAND

We have seen throughout our discussion in earlier chapters how the rapid and sustained growth in outdoor recreation activity has focused attention on the nature of its demand relationships. An understanding of present demands and how they are changing over time has become of immense importance in resource planning and policy formulation.

The analysis of demand for outdoor recreation may be at roughly the same stage that analysis for agricultural commodities was forty or more years ago. In the early 1920's, demand curves were well known to economists, but many doubted that empirical relationships ever could be estimated with any accuracy. During the 1920's, various methods were developed. Later, many of the early empirical results were revealed to be in error. Better data were needed and gradually came into existence as well as more sophisticated and efficient methods of analysis, but today the demand for all agricultural commodities is fairly well known and different workers have obtained empirical measures which are quite consistent. Although debate on agricultural policy may rage, there is general agreement on the basic underlying demand relationships.

Presently available data concerning recreation use are often seriously deficient and are often suspected of being highly inaccurate. A major problem pertains to the most appropriate unit of recreation use. Three major measures are commonly used: visitor day, person visit, and party visit. Each has its usefulness and each is used to some extent.

Visitor days measure the volume of use in a recreation area. They are particularly good in measuring physical volume of use or of wear and tear in the area, and of needed services such as garbage collection and the like. Many organizations administering outdoor recreation areas find visitor days a useful measure of management work load, but this unit of measure is not well suited for demand analysis. Much of the cost of a visit to an outdoor recreation area is the cost of travel (including meals and lodging en route) and equipment. The added cost of an added day at the site may be comparatively small. Average cost per visitor day can be lowered by staying more days, but this raises total cost per person for the whole experience. It is doubtful that cost per visitor day is the most significant way to measure differences in cost of outdoor recreation.

In some respects the person visit is a better measure of the amount of outdoor recreation. It has value to the administrator of the recreation area for it indicates how many different persons he has to deal with. Cost per visit is likely to be a more significant economic measure than is cost per visitor day.

The party visit is perhaps the best measure for demand analysis. In most cases the members of a recreation party are also members of a single family spending money out of a common purse or single income. For them it is the total cost of the whole recreation experience that is most significant, not the cost per person or per person day. Lumping all costs for the whole family for the whole trip into one total may be more meaningful in terms which count in families' decisions about outdoor recreation.

Various kinds of research projects are needed to collect data in various ways and of various kinds. We have only the roughest guesses as to how many individuals the total number of visits represent, for instance. Sample studies have obtained information as to age, family composition, income, and other characteristics of recreationists, but the definitions or class intervals have varied from study to study. Also, the information in these studies is often not comparable with information from more general sources such as census reports. There is little point, however, in asking recreation and administrative agencies to collect, tabulate, and publish better recreation data until "better" can be accurately defined. Research projects in this phase of outdoor recreation deserve a high priority.

Fundamentally the interest in demand studies stems from their importance in explaining and analyzing the regularities and patterns of behavior among individuals in the use of all kinds of recreation areas. That such patterns exist has been demonstrated earlier. However, it is one thing to observe instances of such regularity and have intuitive notions about them; it is quite another thing to relate the regularities to the important determining factors and to have empirically determined estimates of the importance of each factor and of the relationships of one to another and to time-related changes. It is this latter type of information that is in such short supply in the outdoor recreation field but that nevertheless is so useful. Quantitative estimates of demand relations are needed for many aspects of resource allocations. As evidence is accumulated on the structure of demand for outdoor recreation, it will be possible to make meaningful generalizations about recreation which will be enormously helpful in the planning and management of outdoor areas.

Even rule-of-thumb standards of value for recreation areas, as discussed in Chapter 11, must rest on research if they are to be reliable. It is time-consuming and may appear expensive to undertake research for every area for which value estimates are needed. But a well-conceived national program of demand research that began with intensive study of but a few areas would greatly improve the basis for rule-of-thumb guides to the value of resources used for recreation. Recreation demand research should not stop with the study of the first few areas, of course; more refinement, different situations, and improved methodology would each require further studies.

Demand studies could provide valuable, practical guides on many other management issues. They could provide a better basis for estimating probable attendance at an area, or estimating the effect that different fees would have on attendance, for example. The practical utility of demand studies is very great.

RESOURCE EVALUATION AND IMPROVEMENT STUDIES

For outdoor recreation as for any other service or commodity, supply in any meaningful sense must be related to demand. The past upsurges in outdoor recreation activities have been possible only because there were areas and facilities to satisfy that demand. Any projected future increases in recreation use will be realized, at least in large part, if the supply of outdoor recreation areas and facilities expands to accommodate them. Area is not the only problem; there are many other aspects of supply to which research might well be directed.

One line of research on recreation supply is to develop rating scales or systems to measure the inherent attractiveness of different outdoor recreation areas. Even the most casual observation shows that some areas are much more attractive than others; often, however, differences are not as clear or lack specific description or measurement. Some features are readily measurable in quantitative and objective terms; water temperatures, for instance, will condition attractiveness for swimming or will limit the kinds of sport fish that may be produced. Other features are less readily measured in objective terms. For instance, some scenery is outstanding and inspiring to some people but not to others. Yet it would be possible to list the more important natural features of an area and give each of them some kind of rating. The aspects of an area that reflect man's use could also be listed: degree of water pollution, degree of drawdown of artificial reservoirs, accumulated litter, and many others. The greatest difficulty would come in combining data or ratings on individual qualities or characteristics into a summary rating scale; yet this seems both possible and desirable. An

OUTDOOR RECREATION FOR THE FUTURE

area might be rated differently for different uses; an artificial reservoir might be quite suitable for motorboating but unattractive for shore-based activities. In spite of the difficulties, it should be possible to develop specific, and rather objective, rating scales for different outdoor recreation areas and for the major uses of each.[2]

Research is also needed to determine the carrying capacity of various kinds of areas for different kinds of uses. Capacity is closely related to crowding; or, perhaps more generally, to the concept of optimum intensity of use, discussed in Chapter 8. Research should include consideration of methods of increasing carrying capacity. How far can physical layout, vegetative screening, specific structures, or physical improvements increase the ability of an area to serve more people without diminution in satisfaction?

A different but closely allied line of research could be directed toward means of increasing either attractiveness or capacity, or both, for different kinds of areas by use of capital or labor, or both. How far can different kinds of areas "profitably" absorb inputs of capital and labor to produce more or better outdoor recreation at reasonable costs? We suggest that areas differ greatly in this respect; the kind of use also greatly affects the situation. Man-made installations are necessary for intensively used areas but may greatly reduce the value of natural environment and primitive kinds of areas. The investment of manpower and capital is wasted on some areas and extremely productive on others. Any research on this problem should consider the values and satisfactions of the recreation experience; otherwise, what might seem like an increase in capacity might be only a decrease in quality.

Another related line of research might investigate methods of design or management that will reduce or prevent damage to the area or facilities. There are always a few people who damage recreation areas, some unknowingly and some willfully. Education and enforcement would be helpful, and research in this direction should be suggested. But it seems highly probable that design, maintenance, and other aspects of areas and facilities affect mental and emotional attitudes of users, and these also demand research.

Value and quality can be improved by reducing destruction and by encouraging optimum intensity of use. But there are additional factors to which research might be directed. Quality should be considered, and areas should be put to their best use. The use of unique areas of any

[2] Some very imaginative work has been done in this area. See Phillip H. Lewis, "Quality Corridors for Wisconsin," *Landscape Architecture* (January 1964); and Frank C. Craighead, Jr. and John J. Craighead, "River Systems: Recreational Classification, Inventory and Evaluation," *Naturalist,* Journal of the Natural History Society of Minnesota, Vol. 13, No. 2 (Summer 1962), pp. 2–19.

kind for intensive activities, such as camping, would constitute a form of economic and social waste. Relationships between one kind of area and another may be highly significant; for example, the value of the campground in the developed part of a national forest may depend on preservation of the quality of the scenic back country. Actual preservation of recreation quality is a problem for the administrator, but research into what is meant by quality, how quality can be achieved, and what can be gained by it are problems for the researcher.

ALLOCATION OF NATURAL RESOURCES FOR OUTDOOR RECREATION

Competition for natural resources will almost certainly force a more careful evaluation of their value for different uses in the future than has been characteristic in the past. Planners, legislators, and administrators will increasingly ask about the comparative values of resources in different uses. This is not to say that all decisions about resources will be, or perhaps should be, based on measured values alone; this certainly has not been the case in the past. But resource decisions should take account of such values. Research can contribute greatly to measurement of the values involved and thus, indirectly, to much sounder future policies.

One basic kind of research in this general field is the measurement of the physical substitution ratios among the various uses of land. If recreation use of the forest increases, how far and in what ways will this compete with timber harvest or other use? If the number of deer is allowed to increase on the range, how far and in what ways will this impinge upon grazing by domestic livestock? How far is the recreation use of a multiple purpose reservoir reduced or modified by other uses? How far can management practices that would ordinarily be undertaken for one resource use be modified so as to increase the output of the resource for all uses? These are illustrative of the kinds of questions that must be answered by this type of research. Decisions might continue to include factors other than comparative returns. But dependable estimates of such values, based on sound methods worked out through careful research, would surely narrow the range of the present uncertainty and would provide a more objective basis for decision making than now exists.

A closely related but somewhat different line of research could consider the value of specific natural resources for different uses at varying levels of intensity of management. For instance, a federal reservoir area would attract one number and type of visitor, but it would attract another number and perhaps another type of user if improvements such as boat-launching ramps were installed. The value of the natural resource depends in some degree upon the level and type of management of the area. Some management practices may cost more than they will add in value while others may add value far in excess of their cost. In making comparisons of the value of particular natural resources for different uses, it is a net value in which we are interested. Research into the effect of management upon resource values would probably involve several kinds of specialists, and estimates might have to be made for management practices and use intensities not yet experienced in actual operations.

Another important research need is for a better determination of the values of outdoor recreation which accrue to non-users. As we have discussed, there has been much speculation about these values, but little objective research. Such values no doubt exist, but we need to know far more about their nature and importance and how they vary with types of outdoor recreation.

A related line of research should be concerned with the final incidence of benefits and cost from recreation use of natural resources and investments therein. The beneficiaries of recreation use include not only the recreationists themselves, but also those who provide them with services at a price. The benefits of outdoor recreation may be rather widely diffused. But the incidence of costs of providing the outdoor recreation area may be even more diffused. In practice only a small part of the costs are paid directly by the recreation users at the time of use; more is paid by them in the form of taxes, and in many instances taxes are paid to help provide outdoor recreation by people who do not use it. The matter of final incidence of a tax is rather involved, but it is not beyond reasonably accurate measurement.

It would be interesting, and might be revealing, to compare the final incidence of cost with the final benefits from the use of a particular recreation area. Planners, legislators, and others might find useful the results of careful analyses that would show who really pays for outdoor recreation, who gets its benefits, and how the costs and benefits compare.

FINANCING OF OUTDOOR RECREATION

Provision of outdoor recreation costs money, and the difficulties of getting enough public funds allocated to this function may limit the adequacy of the recreation resources. Decisions to allocate or to refuse funds for a public activity are made by political processes; but the provision of facts may aid those processes. In any case, political action and inaction are fit subjects for research in themselves.

One kind of research within this general field is concerned with the equity of various systems of receation and park financing, in contrast with the benefits obtained by users. This is closely related to some of the projects suggested above. A political leader or an administrator wants to know who is going to pay, who is going to benefit, how closely final incidence of costs and benefits coincide or diverge, and other related matters. Facts on these matters are unlikely in themselves to be decisive, but they would be helpful.

Another line of research is a comparative analysis of the financial requirements for recreation as compared with those for other necessary governmental activities in the same unit of government. The typical governmental budget processes show amounts proposed for different functions, and sometimes also show the sources of revenue to support the expenditures. But this provides no real basis for judging the importance or urgency of different kinds of expenditures or the advantages of each. It is possible to do significant research on this problem. When multiple use management is contemplated for a tract of land or water, one use must be balanced against another, with some consideration given to the degree of competition and the degree of complementarity between uses. In the case of different uses of a given amount of public revenue, as in the multiple use case, the benefits are often not directly comparable, or are comparable only with difficulty; yet choices must be made. Research would not obviate the need for choices, but it might delineate more sharply the kinds of choices that could be made. If administrators, legislators, and the public knew which choices were realistically possible and what had to be given up for what, the choices presumably would be more rational in terms of their own goals.

POLITICAL AND INSTITUTIONAL ORGANIZATIONS

Outdoor recreation poses large problems for governments and private organizations. This is a field which has had almost no research. Some research might be directed to an appraisal of current arrangements; other projects might investigate and possibly experiment with new arrangements.

One line of research could be concerned with the relative roles of different levels of government in outdoor recreation research. A first step would be a careful examination of what different governments now do, not only in general but quite specifically. The Outdoor Recreation Resources Review Commission did some of this, but its results were more descriptive than analytical. Government activities include planning, managing, and financing outdoor recreation. How far are these different functions now grouped within the same organizations, and how far are they divided among various levels of government or different units at each level? How far should they be grouped or divided? What special problems arise when these functions are divided? For instance, what are the secondary or indirect effects of grants-in-aid from one level of government to another? Should recreation planning be centered in recreation agencies or in planning agencies? What are the best ways of co-ordinating the recreation planning efforts of various governmental and private groups? These are policy questions, to some extent, but research might unearth facts and suggest lines of action which would be helpful to policymakers.

Another general line of research in this field could study the institutional problems and arrangements for greater public use of private land for outdoor recreation. Although some private landowners make their land freely available for recreation, they should not be expected to do so; neither equity nor economics justifies such action. Saying that landowners should provide recreation for a fee is just a beginning. The problem is a complex one; financial, legal, and administrative aspects must all be considered. How can the individual farmer contact and deal with the individual recreationist, and vice versa? Can the individual farmer provide an adequate recreation opportunity, or must several pool their resources? Can a landowner afford to service and supervise a single recreationist, or must he deal with a group? How can a reasonable level of charges be determined, and will this provide an adequate incentive to farmers and other landowners to provide the land and facilities? What are the legal liabilities of the recreationist and of the landowner? How may each be minimized and perhaps insured against? These are but some of the questions that might be posed for research in this field.

SOME CONCLUSIONS ABOUT RECREATION RESEARCH

As the demand for outdoor recreation increases, research becomes more important. Specific lines of enquiry were suggested above. Here, we list a few broad conclusions about recreation research in general and make some suggestions for improving procedures and organization.

1. The problems of outdoor recreation will be more difficult in the future, and the intuitive approach, under which a man leans heavily on his own experience generalized to a broader situation, simply will not be adequate; research will be even more important than it is now.

2. Usable results from research will flow rather slowly; no miracles can be expected tomorrow. Research workers must develop improved and adequate methodology, test it rigorously under a variety of conditions, and then accumulate a body of research results. Premature reliance on untested research might bring the whole concept of research into disrepute; for the next few years, we shall have to continue to rely

heavily on the intuitive approach which is inadequate for the longer run. But this should not be used as an excuse to delay or underfinance needed research.

3. The most important immediate task of research is devising more useful, more sophisticated, and more imaginative models for analyzing difficult problems. Until these models are developed, more data may be as confusing as helpful. The analytical models must be tested under a variety of conditions; there is no place in this field of intensely practical problems for theorizing which cannot be, or is not, applied.

4. Once better analytical models are developed and tested, data should be collected on a much larger scale and analyzed as fully as possible. The purpose for which data is to be used should be determined before scarce money and manpower resources are spent on its collection. Research studies of the same or similar kinds will help build up a body of research findings that will test the universality of the research techniques and provide sounder guides to planning, administration, and financing.

5. If the field is to be developed rapidly, the push can best come from organizations whose major interest and concern is recreation research. The Bureau of Outdoor Recreation already operates in this area, but it would be useful to have several other organizations with a specialized interest in outdoor recreation research.

6. The establishment of specialized research agencies will not—and we would say should not—eliminate the need for research by specialists in research organizations with other interests as well as outdoor recreation—the Forest Service, forestry schools, land grant colleges, for example. Foresters, wildlife management specialists, park specialists, economists, sociologists, political scientists and others with varied professional backgrounds can contribute a great deal. It is often better to have men who are thoroughly competent in their basic field and who learn about outdoor recreation as they progress in research, than to attempt to develop "recreation researchers" who would then have to learn about economics, political science, and forestry. Men with various professional backgrounds should be encouraged to seek research projects on problems in outdoor recreation, and the specialized recreation research agencies should bring such problems to the attention of these specialists.

7. A better clearinghouse is needed for recreation research. The fragmentation and diversification of the field of recreation research, obvious to anyone who explores it even casually, means that men are often unaware of work being done by others—even those at their own institution or in their own state. We do not attempt to spell out how the clearinghouse function can best be performed, but the need is real.

16

Major Issues of Public Policy

Issues of unresolved public policy are implicit in the discussions of preceding chapters; here they are set forth more explicitly. In this chapter we pose current policy issues as clearly as we can and explore some of their ramifications; but we do not try to solve them, nor do we advocate a line of policy for outdoor recreation in the United States. In the solution of issues of social policy, the value standards and philosophy of the persons concerned may be as critical as the technical and economic aspects of the issue; but the latter set limits or raise problems of cost which often affect the answers. If people are aware of the nature of the policy issues and can understand the practical alternative solutions, then they have a rational basis for making their choices.

In this chapter we consider only the policy issues directly concerned with outdoor recreation.[1] But outdoor recreation will be profoundly influenced by broad, national economic and social policies, and we must base our analyses and plans upon what seem to be the most reasonable trends in population, employment, income, and leisure.

POLICY ISSUES IN DEMAND FOR OUTDOOR RECREATION

Demand is often critical for analysis of problems of resources and resource management. It underlies resource value, and as it is reflected

[1] This chapter draws heavily upon papers given by Marion Clawson at the Western Resources Conference, Boulder, Colorado, in July 1964, and published in *New Horizons for Resources Research: Issues and Methodology* (Boulder: University of Colorado Press, 1965), and at the University of Washington seminar for Natural Resources Public Policy, in October 1964 (unpublished).

in use, it has a greater effect than any other factor on how a resource is managed. If demand is heavy, the resource manager faces one situation, and has certain alternatives open to him; if demand is light, he faces a different situation with quite different alternatives.

Should the nation seek to supply any amount of outdoor recreation that is suggested as likely to be in demand? How far must demands for other services and goods be reconciled with the demand for outdoor recreation when they compete for use of natural resources, capital, labor, or management? How far should government at any level stimulate use by provision of free or nearly free outdoor recreation areas?

If public agencies persist in pricing park and recreation areas at comparatively low levels and at the same time legislative bodies refuse to provide public revenues sufficient to meet the demand so stimulated—a course which, in view of recent history, seems not improbable—how can the available supply of recreation best be rationed among the demands for it? One way, of course, would simply be to allow parks and other areas to get so crowded—and perhaps so dirty also—that enough people would be repelled, and thus demand brought in line with supply. Another would be to set up a system of reservations, especially for relatively extended use. Or people could be forced to queue up, waiting their turn, as now happens at busy seasons at many historical spots. Or entrance fees might be used as rationing devices, perhaps with two or more price arrangements to discourage use at peak time periods and encourage or permit it at other times. Or combinations of these measures could be used.

How far should the nation try to meet the actual or potential demand for outdoor recreation of its lower income and otherwise disadvantaged social groups? As we have noted earlier, the really poor people are unable to afford an auto or to incur the expenses involved in most trips to intermediate and resource-based outdoor recreation areas. It seems probable that no one from the lowest tenth of the income scale has ever visited a remote national park, for instance. But it is also true that these people live in parts of cities where user-oriented parks are least adequate. The frequently advocated program of providing free parks for low-income people is mostly empty talk. Will we, as a nation, try to make a massive effort to remedy this situation, either as part of a general attack on poverty or as a special park and recreation program?

This general issue merges with another. Will parks and recreation areas be made equally available to racial and other minority groups as part of the national effort to eliminate discrimination? Negroes, because of their lower average incomes, have suffered a deficiency in recreation services; but they have also suffered racial discrimination here as in other aspects of modern life, and not merely so in the South. These are major policy issues, with deep emotional, ethical, and moral roots, as well as with serious practical implications for recreation programs at every level of government.

POLICY ISSUES IN THE MAINTENANCE OF THE QUALITY OF THE RECREATION EXPERIENCE

Another major issue of public policy is to retain, as far as possible, the quality of the recreation experience. Each recreation experience has a quality dimension, which may easily be impaired. But it is not easy to define quality; people do not all seek the same experiences in outdoor recreation, even in the same area and even at superficially the same activities. The issue is not a simple one. First of all, whose standards of quality should be maintained—those of the purist, or those of the least discriminating users? Public agencies evade the issue when they say that they should provide what people want, for people usually want what they know, and this reflects what has been provided in the past. Public agencies do have a major responsibility for providing a wide variety of kinds and classes of outdoor recreation, but one might well argue that there is no place in such variety for uses which are destructive or degrading. If the public is exposed to many different kinds of outdoor recreation, and if it is given some education, then perhaps its choices on qualities and kinds can safely be accepted.

Is the public prepared to pay some of the costs involved? It costs money to experiment, to educate, and to administer outdoor recreation areas. Many park agencies have difficulty getting adequate funds for interpretive and other educational programs, yet education of park users is dependent upon enough funds for this purpose. If there is to be an end to dirty parks, someone must be prepared to prevent destructive practices or to clean up the parks, and this too costs money.

Part of the quality of outdoor recreation may well center on the range of choice available. Many people feel with good reason that this range is too constrained, particularly for some segments of the population. They maintain that the cyclist ought to have a better choice than a freeway, for example. This and many other similar situations are no doubt true. This arises not just because existing agencies may be inadequately supported but also because in a sense our institutions and rules have been rigged this way. For example, our institutions and investment guides are such that we will undoubtedly see large investments made to increase reservoir-based water recreation opportunities in the future. Under current conditions or rules, there is little likelihood that the value of more of this type of recreation investment will be seriously compared with the value of alternative recreation opportunities—or even with other means of providing water-based recreation.

The costs of maintaining the quality of the outdoor recreation experience arise in terms other than money. Is the public willing to limit the use of some kinds of park areas to their recreation capacity, however that might be measured and determined? When use exceeds optimum capacity the nature of the recreation experience changes, almost always for the worse. There may also be a change in the nature of the recreation resource. In particular, if the rate of increase in use of some national parks, some historic areas, and some state parks continues as it has in the past, the nature of the recreation experience for which the areas were originally established will be destroyed and the areas will be damaged physically. Some areas simply cannot be used at twenty or more times their present volume of use, which is what will happen if past trends continue another generation, without suffering a drastic change in character.[2] Is the nation willing to face up to the policy issues contained in past and present trends and management practices; or will it allow the quality of the experience to be changed drastically? The problem can be handled, but the public must first decide what it really wants and what it is prepared to pay.

POLICY ISSUES IN FACT COLLECTION AND RESEARCH

The inadequacy of facts and the paucity of research about outdoor recreation have been noted in Chapter 15 as well as elsewhere, and some suggestions given as to the kinds of facts and analyses needed. Nearly everyone would agree on the desirability of more facts and better analyses, although there might be differences of opinion as to the urgency of particular needs. With the increase in outdoor recreation which seems probable for the future, and the large sums that are going to be expended to provide it, a better factual foundation is called for. But how can the nation best get the needed facts about outdoor recreation? How far should this be the responsibility of programs at federal, state, or local levels? Shall it be the responsibility of recreation operating agencies, or of specialized recreation research agencies, or of universities, or of others?

Can the lack of research about outdoor recreation best be overcome by authorizing and directing park and other recreation operating agencies to undertake research, which would be a new and difficult

[2] Marion Clawson, "Our National Parks in the Year 2000," *National Parks Magazine*, Vol. 33, No. 142 (July 1959).

assignment for them? Or by encouraging the establishment of specialized recreation research agencies? If the latter, where should they be fitted into the general governmental structure? Or should general research organizations, especially those which are parts of universities, be encouraged to take up outdoor recreation as one of their fields of inquiry? It is highly probable that more constructive research could be carried out by present research agencies if these would direct their attention toward outdoor recreation as a field of inquiry.[3]

Another related policy issue is whether the nation is prepared to pay the costs for gathering pertinent data and making necessary analyses about outdoor recreation problems. It is true that in the past there have been almost no funds available for research directly in this field. Even the fact gathering of most administrative agencies has been primarily incidental to their administration, not for planning and analytical purposes. Many research administrators and many legislators still do not see these as necessary activities for their respective organizations. It is hoped that this attitude will change. Funds spent for data collection and research may well save much larger sums in land acquisition, land development, planning, and administration generally.

POLICY ISSUES IN EFFECTIVE RECREATION PLANNING

If reasonable economies are to be achieved in future park and outdoor recreation programs, there must be careful planning. Better facts and research will help. But there must also be some mechanism for co-ordinating the activities of the many public agencies and private organizations concerned with outdoor recreation.

Almost every serious and reasonably comprehensive study of outdoor recreation has called attention to the large number of governmental units and private organizations dealing with some part of this field. For each of these, the plans, programs, attitudes, capabilities, areas, and facilities of every other group are a major part of its environment. If there are adequate areas available on a nearby national forest, the local Boy Scout troop may not need its own camp; but, if such areas are not available there, the troop may have no alternative but to buy an area, for instance.

There has been no one effective means of bringing the diverse interests together for planning or even for fact finding. Government and private co-ordinating organizations, including the Bureau of Outdoor Recreation and some state interagency committees, have been influential in certain

[3] Marion Clawson and Jack L. Knetsch, "Outdoor Recreation Research: Some Concepts and Suggested Areas of Study," *Natural Resources Journal* (October 1963).

situations, but, on the whole, efforts in this direction have been few and feeble.

Despite the advantages of co-ordinated planning for outdoor recreation, there is bound to be serious opposition to the kind of centralized planning where the federal government would act for the states, each state for its cities and other subdivisions, government for private groups, and the like. The problem is to get a comprehensive approach without centralized control.

The answer probably must lie in co-operation between government at all levels and private groups. Grants-in-aid from one level of government to another are one way of encouraging co-operation. Pressures from some source are almost critical to make voluntary co-operation proceed to the point where individuals and agencies actually modify their actions. Research which clearly reveals the interrelationships of areas and programs can be a powerful stimulus.

POLICY ISSUES IN RESOURCE ALLOCATION TO RECREATION

How much of its natural resources is the nation prepared to allocate to outdoor recreation? In a multiple-purpose reservoir or in a forest managed for multiple uses, recreation should take its full place as an equal claimant to natural resources. This approach is hampered by problems of measurement; but, as we have indicated, these are not insurmountable.

The technical interrelationships between recreation and other uses of the same resources can be both complex and numerous. How much will increased camping interfere with timber growth and harvest in a forest? Or to what extent must timber growth and harvest be modified to reduce interference with camping, and what will it cost? How much will reservoir drawdown, resulting from hydroelectric or irrigation uses, adversely affect recreation on the reservoir or around its shores? Or how much should reservoir operation be modified in order to maximize outdoor recreation on and around it? These are illustrative of the types of issues that arise. Rarely will the answer be an all-or-none one; instead, it is likely to be a matter of degree—some modification of one use in exchange for some modification of another.

Both the recreation promoters and those who develop resources for other purposes have treated the matter of allocating natural resources to recreation on the basis of comparative economic values in a very gingerly fashion. Each is quite willing to use this approach when he feels it will support his position, i.e., when it is the only way of making a proposed reservoir "economically feasible," or when it supports the establishment of a new park; but each is cautious, not to say, reluctant, about using this approach when the probable value estimates are less clear, and might be adverse to his position.

If outdoor recreation becomes another nonreimbursable purpose of federal development with the federal treasury absorbing all costs allocated to this purpose, then local groups will press for the inclusion of outdoor recreation in resource development projects. The prospect of no direct costs and a sizable increase in local commercial values is an attractive one. Recreation aspects of federal development programs would be much less popular if a state or one of its subdivisions were required to assume part or all of the costs allocated to outdoor recreation. Also, economic analysis might well reveal that the recreation benefits were much less important than anticipated. Government agencies, no less than individuals, are influenced by cost constraints and respond to incentives which can offer opportunities to increase the return from the recreation expenditure.

The matter of charges for outdoor recreation is treated in more detail at the end of this chapter, but it is directly related to the matter of resource allocation for recreation and other purposes. The policy issues for the latter may be rephrased: how far is the public willing to make resource allocations based upon comparative marginal returns or values? Who picks up the check for outdoor recreation? It is our conviction that the answer to the latter question will have a major effect upon the answer to the former one.

POLICY ISSUES ARISING OUT OF THE PROPER ROLE OF GOVERNMENT IN OUTDOOR RECREATION

Government (at some level) may play any one or more roles in the general field of outdoor recreation; it may act as researcher, as planner, as financier, as resource manager, as activity manager or director, as regulator (public health, etc.), and others. In practice, these roles are frequently intermingled and even confused.

Government at some level has typically been the financier. That is, public funds have been put up to acquire, develop, and manage outdoor recreation areas. But the financing role of government can be separated to some degree, perhaps wholly, from the other roles of government in outdoor recreation. A unit of government might plan, acquire, and manage an outdoor recreation area on a self-sustained financial basis; or it might acquire and develop it on one basis, but manage it on another.

Government at some level will often acquire and develop outdoor recreation areas. This is partly because government is dominant in financing recreation; but government has other advantages here also. Many, but not all, levels of government have the power of eminent domain to acquire needed lands for outdoor recreation. Government can often maintain expert staff for recreation area development, as well as sometimes be in a position to make needed capital investment funds available. The various public works programs of the 1930's are responsible for a substantial part of the facilities available for outdoor recreation in this country.

Government at some level may also manage outdoor recreation areas and activities. Various combinations of ownership and management are possible including in some cases, or for some activities, the use of private persons or organizations, such as concessionaires, to manage publicly owned and developed recreation areas or facilities. Typically, however, a unit of government manages an area which it owns and has developed.

Government may serve to provide a degree of regulation for outdoor recreation. Public health considerations, such as water supply, may lead to public control over both public and private recreation areas. The expertise of public health agencies, as well as their traditional role as protectors of the public interest, usually make it advisable for this function to be exercised by such specialized agencies rather than by the recreation agencies. But public health control is not a function of any single level of government.

Few if any of these various functions are, or need be, the function of any particular level of government. There may well be need for a clearer definition of the role of government at different levels. The Outdoor Recreation Resources Review Commission gave considerable attention to this matter, and made a number of sound recommendations about it. No doubt some clarification of respective roles is possible. But it seems impossible that roles could be, still more that they will be, so clearly defined and the definitions so clearly observed in practice that the overlapping in governmental roles will cease. Perhaps an equally or more fruitful approach is to seek better mechanisms for co-ordination among levels of government. Instead of trying to devise firm rules for relations of state parks to metropolitan parks, for instance, some means might be devised for bringing state and metropolitan officials together to consider specific cases, case by case.

POLICY ISSUES IN PUBLIC USE OF PRIVATELY OWNED LAND FOR OUTDOOR RECREATION

There is a vastly larger area of privately owned land than of publicly owned land in this country, and much of it could be used for recreation, either as the primary use or as one of several uses. How can the public use of private land for recreation best be encouraged? What problems will be encountered in doing so?

Private land is especially important for such extensive recreation land uses as hunting. Landowners often want some game harvested, but they do not want to be held legally liable for accidents to hunters on their property; nor do they want to be faced with damage to fences, livestock, or machinery—and many instances of such damage can easily be found, some clearly malicious. Landowners also fear that opening up their land to public travel may cost them some measure of legal control over their roads. These problems point to the need for a better legal basis for permitting public hunting on private land. One device, not tried as far as we know, would be for the state to rent the hunting privileges from the private landowner, for a nominal sum ($1.00 per year), and then allow public hunting, free or for a fee; the state as a tenant would then take over the legal liabilities for damages. A few states have enacted legislation which frees the landowner from damage suits unless he charges a fee. But the legal aspects of public use of private land for hunting clearly need further clarification.

Neither the large landowner (nor the small one) nor the hunter wishes to deal with the other on a retail basis. That is, large timber holding companies would find their task much simplified if they could deal with sportsmen's associations, which would take some responsibility for the actions of their members. Hunters do not wish to deal with a multitude of owners in areas where small land ownerships prevail, but at the same time they do not want to be restricted to a small area. The answer may be a co-operative for hunters and one for landowners, each taking a large measure of responsibility for the actions of its members.

Should hunters have a right to expect hunting on private land to be free of charge? Many seem to think they have a right to hunt free on forest, farm, or other rural property. Not only are they expecting to receive a valuable privilege without charge, or without bearing the costs which they inevitably impose upon the landowner, but they are providing no incentive whatsoever for the landowner to improve or even protect hunting opportunities. Perhaps the time has come for an honest re-examination of this typical attitude toward hunting on private land.

Private landowners may undertake to provide more intensive outdoor recreation opportunities such as camping and fishing as a business venture. Government may help the private landowner with research into the best ways to carry out this activity, by adult education work with landowners, by pricing the use of competing nearby public facilities in a way that avoids undue handicap to the private supplier, and in other ways. The United States Department of Agriculture now has several programs to aid private landowners who wish to develop recreation for the public. Loans are available, and there are various forms of public subsidy for land diversions, construction of water impoundments, and the like. The Small Business Administration has also made loans, on a less than fully commercial basis, to assist in the development of outdoor recreation opportunities, including loans for ski lifts and facilities.

Public aid to private landowners may be the cheapest way to provide additional recreation opportunity, as well as to help solve the income problems of some individuals, but it is not a cure-all. Provision of outdoor recreation for the general public is a difficult and exacting business. Not every piece of worn-out or submarginal farm or forest land is a good recreation area, even if improved, and not every low-income farmer can organize and manage an outdoor recreation business. Success with outdoor recreation business is not inevitable; on the contrary, failures are common. Critical to the success of such a business is an active demand for its services, but, even then, the seasonality of demand may be fatal. Physically desirable areas will increase the prospects for success; but they must be suitably, though economically, improved; and, above all, the business must be skillfully managed.

PAYING FOR PUBLIC OUTDOOR RECREATION

The most actively debated policy issues about outdoor recreation relate to the best way to pay for it. Public outdoor recreation cannot be truly free; some very real costs are incurred, and they must be met in some way. When the total volume of outdoor recreation was much smaller, and much of it could be supplied at low cost partly as a by-product of multiple use public land management, the issue of how recreation was to be paid for was less acute. But, as demand mounts ever higher, the issue cannot continue to be swept under the rug.

In Chapter 14, we explored the whole matter of pricing and paying for outdoor recreation opportunity. In the final analysis, the major policy issue is the degree to which users of outdoor recreation shall pay for it individually and directly as they use it, as compared with raising the necessary revenues collectively by general or special taxes. The extent to which one can demonstrate, or that one believes, that outdoor recreation has broad social effects, in that those who do not partake of it nevertheless benefit because others do engage in it, affects the answer to this policy question. If there are broad benefits—social "externalities," we called them—then it is appropriate that much of the costs of outdoor recreation be met by taxes imposed upon the entire public; to the extent that most or all of the benefits of outdoor recreation accrue to those directly consuming recreation services it is appropriate that

313

more of the costs be met by charges imposed upon the users. Research might help to provide a better basis for judgment than is now available. We may proceed, therefore, to particular consideration of the policy issues involved in systems of user charges designed to pay all or most of the costs of the recreation opportunity. A number of different arguments have been advanced in favor of charges levied directly against the users of public outdoor recreation areas. The major arguments for user charges can be grouped as follows:

Equity arguments. A user charge is perhaps the best way of making the person who lives and pays taxes elsewhere contribute to the cost of the recreation area he uses. In fact, except as his taxes to a higher level of government are used as grants-in-aid to the lower level of government, it is the only way he can so contribute. In addition, equity enters into user charges because only those who use the recreation areas are required to pay. Since a substantial proportion of people do not use certain kinds of outdoor recreation, this argument has considerable practical importance. Without user fees, it might well happen that the poor subsidized the rich in provision of recreation opportunity.

Resource efficiency arguments. If no user charges are levied, the public is invited to use natural resources wastefully. If we administratively establish a zero price on any use of a natural resource, we encourage the public to use it as though it had a zero value. In terms of our earlier demand analysis, the marginal user uses the recreation opportunity to the point where it has no value above his direct costs of getting to it. If, as is usually the case, heavier use takes the form of overcrowding, then satisfaction for all users may well be decreased. The proponents of this resource allocation argument generally suggest that user charges be levied to restrict quantities of outdoor recreation so that the marginal value of the quantity taken is at least as great as the marginal cost of supplying the opportunity. At the least, they would argue that the demand for outdoor recreation should not be artificially stimulated by general public subsidy.

User attitude arguments. It is often argued that users of public outdoor recreation areas abuse such areas, scatter waste and garbage about, and otherwise treat the areas carelessly or destructively, in part because they pay little or nothing for the privilege of using them. Scattered bits of evidence suggest that users are more careful when they pay to use an area, especially if the public agency charging fees then also maintains it better.

Fees as a management tool. Entrance fees or other user charges could be used as a management tool to reduce crowding at particular times and in particular areas. For instance, fees could be charged on days or in seasons of heaviest use, but not at other times, as one inducement to secure a more nearly even time pattern of use; or they could be charged in heavily used areas but not in lightly used ones as a means of spreading use geographically. Levying charges at busy times and none at others would create no administrative problems, but it might be difficult to charge for some areas and not for others, especially within a single park.

Fees to encourage private development. Private provision of outdoor recreation facilities for general public use involves many difficult problems including competition from essentially free public areas. Modest entrance or user fees at public areas would remove one hurdle for private operation.

Pragmatic considerations. The foregoing arguments in favor of user charges are, in practice, likely to be far less effective than the pragmatic one that only in this way will it be possible to raise enough revenue to provide the public outdoor recreation areas demanded. Many park and recreation supporters are strongly opposed to user charges as a matter of principle; but they may reluctantly accept them as the only practical political alternative to an indefinitely inadequate level of appropriations for this purpose. User charges would not necessarily have to raise all of the funds needed for good park provision and maintenance; some contribution from this source would both provide some money and perhaps encourage greater appropriations out of general revenue.

Various arguments, not necessarily consistent with one another, are advanced against the imposition of user charges. One argument is *hardship on poor people,* if a charge is imposed. For the user-oriented type of recreation area, which can be used by many users without any cash costs, this argument makes sense. An entrance fee of as little as a dime would raise a barrier to the use of many city parks, at least for some people. For most other areas, this argument is less cogent. Truly low income people cannot afford to own a car or incur the other expenses of visiting relatively distant outdoor recreation areas. Those who can bear these costs could probably bear a modest entrance charge. A sizable entrance fee would obviously constitute a cost to any user, but so does gasoline.

Administrative infeasibility is another argument against user charges at certain kinds of public outdoor recreation areas. The old way of collecting charges was to have a manned entrance gate or to send a man around the campground, collecting fees. This is an expensive way to collect revenue when the use level is low; in some instances, it has been replaced by less costly methods. In many parks, it would be difficult to collect an entrance fee because the area is open to access from many directions, and users could easily evade a collector—at a playground, for instance. There are many other situations in which it would be difficult or nearly impossible to collect much if any revenue from users of the area.

Some recreation administrators are concerned about the *vulnerability* of user charges to *economic depression*. They fear that, if user charges were their sole or chief source of revenue, they might be in difficult circumstances if attendance fell off during an economic downturn. This may be a dubious argument. If the depression were severe enough to cause a significant decrease in demand, the situation might be no better if operating revenue came from general appropriations, for these would probably be cut. Moreover, if attendance actually declined, most recreation agencies could make some economies in operation without critically weakening their organization on a continuing basis. This argument against user charges would completely lose its force if recreation agencies were allowed to carry modest amounts of unexpended funds forward from one year to the next. If a severe depression did occur, and if a public works program including outdoor recreation were desired, then obviously user fees could not provide the needed funds.

Perhaps the stubbornest opposition to user charges is *philosophical*. Many specialists in outdoor recreation are opposed to user charges as a matter of principle. They argue that parks should be free to all, as schools are free to all; and that the necessary costs should be met in some other way. To some of those who hold this view, the issue is simply not debatable. The orgins of this viewpoint are perhaps remote, but one should not underestimate the passion with which some persons hold it.

Two brief additional points should be made for any consideration of user charges for public outdoor recreation areas. First, all the costs of providing and operating public areas need not be met from one source; user charges, general tax revenue, special taxes, and other sources might be used in combination. This does not solve the policy issues, but the situation is not an all-or-none one. Secondly, as we noted in Chapter 14, a market for both public and private outdoor recreation is beginning to develop; and, generally, we can say that public resistance to paying reasonable user charges is vastly less than many park administrators have feared. The policy issue of how costs *should* be met still remains; but careful management can obviate much of the public resistance to a system of charges, if this is the preferred solution.

Perhaps as important as *whether* to levy a user charge is the question of *how*. The method in each case should be the one appropriate to the goal. Is the objective maximum revenue, or a shift in use from one area or time to another? We have tried to indicate that the way user charges are levied may have a significant effect on the amount or kind of use of the area. If user charges were adopted as a management tool, their efficiency would not be measured just in terms of the amounts of money collected in relation to the collection cost, for instance. A basic consideration is that all the effects, direct and secondary, of any system of collecting user charges should be evaluated, or at least estimated, before any particular system is inaugurated. Inventiveness in management techniques may be as productive in dealing with the problems of revenue collection as they are in overcoming difficulties in other areas.

APPENDIX

EXPENDITURES FOR RECREATION AND EXPENDITURES FOR WHEEL GOODS AND DURABLE SPORTS EQUIPMENT, 1909-62

Year	Personal consumption expenditures for recreation ($ million) (1)	Disposable personal income ($ billion) (2)	Recreation expenditures as percentage of disposable personal income (per cent) (3)	Gross national product, per capita, 1929 prices ($) (4)	Personal consumption expenditures for sports eqpt., etc.[1] ($ million) (5)	Expenditures on sports eqpt., etc.[1] as percentage of disposable income (per cent) (6)
1909	860	26.6	3.2	608		
1914	1,000	29.6	3.4	632		
1919	2,180	63.3	3.4	710		
1921	2,055	60.2	3.4	660		
1923	2,620	69.7	3.8	766		
1925	2,835	73.0	3.9	781		
1927	3,120	77.4	4.0	817		
1929	4,331	83.1	5.2	857	219	0.26
1930	3,990	74.4	5.4	772	172	0.23
1931	3,302	63.8	5.2	721	159	0.25
1932	2,442	48.7	5.0	611	110	0.23
1933	2,202	45.7	4.8	590	93	0.20
1934	2,441	52.0	4.7	639	118	0.23
1935	2,630	58.3	4.5	718	136	0.23
1936	3,020	66.2	4.6	787	171	0.26
1937	3,381	71.0	4.8	846	210	0.30
1938	3,241	65.7	4.9	794	210	0.32
1939	3,452	70.4	4.9	847	228	0.32
1940	3,761	76.1	4.9	916	254	0.33
1941	4,239	93.0	4.6	1,040	314	0.34
1942	4,677	117.5	4.0	1,147	306	0.26
1943	4,961	133.5	3.7	1,245	271	0.20
1944	5,422	146.8	3.7	1,327	323	0.22
1945	6,139	150.4	4.1	1,293	400	0.27
1946	8,621	160.6	5.4	1,179	809	0.50
1947	9,352	170.1	5.5	1,149	972	0.57
1948	9,808	189.3	5.2	1,189	980	0.52
1949	10,122	189.7	5.3	1,147	847	0.45
1950	11,278	207.7	5.4	1,233	878	0.42
1951	11,704	227.5	5.1	1,295	904	0.40
1952	12,257	238.7	5.1	1,317	994	0.42
1953	12,892	252.5	5.1	1,349	1,093	0.43
1954	13,256	256.9	5.2	1,309	1,174	0.46
1955	14,220	274.4	5.2	1,366	1,397	0.51
1956	15,161	292.9	5.2	1,368	1,575	0.54
1957	16,082	308.8	5.2	1,368	1,760	0.57
1958	16,842	317.9	5.3	1,315	1,883	0.59
1959	18,309	337.3	5.4	1,359	2,017	0.60
1960	19,524	350.0	5.5	1,365	2,138	0.61
1961	20,533	364.4	5.6	1,369	2,224	0.61
1962	21,555	385.3	5.6	1,436	2,386	0.62

APPENDIX

[1] Includes expenditures for wheel goods, durable toys, sports equipment, boats, and pleasure aircraft.

SOURCES:

Columns 1 and 5: U.S. Department of Commerce, *Historical Statistics of the United States* (Washington: U.S. Government Printing Office, 1960), p. 224; and *Historical Statistics Continuation and Revisions to 1962*, p. 35.

Column 2: For the years 1909 and 1914, Raymond W. Goldsmith, Dorothy S. Brady, and Horst Mendershausen, *A Study of Saving in the United States*, Vol. III (Princeton: Princeton University Press, 1956), p. 427. For the years 1919–1928, U.S. Department of Commerce, *Historical Statistics of the United States*, p. 139. For the years 1929–59, *Economic Report of the President* (Washington: U.S. Government Printing Office, 1960), p. 170; for 1960–65, *Economic Report*, 1966, p. 216.

Column 4: For the years 1909–54, U.S. Department of Commerce, *Historical Statistics of the United States*, p. 139. The years 1909 and 1914 are annual averages for the 5-year periods 1907–11 and 1912–16, respectively. For the years 1955–59, *Economic Report of the President*, 1960, pp. 130 and 160. Data for the 1909–54 period are not strictly comparable with the 1955–59 period because the 1954 implicit price deflator for the gross national product, used for the latter years, was shifted to a 1929 base. The 1929 implicit price deflator was used for the years between 1909 and 1954.

ESTIMATED EXPENDITURES FOR OUTDOOR RECREATION, AND EXPENDITURES AS PERCENTAGE OF PERSONAL DISPOSABLE INCOME, FISCAL YEARS 1941–59

Fiscal year	Fee paid for hunting licenses ($ thousand) (1)	Fee paid for fishing licenses ($ thousand) (2)	Expenditures on federal duck stamps ($ thousand) (3)	Entrance fees at national and state parks ($ thousand) (4)	Receipts from federal and state concessions ($ thousand) (5)	Receipts from operated facilities in state parks ($ thousand) (6)	Personal consumption expenditures for sports eqpt., etc.[1] ($ million) (7)	Total expenditures: sum of col. (1)–col. (7) ($ million) (8)	Total expenditures as percentage of personal disposable income (per cent) (9)
1941	14,437	11,618	1,254	2,362	407	1,091	284	315	0.38
1942	13,898	10,731	1,432	1,937	500	1,104	310	340	0.33
1943	13,576	10,024	1,376	987	390	1,032	289	316	0.24
1944	13,530	9,810	1,160	525	344	827	297	323	0.23
1945	15,512	10,580	1,475	602	497	1,100	362	392	0.26
1946	19,805	15,004	1,721	1,428	800	1,586	605	645	0.42
1947	28,558	22,667	2,000	2,729	1,391	2,288	891	951	0.58
1948	29,814	27,325	1,706	3,476	1,494	3,023	976	1,043	0.59
1949	34,967	32,658	2,100	3,695	1,592	3,180	914	992	0.52
1950	37,641	34,018	3,884	3,842	1,672	3,286	863	947	0.49
1951	38,139	35,554	3,808	3,846	1,837	4,128	891	978	0.45
1952	36,994	33,610	4,336	4,272	1,950	5,240	949	1,035	0.45
1953	40,551	35,603	4,594	4,796	2,328	6,342	1,043	1,137	0.46
1954	41,505	38,928	4,542	5,820	2,902	7,187	1,134	1,235	0.51
1955	42,791	39,502	4,364	6,786	2,499	7,513	1,286	1,389	0.55
1956	46,638	43,150	4,740	7,199	2,620	8,474	1,703	1,816	0.65
1957	47,847	42,470	4,664	7,379	2,827	9,390	2,051	2,166	0.72
1958	53,608	45,410	4,710	8,275	3,009	10,808	2,128	2,254	0.72
1959	57,811	50,375	6,498	7,994	3,051	11,897	2,270	2,408	0.73

[1] Includes expenditures for wheel goods, durable toys, sports equipment, boats, and pleasure aircraft.

SOURCES:

Columns 1 and 2: Gross cost to hunters and fishermen for licenses. Marion Clawson, *Statistics on Outdoor Recreation* (Washington: Resources for the Future, Inc., 1958), pp. 96–97. Additional data supplied by Fish and Wildlife Service, U.S. Department of the Interior.

Column 3: Estimated expenditures for federal duck stamps derived by multiplying the number of stamps issued by the following fee schedules: 1941 to August 1949, $1.00; September 1949 to July 1958, $2.00; and after August 1, 1958, $3.00. *Ibid.*

Column 4: Revenue from entrance fees for national parks. U.S. Department of the Interior, National Park Service, Branch of Finance, Accounting Operations Section, *General Fund Receipts—Summarization by Fiscal Years.* August 1959. Revenue from entrance fees for state parks, U.S. Department of the Interior, *State Park Statistics,* June 1960, pp. 6–7.

Column 5: *Ibid.*

Column 6: U.S. Department of the Interior, *State Park Statistics,* June 1960, pp. 6–7.

Column 7: U.S. Department of Commerce, *Historical Statistics of the United States* (Washington: U.S. Government Printing Office, 1960), p. 224; U.S. Department of Commerce, *Survey of Current Business,* July 1960, p. 16. Data are not available on a fiscal year basis. Figures are an arithmetic average of two years.

Column 9: *Economic Report of the President* (Washington: U.S. Government Printing Office, 1960), p. 170.

INDEX

(t) = table   (f) = figure

Acreage of recreation areas
  municipal and county parks, 147,
    1960, 198(t); state parks, 152,
    1910–62, 192(f); diversity of size,
    183; growth, *1900–60,* 185(f); fed-
    eral-state-local involvement, 186–
    95, *passim,* 201, comparisons, 198–
    99; nonurban areas, *1960,* 200(t);
    census regions, state and federal,
    202(t)
Advertising, effect on visits, 55, 57
Advertising Council of America, edu-
    cational campaigns, 174
Air travel, 100, 101
Allocation of resources, 299–300, 309–
    10
Anderson, Nels, 11n
Appalachia, 231
Appalachian region, 253

Bancroft, Gertrude, 16n
Barnes, Harry Elmer, 27n
Bayliss, Dudley D., 100n
Benefit-cost analysis
  for estimating land and water values,
    212; for decision making on invest-
    ments, 249–61, 255–60
Berger, Clarence Q., 18n
Bird, Ronald, 206n, 235(t)
Boat "revolution," 134; outboard mo-
    tors, 100
Boating, 25, 56–57, 67, 135
Bogan, R. A., 16n
Boone, Daniel, 169
Brightbill, C. K., 27n
Brooks, Lloyd, 48n
Brown, William G., 49n, 222n
Buffer zones, 155, 157, 162
Bultena, Gordon, 165n
Bureau of Outdoor Recreation, 290,
    292, 303, 308
Bureau of Sport Fisheries and Wildlife,
    190–91, 206
Butcher, Devereaux, 170n, 182n
Butler, George D., 27n, 29n, 30, 30n,
    147, 147n, 148n, 198(t)

California, 72, 73, 85, 147
  standards of recreation areas, 147–
    49; privately owned resources, 206

Campgrounds
  intensity of use, user satisfaction,
    167, 168; private *vs* public, 205–6
Camping, 19, 56, 130, 187
Capital gains, 222–24
Capital costs, higher in future, 262
Castle, Emery, N., 49n, 222n
Charlesworth, James C., 12n
Ciriacy-Wantrup, S. V., 115n
Cities
  movement to, 94–95; older parts,
    lack of recreation facilities, 95;
    standards for recreation areas, 147,
    148. *See also* Outdoor recreation
    areas: user-oriented
City parks, *see* Outdoor recreation
    areas: user-oriented
Clawson, Marion, 36n, 37(t), 49n, 72n,
    74(t), 97n, 102n, 103n, 126n,
    134n, 148n, 152n, 177n, 182n,
    184n, 193n, 213n, 232n, 277n,
    278n, 292n, 304n, 307n, 308n
Cliff, Edward P., 205n
Climate and time pattern of use, 156
Consumption, function of supply and
    demand, 116
Copeland, Lewis C., 235(t)
Cost-benefit analysis, *see* Benefit-cost
    analysis
Costs
  measure of (money, time, travel),
    50, 51, 51(t), 62, 86; and demand
    curve, 47–48, 54, 62; travel costs,
    62, 64n, 71, 74(t), 77, 86, 87,
    106; per visit, 64, 65, 65(t), 66(f),
    71, 72–73, 74(t), 75(f), 76(t);
    shared, 73, 73(f); trips to user-
    oriented areas, difficulty of esti-
    mating, 77; effect of increase, 80,
    80(t); allocation for combined
    visits, difficulties, 83; cost method
    of estimating resource values,
    225–26; and investment consider-
    ations, 249–61; capital costs, high-
    er in future, 262; ways of meeting,
    263–65. *See also* Expenditures, *and
    related tables and figures*
Craighead, Frank C., Jr., 298n
Craighead, John J., 298n
Crutchfield, James A., 226n
Cutten, George Barton, 11n

321

Davis, Robert K., 49n, 214n, 228n
DeGrazia, Sebastian, 11n, 23n
DeHaven, James C., 255n
Demand
  effect of timing and amount of lei-
    sure, 39–40; as applied to outdoor
    recreation, 41, 61–63; elements of
    recreation demand, 43, 45; attend-
    ance at major types of areas,
    years of record, 44(f); effect of
    changes in income, 46; and will-
    ingness of people to pay, 88; in-
    terrelationship characteristics, 89–
    92; and policy issues, 304–6
Demand, future, projections for *1980,
    2000*
  inadequacy of data, 114; aggregate
    demand analysis, 114, ambiguities
    in terms "prices" and "demand,"
    115–16; distinction between de-
    mand and consumption, 116; un-
    certainty of, 116; five projection
    techniques, advantages and disad-
    vantages, 116–26; simple trend
    extension, 117–21, estimates, 119;
    causal forces, socioeconomic, as
    measure of future demand, 121–
    27; satiety, ceiling on demand,
    127–28; ORRRC projections for
    selected activities, 128–31, 130(t);
    "judgment" approach, subjective
    process, 131, 137; user-oriented
    areas, 117–18, 118(f), 119(t),
    121, 122, 134, 134n; intermediate
    areas, 134, 134n, 135; resource
    based areas, 134, 134n, 136–37;
    specific regional and local areas,
    demand over time, 137–40
Demand analysis
  limitations, 86–89, aggregate, 114,
    research on, 295–97; party visit
    best measure, 296
Demand theory, 46, 47, 48
Demand curve(s) or schedule(s)
  definition, 46; expression of data,
    46–50; association with price or
    cost, 47–48; application to out-
    door recreation, hypothetical in-
    termediate area, 48–51, 51(t)(f);
    problems, 62; methodology, 48n–
    49n, money costs per visit to rec-
    reation area, 50, 51(t)(f); elastic-
    inelastic, 52, 54, 69, 84, 85; for
    major income groups, 52, 53(f);
    effect of various demand factors,
    52–58, 53(f), 55(f), 90; for total
    population, 53; location of users
    and of areas, effect, 58–59, 90;
    quantitative, for specific areas,

difficulty, 61; usefulness, 62–63;
  for intermediate areas, specific,
  64–71; for resource oriented areas,
  71–77, for user-oriented areas, 77,
  1910–60, 118(f); for particular
  recreation resource, 77–85, procedure, 78, 79(t)(f), 80(t)(f); limitations, 86–89; four major factors
  affecting demand curve, 93–112;
  user-benefits, estimation, 216–22,
  passim; effect of entrance fees, 283
Depressed areas, economic aid, 230,
  Appalachia, 231, 253
Detroit regional parks, 149
Dewhurst, J. Frederic, and Associates,
  16n, 103, 104n
Dulles, Foster Rhea, 27n
Durant, Henry, 27n

Eckstein, Otto, 255n, 257n, 258n
Economic analysis, applicability to outdoor recreation 45–46. *See also*
  Demand, Demand analysis, Demand curve(s) or schedule(s)
Economic impact of recreation on local
  areas, 230–48
  two kinds of benefits, 231; recipients
    of benefits, 236, 238, 238(t),
    240; typical vacation expenditures,
    (equipment, transportation, travel,
    recreation), 233; travel (food,
    lodging, gas), 233–34, 239, sur-
    veys, 233–34, 235(t); cannot be
    measured by total expenditures,
    239; expenditures stemming from
    facility or area, 240; multiplier
    process, result of expenditure pat-
    terns, 240–43, effect of entrance
    fees, 246; added local government
    costs, taxes, 247–48
Education, 60
  preservation of quality of areas, 165,
    174–75
Educational level of participants, 111–
  12
Engel, Ernest, "law," 109–110
Entrance fees
  included in total costs, 77; effect of
    changes in, 83(f), 88–89; charges,
    90–91, 115, 278, 283; measure in
    attaining quality, 178; effect on
    local community, 246; arguments
    for free entrance, 270–71, 279.
    See also User charges
Evans, John S., 64n, 65(t)
Expenditures, governmental, for public
  outdoor recreation
  federal, direct outlays, regional im-

INDEX

INDEX

effect of distance, 75; user satisfaction, 154(f), 167(f); and quality of area, 167–70; "overcrowding," 169; research on, 295

Investments in facilities and improvements, 113, 158

for existing areas, 159; and cost considerations, public facilities, 249–61; need for investment criteria, 253–55; rules-of-thumb for investment decisions, 261

Ise, John, 182n

Kerr, Clark, 14n

Kerr, John H., Reservoir

visits to, 70, 71(t), 72(f); demand curve for recreation resources, 86, 220, 221; benefits, 258

Kneese, Allen V., 49n

Knetsch, Jack L., 49n, 70n, 161n, 213n, 222n, 292n, 308n

Komarovsky, Mirra, 6n, 27n

Krutilla, John V., 255n, 259n, 275n

Land and Water Conservation Fund, 254

grants under program, 265; source of funds, 278; planning, 290

Landowners, aid to, 312–13

Landsberg, Hans H., 94n

Larrabee, Eric, 6n, 11n

Leisure

in modern America, 11–26; discretionary time, 11, 12, 26; vs recreation, 12; vs work, 13–14; per capita by 2000, 96; trends, 122, 123, 123(f)

Leisure time

timing and size of pieces of, 5, 14–19; retirement, 5, 15, 20, 22(t), 29, 96; annual, 5, 18–19, 22(t), 29; weekend, 18, 19, 20, 22(t), 29; daily, 19, 20, 22(t), 26, 29; vacations, paid, longer, 17, 23, 96, 136, 137, off-season, 171, 247; distribution, 20; increase in, 20, 21(f), 22(t), 23, 24–26, 96; differing views, 23n; competition for, 24; spent in outdoor recreation, 1960, 24–25; changes in, 90; per capita, 96

Lerner, Lionel, 49n, 226n

Lewis and Clark Lake (reservoir), 64

visits to, 65, 65(t), 66, 66(f), 68; demand curve for recreation resources, 81, 81(t), 82(f), 84, 85, 220; benefits, 258

Lewis, Philip H., 298n

Life expectancy, increase, 14; for women, 15

Linduska, Joseph P., 206n

Lucas, Robert C., 153n, 165n, 168n, 180n

Ludlow, William H., 148n

Lund, Richard E., 235(t)

Lundberg, George A., 6n, 27n

Maass, Arthur, 255n

Mack, Ruth P., 102n, 110n

Management and government ownership, 311

Management of recreation areas

intensity of, 55; need for, 153–55; trend toward, 159; multiple use management, 160–62

Manpower for management, 113

Marginal and sub-marginal lands, use as state parks, 193

Margolis, Julius, 259n

Market guides, willingness to pay substitute for, 88, 212, 214, 231, 254

Massachusetts, standards for recreation areas, 149

McInerny, Mary Alice, 6n, 27n

McKean, Roland N., 212n, 218n, 255n

Mead, Margaret, 29n

Mexico, 73

Meyer, Harold D., 27n

Meyersohn, Rolf, 6n, 11n

Michael, Donald, 23n

Miller, Frank, 235(t)

Milliman, Jerome W., 255n

Minority groups, recreational opportunities, 75, 77, 305

Missouri River, 64

Mitchell, Elmer D., 27n

Mueller, Eva, 96n

Multiple Use Act, 188

Mumford, Lewis, 28, 29n

National Association of Counties, on user charges, 277

National forests, 43

visits to, 43, 187; future use, 119(t), 120, 122, 136–37, 185n; multiple use, 160; beginning, 184; acreage, 186. *See also* Outdoor recreation areas: resource oriented

National monuments, *see* Outdoor recreation areas: resource oriented

National Park Service

Mission 66 plan, 133; Director of, 170n, 172n; number and area of parks, 186; expenditures on recre-

INDEX

129n, 130(t); other references to reports, 182n, 197

Pack, Arthur Newton, 11n, 30, 30n
Palmer, Dwight R. G., 101n
Palmer, Edgar Z., 67
Partridge, Bellamy, 97n
Peaking of demand
economic and management problem, 157; measures to control, 170–73, charges, 171–72, 173, off-peak vacations, 171, 171n
Pennsylvania, standards for recreation areas, 149
Playgrounds, *see* Outdoor recreation areas: user-oriented
Policy issues concerned with outdoor recreation, 304–13
"Poor" people
inadequate recreation areas for, 151, 270–71, 305; hardship of user charges, 315
Population
trends, 5, 123, 136, and public policy, 304; age distribution, 5, 94, 95; movement Westward, 5, 94; movement to urban and suburban areas, 5, 94, 95; location of population and recreation areas, factor in demand, 58–59, 90; bases for estimating visits, per capita or per 1,000 base population, 58; causal factor in demand, 93–96, in future demand, 121, 122, 123. *See also various tables and figures*
Prendergast, Joseph, 101n
Prewitt, Roy A., 64n
Pricing and paying for public facilities
public costs, ways of meeting, 263–65, taxes, general and special, 263–64, 265, 313, bond issues, 264, grants-in-aid, 265, direct user charges, 265; arguments for public provision of outdoor recreation, 265–69; free admission, arguments for, 270–71, arguments against, 275; role of government in providing outdoor recreation, 271–72; role of prices in resource management, 273–76; experience with pricing, 276–80; user charges, 265, 279, administrative difficulties, 280–82, effects, 282–84, levying principles, 284–85; policy issues on pricing, 305, on paying, 313–17
Privately owned areas
future demand, inadequacy of data, 114; buffer zones, 155; multiple use, 161; quality, problems, 178–79; price expression of value, 213; policy issues, 311–13, 315
Privately owned forests, 160
Projections of demand: *see* demand, future, projections, *1980, 2000*
Public Works Administration, 193

Quality of recreation
demand factor, 57; preservation, 164–80; appreciation, education in, 165, 174–75; and intensity of use, 167–70; "overcrowding," 169; measures to improve, 170–74, design, 170, 170n, 175–76, off-season vacations, 171, charges, 171–72, 173, "literacy test," 173, ceilings on use, 176–78; entrance and differential fees, 178; private outdoor recreation, problems, 178–79; wilderness areas, problems, 180, 180n, 181; policy issues, 306–7

Racial pattern of urban living, 151
Rationing of recreation areas and facilities, devices, 305
Reclamation Bureau, reservoir areas and shoreline, 190, 190n
Recreation, definition, 6, 6n
Recreation activity, definition, 7
Recreation Advisory Council, 102
Recreation business, 243–44
Reid, Margaret G., 110n
Research needs
phases of recreation experience, 35–36; investment decisions, 261; rules of thumb for estimating resource values, 228–29, 297; agency participation in, 289–92; suggested subjects and areas, 295–302; conclusions, 302–3
Reservoirs, federal, 135
Corps of Engineers, 43, 44, 188, future use, 119(t), 120–21, 122, 127, 134; TVA, 43, 44, future use, 119(t), 121, 122, 134, recreation area, 189, 189n, 190, visits to *1947, 1956, 1964,* 189; value of nearby land, 222–23, 223n; Bureau of Reclamation, 190, 190n
Resort areas, time of use, 156
Retired time, increase, 20, 21(f), 22(t), 23
Retirement areas, use of vacation areas, 247
Retirement leisure, 14, 29; women *vs* men, 15–16; increase, 96

INDEX

Revenues to pay for outdoor recreation
for state park operations, *1941–62*, 194; for added local government costs, 247–48; ways of meeting public costs, 263–65; legislative provision, 305; policy issues, 313, 314

Romney, G. Ott, 11n, 30, 30n

Rest parks, 150, 165

Roads and highways
effect on demand, 55, 56(f), 90, 101–2, 118; scenic highways, 102; highway revolutions of 1920's, 134–35; access, 158

Rules of thumb
standards for estimating resource values, 228–29, 297; for investment decisions, 261

Sapora, Allen V., 27n

Satiety and demand, 53, 127–28

Scale economies for public recreation areas, 266–67

Seasonal use of outdoor recreation facilities, 127, 136, 156
extended use, 247; hazards, 313

Shenandoah national parks
visits to, 75, 75(f); demand curve, various entrance fees, 83(f), 84

Singh, Ajmer, 49n, 222n

Ski lifts and facilities, loans for, 313

Small Business Administration, loans, 313

Snyder, Robert E., 107n

Socioeconomic factors affecting outdoor recreation, 54, 93–112. *See also* Income(s); Leisure; Population; Travel; Travel and transportation

Sorokin, Pitirim A., 18n

Sports, 25. *See also specific sports*

Sports equipment, expenditures, 106, 107, 318(t)

State forests, multiple use, 160. *See also* Outdoor recreation areas, intermediate areas

State park system, attendance, *1947–62*, 194

State parks
future use, 119(t), 120, 122, 134, 135; within Great Plains, 140; time patterns of use, 156. *See also* Outdoor recreation areas: intermediate

Steiner, Jesse Frederick, 27n

Stevenson, Charles, 170n

Stewart, Charles D., 14n

Stieglitz, Harold, 17n

Stoddard, C. H., 37(t), 97n, 126n, 148n

Sullivan, Pa., recreation expenditure study, 242–43

Supply of recreation resources, 143–207
use of resources, 145–63; adequacy of areas, standards, 146–50, role of location, 150–53; intensity and concentration of recreation activities, 153–55, user satisfaction, 154(f), special problems, 155; time patterns of recreation activity (seasonal, daily, climatic, peaking), 155–57; substitution of capital, labor and management for resources, 157–60, investment and planning, 158, 159, "turmoil" costs 160, 163; multiple use management and recreation, 160–62; future requirements, 162–63; evaluation, research on rating scales, 297–98

Swamps, conversion of, 153

Swanson Lake, Nebraska
visits to, 68, 69(t); regression analysis of visit rates, equation, 68n

Taves, Martin, 165n

Taxes
effects of recreational development, 247; to meet local government costs, 247–48; general and special, policy issues, 263, 264, 265, 313

Taylor, Gordon D., 138n

Theobald, Robert, 23n

Tiebout, Charles M., 241n

Tilden, Freeman, 182n

Time budget, national, 19–26; *1900, 1950, 2000*, 20, 21(f), 22(t), 23

Time budgets, competition for the individual's time, 19, 24, 26

Tobin, Austin J., 101n

Tourism, as investment opportunity, 230, 232, 248

Travel
demand value other than costs, 86; increase, *1930–60*, 122, 123(f)

Travel facilities
factor in demand, 54; revolutionary changes, 99, 100, 136, 137

Travel and transportation
increase in travel, 5, 49, 97–98, 99; effect on outdoor recreation (time costs, character), 96–102; typical one-way distances, 98–99; costs of travel, *see* Costs

Trecker, Edgar W., Jr., 165n, 235(t)

Trice, Andrew H., 49n